This is the first study of French–American relations in the critical postwar period, 1945–54, that makes use of recently opened diplomatic archives and personal papers in France and the United States. Irwin Wall examines the American role in French diplomacy, economic reconstruction, military policy, politics, and the reshaping of French society from labor unions to consumer tastes and films. He places particular emphasis on American attempts to combat the influence of French communism and achieve a stable, centrist regime avoiding the extremes of right and left.

The United States and the Making of
Postwar France, 1945–1954

The United States and the Making of Postwar France, 1945–1954

IRWIN M. WALL

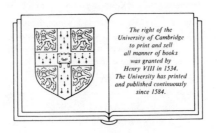

The right of the
University of Cambridge
to print and sell
all manner of books
was granted by
Henry VIII in 1534.
The University has printed
and published continuously
since 1584.

CAMBRIDGE UNIVERSITY PRESS
Cambridge
New York   Port Chester   Melbourne   Sydney

DC
404
.W3513
1991

The original version of this book was published by Editions André Balland
in Paris in 1989 under the title *L'influence américaine sur la politique
française, 1945–1954.*
Published by the Press Syndicate of the University of Cambridge
The Pitt Building, Trumpington Street, Cambridge CB2 1RP
40 West 20th Street, New York, NY 10011, USA
10 Stamford Road, Oakleigh, Melbourne 3166, Australia

© Cambridge University Press 1991

First published 1991

Printed in the United States of America

Library of Congress Cataloging-in-Publication Data
Wall, Irwin M.
[Influence américaine sur la politique française. English]
The United States and the making of postwar France, 1945–1954 /
Irwin M. Wall.
p. cm.
Translation of: L'influence américaine sur la politique française.
Includes bibliographical references.
ISBN 0-521-40217-4
1. France – Foreign relations – United States. 2. United States –
Foreign relations – France. 3. France – Politics and
government – 1945–1958. 4. France – Civilization – American
influences. 5. France – History, Military – 20th century. I. Title.
DC404.W3513 1991
327.44073 – dc20
90-47868
CIP

British Library Cataloguing in Publication Data
Wall, Irwin M.
The United States and the making of postwar France, 1945–1954.
1. France. Relations with United States, history 2.
United States. Relations with France, history
I. Title II. [L'influence américaine sur la politique
française. *English*]
303.48244073

ISBN 0-521-40217-4 hardback

22421996

Contents

Acknowledgments

ANY PROJECT OF THIS LENGTH involves the accumulation of a great many obligations. It is a pleasure to be able finally to acknowledge them in print. Two persons have had a particularly intimate relationship with this work. Françoise Adelstain originally suggested the topic, and her support and encouragement were unflagging every step of the way. I can only hope the result corresponds at least partially to the firm belief she held that a book on French–American relations during the postwar period was badly needed. Philippe-Etienne Raviart, a dear friend of many years, agreed to do the translation for the French edition, but in fact did much more – editing, criticizing, advising, and providing the general moral support any author needs. Indeed, those able to read the French version may find that the translation is an improvement on the English original. Thanks also to Naik Raviart for hosting my several working visits with such grace.

A number of persons consented to interviews. While the information they provided is rarely acknowledged in the footnotes, it greatly assisted me in providing the kind of sympathetic understanding of the period and confidence necessary in reconstructing a very complex and difficult story. I want to thank Georgette Elgey, Paul-Marie de la Gorce, Pierre Uri, François Bloch-Lainé, Guillaume Guindey, Robert Marjolin, and Michel Drancourt, for sharing generously of their time and memories. On the American side, Gordon Wright, Henry Labouisse, and Ambassador C. Douglas Dillon did the same.

My research was ably assisted by a great many archivists and librarians. It is a pleasure to acknowledge the help of Sally Marks and Kathy Nicastro of the Diplomatic Branch of the National Archives, Washington, DC, and equally of Mesdames Bonazzi and Irigoin of the Section Contemporaine, Archives Nationales, Paris. Thanks also to the staffs of the Quai d'Orsay, the Biliothèque Nationale, the Foundation Jean Monnet in Lausanne, Switzerland, the Harry S Truman Library, Independence, Missouri, the Dwight D. Eisenhower Library, Abilene, Kansas, the Lyndon B. Johnson Library, Austin, Texas, the State Historical Society, Madison, Wisconsin, the AFL-CIO Archive, Washington, DC, the ILGWU Archive, New York, and proverbially last, but not at all least, the Library of the University of California, Riverside. My travel was assisted by a generous advance by my French publisher, André Balland, and by several grants from the Research Committee of the Academic Senate of the University of California, Riverside. Portions of the manuscript were read and commented upon by Kim Munholland, John Sweets, Richard Kuisel, André Kaspi, Norman Ravitch, and Kenneth Barkin. Vance Mitchell and William and Sarah Hughes both helped with invaluable research assistance, and Bill read carefully and commented on the whole. Sarah Neiman, Annette Laing, and Teresa Munro helped with the editing. The errors, alas, are mine alone.

The greatest thanks go to those closest to me, Sarah and Alexandra Wall. They had more to do with the book's completion than anyone.

Abbreviations

ACC	Allied Control Commission
AFL	American Federation of Labor
AFP	Agence France-Press
AN	Archives Nationales
AS	Associated States (of Indochina)
CFTC	Confédération Française des Travailleurs Chrétiens
CGT	Confédération Générale du Travail
CIA	Central Intelligence Agency
CIG	Central Intelligence Group
CIO	Congress of Industrial Organizations
CNR	Conseil National de la Résistance
ECA	Economic Cooperation Administration
ECSC	European Coal and Steel Community
EDC	European Defense Community
ERP	European Recovery Program
FO	Force Ouvrière
FRUS	Foreign Relations of the United States
FTUC	Free Trade Union Committee
GATT	General Agreement on Tariffs and Trade
ILGWU	International Ladies' Garment Workers Union
IMF	International Monetary Fund
JCS	Joint Chiefs of Staff
MAAG	Military Assistance and Advisory Group
MAE	Ministère des Affaires Etrangères
MDAP	Mutual Defense and Assistance Pact
MPA	Motion Picture Association
MRP	Mouvement Républicain Populaire
MSA	Mutual Security Agency
NAC	National Advisory Council
NARA	National Archives and Records Administration
NATO	North Atlantic Treaty Organization
NSC	National Security Council
OEEC	Organization of European Economic Cooperation

OSP	Off Shore Procurement
OSR	Office of the Special Representative
OSS	Office of Strategic Services
PCF	Parti Communiste Français
PPS	Policy Planning Staff
PSB	Psychological Strategy Board
PTT	Poste, Téléphone et Télégraphe
RPF	Rassemblement du Peuple Français
SHSW	State Historical Society of Wisconsin
SNCF	Société Nationale des Chemins de Fer
STEM	Special Technical and Economic Mission
SWNCC	State War and Navy Coordinating Committee
TCC	Temporary Council Committee
USIA	United States Information Agency
USIS	United States Information Services
WFTU	World Federation of Trade Unions

Introduction

THE UNITED STATES emerged from the Second World War as the preponderant economic and military power in the world. Western Europe lay weakened and in large part destroyed; the Soviet Union, which suffered enormous devastation itself, shared military hegemony in Europe with the Americans. Under these conditions it was virtually inevitable that the United States would play an enormous role in the process of European reconstruction. American influence in the reshaping of France was correspondingly great. In the absence of serious historical study until recently, the subject has become clouded by political partisanship and mythology. Studies abound with titles that announce their theses: *L'empire américaine* or *La France colonisée*. It is axiomatic in some circles that the United States purged the Communists from the French government in 1947, organized the non-Communist labor union Force Ouvrière, forcefully integrated France into a Western bloc of its own making, and imposed upon the unwilling French its own model of organized, consumer-oriented, capitalism. Whatever the degree of truth in such formulations, the reality was more complex. These conclusions were reached without benefit of government documents, most of which have become available in the last decade up to 1954 and beyond. It is now possible to put them to test. French historians have begun to tap sources available in France; until now virtually nothing has been done with benefit of American sources.

Any study of the American role in France must take into account at least four different, distinct, yet interrelated aspects. There is first the conventional diplomatic record. France and the United States became military allies in the North Atlantic Treaty Organization, cooperated in their policies vis-à-vis the USSR and European integration, and fought together in two wars, in Korea and Indochina. Given the preponderance of American power, it was to be expected that the French role would be one of supplicant and junior partner. Yet the relationship remained characterized by the usual crises,

I

tensions, and sovereign disputes and jealousies that govern diplomatic relations between nations in the most normal of times. The American and French republics had a 150-year history of troubled friendship upon which they could draw and which continued to shape the nature of their postwar relations. Diplomats of both nations made continued reference to it on any and every suitable occasion.

Diplomacy was complicated by a new and unprecedented economic relationship between the two countries, which took the form of a vast economic assistance program. American aid began with a conventional reconstruction loan in 1946. But with the onset of the cold war and the foreign payments and exchange crisis of the following year, it took the innovative form of the Marshall Plan, which involved sixteen nations in a scheme of reciprocal obligations with the United States and each other. The Marshall Plan put international economic relations on a new level, created a new international bureaucratic framework, and accorded the United States through bilateral treaties and its aid missions, unprecedented means of influencing directly the postwar economic development of the nations of Western Europe. France was the single greatest recipient of Marshall Plan aid, the most important in the American view and even more central in the American military assistance program for Western Europe that followed. Between the Marshall Plan, military aid, direct budgetary assistance, and American help to France in defraying the cost of the Indochina War, American aid approached or exceeded one billion dollars per year for the entire period between 1945 and 1954. Such aid levels, in the context of the extreme penury of the postwar period, could not help but have the most profound effect on French economic development, international relations, and internal politics.

A third level of relations thus involved American intervention in French internal affairs. The political system of the Fourth Republic facilitated external influence.[1] After a brief period of a strong provisional executive power under de Gaulle from 1944 to 1946, the resurgent parties wrote a new constitution that reproduced many of the unstable features of the prewar regime. A largely ceremonial president, elected by the National Assembly and Council of the Republic (Senate) in joint session, enjoyed only the power to select the *Président du Conseil* or premier, who depended upon a majority in the lower house. A multiparty system, in which no party was able to get more than 28 percent of the vote at most, meant the government must be formed by a coalition, in which agreement was of necessity arrived at by hard bargaining and could easily fail at any time, depending upon which issues were paramount. Governments were thus unstable and fell with alarming frequency; and the conflicting ambitions and individual importance of the deputies, whose votes were critical in forming new govern-

---

[1]   The best history of the Fourth Republic is by Jean-Pierre Rioux, *The Fourth Republic, 1944–1958*, trans. Godfrey Rogers (Cambridge: Cambridge University Press, 1987).

ments, made them individually and in groups unusually susceptible to the appeals of pressure groups of all kinds, both internal and external. The party system was roughly hexagonal, with the two largest parties after 1947 located on the extremes and hostile to the system itself. On the left the Communists retreated into enforced and bitter isolation; on the right the Gaullists took on the appearance of an authoritarian threat to the Republic. The four parties that supported the regime were virtually forced to make coalitions with one another in the hope of preserving democracy, but they reflected deep divisions on the issues. On the moderate left, the Socialists and Christian Democrats (Mouvement Républicain Populaire) largely agreed on the construction of the welfare state but were bitterly divided on clerical issues. On the moderate right, the prewar Radical party and Independents were largely driven by ambition for power but reflected the interests of economic groups, both industrial and modernist, and those hostile to modernization, in particular a backward peasantry and urban commercial class of small businessmen.

The issues were complicated by the cold war, Washington's fear of communism, and the cascade of governments in France under the constitution of the Fourth Republic. The Americans hoped for a stable, centrist regime, free of either of the extremes represented by the Communists, dangerously strong in the American view, and de Gaulle, whose political program they tended to equate with fascism. The multiplicity of parties and instability of cabinets afforded astute American ambassadors unprecedented leverage for intervening directly in French political crises. In general the Americans were reluctant about exercising their newly discovered power, and in many cases they found it did not go as far as they might have wished. It is notoriously untrue, for example, that Washington forced the French to get rid of the Communists under the coalition government of the Socialist Paul Ramadier in May 1947. In fact the Americans watched that crisis unfold from a distance, although they were privileged with inside information as it unfolded, and it occurred at a time when Washington was still of two minds as to whether the Communists were not more useful inside the government as a hedge against social instability. But a year later the American ambassador had discovered the extent of his influence and regularly intervened with French politicians to warn them against the return of the Communists to power or the overthrow of governments of which Washington especially approved. In these admonishments economic aid and its possible interruption were regularly brandished as a weapon. Although Washington had influence, however, it rarely could have its way. Rather, U.S. influence became one of the many factors governing the outcome of French political crises and rarely the determining one. The Americans in France became one more pressure group, albeit a powerful one, with which French politicians had to contend.

There was a second realm in which the Americans tried to influence internal French developments, by the direct influence upon and manipulation of French public opinion. Here the documents available allow some new light to be shed on American activities, although many facets remain shrouded in darkness. The record of extensive American support for non-Communist labor, at least in its formative years until 1950, is now available. What the support accomplished is another matter, for the Americans were never happy with the splintered situation in the French labor movement and their best efforts failed to correct it. French labor leaders took Washington's help but never its orders, and the structure of the French trade union movement remained shaped by indigenous historical traditions. There can be no doubt, however, that American assistance was of critical importance in the survival of Force Ouvrière at a dangerous moment in its early history. A vast anti-Communist propaganda offensive was mounted in France by Washington as well. Some manifestations of it were the sensational Kravchenko case, the subsidization of the anti-Communist peace movement *Paix et Liberté*, and the hidden activities authorized by the Psychological Strategy Board. The extent of American attempts to purchase influence on French publications and the media remains hidden in the archives of the Central Intelligence Agency, which under present law cannot be forced to release the files of its operational divisions.

A final manifestation of American influence lay in the realm of mass culture. Much of what passed and passes for Americanization in France is, instead, modernization. France could not avoid becoming more like America as it adopted the trappings of the consumer society. Americans did attempt to influence directly the shaping of the French mentality by the export of films, the exemplary presence of the American military, and the investments by American businesses in France. But neither the cultivation of the media nor the attempts at the Coca-colonization of French tastes in soft drinks were especially successful or significant. Of greater importance were the export of American methods to increase productivity through technical assistance programs, and the emergence of the American model as one suitable for emulation or imitation by French modernizers. Washington tried to steer French modernization efforts toward its own model of free enterprise. But the French pursued their own efforts in the more structured framework of the Monnet Plan. These issues have been and are being explored in greater detail by other historians.[2]

The unprecedented extent of American influence occurred primarily be-

---

[2]   In particular, the work of Richard Kuisel now under way and his *Capitalism and the State in Modern France* (New York: Cambridge University Press, 1981). See also Michael Hogan, *The Marshall Plan: America, Britain, and the Reconstruction of Western Europe, 1947–1952* (New York: Cambridge University Press, 1987), Charles Maier, *In Search of Stability: Explorations in Historical Political Economy* (New York: Cambridge University Press, 1987), and François Bloch-Lainé and Jean Bouvier, *La France Restaurée, 1944–54: Dialogue sur les choix d'une modernisation* (Paris: Fayard, 1986).

cause France was a central battleground in the cold war. France was not, however, despite its aspirations, a focus of strategic decision making in the conflict, a role reserved for Washington. A study of American influence in France therefore inserts itself only marginally into the central questions of cold war historiography. The debate between traditionalists and revisionists has long since been transcended by the appearance of synthetic works that offer a more balanced picture stressing the responsibility of both sides and the limitations of the "mentalités" of politicians of the era.[3] Further recent work has gone beyond this to emphasize the European contribution to the outbreak of the cold war.[4] The present work seeks to reinforce that perspective. For marginal as they may have been to decision making in Washington, French elites needed no tutoring in anti-Communism. Their zeal in this area was homegrown. As a consequence it is necessary to point out the extent to which the United States was drawn into the network of Western institutions and alliances of the postwar era rather than, as is more commonly depicted, its role as a creator or innovator.

This work has further inserted itself into an internal debate between French scholars about American influence in France. The thesis of extensive American interference has been given scholarly formulation in the extensive writings of Annie Lacroix; a counterargument was carefully developed by Jean Bouvier and François Bloch-Lainé. A balanced middle ground may be found in the articles and thesis of Gérard Bossuat.[5] The French edition of this book has been used to reinforce the theses of both camps. Reviewers in *Le Monde* and *L'Express* have stressed the limited nature of the conclusions reached about what American influence accomplished; those in *Le Monde Diplomatique* and *L'Humanité* have dwelled on the extensive and often heavy-handed American presence and activity in France.[6] These reviews are not necessarily contradictory; American influence was both pervasive and ineffective at once.

A study of that influence thus invites several reflections. I have eschewed any attempt to characterize American–French relations in the postwar era by a label. France was not a colony or a protectorate, and the use of such terms can only have a polemical intent. Nor is it true, as John L. Harper writes of the Italian case, that the American umbrella brought France a

---

3 See Vojtech Mastny, *Russia's Road to the Cold War* (New York: Columbia University Press, 1979), Daniel Yergin, *A Shattered Peace* (Boston: Houghton Mifflin, 1979), and Jean Elleinstein, *Goliath contre Goliath, Histoire des relations américano–soviétiques. I: L'Enfance des grands (1941–1949)* (Paris: Fayard, 1986).
4 For example, Victor Rothwell, *Britain and the Cold War, 1941–47* (London: Jonathan Cape, 1982), and Terry H. Anderson, *The United States, Great Britain, and the Cold War, 1944–1947* (Columbia: University of Missouri Press, 1981).
5 See the bibliography for a complete listing of the works of these scholars.
6 See reviews by André Laurens, *Le Monde*, June 18–19, 1989; Jacques Nobecourt, *L'Express*, no. 1986, July 28–August 3, 1989; Paul-Marie De La Gorce, *Le Monde Diplomatique*, August 1989; and Alain Guérin in *L'Humanité*, November 9, 1989.

"parenthesis from history," or a respite from the trials and rigors of national independence.[7] France was not Italy, and it could not be so easily manipulated as that defeated and impoverished nation. Nor was France Great Britain, however, where the Americans exercised little influence even in the use of the dollars they so generously infused into the national economy. American influence in France was unusually strong, powerful, direct, felt more concretely from day to day than at any previous time in the national experience or in any period since. American–French relations until 1954 fit into a category of their own, unlike the relationship between France and any other nation, infinitely more important and frought with consequences. It is no exaggeration to say that the history of the Fourth Republic needs to be rewritten to take that influence into account.

It is one thing to demonstrate influence, however, and another to measure its effect. Influence is not quantifiable. Nor is it ever justified to draw a simple relationship of cause and effect. One can cite many examples of the French doing precisely what the Americans urged them to do, but it was rarely demonstrable that the French were reacting to American pressures rather than those from within their own society, or as the case may be, from other nations. There are also incidents in which American pressures had an effect precisely the opposite from that intended, preventing the French from doing what they freely would have done otherwise, for fear of negative publicity. Writing about French internal politics from the American perspective is an invitation to exaggerate the importance of that perspective, away from which the reader should be forewarned.

Foreign influence on internal French politics, economics, and society has rarely been absent from the French scene, moreover. Allan Mitchell has demonstrated the extent to which Adolphe Thiers ruled France after the Franco–Prussian war by dint of the support he received from Berlin as a guarantor of the terms of the peace; an overt press campaign in Berlin warned the French of the consequences of his fall from power.[8] Washington never permitted itself so crude a manifestation of influence. In 1938, following Germany's absorption of Austria, London did not hesitate to inform Daladier that Joseph Paul-Boncour was unacceptable as French foreign minister because of his hard-line attitude toward Berlin. But both of these incidents pale beside the shameful German domination of France during the war and the obsequiousness of Vichy. It is perhaps worth stressing that the emergence of France from such domination, while leading to the proud show of independence of a de Gaulle, nevertheless left most of his countrymen chastened by a demonstration of the opposite, their dependence on a benevolent foreign power in order to maintain their endangered freedoms.

[7] John L. Harper, *America and the Reconstruction of Italy* (New York: Cambridge University Press, 1986).
[8] Allan Mitchell, *The German Influence in France after 1890: The Formation of the French Republic,* (Durham: University of North Carolina Press, 1979).

That dependence was built into the structure of the postwar world, the consequence of a war that impoverished almost all those nations that fought in it with the exception of the United States. At war's end France, like the rest of Western Europe, faced enormous shortages that could be met only from America. France was also strongly influenced by the Soviet Union through the internal strength of the French Communist party. The strength of the French Communists was such that it appeared for a time that no government could be formed without the party's cooperation, and that internal French social stability depended upon its willingness to maintain labor peace. These policies in turn were believed to depend upon the strategic choices of the USSR. The postwar French elite was virtually unanimous in this view, which is mirrored in the American diplomatic documents. It remains today the common belief of most historians.[9] It is hardly surprising that those same elites turned to American intervention in France as a means of freeing themselves from dependence on the whims of the Soviet Union and Stalin.

Questions of internal French social structure became linked to external geopolitical considerations, but this, too, was built into the structure of international relations in the period. A policy of French reconstruction based on egalitarian sharing of burdens in full independence would have fulfilled the heritage of the Resistance. But such policies were foreclosed to the French democratic left because they implied the cooperation of the Communists, and hence a disproportionate level of Soviet influence in the country if not outright absorption of France into the Soviet bloc. Those on the left who favored such a policy found themselves instead thrown into the arms of the Americans in order to avoid the apparent Soviet danger. American assistance did enable the French elites to dispense with Communist cooperation in the task of economic reconstruction. But it also helped them to carry out that reconstruction on the basis of existing social hierarchies and structures of power. The non-Communist left, faced with a choice between social inequality and Soviet domination, chose inequality because it was tempered by political freedom. Paradoxically, American observers criticized French social inequality and favored a policy based upon the hegemony of the non-Communist left. The Americans could not bring about such a policy, however. Powerful as they were, their choices too were limited by the existing distribution of power and wealth on the French scene.

The peculiarities of American influence do not stop there. Its analysis is made more complex by the nature of the internal American political process. Washington's many bureaucratic agencies did not speak with one voice. The State and Defense departments pursued their own agendas, and each was answerable to a Congress itself deeply divided. When the reconstruc-

---

9   For a contrary view, see Irwin M. Wall, *French Communism in the Era of Stalin: The Quest for Unity and Integration, 1945–1962* (Westport, CT: Greenwood Press, 1983).

tion of Germany became American policy, the Defense Department wished to rush ahead pell-mell, while the State Department temporized for fear of adversely affecting relations with France. When economic aid to Europe became American policy in the form of the Marshall Plan, Congress put that aid under the administration of a new agency, the Economic Cooperation Administration (ECA), which reflected the financial and fiscal conservatism of the businessmen and industrialists who ran it. While the State Department urged pay increases on the French in the hope of strengthening the non-Communist left, the ECA pressed for higher taxes, restraint on wages, and fiscal conservatism in order to prevent inflation. When one speaks of American influence in the postwar era, it is often appropriate to ask which Americans one means.

There was little the French could do to emancipate themselves from American tutelage during the period of the Marshall Plan, from 1948 to 1950. The issue was the acquisition of essential foodstuffs and raw materials without which the economy would collapse, yet for which Paris did not have the means to pay. The willingness of the Americans to provide these products and the ways in which the French used the products provide a central focus to the first part of the story. A turning point occurred in 1949–50 as economic assistance was scaled down to make room for a military buildup. France appeared as dependent on American military largesse as it had been for foodstuffs and raw materials. But the necessity of military aid was conditioned by diplomatic constraints and the reality of France's insertion into NATO and the Western bloc. Clearly that dependence could be lessened if international relations took a turn for the better and the consequence need for weapons was reduced. From 1950 on, French dependence on the United States appeared less a reflection of painful economic reality than the consequence of cold war policies and unbridled colonial warfare. Consciousness of this emerged in the phenomenon of neutralism and the struggle against the Indochina conflict. With this realization, and the growing ability of France to manage its economy without help, it became possible to foresee an end to the existing subordination to Washington.

France's dependence on the United States was further exaggerated by the colonial consensus of the French elite, the widespread belief that without its colonial empire France faced a future of decadance and decline to the status of a second class power. To fight its colonial war in Indochina France had to convince Washington of that conflict's relevance to the cold war against communism. Here again the Americans discovered the structural limits of their power. They provided the means for France to fight a war they had initially opposed because they favored the independence of colonial peoples. But they could do nothing to force France to grant that independence. The French soon perceived that their dependence on Washington was aggravated by their colonial ambitions and could be lessened by an end to the conflict. At the same time they became aware that they enjoyed a greater margin for maneuver in East–West diplomacy in proportion to their willingness to sacrifice the enormous amounts of military aid Washington dispensed. This new consciousness came to the fore with defeat in Indochina and the government of Pierre Mendès France. In the events of 1954 one can discern a turning point, in which the unusual dependence of the postwar period came to an end, and more or less normal international relations were resumed.

Within all these constraints there was room for decision. The enormity of American influence was written into the postwar structure; how it would be exercised was not. Washington's relations with specific French elites, groups, parties, and personalities, its subjective appreciation of the purpose and value of each, and its actions consequent upon that evaluation, all remain the subject of analysis. It is with these questions that this study remains concerned.

It is perhaps pertinent to make some remark about the bane of the historian, moral judgment. At every point in this analysis the reader may feel constrained to ask whether this action was proper, or that policy constituted a violation of French sovereignty. The notion of sovereignty as the ultimate value that no action in the international relations of independent states can be allowed to violate was the cardinal rule governing the actions of statesmen. It was no less an artificial concept. Nations sacrifice a portion of their sovereignty every time they make an agreement or sign a treaty or enter into an alliance, indeed every time they act on the international scene. The Americans seemed most aware of this reality in the postwar world – they most fervently propagated the message of global interdependence and argued that the prosperity of all was dependent upon the reconstruction of an international system of trade, payments, and mutual obligation. The specific system they favored may have been the one that most conformed to their subjective appreciation of their interests, but they were perfectly reasonable in arguing that some system was necessary. The same consideration should be brought to bear on the question of less tangible questions of influence, political, economic, or cultural. Such influences are part of the stuff of international relations and occur by virtue of nations and cultures being aware of one another and inhabitants of the same planet. Books will no doubt continue to be written about the perils of "Franglais," the defense of the *chanson* against the inroads of rock music, and like subjects. They have their place – as descriptions of the natural order of things. Very little of their subject matter is susceptible to analysis in terms of freely made decisions of historical actors.

The focus of this book then is not so much American influence, which is taken for granted, but the constraints within which it operated and how it was exercised and reacted to by the political figures involved. Even within these limits it is a fascinating story.

1

The diplomatic heritage

I   A TROUBLED LEGACY

BETWEEN 1947 AND 1954 the United States and France entered into an intimate relationship characterized by unprecedented American involvement in French internal affairs. Both peoples harbored cultural stereotypes about the other, and their diplomatic legacy ill prepared them for their new relationship. Antinomies in the two cultures became exaggerated through confrontation: French Cartesianism versus American pragmatism, statism versus private initiative, centralization versus decentralization, a revolutionary myth versus a carefully cultivated myth of national consensus.[1] The United States became the standard of modernization for most nations in the postwar era. The French blamed their traditions for their nation's relative backwardness, and were invited to internalize an American image of themselves as feudal, archaic, politically unstable, and economically stagnant, a "stalemate society."[2]

America's prestige and wealth did not efface a negative French image of the United States as excessively mechanized, devoted to efficiency and rationalization to the neglect of humane values, in short materialist, capitalist, and imperialist. A parallel view was that of a drab, conventional culture, devoid of individualism, "A dictatorship without a dictator, exercised by everyone over everyone else."[3] America was regarded as uncultured, a society of overgrown children imbued with naive optimism, a country of prag-

---

[1] Jacques Thibau, *La France Colonisée* (Paris: Flammarion, 1980).

[2] Stanley Hoffmann, *In Search of France* (New York: Harper & Row, 1964). Similar theories find their way into French academic circles, as Thibau points out, in the works of Michel Crozier.

[3] Albert Beguin, quoted in Jacques Freymond, "America in European Eyes," *Annals of the American Academy of Political and Social Science*, 295 (September 1954): 33–41.

matists devoid of theoretical understanding. Americans were convinced of their own superiority and impervious to the wisdom born of experience that characterized the old world.

To Americans, the French were a nation of petit bourgeois, tight fisted and cautious, characterized by cynicism and sarcasm, fickleness and intense nationalism. John Adams wrote in 1778 that France was a nation of luxury, dissipation, and effeminacy, and little would seem to have occurred in the next 150 years to change his countrymen's minds. The French became known for their luxurious clothes, artistic achievements, and wines and cheeses, while German industrial products were the most prized. Underlying all was a preference for Anglo-Saxon and Teuton over Latin and Slav; "the niggers [wogs] begin at Calais."[4]

A further disadvantage plagued the French in their dealings with the United States: Alone among the European nations, they lacked a constituency in America. Encounters between the Americans and the French tended to reinforce stereotypes. After both world wars, American troops stationed in France complained of price gouging, surly attitudes, hostility, and indifference.[5] Few such problems were reported when "GIs" interacted with the English, or even the defeated Germans. A minority sentiment of Francophilia has always existed in America, fostered in the main by a cultural and academic elite. But America has a popular tradition of antielitism and anti-intellectualism, which in consequence also works against the French.

A carefully fostered myth of Franco–American friendship enduring over 200 years is belied by the historical record of an often strained and troubled relationship. France was America's oldest ally, and with the brief exception of the November 1942 landings in North Africa, French and American troops have never fired on each other in anger. The historic friendship is evoked by politicians of the two countries on every suitable occasion. In 1983 President Mitterrand was the only foreign head of state invited to the bicentennial celebration of the Battle of Yorktown. In 1986 he returned to the United States to help commemorate 100 years since France presented the United States with the Statue of Liberty. But conflict, suspicion, mistrust, verbal missives, and rumors of war have been the common stuff of Franco–American relations since the founding of the American republic.[6] France was angered by American neutrality in its revolutionary wars. It supported

---

[4]   Crane Brinton, *The Americans and the French* (Cambridge, MA.: Harvard University Press, 1968).

[5]   On the post–World War I incidents, see Henry Blumenthal, *Illusion and Reality in Franco–American Diplomacy, 1914–45* (Baton Rouge: Louisiana State University Press, 1986), p. 74, and see below.

[6]   Marvin Zahniser, *Uncertain Friendship: American–French Diplomatic Relations through the Cold War* (New York: John Wiley and Sons, 1975). See also the classic account by Jean-Baptiste Duroselle, *La France et les Etats Unis des Origines à nos jours* (Paris: Seuil, 1976).

the independence of Texas from the United States and the Confederacy during the Civil War. Napoleon III's ill-fated attempt to conquer Mexico was deeply resented in Washington. Under the Third Republic there was only moderate improvement; the French attempt to build a canal across the Panama isthmus was the source of friction, as was France's sympathy for Spain during the Spanish–American war.

The United States entered World War I more out of sympathy with England than with France, although economic ties of trade and loans had by 1917 bound up American prosperity with both countries. To be sure, French feats of arms during the war evoked admiration and favorable propaganda in the United States. Note the absurdly favorable doggerel by Henry Van Dyke:

> Give us a name to fill the mind
> With stirring thoughts that lead mankind
> A name like a star, a name of light
> I give you France.[7]

But America entered the war as an "Associated," not an "Allied" power. A rebuilt Germany was perceived in Washington, after both world wars, as the key to any renewed prosperity for Europe and the world. The United States resisted French territorial demands in the Rhineland and the Ruhr; nor would it recognize any link between French indebtedness and German reparations. The French argued that they had fought the war on behalf of a common cause: Were not the rivers of French blood spilled over four years repayment enough for a few American billions?[8] But Washington demanded it be paid in full. After the Second World War the United States again blocked French aspirations in the Rhineland and the Ruhr, and the refrain of "French blood for American money" poisoned efforts to build a common front against communism in the French phase of the Indochina War.

Anger and recrimination characterized Franco–American relations through the 1920s. France obstructed Washington's disarmament schemes and the United States objected to France's invasion of the Ruhr. President Harding remarked to an astonished Clemenceau visiting in Washington in December 1922 that "Germany's defeat might be the greatest tragedy in history." The United States sought to restore the prosperity of Germany, and the French accepted with ill grace the Dawes Plan of 1924 and the Young Plan of 1929, each of which lowered the amount of German reparations France could expect to receive.[9] The French resisted negotiating a settlement of their war

---

[7] Cited by Zahniser, *Uncertain Friendship;* the poem dates from 1917.
[8] Blumenthal, *Illusion and Reality in Franco–American Diplomacy,* pp. 83–4.
[9] See Stephen Schuker, *The End of French Predominance in Europe: The Financial Crisis of 1924 and the Adoption of the Dawes Plan* (Chapel Hill: University of North Carolina Press, 1976), and Melvyn P. Leffler, *The Elusive Quest: America's Pursuit*

debts with Washington, finally signing an agreement in 1929. Another pattern can be discerned in European efforts to involve the United States in the affairs of the old continent while minimizing American influence. The Kellog–Briand pact to renounce war originated in April 1927 as a French bilateral proposal to Washington and was clearly meant to imply a special relationship between the two nations if not an alliance, but Secretary of State Kellog effectively parried it by proposing a general (and meaningless) agreement open to all.[10]

In December 1932 the French Chamber of Deputies defaulted on a minimal interest payment to the United States. In 1934 Congress responded with the Johnson Act, which prohibited American loans to any nation that had defaulted on debt payments. Together with American neutrality legislation, and the strong pro-appeasement sentiment in the State Department, the act greatly inhibited French efforts to draw the United States into European security arrangements in the 1930s.[11] The United States refused to embargo oil to Italy during the Ethiopian crisis, took a hands-off attitude toward the German remilitarization of the Rhineland, and said it would not trade with either side in the Spanish Civil War, a policy that greatly harmed Spain's legal Republican government. American unwillingness to intervene at all in European efforts to stop fascist aggression greatly strengthened the forces of appeasement in the democracies.

Léon Blum's Popular Front government nevertheless sought the closest possible relationship to the United States and England; Blum was an Atlanticist before his time. His policy was logical in view of the perceived unreliability of France's alliance with Russia, in light of the purges taking place in that country. But Washington obliged Blum to forgo exchange controls on the franc and postpone a devaluation, the need for which was painfully apparent when he came to power in June 1936. This is not to say that Blum would have devalued without Washington's pressure, but the pursuit of an American connection may, in the long run, still have done the Popular Front more harm than good. Blum passionately admired Roosevelt and the New Deal, which he saw as similar to his own Popular Front experiment.[12] While the American State Department regarded Blum at this time as a radical revolutionary, Roosevelt privately at least in part reciprocated Blum's feelings:

        of European Stability and French Security, 1919–1933 (Chapel Hill: University of
        North Carolina Press, 1979).
10   Blumenthal, *Illusion and Reality in Franco–American Diplomacy*, pp. 135–47.
11   On American appeasement see Arnold A. Offner, *The Origins of the Second World
        War: American Foreign Policy and World Politics, 1917–1941* (New York: Praeger,
        1975).
12   Jean Lacouture, *Léon Blum* (Paris: Seuil, 1977). René Girault, "Léon Blum, la déval-
        uation de 1936 et la conduite de la politique extérieure de la France," *Relations
        Internationales*, 13 (Spring 1978): 91–109. Joel Colton, *Léon Blum: Humanist in
        Politics* (New York: Knopf, 1968).

Of course I cannot say anything to even intimate that I am in favor of Blum –
but if Blum can be kept there for a while he may be able to do certain things
that almost every nation in the world has done.[13]

Upon taking office, Blum dispatched Emmanuel Monick, his financial attaché in London, to Washington to begin negotiations on an international
currency "alignment." The French devaluation was finally negotiated between Paris, London, and Washington in September 1936, but by that time
it was probably too late; much capital had already left the country and the
benefit of surprise was lost. Blum nevertheless took satisfaction in an unprecedented international agreement moving toward the stabilization of
currencies.

Blum further proposed to American Ambassador Bullitt that the United
States, France, and England agree to reduce all trade restrictions, renounce
exchange controls, and grant most favored nation status to any nation willing to join with them.[14] Earlier, Secretary of State Cordell Hull told the
French ambassador that $15 billion to $25 billion of world trade needed to
be restored to overcome the depression, or in their economic distress, people
would "enthrone dictators." Minister of Commerce Georges Bonnet replied
that he also favored a liberal trade policy as the only way to the salvation
of the world, or economic nationalism would lead to the ruin of all.[15] Some
measure of free trade represented the consensus in the 1930s of the French
political elite of both right and left. The French proposals show an early
willingness to abandon traditional state controls, or *dirigisme,* in the interest of allied solidarity. They challenge a school of historiography of the
postwar era that attributes such ideas to the Americans alone as a manifestation of their imperialism.[16]

Blum took Ambassador Bullitt into his confidence and helped make the
American embassy a focal point of power and influence in French political
life. This pattern persisted into the postwar era. William Bullitt was the first
of a succession of powerful American ambassadors including William Leahy
(to Vichy), Jefferson Caffery, David Bruce, and C. Douglas Dillon. Bullitt
was a confidant of Franklin Roosevelt, a francophile who spoke the language, and an accomplished diplomat who had served in the USSR – all of
which made him much sought after by French politicians of the right and

[13] Quoted in Martin Weil, *A Pretty Good Club: The Founding Fathers of the U.S.
Foreign Service* (New York: Norton, 1978), p. 89.

[14] Foreign Relations of the United States, 1936, vol. II, Europe, France (Washington,
DC: U.S. Government Printing Office, 1954), October 30, 1936, pp. 95–6. Hereinafter FRUS.

[15] FRUS, 1936, II, Europe, France, January 30, 1936, pp. 86–7, April 2, 1936, pp.
102–3.

[16] See, for example, in France the works of Annie Lacroix-Riz and in the United States
the writings of Gabriel and Joyce Kolko, listed in the bibliography.

left. Blum himself, in an unprecedented act, appeared at the American embassy following Roosevelt's November 1936 election victory, embraced Bullitt,
and expressed his overwhelming joy at the election's outcome.[17] Bullitt reported to Roosevelt that he had established the closest personal relations
with Blum and Foreign Minister Delbos. Bullitt could see them whenever he
wished, and they spoke to him with total frankness and candor. But like his
State department colleagues, Bullitt favored appeasement. He believed that
a Franco–German reconciliation was possible on the basis of antibolshev-
ism and necessary for the preservation of European civilization. He warned
FDR that the French government sought the closest possible relationship
with the United States because they were "hoping to involve us in war."[18]

Bullitt enjoyed the same relationship with Daladier as with Blum. Daladier regularly asked Bullitt for advice and appeared too often ready to follow it. He asked Bullitt to take his children to the United States in the event
of war and asked Roosevelt on the telephone, perhaps not entirely in jest,
whether he could take Bullitt as the French minister of foreign affairs. But
Daladier's intimacy was misplaced. Hitler's *Anschluss* with Austria was
welcomed in the American State Department by Assistant Secretary Berle,
who saw in it national self-determination and the needed acquisition by
Germany of markets and raw materials, the absence of which was likely to
make her turn toward war.[19] Berle further counseled British and French
concessions to Hitler on the Czech question. Bullitt agreed, warning that
war would result in "the complete destruction of Western Europe and bolshevism from one end of the continent to the other."[20] American pressure
during the Munich crisis was in favor of peace and the acceptance of German demands. Bullitt, under French pressure, asked authorization from Hull
to state that "no one could predict" what America would do in case of a
European war, but even this was denied.[21] Bullitt wrote Roosevelt that the
French "dreamed" that the collaboration of England, France, and the United
States could impose a peace upon Germany, but Bullitt thought that "we
ought to make it clear that the United States, like God, helps those who help
themselves."[22] The analogy became an American staple of the postwar era.

The French did not lose hope of securing American involvement in their
affairs. The premier's office received nervous reports about American public

[17] Orville H. Bullitt, ed., *For the President, Personal and Secret: Correspondence be-
     tween Franklin D. Roosevelt and William C. Bullitt* (Boston: Houghton Mifflin, 1972),
     p. 181.
[18] Ibid., pp. 184, 196.
[19] Blumenthal, *Illusion and Reality in Franco–American Diplomacy*, p. 241.
[20] Bullitt, *For the President*, pp. 245, 267.
[21] John McVicker Haight, Jr., "France, the United States, and the Munich Crisis," *Jour-
     nal of Modern History*, 34, no. 4 (December 1960): 340–58. On the other hand
     Bullitt had to warn Daladier that in the event of war the United States could not sell
     France any arms.
[22] Bullitt, *For the President*, p. 206.

opinion with regard to France (55% of Americans favored England, 11% only France, and 8% Germany among European countries in July 1938). No favor requested by Americans was too small to receive the highest attention.[23] Bullitt did help the French in the purchase of American airplanes. In May 1938 he suggested that Daladier send Jean Monnet to the United States on a purchasing mission, recommending Monnet to Roosevelt as "an intimate friend of mine for many years whom I trust as a brother."[24] Monnet, perhaps the most important figure in French–American relations in the postwar era, had extensive American connections and experience. He had worked with Blair Company Investment Bankers of New York on international loan transactions in the 1920s, and was a founding partner of Bank of America. Monnet's mission was facilitated by Roosevelt, who had to overcome the opposition of the army air corps to the release of its new model planes, and the hostility of Congress. Monnet also had to face sniping at home by Bonnet and Reynaud, who thought French gold more useful than attack planes in the event of war. FDR ordered air corps chief General Arnold to release the new Douglas attack bomber to the French or resign.[25]

The French purchasing team, which included two future prime ministers of France, René Pleven and René Mayer, placed orders for 555 airplanes in 1939 and another 1,000 in 1940. The French invested heavily in the expansion of American plants and planned to produce their Amiot bomber in the United States, where manufacturing facilities would remain secure from German attack. Many hundreds of American planes were delivered to France before the outbreak of war, although not nearly enough to affect the outcome of the Battle of France. Most of them rusted in North Africa and Martinique for the remainder of the war. The rest of those on order were taken by the British, to whom Monnet transferred his services after the fall of France.

Bullitt remained in intimate contact with French government officials through the outbreak of the war. He suggested that the French government make a token debt payment, in exchange for which Washington would lift its ban on new loans. The French were willing to sweeten the offer with the lease of bases to the United States on their Pacific Island possessions.[26] Washington, however, remained unreceptive. During the August 1939 crisis over Danzig, Bullitt reported his intimacy with Daladier in unflattering terms:

23 Thus the request of a Professor Schnurer, who taught French at Antioch College, a small liberal arts college in the Midwest, to take a group of students on a camping tour of the French countryside and meet with French students, merited a message from the Prime Minister Chautemps to several prefects counseling a welcome to the "très francophile" professor. See Archives Nationales, Section Contemporaine, F60, 169, Etats Unis; Questions Politiques (July 27, 1938).
24 Bullitt, *For the President*, p. 299.
25 John M. Haight, Jr., *American Aid to France, 1938–1940* (New York: Atheneum, 1970), p. 92 and passim.
26 Bullitt, *For the President*, p. 335.

"I have seen Daladier constantly and intimately throughout this crisis . . . there is nothing he doesn't say . . . he has an altogether too exalted idea of my own value, asks my judgment about nearly everything . . . and is apt to do what I advise." Bullitt continued to urge help to the French and told Roosevelt that Washington's failure to revise neutrality legislation was an encouragement to the Germans to begin a conflict. But Washington was not realistically a factor in the war's outbreak, with or without neutrality legislation.[27]

FDR's reaction to the coming of war was to demonstrate sympathy for Britain and France, and press Congress for the repeal of neutrality legislation. Nevertheless, he felt constrained to undertake several peace initiatives, and dispatched Under Secretary of State Sumner Welles to Europe in February 1940 to see the belligerents about the possibility of a negotiated peace that could only have been based upon the status quo.[28] Chamberlain rebuffed Welles contemptuously, as did Hitler. Daladier told Welles that France's minimum conditions for peace included the restoration of the sovereignty and territorial integrity of Poland and Czechoslovakia. Bullitt reported that the Welles mission had made the most terrible impression, leaving Daladier with the idea that "you [Roosevelt] think Hitler cannot be beaten and want an end to the war."

Bullitt was with Daladier on May 15, 1940, when the defense minister received a telephone report from General Gamelin of the German breakthrough at the Meuse. Daladier urged a counterattack, which Gamelin said was impossible: "It seems obvious (wrote Bullitt) that unless God grants a miracle as at the time of the Battle of the Marne, the French army will be crushed utterly." On June 9, 1940 Prime Minister Paul Reynaud announced to Bullitt the departure of the French government from Paris, asking the ambassador to accompany it to its new location. Bullitt declined, citing the "tradition" of the American ambassador acting as self-styled "protector" of the city.[29] Roosevelt ordered Bullitt to follow the French government, but the ambassador again refused, urging that his deputy, Anthony Biddle, be sent in his place. Bullitt could not run away from anything and be himself, he said, "J'y suis, j'y reste."[30]

Nothing the American ambassador subsequently did engendered more criticism than this final act. Hull, with restrained anger at the contravening of his orders, termed it unfortunate. Charles de Gaulle strongly criticized

---

[27] See Robert Dallek, *Franklin D. Roosevelt and American Foreign Policy, 1932–1945* (New York: Oxford University Press, 1979).

[28] Offner, *The Origins of the Second World War*, pp. 166–9. Bullitt, *For the President*, p. 393.

[29] American ambassadors Elihu Washburne and Myron Herrick had remained in Paris during the Franco–Prussian and First World wars.

[30] Bullitt, *For the President*, p. 466. "Here I am and here I stay," said by Marshal MacMahon at Malikoff in the Crimea.

Bullitt in his memoirs, and Jean Chauvel of the Quai d'Orsay also thought the presence of the ambassador at Tours and Bordeaux might have made a difference: "Having been absent by choice, he perhaps missed a rendezvous with destiny."[31] H. Freeman Matthews was even more categorical about the French government's decision to seek an armistice rather than fight on: "If there was one man who, with his enjoyment of French confidence and dynamic personality, might at one or two critical moments have succeeded in giving the necessary push to swing the scales, that man was Ambassador Bullitt."[32]

The French government nevertheless tried to involve the Americans in the Battle of France. Biddle and Matthews saw Reynaud four times in one day at Tours, to listen to his appeals for at least the promise of eventual American participation in the war. Knowledge that America would fight, Reynaud claimed, would enable the French government to depart for North Africa confident of victory in the long run. But much of Reynaud's histrionic posing was simply for effect; everyone knew the Americans would do nothing. Moreover, Matthews and Biddle could not help but observe the ubiquitous presence of Reynaud's mistress, Helène des Portes, whose influence was working strongly in the direction of an armistice with the Germans. Never ceasing her pleas for capitulation, Matthews reported, "she spent one whole hour weeping in my office one afternoon in a futile endeavor to get us to support her stand." Matthews watched Reynaud turn "ashen gray with panic" as news poured in from the front, while the influence of presidents of the Chamber and Senate, Eduard Herriot and Jules Jeanneney, and the minister of the interior, the "cold-blooded Jew [Georges] Mandel," all of whom were in favor of resistance, ebbed away.[33]

In Paris Bullitt helped get the capital declared an open city. There is no evidence to suggest he could or would have advised the French government to resist had he followed Reynaud to Tours. On the contrary, the ease with which Washington accepted the establishment of the Vichy regime, and the studious contempt with which the State Department regarded the appeal for Resistance of the little-known Charles de Gaulle, suggest that the United States shared in the "decadence" it held responsible for France's collapse. Bullitt supported the continuation of relations with Vichy, while Washington contented itself with what it was able to achieve. The Americans believed that the French fleet, in part because of a blunt warning by Roosevelt,

31 *The War Memoirs of Charles de Gaulle,* vol. 1 (New York: Simon and Schuster, 1959); Jean Chauvel, *Commentaire,* I: *De Vienne à Alger (1938–1944)* [Paris: Fayard, 1971], pp. 216–7.
32 National Archives and Records Administration (hereinafter NARA), General Records of the Department of State, Matthews–Hickerson File, Microfilm Reel 13, August 14, 1940, and in his critique of William Langer's *Our Vichy Gamble,* January 17, 1945.
33 NARA, Matthews–Hickerson File, Microfilm Reel 13, August 14, 1940.

was kept out of German hands (although Darlan would probably not have permitted its surrender in any case), and the Germans as yet showed no interest in the French empire. The fleet and empire seemed sufficient reason for the conservative diplomats in the State Department to continue doing business with Vichy. Pétain's regime contained the traditional elites of French society with whom the State Department was accustomed to deal. The corresponding hostility with which the United States came to regard the so-called Free French, as Secretary of State Hull was to term them, was the corollary of America's Vichy policy and did much to set the pattern of American–French relations in the postwar period.

II THE UNITED STATES, VICHY, AND THE FREE FRENCH

In 1947 the distinguished historian William Langer published a defense of American policy with regard to Vichy France titled "Our Vichy Gamble."[34] Langer's work was commissioned, and he was given access to State Department documents that otherwise remained closed to researchers for the next thirty years. He argued that the United States entered into a risky and morally repugnant relationship with the Pétain regime because of overriding national security concerns. The Americans were concerned that the French fleet and possessions in North Africa stay out of German hands, and they hoped to pressure Vichy against joining the war on the German side against England.

Several other considerations worked in favor of Washington's so-called Vichy gamble. An American presence could weigh in internal power struggles in Vichy. It was believed that Marshal Pétain (code-named "Popeye") was fundamentally anti-German but that pressure in favor of collaboration came from his ministers, in particular the sinister Pierre Laval ("Black Peter"). Admiral Leahy was sent as ambassador with instructions to become as close to Pétain as possible and keep him informed about the actions of his subordinates. Reportedly lucid for only half the day due to age, Pétain, the Americans believed, could not keep close supervision over French affairs (code-named the "Frog Pond").[35] Washington picked up valuable intelligence in Vichy, some of it passed on by American sympathizers in the French administration and the intelligence services of the Deuxième Bureau. Finally, the Americans believed that General Weygand would eventually bring North Africa over to the allies. Robert Murphy was sent to North Africa to cultivate Weygand, who allowed American intelligence agents to operate

---

[34] New York: Alfred A. Knopf, 1947.
[35] William D. Leahy, *I Was There* (New York: McGraw-Hill, 1950), pp. 6–7. The code names appear in the Matthews–Hickerson File, NARA.

freely in the guise of food-aid administrators. In this way, according to Langer, the ground was prepared for the allied invasion of North Africa, carried out with little or no French resistance in November 1942.[36]

But there was more to American policy toward Vichy than realpolitik. Immediately after the fall of France, a consensus formed in the United States that the catastrophe had occurred because of French internal weakness rather than military defeat. National complacency, self-indulgence, and a fifth column were responsible, a weakness of the nation's moral fiber in the face of the threat of totalitarianism.[37] French democracy, rather than the fascist regimes, was regarded in Washington as morally decadent, and to many observers France appeared ready for a national revolution. There was no "Vichy gamble"; America's Vichy policy was instead the logical culmination of isolation and appeasement, and it expressed the beliefs and prejudices of those who implemented it. State Department officials feared and disliked bolshevism much more than they did nazism in the 1930s, and Bullitt was no exception. He shared the fears of conservative French politicians that Paris would succumb to communist revolution while awaiting the German armies. Franklin Roosevelt had long been contemptuous of France and critical of the Third Republic. He thought France needed to Americanize its political system by installing a stable executive and limiting the number of political parties. His hope that Pétain might be the instrument of needed change might well account for his initial message of "sympathy and understanding" to the marshal, and praise of Pétain's "steadfast courage and determination in pursuit of a free and independent France."[38]

Admiral Leahy developed a genuine sympathy for the marshal. If Leahy could not tolerate Laval, he was equally bitter with regard to de Gaulle, and advised against the United States entering into relations with the Free French: "The radical Gaullists whom I have met do not have the stability, intelligence, and popular standing in their communities that should be necessary to succeed in their announced purpose."[39] Leahy attributed the Gaullist pressure in the United States to "a group of Jews and Communists in this country who feared Darlan's 'fascist' attitude." Robert Murphy, of German-Irish and devoutly Catholic background, displayed sympathy for assorted right wing politicians and schemers who permeated the Vichy regime; Murphy personally "liked" Admiral Darlan. Franklin Roosevelt also showed sympathy for Darlan, whose son was stricken with polio just before

---

[36] Robert Murphy, *Diplomat among Warriors* (Garden City, NY: Doubleday, 1964). Langer, *Our Vichy Gamble.*

[37] Julian Hurstfield, *America and the French Nation, 1939–1945* (Chapel Hill: University of North Carolina Press, 1986), pp. 31–7.

[38] Milton Viorst, *Hostile Allies: FDR and Charles de Gaulle* (New York: Macmillan, 1965), p. 55.

[39] Leahy, *I Was There*, p. 42.

the North Africa landings. The president arranged treatment for the younger Darlan in Warm Springs, Georgia. Murphy inveighed against the Popular Front, held Blum responsible for French unpreparedness in 1940, and blamed Vichy antisemitism on the large number of Jews in the French Communist party. Murphy arranged to bring back Marcel Peyrouton from his post as ambassador to Argentina so he could serve as an administrator in North Africa, citing the experience and "anti-German" sentiment of the former minister of the interior under Vichy.[40]

The "normality" of American relations with Vichy continued despite the removal of General Weygand; Leahy protested, but Pétain told him German pressure had been too much to resist. A review of the Vichy policy in Washington concluded that despite Weygand's dismissal, there was no alternative to its continuance. Any alternative meant pushing Vichy even further toward collaboration.[41] The return of Laval to power in the spring of 1942 did lead to the recall of Leahy, who by that time had given up on the policy. Pétain was then told that the appointment of Laval "would make it impossible for America to continue its attitude of helpfulness to France," but the marshal ignored the warning. Still there was no change in Washington's attitude toward French affairs.

The Darlan affair at the time of the North African landings should offer little mystery. In the summer of 1942 the Americans had identified General Giraud, whose dashing escape from a German prison camp captured the imagination of Roosevelt, as the best candidate to administer the French territories slated to come under their tutelage. Giraud's politics, however, differed little from those of Vichy. He was brought to Gibralter too late to be of use in the landings, and then proved to be absurdly obstinate, insisting upon sole command of the allied forces. Darlan, on the other hand, was in Algiers "fortuitously" when the landings took place, so the Americans turned to him. Murphy tried to organize several internal coups, with the assistance of Jacques Lemaigre-Debreuil, which were meant to bring sympathizers to power in North Africa in order to nullify anticipated resistance to the landings. They were ill-timed, however, and quickly failed. There seemed no remaining choice but to appeal to Darlan in an effort to head off French resistance to the landing of American forces. Darlan, approached by Murphy, in turn appealed to the Marshal, during which time French forces fired on the Americans and several thousand casualties were suffered on both sides.

Darlan ultimately claimed he had Pétain's authority to call off resistance

---

[40]   Martin Weil, *A Pretty Good Club*, p. 123; Murphy, *Diplomat among Warriors*, pp. 128–30.

[41]   An ironic claim in view of what is now known of Vichy's many offers of collaboration that were spurned by the Germans. See Robert Paxton, *Vichy France: Old Guard and New Order, 1940–1944* (New York: Norton, 1975).

to the Americans, in exchange for which the United States simply allowed the continuation of the Vichy regime in North Africa under his authority: "Vichyism under American protectorate." The Darlan deal, like the "Vichy gamble" of which it was a continuation, was an abject failure. Darlan neither delivered the French fleet, which was scuttled in its harbor at Toulon, nor smoothed the allied landings. Moreover it was not lost on the Free French, with whom Washington would not deal officially because their democratic character had not been demonstrated, that no such scruples apparently applied to a collaborator and a fascist.[42] Little wonder then that the murder of Darlan on Christmas day, 1942, was termed by American General Mark Clark an "act of Providence, the lancing of a boil." But even Darlan's murder did not force a reconsideration of the Vichy policy, by this time the object of widespread protest by liberal public opinion in the United States – a policy from which even the British had felt it necessary to dissociate themselves. Vichy repressive legislation remained intact in North Africa under General Giraud despite the supervision of the American military occupation.[43]

American antipathy to de Gaulle was the counterpart of the carefully cultivated relations with Vichy. Roosevelt's problems with the general have commonly been attributed to differences in their characters, but they shared a deep sense of mission and often arrogant authoritarianism that made them intolerant of opposition. De Gaulle had the same personal problems with Churchill as with Roosevelt, and more than once, the British prime minister agreed with the American president that the French general must be eliminated from the scene. Churchill was dissuaded from his antipathy to de Gaulle, however, by the British war cabinet, which had a profound sense of the need for a restored and strengthened France as a guarantee to British security on the continent once the war ended.[44]

Differences were compounded by the French need to establish a sense of identity and strengthened dignity in opposition to "les Anglo-Saxons." The Free French were granted lend-lease aid in July 1941 and allowed permanent representation in Washington from November, in recognition of their control over sections of the French empire. In New Caledonia an arrangement was worked out for the landing of an American force to defend the island against the Japanese. No sooner had U.S. forces arrived, however, than they found themselves involved in a local dispute between Governor Henri Sautot, and the emissary of de Gaulle sent to replace him, Admiral

---

42   *The War Memoirs of Charles de Gaulle,* vol. II: *Unity,* p. 53.
43   The story of the Darlan affair has been told in numerous works. Langer's account is still accurate. Clark is quoted in Viorst, *Hostile Allies,* p. 130. Washington always believed, however, that the Gaullists were responsible for the assassination.
44   On de Gaulle's relations with Great Britain see François Kersaudy, *De Gaulle et Churchill* (Paris: Plon, 1981).

Thierry d'Argenlieu.[45] When angry islanders temporarily arrested d'Argenlieu and restored Sautot, de Gaulle charged the Americans with interference and imperialism. American anticolonialism was interpreted during the war by both Churchill and de Gaulle as masking the imperialism of Washington, which allegedly wished to penetrate the colonial empires of its rivals once the war was ended.[46]

Murphy attributed Roosevelt's contempt for the Free French to their part in the failed attempt to take Dakar in September 1940, although the British shared responsibility for that fiasco.[47] De Gaulle's move to take over the islands of Saint-Pierre and Miquelon off the Canadian Atlantic coast in December 1941 angered Washington, which had given assurances to Vichy against any transfer of sovereignty over French possessions in the American hemisphere. Hull's intemperate reference to the "so-called Free French" on that occasion caused a storm of criticism among liberals in the United States who were critical of American dealings with Vichy and early rallied to the Gaullist banner. Hull's amour propre was wounded by the incident, which also pitted the Roosevelt administration against the liberal constituency to which it normally looked for support.[48] The vocal anti-Gaullism of much of the French community in exile in America also worked strongly against the interests of the Free French. Most prominent among them was Alexis Leger, former secretary general of the French Ministry of Foreign Affairs, who advised the State Department on European policy and influenced it against de Gaulle. The Free French delegation in Washington was also ill-served by its head, Adrien Tixier, who often took administration officials into his confidence when expressing his own doubts about de Gaulle.[49] The Darlan affair was thus only the latest and worst of a series of clashes between the Free French and Washington. Received by Roosevelt on November 20, 1942, André Philip protested the arrangement with Darlan: "We are not a colony. the American government will never make us accept the authority of traitors."[50] FDR replied angrily that the American government would deal with whom it wished. The president confided to Murphy at Casablanca that he much preferred Vichy officials to the obstreperous Free French.[51]

Yet none of these reasons appears sufficient to explain an antipathy to the Free French that continued in Washington long after the Vichy policy

[45]　Kim Munholland, "The Trials of the Free French in New Caledonia, 1940–1942," *French Historical Studies*, 14, no. 4 (Fall 1986): 547–79.

[46]　William Roger Louis, *Imperialism at Bay, 1941–45: The United States and the Decolonization of the British Empire* (Oxford: The Clarendon Press, 1977).

[47]　Murphy, *Diplomat among Warriors*, p. 77; Kersaudy, *De Gaulle et Churchill*, pp. 82–7.

[48]　Hurstfield, *America and the French Nation*, pp. 173–83.

[49]　Raoul Aiglion, *De Gaulle et Roosevelt* (Paris: Plon, 1984).

[50]　Viorst, *Hostile Allies*, p. 130.

[51]　Murphy, *Diplomat among Warriors*, p. 181.

had been abandoned. The United States continued its attempt to install its own candidate, General Giraud, as head of the French Committee of National Liberation, and refused to recognize the Committee's transformation into a provisional government. Washington excluded the Committee from plans for the Normandy invasion and proceeded with plans for a military government of France, until such time as the French proved they were able to choose a government for themselves. Roosevelt fancied himself, not the Free French, as the custodian of French sovereignty once the Vichy option was abandoned. Interestingly, this attitude did much to cement Resistance support for de Gaulle – Resisters feared the idea of an American military government as much as Vichy or the Germans, who were assumed to be vanishing from the scene in any case.[52] Roosevelt finally invited de Gaulle to join the Giraud regime at Casablanca in January 1943, bowing to American public opinion and recognizing the extensive colonial territories the Free French controlled. But FDR failed to endear himself to de Gaulle, referring to a "shotgun wedding" between the two generals, and comparing France to a child "unable to fend for itself," over which the allies proposed to act as guardians until the war was over.[53]

The basis of American antipathy to the Free French went beyond objections to de Gaulle, to the substance of American hopes and expectations about the future political and social order of France at the end of the war. The United States was not happy with either alternative, Pétain or de Gaulle. To be sure, the Office of Strategic Services (OSS) was generally favorable to de Gaulle, and Eisenhower wanted to deal with him for pragmatic reasons. But both Hull and Roosevelt rejected this advice, regarding both as military dictators, equally repugnant politically. In social terms, the Americans preferred Pétain, who represented the traditional elites in France with whom the State Department was accustomed to doing business and with whom it hoped to resume its relations after the war, while around de Gaulle there was the distinct aroma of political radicalism and social revolution.

In a January 1944 report on the "Reasons underlying this government's lack of confidence in de Gaulle," the State Department complained of vitriolic anti-Americanism among the Free French and their subordination of military to "political goals." They exhibited a narrow, chauvinistic nationalism, posed the "threat of dictatorship," and displayed "subservience to the Russians."[54] Alexis Leger described de Gaulle's democratic claims as the "sheerest propaganda," and the General's methods as "similar to those of Hitler." De Gaulle was emotionally unstable, and exercised brutal control over his followers through the use of torture. A September 1943 report on the French Resistance declared that politically and economically "he seeks

52   See John F. Sweets, *The Politics of Resistance in France* (De Kalb: Northern Illinois University Press, 1976).
53   Don Cook, *Charles de Gaulle* (New York: 1984), p. 168.
54   NARA, Matthews–Hickerson File, Microfilm Reel 13, January 1944.

a military socialistic dictatorship in alliance with the Communist party."[55]
Pierre Cot, returning from a mission to Washington in January 1943, warned
the Gaullist leadership that the State Department regarded it as Communist
influenced.[56] Washington could not prevent the admission of de Gaulle into
a reorganized French Committee of National Liberation, but Matthews expected Murphy and Monnet to "harness" de Gaulle in the Committee, where
his only sure vote was "the rabid [André] Philip." The Americans feared
that the general would attempt a military putsch in Algiers. As a precaution,
Matthews urged Murphy to hold up authority for de Gaulle's "little play-
mates," Diethelm, Soustelle ("the propagandist"), and Passy and Pelebon
("the killers") to leave London for Algiers, for these were people who would
"stop at nothing," and Algiers would be a "fertile field for their gunplay."
In London, Matthews investigated murky affairs involving the Free French
and reported in detail on the Dufour case, which he regarded as proof of de
Gaulle's "fascist tendencies." (Dufour sued the Free French in British courts,
claiming that he had been tortured on suspicion of being a spy for the British.[57]) De Gaulle claimed the case had been concocted by British Intelligence
and American Secret Services in order to "splatter filth on me."

Jean Monnet was sent to Algiers by the Americans to act as a political
adviser to the inept Giraud and to "harness" de Gaulle. Monnet enjoyed
the confidence of many highly placed Americans, but Hull did not trust
Monnet and warned against sending him, and it seems clear that Monnet
did eventually change sides in Algiers, recognizing the greater political abil-
ities of de Gaulle. Monnet loyally did his best to democratize the Giraud
regime and to bring about a fusion between it and the Free French.[58] But he
could not prevent Giraud from being maneuvered out of his position of
authority by the more politically astute de Gaulle. Murphy was bitter at this
turn of events, but Monnet was impressed by the loyalty to de Gaulle declared by the National Council of the Resistance on May 15, 1943. Washington was not.[59]

The Americans resisted concluding that the future government of France
had been decided, and would not contribute to de Gaulle's claim by accord-

[55] Ibid., September 1943.
[56] Hervé Alphand, *L'Etonnement d'être: Journal 1937–1973* (Paris: Fayard, 1977), p.
      142.
[57] Hurstfield, *America and the French Nation*, p. 193. The State Department even planted
      an article about the case in the *Reader's Digest* in order to counter pro-Gaullist sen-
      timent in the United States.
[58] André Kaspi, *La Mission de Jean Monnet à Alger, Mars–Octobre, 1943* (Paris: Pub-
      lications de la Sorbonne, 1971).
[59] Murphy, *Diplomat among Warriors*, 181. Monnet, in his memoirs, confirms Mur-
      phy's account of what happened, and it is clear de Gaulle would never have kept him
      on had he not supported the general against Giraud: Jean Monnet, *Memoires* (Paris:
      Fayard, 1976), 199. Hervé Alphand also remarked that Monnet did "invaluable work
      for us": *L'Etonnement d'être*, p. 173.

ing him prior recognition. American policy had been charted in informal discussions of the President's Advisory Commission on Postwar Foreign Policy, which consisted of academicians, journalists, and other prominent persons selected to develop policies toward the various European countries after the war. In a February 26, 1943 meeting devoted to France, the Commission described the options as: (1) an authoritarian, Vichy-type regime, (2) a Communist or Popular Front regime, or (3) a new, democratic, Fourth Republic, which would have "markedly socialistic trends."[60] The United States could not choose either a hands-off policy, rejected as impossible in practice, or the recognition of a provisional civil government outside of France, equally objectionable because the French were said to dislike military men and emigrés in politics, proscriptions that applied to both Giraud and de Gaulle. The only remaining policy, the Commission agreed, was "indirect encouragement to moderate elements" in France, while the United States undertook to ensure conditions necessary for a free choice by the French people by means of a "long period of military occupation." The eminent historian Shepard B. Clough noted that income disparities in France were extreme, and expressed the fear that social inequality augured ill for political stability in the country. But other members of the Commission rejected Clough's analysis as going beyond the range of options with which it was appropriate for the United States to be involved. On the other hand *New York Times* columnist Anne Hare McCormick insisted that "France could have any government it wanted ... even a Communist regime. The United States laid down only the conditions that it be freely chosen by the French people. Any government which guaranteed a bill of rights to which all United Nations members subscribed would be satisfactory for France."

At the Tehran conference of the Big Three in November 1943, Stalin and FDR agreed that France after the war could not be restored to Great Power status. For Stalin the Vichy regime represented the "real" France; FDR agreed, and declared that no Frenchman over age 40 should be allowed to participate in the administration of his country: They were all corrupt. "The first necessity for the French, not only for the government but for the people as well, was to become honest citizens." Both agreed as a matter of course that Indochina should not be returned to France. But whatever FDR's preferences with regard to the evolution of the Free French, he could not influence its development. De Gaulle easily outmaneuvered Giraud in Algiers, and even as Stalin and Roosevelt spoke, the outcome was already determined.[61]

The Americans nevertheless resented Giraud's elimination; on April 6, 1944 Murphy noted that with his demise "American prestige has suffered a

---

60 NARA, Record Group 59, Records of Harley A. Notter, Records of the Advisory Commission on Post-War Foreign Police, Division of Political Studies, T Minutes 41 and 42, February 26 and March 5, 1943.
61 John D. Wheeler-Bennett and Anthony Nicholls, *A Semblance of Peace: The Political Settlement after the Second World War* (New York: Norton, 1974), p. 144.

distinct setback in recent months," a discreet reference to the general's obvious incompetence. Disturbed by rumors of American interest in a possible
revival of the Vichy regime, Washington issued several statements insisting
that the United States would have no further relations with Vichy "except
for the purpose of abolishing it." On the other hand, the Americans continued to reject any hint of recognition of the Committee. Monnet's expectation of recognition represented "misunderstanding, wishful thinking, or desire to please." General Eisenhower was authorized, prior to the Normandy
landings, to "consult with the French Committee of National Liberation
and authorize them in your discretion to select and install the personnel
necessary for [a French] administration," but he was not to limit such personnel to the Committee, nor take any step that implied official recognition
of it. To Churchill's entreaties on behalf of the Committee, FDR wrote that
he was unable to recognize any government of France until the French people had the opportunity for a free choice. The French were expected to
"subordinate political activity to the necessity for unity in ejecting and de-
stroying the enemy."[62]

Roosevelt objected when the French National Committee declared itself
to be the "Provisional Government of the French Republic" on May 16,
1944. Under Secretary of State James Dunn told Monnet the United States
would not deal with any "Provisional Government," the creation of which
made for "difficult questions" that "it would seem highly desirable to avoid."[63]
FDR told Churchill that recognition would amount to imposing de Gaulle
on the French people, and instructed his representative, Selden Chapin, that
de Gaulle would be welcome if he wished to come to Washington but was
not a head of state and could not be invited. On June 4, 1944 Murphy
revealed his continued dislike of the Gaullists, whose propaganda was
"marked by suspicion of Anglo–American motives and harping criticism of
our military, economic, and financial and political performance." Noting
French rumors of alleged American designs on North Africa, Murphy wrote
that "We fared as well under the Vichy press, as rotten as it was. Under the
present system of course we are permitted to supply the newsprint."[64]

Another measure of American hostility to the Gaullist movement lay in
the contrasting treatment of Vichy and the Free French on the colonial question. In its dealings with Pétain and then Darlan, the United States gave
formal assurances of its intent to preserve the integrity of the French empire.[65] The promises appeared to be inconsistent with the goals enunciated

[62] FRUS, 1944, III, British Commonwealth and Europe, France, January 14, 1944, pp.
     641–2; April 6, 1944, p. 671; April 8, 1944, pp. 673–7.
[63] FRUS, 1944, III, France, May 16, 1944, p. 690.
[64] FRUS, 1944, III, France, May 27, 1944, p. 692; May 31, 1944, pp. 693–4; June 4,
     1944, pp. 697–8.
[65] "Official Statements and Views Regarding the Free French and the French Empire,"
     Matthews–Hickerson File, NARA, Microfilm Reel 13, January 1944.

in the Atlantic Charter, but these remained ambiguous, and Roosevelt had never meant to imply immediate independence for colonial peoples, but rather a long period of tutelage under United Nations' trusteeship, the nature of which had yet to be defined.[66] Roosevelt's attitude toward the French colonies changed at the time of the Casablanca meeting, just as de Gaulle merged his movement with Giraud's. Moroccan poverty impressed the president, who referred to it again and again, arguing that the French must be held accountable to an international organization for the level of illiteracy, death rates, and health conditions in the protectorate. To the sultan, whom FDR accorded the honors of a head of state at a dinner in Casablanca, Roosevelt talked of making the deserts bloom, and promised independence.[67] To Murphy, FDR said he did not intend to restore the French empire, which was an "outrage." FDR saw no reason why a population that was 90 percent Moors should be run permanently by France.

About Indochina, Roosevelt complained that the French had been there for 100 years, and "the population was worse off than at the beginning." An American military inquiry into the condition of French islands in the Pacific concluded that the French administration there was very bad and the population disaffected, and that the area should be ceded to the United States, the leading power responsible for security in the region.[68] Perplexed by FDR's attitude, Hull sent the president a memo on January 24, 1944, noting prior American commitments to the integrity of the French empire made to Vichy and Admiral Darlan, and the contradiction with FDR's recent statements on Indochina. The president reaffirmed his opposition to French colonial rule, adding that "France has milked it [Indochina] for 100 years. The people of Indochina are entitled to something better than that."[69] Only in the spring of 1945 did evidence appear of a shift in the American attitude toward a greater readiness to accept France's return to its colonies.

During the Normandy landings, de Gaulle angrily rejected the Allies' plans to introduce a special occupation currency, repudiated the text of a declaration calling upon the French to welcome and collaborate with Allied troops, and refused to supply liaison personnel to Allied forces until the status of the Provisional Government had been settled. The consolidation of Gaullist power in the metropole occurred very rapidly. From the very first appearance of the General on French soil, the spontaneous acclaim of the population made clear where future authority in France was to lie.[70] De Gaulle found a ready ally in the apolitical General Eisenhower, whose main concern at the time of the Normandy invasion, as in North Africa in 1942, was

[66] Louis, *Imperialism at Bay*, passim.
[67] Murphy, *Diplomat among Warriors*, p. 84.
[68] Louis, *Imperialism at Bay*, pp. 269–83.
[69] FRUS, 1944, III, France, January 24, 1944, p. 773.
[70] See Charles Louis Foulon, *Le pouvoir en province à la libération* (Paris: Armand Colin, 1975).

the security of the area behind Allied lines. Eisenhower had won the confidence of the Free French by December 1943, and he turned readily to the Provisional Government to administer the liberated areas, magnanimously turning the liberation of Paris over to General Leclerc's Second Armored Division.[71] In the meantime, de Gaulle consolidated his authority in the liberated areas. His trip to Washington in July 1944 was a success, and he returned home with de facto recognition of the Provisional Government.[72] Chapin argued for de jure recognition on September 15, 1944. The regime was republican, he said, universally acknowledged, and it was acting with tolerance and restraint. Further refusal of recognition caused anti-Americanism among the French and accomplished no other purpose. "We shall have to extend recognition . . . no more appropriate moment could be chosen than the present when enthusiasm for USA is at the crest."[73] Recognition remained "under study" in Washington; however, it came on October 23, 1944 following a plea from Eisenhower, who cited the necessity for security in his rear lines.

But there was to be no real end of contentiousness between de Gaulle and the Americans until the general finally resigned in January 1946. In January 1945, Foreign Minister Georges Bidault protested the peremptory American move onto the uninhabited Clipperton Island, off the coast of Mexico, where the French claimed sovereignty. Bidault protested that the action was "humiliating. . . . We are so anxious to cooperate with you, but sometimes you do not make it easy." Acting Secretary of State Grew suggested that the United States back down on this question, given "the basic weakness of our position . . . [the issue] could seriously and needlessly impair our relations with the French."[74] French access was granted and their sovereignty recognized on March 21. On the German front, de Gaulle refused to allow his forces to evacuate the "sacred ground" of Strasbourg when ordered to do so for logistical reasons by General Eisenhower. In this decision de Gaulle had the support of Churchill; recognizing that his authority over the French troops was purely formal, Eisenhower elected to avoid a command crisis and backed down. French troops set up a military government in Stuttgart, in an attempt to lay claim to a zone of occupation in Germany, only to find themselves ordered out by the Americans. De Gaulle was "grievously shocked" by the Stuttgart incident, the new American ambassador, Jefferson Caffery, wrote, finding in the American action an "offense to the French army, as well as to the French government and people." Simultaneously, the joint chiefs of staff recommended that the United States terminate French re-

---

[71] David Eisenhower, *Eisenhower at War, 1943–1945* (New York: Random House, 1986), pp. 163–4.
[72] FRUS, 1944, III, France, July 10, 1944, pp. 723–5.
[73] FRUS, 1944, III, France, September 15, 1944, p. 734.
[74] FRUS, 1945, IV, Europe, France, January 22, 1945, pp. 788–9, January 26, 1945, 789–90.

armament, since it was no longer serving any useful purpose in the war.[75] Hull advised FDR to use the growing financial dependence of the French on Washington as a means "to do what you may think necessary from time to time in the light of French behavior."[76] FDR, and Truman after him, took that lesson to heart.

Piqued by the failure of the Big Three to invite him to Yalta, de Gaulle haughtily refused FDR's "summons" to meet him in Algiers, where the American president stopped during his return voyage. "How could I agree to be summoned to a point on the national territory by a foreign chief of state?" de Gaulle asked.[77] The incident, which caused a sensation, was surrounded by confusion. In February 1945 Bidault told Harry Hopkins that FDR should not seek to see de Gaulle immediately before or after a conference of the Big Three to which the French were not invited. Hopkins objected to Bidault's remark, and said that he would not want to transmit such a message to Washington. The next day Bidault reversed himself, telling Hopkins that de Gaulle would indeed be delighted to see the president before his return to the United States. The French only needed to be notified of the time and place.[78] Caffery was pleased by the aftermath of de Gaulle's apparent snub of Roosevelt, the first incident in which de Gaulle's followers appeared to question his judgment and previous "infallibility." The French were, for once, "contrite." FDR was furious, referring to de Gaulle as a "prima donna," and had to be restrained by Hopkins and Charles Bohlen from issuing an insulting public reply of his own: "We can all admit [privately] that de Gaulle is one of the biggest sons of bitches who ever straddled a pot," Bohlen remarked, to presidential laughter.[79]

In May 1945 relations were strained by the annexationist behavior of French forces in the Val d'Aosta region of Italy, and by apparent French aims to retain their prewar imperial positions in Syria and Lebanon. French troops refused to withdraw from the Val d'Aosta and reportedly spread word to the population that the Allies expected a vote to join France.[80] The Americans complained to Bidault, who referred to some necessary minor "rectifications" of the frontier, privately confided his unhappiness with de Gaulle's behavior, and generally tried to make light of the issue. De Gaulle took the issue seriously, however, remembering Italy's attack on France with

---

75 FRUS, 1945, IV, France, April 28, 1945, p. 681. Eisenhower, *Eisenhower at War*, pp. 602–3, 776.
76 FRUS, 1944, III, France, September 11, 1944, p. 761.
77 Memoirs, III, *Salvation*, 99.
78 FRUS, 1945, IV, France, January 30, 1945, pp. 667–9, February 2, 1945, p. 761. See the account by Ambassador Henri Bonnet in Ministère des Affaires Etrangères (Quai d'Orsay), B Amérique, 119, May 3, 1945. Hereinafter MAE.
79 Charles Bohlen, *Witness to History* (New York: Norton, 1973), p. 208.
80 FRUS, 1945, IV, France, May 17, 1945, p. 729, May 19, 1945, p. 730, May 20, 1945, pp. 731–2.

Germany in 1940, a matter that was of no concern to the Americans who wanted to postpone settlement of all territorial grievances until after the war. The incident soon reached the crisis stage: on June 5, 1945 President Truman formally insisted on French withdrawal from the Val d'Aosta region, threatening "grave consequences" and again resorting to the aid weapon:

> [I note] the unbelievable threat that French soldiers bearing American arms will combat American and allied soldiers whose efforts and sacrifices have so recently and successfully contributed to the liberation of France itself. I beg you to withdraw ... before I acquaint the people of the United States with this situation. While this threat by the French government is outstanding against American soldiers I regret ... no further issues of military equipment or munitions can be made to French troops.[81]

General Juin notified the allies that de Gaulle was seeking a face-saving way out of the crisis on June 9. De Gaulle's position, Juin confided, was "unreasonable and impetuous," and all in the French cabinet were out of sympathy with him. Churchill was exasperated; he could not deal with de Gaulle, he told Truman, but "if de Gaulle is to be thrown out, it has to be by the French people and not by outsiders."[82] In 1954 the British and Americans were again to confer about ridding France of a leader with whom they could not deal, Pierre Mendès France (see Chapter 9, II). On June 11, 1945 French forces withdrew from the Val d'Aosta, and the French government agreed to a face-saving formula demilitarizing the Italian frontier.

In March 1945 the State Department informed French embassy counselor Francis Lacoste that the United States would oppose any postwar attempt by France to assert "special privileges" in Syria or Lebanon, the independence of which it recognized. Late in April, Paris protested American intentions to supply arms to the Syrians, while Washington objected to planned French movement of troops there. In May the situation exploded into crisis: Acting Secretary Grew instructed Caffery to warn the French against further troop transfers. Loy Henderson of the Middle East desk accused Paris of using tactics similar "to the Japanese in Manchukuo and the Italians in Ethiopia." On May 26 an American note asked Paris for a "review" of French policy in Syria and Lebanon.[83] On May 29 the French government replied that its small-scale troop movements were merely for "relief and deployment," and that its aim was simply to negotiate with the Syrians questions directly concerning France. But there were no signs of negotiations. Instead, French troops were reported to be shelling Damascus; Loy Henderson characterized the situation as "open warfare," with Paris in violation of the United Nations charter, and the entire Middle East seemed likely to become

---

[81] FRUS, 1945, IV, France, June 6, 1945, p. 735.

[82] FRUS, 1945, IV, France, June 9, 1945, pp. 737–40.

[83] FRUS, 1945, VIII, Near East and Africa, March 10, April 26, May 4, 16, 23, 26, 1945, pp. 1054–75, 1090–5.

inflamed against the Western powers. Indeed, both Syria and Iraq repeatedly protested French behavior to Washington. Secretary of State Edward R. Stettinius urged Truman to appeal to de Gaulle directly, while Winston Churchill notified the president of his intention to send British troops into Syria to "restore order," and requested American support. As in the Val d'Aosta crisis, Truman acted decisively against the French. Planning for de Gaulle's impending trip to Washington was postponed, the president approved the British intervention, and a blunt warning was sent to the French leader. Meanwhile, without waiting for the American response, Churchill ordered in British troops. French troops were ordered to cease operations and confine themselves to barracks, and on June 2 de Gaulle agreed to a cease fire. Caffery reported that de Gaulle was "infuriated and humiliated" by the British action, as he may well have been some weeks later as well, when Washington rejected his face-saving plan for a Four-Power conference on the Middle East, including the Soviets.[84]

Despite these incidents, neither nation would permit its basic ties to the other to be obscured, or repudiate its clear need for the other in the postwar period. While the crisis raged, on May 5, Caffery had a frank exchange of views with de Gaulle which pointed the way toward a transcendance of their wartime jealousies and established the framework for postwar cooperation. De Gaulle confided to the American ambassador his fears that the Russians were powerful enough to take over the whole European continent. "I would much rather work with the USA than any other country," the General said, "but if I cannot work with you I must work with the Soviets in order to survive even if it is only for a while and even if in the long run they gobble us up too." De Gaulle complained that the Americans appeared to have written off France – to think that France was again going to fall, as in 1940 – "and perhaps you are right, but she would not fall if you helped her." De Gaulle recognized the geopolitical realities of the postwar era, and feared that a weakened France would become a battleground in an emerging American–Soviet struggle. Caffery replied with assurances of the American desire for a strong France, casting his phrases in terms of economics: The United States desired French prosperity because of "our desire to export and we cannot export if you are not prosperous enough to buy."

It was to remain characteristic of the immediate postwar era, and a source of Franco–American misunderstandings, that Paris thought geopolitically, while the Americans saw the world in terms of economics. Caffery reported that it was a frank and friendly exchange, however, the general rising from his seat, as was his usual practice, to accompany the ambassador to the door.[85] It was in terms of economics blending gradually into geopolitics that

---

84 FRUS, 1945, VIII, Near East and Africa, May 29, 30, 31, 1945, pp. 1112–26; June 1, 2, 3, 8, 20, 1945, pp. 1129–49; October 2, 1945, pp. 1169–70.
85 FRUS, 1945, IV, France, May 5, 1945, pp. 685–7.

the American–French dialogue on European reconstruction after the war was to be conducted; and a veneer of cordiality and friendship, however forced, overcame the petty irritants and recriminations of the past. But an important precedent had been established during the war years. The Americans had tried to, and discovered that they could not, make and break French regimes. But they had also become accustomed to the exercise of an unprecedented degree of meddling in internal French affairs. This was forgotten in the immediate postwar era, when for a brief time it was believed that "bringing the boys home" could be a prelude to the peaceful construction of a new normality. In 1947 the Americans returned, to be involved with French politics again, and for many years to come.

2

The postwar years:
Independence compromised

I ECONOMIC DEPENDENCE
AND POLITICAL DISCORD

FRENCH FOREIGN POLICY in the years immediately after the war was based on an apparently unresolvable contradiction. Security needs dictated the pursuit of policies designed to obtain the political disunity of Germany and its future economic weakness vis-à-vis a restored France. French economic realities – the severe economic dislocation, disruption, and absolute deprivation caused by the war – dictated a policy of dependence on the United States. The United States alone could provide the imports France needed to maintain a minimum level of subsistence while attempting to reconstruct and modernize its economy. But the price of American assistance soon revealed itself to be French acquiescence in the reconstruction of Germany. At the war's end American policy toward Germany remained fluid, and the widespread belief in both France and the United States in the continued cordiality of relations between the Soviet Union and the West, permitted the French to mask this contradiction. France persisted in the belief that it could pursue its security needs despite its economic dependence on the United States. As American suspicion of Russia grew, however, the traditional American conviction of its need for a strong Germany in Europe as a trading partner reasserted itself, and the French found it increasingly difficult to continue pursuing German weakness and American credits simultaneously. The contradiction was revealed most dramatically in the Blum–Byrnes negotiations of 1946, which the French hoped would provide a substantial loan of several billion dollars to finance the Monnet Plan for economic reconstruction and modernization. The French came home from Washington with their hopes dashed. Washington would not lend anything near the amount the French requested, in large part because France would not bend to American will on the German question.

35

As this fundamental contradiction sharpened, the French political system underwent a transition from a quasi-authoritarian regime based on the personal charisma of Charles de Gaulle toward a revival of traditional republican politics based on the prewar pattern. The Fourth Republic was established after partisan political struggle, rejection by the voters of an initial constitutional draft, and with minority participation of an electorate tired of the repeated calls made upon it. It repeated many of the political defects associated with the Third Republic. The resignation of de Gaulle in January 1946, weakness of the executive, and political instability resulting from political challenges from the extreme right and left, provided a fertile field for pressure groups of all kinds, domestic and foreign, to influence political decision making. The poverty of the country and economic dependence on the United States, unquestioned even by the Communists until 1947, allowed the U.S. embassy to become one of the most important pressure groups in the country. The importance of the American embassy emerged gradually, as a natural consequence of American economic weight and strategic significance in the postwar period. It was due as much to the pull of the French as opposed to the push of the Americans, who often found themselves willy-nilly mixed up in French internal rivalries they would have preferred to avoid. As American preferences for one or another French policy, or even politician, became known, French protagonists sought to use American desires to their advantage, and even bargained with the embassy directly in quest of American support and intervention. One may see the embassy gradually becoming more involved in French politics during 1946, and during 1947 assuming what often appeared to be a central role.

While de Gaulle was jealously demonstrating French independence of the United States in 1944 and 1945, Jean Monnet, with the general's blessing, was setting down the basis of French economic dependence. In November 1944 Monnet set the contours of a French import program designed to continue in effect through January 1, 1946. Most of France's needs, 50 percent of food and agricultural imports, 25 percent of coal and other raw materials, 80 percent of semifinished, and 90 percent of finished goods were expected to come from the United States.[1] American aid was intended in the short run to enable the French to take their place in the war alongside the Anglo-Saxon powers; in the long run, to provide for the economic modernization and reconstruction of the country.

---

[1]   Archives Nationales, hereinafter A.N., F60, November 10, 1944, Memo by Jean Monnet. See also, Philippe Mioche, *Le Plan Monnet: Genèse et elaboration* (Paris: Publications de la Sorbonne, 1987), pp. 77–9. For a thorough treatment of French foreign policy from 1945 to 1949, see John W. Young, *France, the Cold War, and the Western Alliance: French Foreign Policy and Postwar Europe, 1944–49* (New York: St. Martin's Press, 1990).

The initial French slide into economic dependence on the United States was a consequence of the war. It was not reflected in any immediate improvement in relations between the Americans and the Free French. Friction was manifest on both continents. In New York, where the French Supply Council came to employ a bureaucracy of some 1,200 persons to make its purchases, monopoly trading practices incurred the hostility of American businessmen, who complained of rigid bureaucratic procedures and delays in contracts while awaiting final French government authorization. They demanded that the French government revert to the prewar pattern of private trading.[2] In France American soldiers complained of profiteering and price gouging by French shopkeepers, while the Ministry of Foreign Affairs worried that the GIs' "profound bitterness is reflected in their correspondence and will probably be echoed before long in the whole country and in Congress."[3] A report by a "francophile" American French-speaking officer spoke of American perceptions of the French as mercenary, lazy, poor workers, morally deficient, filthy, dishonest, and seething with anti-American hostility. From the French side things were little better. The French, he said, suffered wounded pride, humiliation from Americans who treated them "like children," and resented American requisitions of luxury hotels, baptizing the Supreme Headquarters Allied European Forces (SHAEF) as "Société Hotelière des Américains en France."[4] American soldiers allegedly coddled German war prisoners, and showered them with chocolate, coffee, and cigarettes, while the French received nothing. The GIs were described as drunken, rapine, mannerless, reckless in their driving, and hostile to the French.

With the war's end, the American administration, following the letter of the Lend-Lease law, immediately cut off the flow of arms and supplies to the Allies. The Russians interpreted the cessation of Lend-Lease as a hostile act directed against themselves, but the outcry from the French was equally shrill. French ambassador Henri Bonnet was instructed to inquire at once into the reasons for the termination of lend-lease; not for the first time, Paris accepted with ill grace the literal application of American legal requirements in Washington's diplomacy.[5] The Americans realized, however, that they could not abruptly cut the Allies' lifeline. The war's end brought a change in the financing rather than a cessation of the shipments upon which the French economy depended. Orders already placed were filled, while new requests were to be negotiated and financed by the Export-Import Bank. Immediate credit was granted to the French for $316 million, and a supplementary "lend-lease takeout loan" of $550 million was extended to them

2 A.N., F60, 920, Minutes of the French Supply Council, January 22, 1945.
3 A.N., F60, 921, January 15, 1945, telegram from the Ministère des Affaires Etrangères.
4 Ministère des Affaires Etrangères (MAE), B Amérique, 119, July 28, 1945.
5 A.N. F60, 921, July 15, 18, 20, 1945.

in December 1945, permitting completion of lend-lease through 1946 as originally projected.

On the occasion of both loans, the French exchanged diplomatic notes with Washington expressing the mutual intent of the two countries to relax exchange controls and eliminate quotas, end discrimination in restraint of trade, and reduce tariffs, while doing everything they could to accomplish the ultimate goal of free international trade. American insistence on the establishment of a system of free international trade and payments is often regarded as the linchpin of a plan for hegemony. Washington required the rest of the world to accept free trade as the price for its postwar economic assistance.[6] But similar objectives were shared by many European leaders of the period. Free trade principles had become a pious affirmation to which the French fully subscribed and which they repeated on every suitable occasion. French leaders held protectionism responsible for the depression of the 1930s and a long history of French economic stagnation and industrial decline. The virtues of larger markets of international dimensions seemed obvious to everyone. Was not American economic preponderance to be explained by the availability of a market of continental size? Tariff wars, bilateral trade agreements, and policies of autarchy were, on the other hand, the rejected policies of fascist and totalitarian powers.[7] Moreover, France had subscribed to such principles as early as the Atlantic Charter. The goal of free trade was written into the Lend-Lease agreements of February 1945, reaffirmed in an exchange of notes consequent upon the negotiations of the $550 million loan of December 1945, and repeated again on the occasion of the Blum–Byrnes negotiations of 1946.

There was one caveat, however, which Washington understood and accepted. The French could not participate in a free system of international trade and payments until their economy had been restored to strength and its projected deficits, which were expected to run into the billions of dollars, were financed. The Quai d'Orsay specified that it desired to return to more liberal exchange and trade, but it did not promise to do so.[8] Jean Monnet was able to get the United States to separate any demand for progress toward free trade from the $550 million loan of December 1945. The Americans wanted the French to enter into international negotiations for a general agreement on trade and payments, but Paris insisted that the United States first agree to bilateral negotiations with France devoted to an examination of the whole of the projected French deficit for the coming four years. Washington agreed to the French demand in November 1945, and the Blum–Byrnes talks came about at French request. France's needs, first economi-

6   Joyce and Gabriel Kolko, *The Limits of Power: The World and United States Foreign Policy, 1945–1954* (New York: Harper & Row, 1972).
7   See Michel Margairaz, "Autour des accords Blum–Byrnes: Jean Monnet entre le consensus national et le consensus atlantique," *Histoire, Economie et Société*, 3 (1982): 486–9. Also Mioche, *Le Plan Monnet*, pp. 79–82.
8   A.N. F60, 921, January 15, 1945.

cally, then militarily, provided the impetus for American involvement in French, and European, affairs.[9]

On November 14, 1945 Caffery reported that the French had made a decision of major import "toward multi-lateral trade with all its domestic economic implications," and recommended that Washington agree to negotiations.[10] His optimism was short lived, however. Before the negotiations could begin, the political situation was radically changed by the elections of October 1945, and Communists, having emerged as one of the three major Frendi political parties, assumed most of the major economic positions in the French cabinet. The new left-wing coalition, Caffery warned, had many "closed economy aspects difficult to reconcile with American commercial policy objectives," or with the concessions needed from the French government in order to achieve them. "I desire to emphasize my conclusion that political developments have multiplied dangers inherent in any procedure which would permit French–American discussions to take place unless there was discussion simultaneously of commercial policy and specific trade problems," the ambassador added.[11]

The talks were jeopardized further by the differences between the United States and France on the German question. French policy with regard to postwar Germany had hardened into a set of specific demands – decentralization, military occupation of the Rhineland, and internationalization of the Ruhr – while American policy swung from one extreme to the other. The Morgenthau Plan, which would have created a decentralized, pastoral Germany, had been endorsed by Roosevelt in the late stages of the war. With the occupation of Germany, however, it rapidly gave way to a directly opposing policy of reconstructing Germany both economically and politically, which was clearly in effect by the fall of 1945. When Foreign Minister Georges Bidault visited Washington in May 1945, on his way home from the founding conference of the United Nations in San Francisco, he found a relatively sympathetic reception to his ideas from President Truman. But when Bidault returned to Washington with General de Gaulle in August 1945, they found the situation to be quite different. American officials told the French, off the record, of their dissatisfaction with the French policy of playing a "double game" between the United States and the USSR.

Bidault found himself being lectured by Secretary of State Byrnes on a myriad of problems. France should abandon all hope of getting reparations from Germany. The United States would neither recommence the errors of the previous war, nor spend a single dollar to finance German reparations payments.[12] Byrnes complained of high tariff walls around France and an

---

9   MAE, Direction des Affaires Economiques, 194, Dr. 5, October 16 and November 8, 1945.

10 Foreign Relations of the United States (FRUS), 1945, IV, Europe, France, November 8, 1945, p. 772.

11 FRUS, 1945, IV, Europe, France, November 25, 1945, pp. 773–4.

12 A.N., 457 AP 80 (1), Papiers Georges Bidault, August 13, 1985.

artificially high rate of exchange for the franc. Bidault would not discuss the rate of the franc, but he did partially repudiate autarchy. When possible, France would adopt "a regime of freedom in the modern sense of the word, that is to say, tempered by discipline." On the German question, Bidault pointed out that Germany had already been "amputated" in the east at Russian insistence. Why not in the west as well? The Americans were proposing the establishment of centralized services for the post and transport in Germany, while France had not been consulted. American policy prefigured the creation of a unified, centralized, German state that would bring the Russians into the affairs of the Western zones and establish Soviet power on the borders of France. Bidault protested these policies, but to little avail. Truman was even more blunt the next day with General de Gaulle. There would be no internationalization of the Ruhr as demanded by the French, the president said, nor should Paris exaggerate the German danger on the Rhine. The United States was prepared to guarantee the security and prosperity of France, but no French territorial claims against Germany could be considered. Truman also complained of attacks on the United States in the French press and a rude, inhospitable climate for American businessmen in Paris.

Policy differences over Germany were translated into practical disagreements there. In November 1945 French delegates in Berlin found themselves facing the combined agreement of American, British, and Soviet delegates to the reduction of German monthly coal exports to Paris from 1.2 million to 900,000 tons. Truman had explicitly promised to give priority to the needs of liberated Europe over those of Germany; it was inadmissible from the French point of view that Germany have as much coal per capita as France.[13] Alphand protested in Washington, and was told that the problem was lack of transport facilities in Germany. He could not accept this explanation: "Problems of transportation must not be allowed to prevent the application of the principle [of French priority]." But the Cartesian French found themselves confronted with stubborn American pragmatism. Consul Francis Lacoste received a lecture on the subject from the Americans. France would do better to argue from the concrete impact of the lack of coal on its economy, he was told, rather than to phrase its demands in terms of principle. General Clay reaffirmed that the problem was transportation and violently upbraided the French for their refusal to agree to the establishment of a combined transport authority in Germany. Paris had to accept the reduced coal deliveries, and despite Washington's assurances, they did not increase in succeeding months.

There were disagreements between the American and French zones in Germany as well. It was an American officer who saw fit to complain about the discourtesy of his countrymen toward the French when they visited the

---

[13]   MAE, Y 1944–9, Internationale, Charbon, 89, November 3, 8, 12, 17, 19, 1945.

American zone; in contrast, Americans visiting the French zone were always received correctly and cordially by their hosts. Moreover, the Americans undermined French authority in Germany, listening sympathetically to German complaints while on tour, and inciting the Germans against the French occupation authorities. Suspicious of the role of Communists in the French zone, American military intelligence decided to spy on the activities of occupation authorities there, employing a network of former Nazis, headed by Klaus Barbie, the infamous "butcher of Lyon," for the purpose. Barbie's mission was to "infiltrate secret services in the French occupation zone"; he remained in American employ until 1950, and his reports were considered to be of value. When the French got around to requesting his extradition, American authorities demurred, fearing that he would inform on American activities in the French zone once in Paris. Barbie was therefore sent down the "rat line," an illegal escape route for former Nazis, eventually settling in Bolivia, until his extradition in the 1980s.[14]

In February 1946 the United States formally requested Paris to reconsider its opposition to the creation of centralized services in Germany. Byrnes protested to Bonnet in the strongest terms the French use of their "veto power" on the Allied Control Commission in Germany, while Under Secretary of State Acheson warned the French that deliveries of German coal to France were "handicapped" by French obstruction.[15] French hopes of receiving enough funds to finance their expected deficit for four years and achieve the modernization of the country were in jeopardy.

On January 20, 1946, the eve of the negotiations, de Gaulle resigned. To be sure, there was no great love for the general in Washington. But because he had come to be considered a valued bulwark against communism, his authoritarian strain was overlooked. On August 31, 1945 Bidault was assured by James Dunn, Freeman Matthews, and Charles Bohlen that "the existence of a strong France is an axiom of present American policy." Because the United States feared the extreme left, it wished to help consolidate the present French government.[16] De Gaulle, for his part, began making overtures toward better relations with Washington in the latter part of 1945. On November 20, 1945 Colonel Dewavrin, alias Passy, who was de Gaulle's intelligence chief, called at the American embassy with a message concerning the general's desire to eliminate Franco–American misunderstanding.

14 Central Intelligence Agency, Archives, Report on Klaus Barbie, February 23, 1951. *Klaus Barbie and the United States Government: A Report to the Attorney General of the United States.* Presented by Allan A. Ryan, Jr. (Washington, D.C.: 1983). This official investigation concluded that American military intelligence acted without authorization of Occupation authorities and were guilty of obstruction of justice.

15 MAE, Y 1944–9, Internationale, Charbon, 89, December 4, 5, 1945, March 22, 1946. Also NARA, Matthews–Hickerson File, Microfilm Reel 10, February 6 and March 12, 1946.

16 A.N., 457 AP 80 (1), Papiers Georges Bidault, August 31, 1945.

De Gaulle understood that French foreign policy must be close to that of the United States if it wished to survive. France must get along with America, like it or not; the German question was "secondary to the Russian" and must not be allowed to interfere with relations.[17] Dewavrin tried to reassure Caffery about the new French government. He explained that de Gaulle intended to play the three major parties off against one another. The general could count on the Mouvement Républicain Populaire (MRP) and the Socialists to support his foreign policy and the Communists would not be allowed to occupy any key ministries. They would be offered technical posts such as the economy and agriculture.[18] This was appreciated in Washington as a "remarkable solution" to the Communist problem. On December 4, 1945 René Pleven, de Gaulle's finance minister, called at the Embassy to assure the ambassador that the nationalization of several French banks would have no effect on American interests. On December 9 Guillaume Guindey of the French Treasury told Caffery that France was ready to ratify the Bretton Woods agreements and devalue the franc, as Washington wished.[19] Earlier the French had agreed to sign an aviation convention and not to increase tariffs and quotas pending international negotiations on trade and payments.

The Americans were kept informed about the general's plans to resign. On January 10, 1946 Caffery noted disillusionment and discouragement on the part of the French population with the regime. The food shortages and ineffectiveness and incompetence of the government were harming de Gaulle's prestige. A political crisis was likely, although not until January 15.[20] A report by the Office of Strategic Services a few days later, evaluated the general's support at 40 percent of the population, down from 67 percent a year earlier. The report predicted the general would resign and try to "presidentialize" the regime.[21] On January 18, 1946 Gaston Palewski, de Gaulle's closest confidant, who became the regular intermediary between the general and the ambassador, reported to Caffery that de Gaulle was ready to give up his office in response to the maneuvers of the Communists and others against him. If he resigned, it would be in order to take his struggle against the political parties to the country, and he would not surrender to the Parti Communiste Français (PCF) without a fight.[22] Finally, Caffery reported on January 20 that "sources close to de Gaulle say he is fed up and will re-

---

17   National Archives and Records Administration, State Department Decimal File, Record Group 59 (NARA), 851.51/11-2045, November 20, 1945.
18   In effect, following the October 1945 elections, de Gaulle announced that the Communists, because of their foreign ties, were ineligible for the ministries affecting foreign policy, which he defined as Foreign Affairs, Defense, and the Interior.
19   NARA, 851.51/12-445, December 4, 1945; 851.51/12-945, December 9, 1945; MAE, B Amérique, 119, November 26, 1945.
20   NARA, 851.00/1-1046, January 10, 1946.
21   NARA, 851.00/1-1546, January 15, 1946.
22   NARA, 851.00/1-1846, January 18, 1946.

sign." But the general's entourage assured the ambassador on January 28 that he would be back in power within six months.[23]

Fear of the unknown and preference for the status quo became the governing principles in Washington's responses to French cabinet crises. When new governments were formed, the American reaction was invariably satisfaction that the crisis had been successfully overcome and hopes that the new cabinet would find a measure of stability. The Socialist-directed Gouin government was received positively in Washington. American opinion of the French Socialists had been evolving for some time. Initially they had been regarded with hostility and mild distaste. On the occasion of Léon Blum's return to France after his release from Buchenwald, the State Department rejected as "inappropriate" embassy suggestions that a message of congratulations be sent to the Socialist leader, because "Mr. Stettinius does not know Mr. Blum."[24] But wiser heads prevailed, and congratulations were sent to both Blum and Herriot on behalf of both the president and the secretary of state. On May 10 Caffery reported to Washington a conversation with Daniel Mayer, secretary general of the Socialist party, whom Caffery described as representing that part of the Socialist party that was "very narrow and doctrinaire in its outlook," and distrustful of the United States for its "economic imperialism." Mayer warned Caffery that the SFIO would fight any attempt by the American government to block nationalizations in France, and he criticized American stinginess with economic aid. Caffery responded angrily that Mayer's ignorance of the United States and its policies was "appalling."[25]

Blum called at the embassy on May 22, perhaps hoping to correct the bad impression Mayer had made. He thanked Caffery for the role American troops played in his liberation and assured the ambassador of his "ardent desire to work closely with us." The war had caused Blum to become an even more passionate admirer of the American political system. Caffery in turn became one of Blum's most sincere admirers. Blum was stiffening the Socialists in their ardor to oppose the Communists; he was "the only first-rate man in the Socialist party" and extremely intelligent and friendly to the United States. If Washington was prepared to deal with a Socialist-led government in France, it was largely because Blum's influence in his party was believed to be paramount.[26]

Bonnet reported the State Department's "profound satisfaction" with the formation of the Gouin government in January 1946, and hopes that Gouin would remain in power until the elections. "They welcome with equal fervor [his] financial program."[27] Byrnes saw "no adverse effect on Depart-

23 NARA, 851.00/1-2046, January 20, 1946; 1-2846, January 28, 1946.
24 NARA, 851.00/5-745, May 7, 1945.
25 NARA, 851.00/5-1045, May 10, 1945.
26 NARA, 851.00/1-2346, January 23, 1946.
27 MAE, B Amérique, 119, January 28, 1946.

ment views due to the change in the French government," and hoped a strengthening of the French economic position would increase prospects of the servicing of U.S. credits.[28] In Paris financial officer Ivan White recommended a loan to France on the order of at least one billion dollars, terming the Gouin government "one of the few hopeful developments in many months." White said that de Gaulle's military policies were excessive and Pleven's financial policies too permissive; André Philip, the new minister of finance, pledged to reduce military spending, raise taxes, and block some deposits, policies that made more sense than those of either the Gaullists or the Communists and were desirable "from the French standpoint and our own."[29]

Washington's attitude toward both the Gaullists and the Socialists was governed by the lurking spectre of French communism. The Parti Communiste Français was regarded in Washington as a powerful, disciplined, totalitarian political machine slavishly obedient to Moscow. The party was believed to be extraordinarily strong because of its control over significant elements of the working class and its extensive underground organization. Based on former Resistance fighters and Spanish Civil War veterans and led by a guerrilla leader of the Resistance, Léon Mauvais, the PCF's paramilitary force was believed to have hidden extensive caches of arms, which it could use when and if the Soviet Union called for an insurrection in France. If the French Communists were currently pursuing moderate, apparently democratic tactics, it was because these policies suited the immediate goals of the USSR. At a moment's notice the party was prepared to revert to a revolutionary line, paralyze the economy by means of strikes, and violently seize control of the state. In the short run the party was governed by Moscow's desire not to antagonize the United States, which was not, however, a cause for Washington to be complacent. The immense prestige the party had gained as a consequence of its role in the Resistance gave it tremendous leverage with which to operate within the democratic political system. The party's immense popularity, which dictated its inclusion in the government, afforded it the means to take power legally by use of "Trojan horse" techniques, building an elaborate power base in the machinery of the state: the nationalized enterprises, government bureaucracy, army, and police.[30]

The pessimistic outlook on the PCF, which prevailed in the State Department, and to which Caffery's conservative Irish-Catholic origins inclined him, was criticized by lesser officials in the Paris embassy. Among these there were several analysts, some who came from the OSS, a few with academic backgrounds and more liberal political views, who saw the French

---

[28] NARA, 851.51/2-446, February 4, 1946.
[29] NARA, 851.51/2-1146, February 11, 1946.
[30] Edward Rice-Maximin, "The United States and the French Left, 1945–1949: The View from the State Department," *Journal of Contemporary History*, 19 (1984): 729–47.

left differently. Gordon Wright worked in the embassy as a political analyst, developed sympathies with the Socialist party, on whose activities he authored many reports, and helped convince embassy personnel that they could work with the Socialists.[31] Labor attaché Richard Eldridge was a sophisticated observer of the Communist party and the labor unions and maintained a wide base of contacts within the French labor movement, including the Communists.

The Communists were aware of their unfavorable image in Washington and concerned to improve it so long as Soviet–American relations continued to be cordial and Washington promised to be a lucrative source of funds for French economic development. Party officials regularly fed the embassy information on the party line and clarifications of Communist policy. These regularly stressed the party's moderation. On June 20, 1945 Jacques Duclos explained to an embassy informant the nature of the Communist party's Popular Front policies and the party's commitment to the program of the National Council of the Resistance. Duclos stressed the PCF's desire to work closely with the Socialists, stating that the Communists would accept almost any conditions in their effort to achieve unity of the left. The next day, Frachon told Eldridge that any labor unrest in France was the fault of management or the government: "It is we who prevented a general strike."[32] Frachon minimized the importance of the idea of the "dictatorship of the proletariat" in Communist doctrine, stressed the party's commitment to democracy, and proudly declared: "Today, there are no strikes in France."

The embassy was unconvinced by these declarations, all of which it could equally read in *L'Humanité*. The Americans feared that the Communists would revert to causing strikes once they had consolidated their control over the CGT, a process the embassy nervously monitored. American analysts were disturbed by publication of the "Duclos letter" in April 1945, in which the French Communist leader criticized the moderate policies of Earl Browder, the head of the American Communist party. Duclos's missive was believed to herald adoption of a revolutionary line by all Communist parties in the West now that the war was over. Frachon tried to disabuse Eldridge of this idea, assuring the American that the CGT would mobilize to counter all strike agitation in France. Strikes were only advocated by reactionaries who were seeking to sabotage the work of French economic reconstruction.[33] The PCF's policy was to mobilize the workers around the program of the Conseil National de la Resistance; neither the Communist nor the Socialist party programs were the immediate objectives. The Communist party denounced "all those who seek to trouble our relationship with the United States, the United Kingdom, and the USSR."

[31] Personal interview, December 2, 1985.
[32] NARA, 851.00/6-2045, June 20, 1045; 851.00/6–2145, June 21, 1945.
[33] NARA, 851.00/5-2145, May 21, 1945; 851.00/8–1045, August 10, 1945.

Fortified by Frachon's assurances, Caffery denounced reports received by American military intelligence in France which depicted the Communist party as planning a coup. These reports, he said, were being fed to naive military officers by French rightists in search of subsidies for their own political purposes. They had often approached the embassy with the same information. Caffery expressed his doubts that the Communists would attempt a coup when they had everything to gain by working within the democratic process.[34] Nevertheless, Washington panicked when military intelligence forwarded another of these reports on May 3, 1946. The report insisted that the PCF would attempt a coup in the event that the June 1946 constitutional referendum turned out unfavorably to the party.[35] Washington's fear was intensified by an earlier OSS report warning of Communist guerrillas amassed in the French departments on the Spanish frontier. Communists were said to be in control of factories and the transportation network in the region, and had infiltrated the police and army rendering them of doubtful loyalty.[36] Reacting to the May 3 report, Secretary of War Robert P. Patterson proposed to President Truman that the American military commander in Europe, General Joseph McNarney, be given authority "to effect movement of troops into France in case of serious disturbance there." U.S. forces would intervene for the purpose of protecting American supply lines and installations in France relevant to the American military occupation of Germany, but were to be prohibited from taking part "in French internal conflict" that might occur.

John Hickerson, at the State Department's European desk, thought the idea absurd: The Communists would not try a coup because they were counting on legal methods to bring them to power. U.S. troops could be supplied through German ports whatever happened in France, and should the telegram become public it would appear to be a blatant intervention in French affairs that would offer the Soviets a similar excuse to intervene.[37] Caffery again stressed the Communists' emphasis on legal methods; they hoped to come to power by peaceful means through grasping the "levers of command" in the administration and bringing about the "disintegration of the bourgeois state apparatus." But Truman overruled State Department objections and gave General McNarney the recommended authorization. During Washington's crisis, Léon Blum and Jean Monnet were in the capital to conclude the loan negotiations. There is no evidence that they were aware of the panic, nor did these events appear to have influenced the negotiations.

Curiously, Maurice Thorez acted as if he were aware of the reports, and went out of his way to assure Caffery personally on May 7, 1946 that the

[34] NARA, 851.00/3-1446, March 14, 1946.
[35] NARA, 851.00/5-346, May 3, 1946.
[36] Archives of the Central Intelligence Agency, also labeled 851.00B/4-2946, report dated March 1946.
[37] NARA, 851.00/5-646, May 5, 1946.

Communist party was not concerned by the referendum defeat, expected a success in the June 5 elections, and would continue its policies of stimulating productivity in France while preventing strikes.[38] But on June 4, Robert Murphy, now political adviser to General Clay in Germany, cabled yet another report, allegedly obtained from military intelligence in Brussels, stating that Laurent Casanova, who was also believed to be a leader of Communist paramilitary forces, had urged the PCF Politburo to seize power in France. Matthews angrily cabled Murphy, whose ties to French rightists from Vichy days remained current, that "your source is phony"; the extreme right in France was again trying to stir up trouble in an effort to get U.S. funds.[39] Murphy reported that Maurice Thorez, in a meeting of the Political Bureau, angrily referred to stories that Washington had pressured Léon Blum to remove the Communists from the French government. Such rumors were never substantiated. They originated with Agence France-Presse (AFP) Washington correspondant Jean Davidson, according to whom Secretary of the Treasury Vinson asked for a formal promise from Blum that the Socialists would lead the French cabinet in efforts to remove the Communists from all important posts they occupied in the French government.[40] Davidson's report, denied by the State Department, was never printed, because he could not get it corroborated from any other source. Could it have originated from those same right-wing sources that were feeding Murphy his information? The embassy believed that the political right was trying to sabotage the Blum mission in Washington; reports such as these would have been an ideal way to do so.

Contrary to Davidson's report, and despite Washington's uneasiness with the Communist problem in France, it was not the State Department's policy to seek the PCF's removal from the French government. The department feared the Communists much more outside the government than within. On November 14, 1946 Caffery criticized "loose talk" about excluding the Communists from participation in the French government. Such aims, he said, were irresponsible since Communist control of the Confédération Générale du Travail (CGT) was sufficient to allow the party to paralyze the government if it wished. The party had strength enough to seize power almost at any time since it had infiltrated the aviation industry, police, and army. Marcel Paul, Communist minister of industrial production, controlled all access to gasoline and tires in France. The party had an extensive paramilitary capability in its Resistance cadres and the veterans of the International Brigades. But the PCF preferred to come to power legally because Moscow feared active American intervention and war in case of an attempted Communist coup in France. In short, the only thing blocking a

---

[38] NARA, 851.00/5-746, May 7, 1946.
[39] NARA, 851.00/6-446, June 4, 1946.
[40] Jean Davidson, *Corréspondant à Washington, 1945–1953* (Paris: Seuil, 1954), p. 18.

Communist seizure of power in France, Caffery said, was American posses-
sion of the atomic bomb.[41] Thorez's London *Times* interview, in which the
Communist leader opened the perspective of a peaceful transition to socialism in France different from the Soviet model, reflected "higher Stalinist
strategy" and was designed to "embrace the enemy the better to strangle
him." The PCF possessed both the power and the tactics necessary to come
to power in Paris, and "no force in France at this juncture appears capable
of arresting the advance of this Soviet Trojan horse."[42]

The newly created Central Intelligence Group (CIG), immediate predecessor of the CIA, challenged Caffery's estimate of the party's strength, however. The CIG agreed that while no French government could be formed at
the present juncture without PCF participation, "there is reason to doubt,
however, that the Communists are able at will to seize power in France by
a coup d'état." The army would remain loyal to the Republican regime, and
there were rightist paramilitary forces that were well-armed and could step
in to neutralize Communist groups. The situation was indeed of "the utmost
gravity," but no immediate Communist coup was to be feared.[43]

Both of these analyses led to conclusions of American impotence. The
situation in France was desperate but could not be corrected by means of
any American action. The attempt by Washington to weigh positively in the
internal politics of the European nations had to await the turn toward cold
war militancy in 1947, the Marshall Plan and the forging of the necessary
economic weapons, and the establishment of the CIA with its operations
division. Even then a measure of American desperation in the face of what
was seen to be overwhelming Communist power can be seen in the initial
CIA plans to organize potential resistance groups or "stay-behind nets" in
the various West European nations, to be activated in the event of Soviet
military occupation of Western Europe.[44] In a similar pessimistic vein, the
American embassy maintained emergency plans for the evacuation of France
by all resident Americans and tourists in case of a Soviet attack accompanied by a Communist coup.

Curiously, the American Federation of Labor was ahead of both the State
Department and the CIA in 1945–46 in attempting to provide a response
to the preponderance of Communist power in France. In the fall of 1945,
the AFL sent Irving Brown to Europe as its representative with the task of
organizing the non-Communist unions and providing them financial support. Brown set immediately to work, but in the beginning he operated on
a shoestring. Only after 1947, when the State Department and the CIA be-

[41]   NARA, 851.00/11-1466, November 14, 1946.
[42]   NARA, 851.00/11-2046, November 20, 1946.
[43]   Truman Library, President's Secretary's Files, Intelligence File, Box 249, Memo-
       randa, 1945–1949 (Folder 4-48), November 26, 1946.
[44]   William Colby and Peter Forbath, *Honorable Men: My Life in the CIA* (New York:
       Simon and Schuster, 1978), pp. 81–97.

came active as well, did his efforts begin to make any difference. In the interim, France's Communist problem seemed to be only minimally amenable to American influence as the United States attempted to decide how to respond to the French request for an extensive reconstruction credit. Was it worthwhile to gamble on a huge credit in the hope of strengthening the Socialists? Or might it not be better to offer very little, in the hope French disappointment might rebound to the benefit of the moderates? Worse, might a big credit turn out to be entirely wasted in the event France became Communist? These questions were very much on American minds as the Blum mission made its way to Washington.

II THE BLUM–BYRNES ACCORDS

On January 23, 1946 Léon Blum sent a confidential message to Jefferson Caffery informing him that he, Blum, would soon be leaving for Washington to explain the immensity of French needs in connection with the contemplated reconstruction loan and, Caffery wrote, to "convince the Americans that France has not gone red."[45] The previous October the Export-Import Bank had approved a $550 million dollar credit to France. Noting that the French were anticipating a much larger request for a reconstruction loan, Secretary of State Byrnes remarked that "There should therefore be several opportunities in the future to link policy questions with credits to the extent that it is desirable to do so."[46] Several policy questions were at issue. The United States wanted the franc devalued, an end to restrictive trade practices, and some movement toward free currency exchange: "[We must] lend support to those in the French Government who are at present inclined towards a liberal commercial policy." Washington wanted freedom to export American films to France, a more liberal policy on American investments, a way to dispose of American war surplus materials in France, and finally, commercial access to the French Empire.[47]

More important, Washington hoped Blum's visit would signal a change of French policy in Germany. The German question had caused a deterioration of relations that threatened French hopes for a loan. In September 1945 the French refused to allow the extension of central administrative services into their zone; in October they blocked proposals in the Allied Control Commission to establish unified transportation, communications, and postal systems. By November the French were systematically using the "veto power" granted them when the Americans had originally agreed to a separate occupation zone for France. By systematic obstruction of American aims in Germany, Paris was trying to force recognition of its claims for

---

[45] NARA, 851.00/1-2346, January 23, 1946.
[46] NARA, 851.51/10-845, October 8, 1945.
[47] NARA, 851.51/10-3145, October 31, 1945.

separation of the Rhine, internationalization of the Ruhr, and economic integration of the Saar with France. The result was the frustration of American policy in Germany, which was to reconstruct that country as the economic center of a restored and revitalized Western Europe and a bulwark against Soviet Russia.[48] The French were informed that Blum would be expected to bring some concessions with him on the German question in exchange for whatever financial accommodation the Americans were prepared to make.[49] Caffery said he feared a failure of the Blum mission unless Bidault's response to Byrnes on the German question was favorable.

But Blum came to Washington without any concessions to offer. The French would repeat their declarations in favor of free trade, which were already on record, but they would make no commitments unless the whole of their projected deficit were met.[50] Bidault refused categorically Byrnes's request for reconsideration of the French position in Germany and responded instead with threats of his own. The failure of the Blum mission, he declared, "would not imply a revision or reorientation of our foreign policy on the diplomatic plane, but almost inevitably we would be constrained to organize our economic policy in different directions."[51] Why, then, given Bidault's intransigence, should the French have hoped for success from the Blum mission? First, the French had before them the example of the British loan. The British had received $3.75 billion from Washington at favorable interest rates, and although the loan was hedged with restrictions – notably the British had to promise to ease exchange controls within one year – there were also numerous escape clauses, leading the French to consider the loan a success for London. Jean Monnet lost no time in informing the U.S. Embassy that "France was just as important as Britain" in the scheme of things.[52] Second, it was widely believed by Marxists and non-Marxists alike that the United States needed to export in order to avert a postwar depression.[53] Third, the French counted on the Monnet Plan to impress the Americans that their money would be put to good use.[54] Finally, there was the choice of Léon Blum himself, the persuasive and eloquent elder statesman of French politics, who enjoyed a good deal of admiration among New Dealers in Washington and whose Jewish origins and incarceration in Buchenwald during

48 John Gimbel, *The Origins of the Marshall Plan* (Stanford, CA: Stanford University Press, 1976), pp. 4, 59–64, 87–90.
49 NARA, Matthews–Hickerson File, Microfilm Reel 10, March 12, 1946. A.N., Papiers Georges Bidault, 735 (2), February 6 and 20, 1946.
50 A.N., F60, 923. Instructions to Léon Blum.
51 A.N., 457 AP 80 (2), Papiers Georges Bidault, March 21, 1946. MAE, A 194, 5, March 22, 1946.
52 MAE, A 194, 5, "L'Accord anglo–américaine du 6 décembre 1946." by Paul Calvet, December 16, 1945. NARA, 851.51/1-1546, January 15, 1946.
53 MAE, A 194, 5, April 9, 1945, February 21, 1945.
54 Monnet Papers, Fondation Jean Monnet (Lausanne), 4/5/2. Monnet argued repeatedly for the interconnection between the loan and the plan.

the war were expected to arouse American sympathies and dramatize the role of France as victim of German aggression.

Unfortunately from the French viewpoint, none of these hopes or expectations developed quite as foreseen. The Americans made it clear that they regarded the British loan as unique because of that country's Commonwealth obligations, the role of sterling as an international currency, and Britain's role as wartime partner. Underlying these considerations was the unstated "special relationship" between the Anglo-Saxon powers from which the French were always to feel excluded, even after they were formally admitted to the charmed circle of the postwar Big Three. Moreover, the mood of Congress was hostile to foreign loans and even the British loan was in trouble. A treasury loan for any other nation was simply out of the question. The National Advisory Council (NAC), charged with the task of ruling on all foreign loan requests, decided as early as January 30, 1946 that the French could receive only an Export-Import Bank loan, the maximum amount of which would be in the vicinity of $500 million.[55] French negotiators should be warned of that unhappy fact before they left for the United States. As a consequence, the NAC noted, there was little hope of getting the French to revise their position on Germany in consideration of so paltry an amount: "We have no bargaining power." Whatever leverage the Americans enjoyed had been lost when they granted the French a $550 million line of credit in December 1945.

French hopes that the United States needed to export also proved deceptive. All the industrial economies of Europe in 1946 were experiencing full employment amid their scarcity, while in the United States there was a boom in progress. Backlogs for some foreign orders were taking two years and more to fill. Depression was not in fact to occur during the immediate postwar period, and the United States experienced only a mild recession in 1949.[56] The Monnet Plan was conceived with the United States in mind as the source of French modernization funds, as were almost all other postwar reconstruction plans everywhere in Western Europe. The text of the Monnet Plan acknowledged the need for American funding, and even anticipated the Marshall Plan in its suggestion that the "counterpart" in francs of American loans be reserved for internal investment.[57] But the Monnet Plan had another agenda which Washington recognized and did not endorse. The plan was designed to have France displace Germany as the major steel producer

55 NARA, Main Decimal File, 711.51/1-3046, January 30, 1946.
56 Alan Milward, *The Reconstruction of Western Europe, 1945–1951* (London: Methuen, 1984).
57 A.N., F60, 692, Archives du Cabinet Ramadier, Rapport de Jean Monnet sur le Premier Plan, November 1946. As the date of this text indicates, Monnet did not have a full-blown plan ready when he came to Washington, and the influence of the plan on the Blum–Byrnes talks and the American roles in the development of the plan, have been vastly exaggerated. See Mioche, *Le Plan Monnet*, pp. 127–35.

in Western Europe.[58] Consequently, Byrnes marked those parts of the French import plan designated for heavy industrial equipment for special "screening." Paris was to be restricted to its basic needs. Press reports in Washington during the negotiations also highlighted French national ambitions as outlined in the Plan.[59] Moreover, Washington was also critical of the plan's inflationary character and its unilateral emphasis on heavy industry to the virtual exclusion of consumer goods, especially housing. For the State Department, the plan's inattention to consumer interests made it a recipe for increasing the appeal of French communism.

The choice of Blum as negotiator occasioned some comment. Bidault was reported to be furious at Gouin for having bypassed him as foreign minister, and it was to mollify Bidault that Blum was finally placed under the Quai's formal instructions. In the United States there was some curious and satirical reaction, demonstrating that the old view of Blum as the flaming radical had not entirely disappeared. American capitalist suspicion of the venerable socialist was evident in a *Wall Street Journal* article titled "When Karl Marx Calls on Santa Claus." A highly placed American told the French of his astonishment: Americans regarded loans as commercial transactions and "business and socialism don't mix."[60] Blum was aware of the paradox and revised his public speeches accordingly, deleting references to socialism or collectivism and replacing them with more neutral terms like *dirigisme*, or planning.[61] Whatever their suspicions, however, the Americans were acutely aware of Blum's importance in French politics. H. Freeman Matthews suggested Blum receive honors appropriate to a head of state, including residence at Blair House, "particularly in view of the fact that the French may be preparing to ask for considerably more than we may be in a position to grant."[62] Blum's eloquence was not lost on the Americans, despite his inadequate command of English. Press reports were uniformly favorable. The *New York Times* commented that "none among the great wartime figures who have visited New York towers above Blum in spiritual stature." He was the "epitome of those qualities we admire most in the French: their courage, their flashing intelligence, their love of freedom, their humanity. France could not have sent us a better advocate." In New York Blum was reported to have wept in face of the tributes he received.[63] Blum's qualities

[58] Frances Lynch, "Resolving the Paradox of the Monnet Plan: National and International Planning in French Reconstruction," *Economic History Review*, 37, no. 2 (May 1984), pp. 229–43.

[59] NARA, 851.51/4-1046, April 10, 1946. Monnet Papers, 4/8/217, May 19, 1946, *Washington Post* article titled, "U.S. Backs France in Try for Reich's Old Steel Trade."

[60] MAE, A 194, 5, February 11, 1946.

[61] Fonds Léon Blum, Fondation Nationale des Sciences Politiques, 4, Bl 1, Dr. 6.

[62] NARA, 851.51/2-2546, February 25, 1946.

[63] Monnet Papers, 4/8/95, *New York Times*, April 15, 1946.

may have won the French some sympathy, but they did not shake loose any more money.

Washington was at a loss as how to deal with the French negotiators. The State Department kept a nervous eye on the French internal political situation and argued for the largest possible loan, hoping to provide the Socialists with a political success that could be translated into an election victory in June. But the War Department took the opposite tack, advising that the loan negotiations be used to punish the French for their obstruction in Germany. General Clay asked that increased pressure be placed on the French government, but the State Department feared that Bidault might be forced to resign and the French government would fall. Clay asked that wheat shipments to France be halted, but no suggestion, from the Department's point of view, could have been more ill-timed. Maurice Thorez, PCF general secretary and minister of state in the Gouin government, had warned that American credits represented a threat to French independence. Thorez approached the Russian government in an effort to secure shipments of Soviet wheat to meet the French shortage.[64] Word of Thorez's action got out, and Bonnet had to protest rumors to the effect that Washington might cut its allocation to France in view of Russian deliveries that were equally needed. The Communists reaped a propaganda bonanza from the announcement that the Soviet Union had agreed to ship 500,000 tons of grains to France. Caffery pleaded that an American shipment be readied at once, while Matthews, noting the reduction of the French bread ration to 250 grams per day, warned that increased shipments of wheat were necessary "if serious political consequences are to be avoided. If assistance . . . can be forthcoming the position of the anti-Communist elements in France will be immeasurably strengthened." Soviet Ambassador Bogomolov staged a media event by personally welcoming a Soviet freighter full of wheat at Marseilles, while the Americans lamely issued a statement underlining their own greater generosity since the war.

Early in the negotiations Washington tried to raise questions about French nationalization policy. Washington feared that the French, and the Europeans, might construct closed, autarchic economies in the postwar period that were resistant to American penetration.[65] The French replied bluntly that they saw no utility in discussion of policies that were already a matter of public record, and at their insistence, nationalization was withdrawn from the agenda. The best the Americans could obtain was a public statement by Blum noting that any French takeover of American property would be fully compensated.[66]

[64] NARA, 851.5018/2-2446, February 24, 1946; 2-2746, February 27, 1946; 3-646, March 6, 1946; 3-1246, March 12, 1946; 3-1346, March 13, 1946.
[65] Joyce and Gabriel Kolko, *The Limits of Power*, passim.
[66] A.N., F60, 923, Rapport de la sous-commission de l'Assemblée Nationale.

The only positive advantage the French enjoyed in the loan negotiations paradoxically stemmed from their fragile internal political situation and Washington's belief in the danger of a Communist coup in Paris. But even here, disagreement occurred in Washington over how to handle this volatile issue. Caffery pleaded for a generous credit to France on political rather than financial grounds. The internal political situation was "deteriorating." To refuse or reduce the loan request "will pull out one of the last props of hope from those in France who want to see her remain independent and democratic."[67] Byrnes, regretting the unavailability of more funds, nevertheless said he was impressed by French needs and understood the necessity of giving the French the "appearance of success." Caffery returned to the attack on April 4. The Socialist showing in the elections, he argued, depended on the degree of Léon Blum's success in obtaining credits. It was important to strengthen Blum's leadership: "We must strengthen the elements with whom we can work." Generous credits would strengthen all those who "share our basic conceptions;" if the United States lost interest, the French would feel abandoned and turn to the Communists.[68] But Caffery's views were not universally shared. A circular letter to all American consulates in France noted that a large loan would certainly be exploited by the Socialists. Failure or delay in the loan talks, however, would be used by French political moderates as evidence of American opposition to the policies of the present left-wing coalition and the need for a shift to the right, which was in the American interest. Arguably this is what actually happened in the elections, which strengthened the MRP in comparison to the Socialists, while Communist support remained unchanged.[69] Bidault replaced Gouin as head of the French government in June 1945, and French politics assumed a more conservative bent.

Similar arguments went on in the National Advisory Council. William Clayton argued for very generous financial assistance: A decision against a substantial loan would be a "catastrophe." Clayton thought a scaled-down French request of $2 billion could be met through an Export-Import Bank loan of $650 million, the cancellation of existing debts of another $650 million, and the promise of an additional $800 million to $1 billion loan from the World Bank a year later. William M. Martin of the Federal Reserve thought this amount was too much for the Export-Import Bank to handle, but Clayton disagreed, arguing for the transfer to the French of funds held in reserve for an eventual loan to Moscow.[70] At the May 6 meeting of the NAC Clayton noted that the defeat of the constitutional project in the recent referendum had brought a welcome shift to the right in French politics. But Marriner Eccles, chairman of the Federal Reserve, said he "would dis-

---

67 NARA, 851.51/2-946, February 9, 1946.
68 NARA, 851.00/4-446, April 4, 1946.
69 NARA, 851.51/5-246, May 2, 1946; 851.00/2-1346, February 13, 1946.
70 FRUS, 1946, V, France, April 25, 1946, pp. 440–6.

like to have the American government accused of undertaking to buy a foreign election. We are concerned with getting countries back on their feet rather than as to whether the government is socialist, communistic, or a capitalist democracy." Eccles feared that the loan might cause a negative reaction against the parties identified with the United States in the June 5 elections. Was the Council equally prepared to extend the loan to a Socialist–Communist coalition that might emerge victorious? Clayton replied in no uncertain terms that the United States would go ahead with the loan in any case. A reconstruction loan had already been made to Poland and it was "hardly conceivable that France would go further to the left than Poland." [71] But many continued to worry that a loan made in the interest of strengthening still capitalist France might paradoxically work to the benefit of a Communist regime that would come to power there.

The final terms of the Blum–Byrnes accords were not regarded as a success by the French, although many went to great lengths to make them appear as such. The French received a new loan of $650 million from the Export-Import Bank as originally expected. [72] In addition, some $2.8 billion of lend-lease obligations were cancelled, but it had been understood prior to the negotiations that Washington would not require repayment for its wartime aid. Deliveries in the pipeline to France since the cancellation of lend-lease were consolidated into a new loan of $420 million, to which another $300 million were added as charges for American surplus goods left behind in France. Finally, the United States promised to support a French request for a further $500 million loan from the World Bank, scheduled to begin operation within a year. Although the total granted or promised the French could be "dressed up" to look like almost $2 billion, the reality was that only $650 million represented "new money," while Paris had been hoping for $3 billion. The lend-lease and surplus represented war goods "already consumed" and the World Bank loan was hardly assured. Later developments bore out the Quai's pessimistic analysis.

France did not receive the means to finance the Monnet Plan, despite the claims of Monnet later that the loan was predicated on the plan and therefore France had a "moral obligation" to live up to it. [73] The $650 million enabled France to survive another winter, but barely. Within months a financial crisis again loomed, imports were threatened, and the French were back in Washington with further requests. The somber future was clear to the French at the later stages of the negotiations. Near desperation, Blum appealed to Secretary Byrnes, only distantly involved in the negotiations, and to President Truman, who was not involved at all. From the president, Blum received assurances that the American negotiators would be instructed

[71] FRUS, 1946, V, France, May 2, 1945, pp. 441–5.
[72] A.N., F60, 923, Accords Blum–Byrnes, Exposé. Rapport du Comité des Affaires Etrangères par M. Gorse, July 30, 1946.
[73] Fondation Jean Monnet, Papiers Jean Monnet, 4/5/2.

to be more forthcoming. From the secretary, Blum received a laconic observation that all negotiations carried their disappointments.[74] Gouin told Blum
to break off negotiations and return home to "report" in the event the result
appeared unsatisfactory to him, but Blum, free to use his own judgment,
finally decided to sign.[75]

The stickiest part of the negotiations related to minor issues; the evaluation of American war surplus goods in France and the matter of the access
of American films to the French market. The Americans valued the war
surplus at $325 million; the French, realizing that the cost to Washington
of bringing these materials home for storage was more than their real worth,
offered $175 million.[76] The Americans refused to compromise and $300
million was added to the French debt. The often bitter and protracted negotiations over what appeared to be a minor matter, the motion picture
industry, defy explanation in simple terms of economics. The French were
forced to accept more American films than they wished, and as a consequence of the Blum–Byrnes agreements the French came to believe that the
postwar recovery of their film industry was prevented by American cultural
imperialism. The myth was in part based on a misunderstanding of the text
of the agreement, which set aside a minimum of four weeks out of every
thirteen, not a maximum as was commonly believed, during which theaters
were required to show French films (on Blum–Byrnes and French film, see
Chapter 4, II). Nevertheless, a *legende noire* developed around the alleged
imperialism of Hollywood, and the American insistence upon a "free flow
of information" as a means to export the American way of life.[77]

Despite the disappointing conclusion of the Blum–Byrnes negotiations, it
has been argued that they represented a crucial step in the integration of
France into an anti-Soviet Western bloc dominated by Washington, the contours of which later became clearer with the establishment of the Marshall
Plan and Atlantic Alliance.[78] But the accords had no such effect on French
foreign policy. The continued dependence of the French on American imports, for which Paris lacked the ability to pay, for the time being only
sharpened the contradictions inherent in a foreign policy that increasingly

[74] FRUS, 1946, V, *France*, May 23, 1946, pp. 451–2. Matthews–Hickerson File, Reel
10, April 18, 1946.
[75] MAE, A 194, 5, May 25, 1946.
[76] MAE, 194, 5, May 26, 1946.
[77] Jacques Thibau, *La France colonisée* (Paris, Flammarion, 1980), p. 69 ff. Charles
Ford argues French films were well protected: *Histoire du Cinema français contem-
porain, 1945–77* (Paris: France-Empire, 1977). The best recent analysis is Jacques
Portes, "Les Origines de la légende noir des accords Blum–Byrnes sur le cinema,"
Revue d'histoire Moderne et Contemporaine, 33 (April–June 1986): 314–29. Other
aspects of this controversy are examined in Chapter 4, II.
[78] Annie Lacroix-Riz, "Négociation et signature des accords Blum–Byrnes (octobre 1945–
mai 1946) d'après les Archives du ministère des Affaires étrangères," *Revue d'histoire
moderne et contemporaine,* 31 (July–September 1984):417–48.

diverged from Washington. Gouin, and Blum, had hoped to offer concessions on the German question in exchange for a substantial loan, but Washington could not offer more than the minimum credit extended, and the Socialists could not deliver either given the hard line on Germany adopted by the MRP and the Communists. The French cabinet was believed in Washington to be on the edge of crisis in April 1946, because of a Gouin–Bidault argument over concessions on Germany.[79] But Bidault won, and his hard line was rewarded by the electorate, which gave the MRP and the PCF gains at Socialist expense in June. The American embassy sadly concluded that Bidault emerged from those elections very much the man of the hour, his stature and statesmanlike image enhanced, precisely because he was the advocate of the harder line on Germany.[80]

Bidault was held in low esteem in Washington, where he was regarded as ambitious and cynically prepared to work with the Communists. Caffery noted that the British also thought him to be a man of limited outlook and ability. His foreign policy was thought too favorable to the Russians due to Communist influence. The Quai d'Orsay was aware of the considerable irritation in Washington over Bidault's attempts to act as a "bridge" between it and Moscow. During the crisis over the Russian failure to withdraw their troops from Iran, Paris was regarded as sympathetic to the Soviet position. Bidault's attempts to win Washington's support for an anti-Franco policy further angered Washington, eager at this juncture to forge better relations with Spain. Bidault was also disliked for crudely seeking to use the French internal situation to blackmail Washington, a perception that occurred repeatedly throughout his long tenure in the Quai d'Orsay. Thus French embassy officials told Under Secretary of State Acheson that unless Bidault received American support for his Spanish policy, he might be forced to resign. Acheson replied that he found all this very interesting, but had to excuse himself to attend another meeting.[81]

Eleanor Roosevelt voiced American liberal concerns over French refugee policy, charging that Russian, Yugoslav, and Bulgarian nationals under French control were being inhumanly treated and forceably repatriated. The Quai reported that her remarks reflected American and British concern that the French desired agreement with Moscow, even at the price of sacrificing human rights, for reasons of internal politics. The French protested that they were unable to refuse Russian requests out of concern for Alsace-Lorraine war prisoners in the USSR, the repatriation of whom Paris was trying to obtain.[82] More seriously, "confirmed" intelligence from French diplomats in Portugal quoted American envoys in Lisbon as saying that the United States had no plans to defend France in case of a Soviet invasion of Western

[79] Monnet Papers, 4/8/32, April 25, 1946.
[80] NARA, 851.51/6-346, June 3, 1946; 6-446, June 4, 1946.
[81] Matthews–Hickerson File, Microfilm Reel 13, March 27, 1946.
[82] MAE, B Amérique, 119, July 4, 1946.

Europe. The Americans would rather fall back to a defensive line in the Pyrenees because they regarded only Britain, Spain, and Portugal as reliable allies. The reports were correct: American military plans were predicated on the idea that France and Germany could not be defended successfully against a Soviet attack (see Chapter 3). American suspicion of the French was allegedly shared by the English, many of whom, Paris feared, regarded Paris as "un peu trop sous l'influence russe." London was said to fear that in case of war France, under Soviet influence, would try to deny Britain passage through the Straits of Gibralter.[83]

The American view of France was evolving, however, in a direction that Paris would eventually find to be less ominous. Changing views of American policymakers were evident in a "Policy and Information Statement on France" circulated internally by the State Department on September 15, 1946.[84] The French were wrong if they believed that Washington had written off France. On the contrary, France held a "paramount strategic importance" in wars in which American interests had been menaced in the past. At present, the "world drama of Soviet expansion" was being played out in France, and Washington did believe that the France Communist party had a "veto power" on both domestic and foreign policies of the French government. However, it was in the interest of the United States to assist France both morally and physically to regain its former strength and influence, because the political health of the nation lay in its economic well-being. In its dogged insistence on the simple equation between poverty and Marxism the State Department often demonstrated that it had assimilated a crude Marxism all its own in its view of human affairs.

Every effort must be made to convince Paris of the necessity to reconstruct Germany, but the French must not be presented with any faits accomplis. Washington appreciated that Paris favored free trade, but recognized that it must continue protection for a transitional period of several years.[85] The most interesting aspect of the report was its discussion of French attitudes toward the United States. The French understanding of America was shaped by humiliation, touchiness, jealousy, and an "inferiority complex," according to the State Department. The latter phrase appears ad nauseum in American diplomatic correspondance of the period. In consequence, the French were said to have a "warped" view of the United States, regarding Americans as hedonistic, materialistic, selfish, and predatory; the French consistently deprecated American culture and "distorted our values." Anti-Americanism, according to a time-honored American shibboleth, was the property of the political extremes of the right and left. America's natural allies in France were found among the "common people" and in industrial

[83]   MAE, B Amérique, 119, August 13, 1946. "A bit too much under Russian influence."
[84]   NARA, Main Decimal File, 711.51/9-1546, September 15, 1946.
[85]   Ibid.

and financial circles. However, American policy must be careful not to ally itself with reactionary business and wealthy elements against the interests of the masses, "upon whose confidence and friendliness our position and authority must depend."

Of equal interest was George Kennan's critique of a draft of the State Department's French Policy and Information Report. Kennan tried to integrate France into the general scheme of containment, adumbrated in his famous "long telegram" from Moscow in February 1946, and later enshrined in the equally renowned "X" article in *Foreign Affairs*. Kennan criticized the West European desk of the State Department for giving insufficient attention to the reality of Soviet power in French internal affairs.[86] The French Communist party, he said, was the strongest single force in French life, dominated by the USSR, and could be expected to oppose vehemently all American influence in the country and "seal off" France. The USSR intended to weaken France in order to render it susceptible to Soviet domination. The French people, however, did not understand Communist aims, which explained the party's broad support. An "objective, factual" knowledge of the USSR must be brought to the French people, presumably by American initiative through psychological warfare. "Our relations with France," Kennan insisted, "will be vitally affected by the extent to which the French people get a realistic view of the USSR."

Perhaps reacting to the disquieting reports from the Quai concerning American impatience with his foreign policy, Bidault let it be known to Caffery that he, Bidault, "no longer believed that France can be an intermediary between the USA and the USSR." Nor did Bidault think he could work with the Communists over the long term; he expected to eliminate the Communists from the French government within the next six months.[87] This was the first of many such confidential assurances that the ambassador was to receive in coming months. Conservative French politicians would like nothing better than to govern without the Communists and would do so as soon as they were strong enough – a hint that Washington could help to provide that strength through economic aid. The Socialists also tried to reassure the ambassador: Caffery was warned that the Mollet group would be able to defeat Daniel Mayer and Léon Blum and take control of the SFIO at the next party congress. The Americans need not worry, however, for Mollet's people had no Communist sympathies, "and desired above all to be friendly to the United States."[88]

But disturbing news began to come from the political right. Reacting to De Gaulle's Bayeux speech, in which the general announced his plans to establish a presidential regime in France, Caffery wondered whether de Gaulle

---

[86] NARA, 711.51/4-146, April 1, 1946.
[87] NARA, 851.00/8-2446, August 24, 1946.
[88] NARA, 851.00/8-2746, August 27, 1946.

did not really intend to carry out a coup d'état. Bidault confided that de Gaulle worried him by "waiting in the wings for me to make a mess"; he had approached de Gaulle in hope of an alliance, but the general gave him the "brush off." Caffery concluded that de Gaulle hoped the government would fail and the economy collapse, after which he would be recalled to power, once again to play the role of savior. The "self-satisfaction and smug assurance" of the Gaullists was shocking, as was their idea of "skipping nimbly over constitutional barriers with no thought that he [de Gaulle] is playing the Communist game." The Gaullists were purely and simply helping in the political and economic disintegration of France, and Caffery could not find anyone in their circle who demonstrated any disinterest, talent, or concern for the national interest.

Following the November elections, Caffery feared that Thorez would be able to form a government. Washington was relieved when Blum formed his temporary homogeneous Socialist government and Vincent Auriol was elected to the presidency, both Socialist leaders being regarded as friendly to the United States. Caffery wanted to see Blum continue in power in order to keep the Communists out. But on January 12, 1947 Bidault told Caffery that he expected to form the next government, venturing to remark that he thought that Thorez and Duclos were not in Moscow's good graces: "As you know, Thorez has always been very cooperative with me."[89] Caffery was alarmed; again flirting with the Communists, Bidault "would like to play on our side," but at this time found it "inexpedient." Meanwhile, Blum told Caffery that he could not continue in office: "I am worn out. There must be another 'providential man' in France. If I stay, I fritter away my prestige," the Socialist leader said. Bonnet reported satisfaction in Washington with the succession of Blum by Ramadier in January 1947. But the French ambassador was misinformed in reporting that Bidault's return as foreign affairs minister was welcomed, and that François Billoux, the new Communist minister of defense, was regarded favorably as well.[90] It was true, though, that Washington still thought it better that the Communists participate in the government than that they attempt to paralyze the French economy from without. That was shortly to change, however.

Washington continued to be standoffish with economic assistance to the French. In November 1946 Emmanuel Monick, governor of the Bank of France, had approached Ivan White to say that the French financial situation was undergoing severe deterioration and again approaching a critical point. In order to control labor unrest, Communist participation in the government remained essential, but they could be kept in ministries "of the health type." France must pursue the World Bank loan promised in the

[89] NARA, 851.00/11-2146, November 21, 1946; 1-1247, January 12, 1947.
[90] NARA, 851.00/1-1747, January 17, 1947. MAE, B Amérique, 120, January 23, 1947.

Blum–Byrnes agreements to retain its financial health.[91] In December Bonnet and Baumgartner met with State Department officials to discuss the loan and discovered Washington had extreme reservations in granting the promised credit. Clayton said the American government could not make any commitment on behalf of the World Bank, nor was it clear that the American representatives would support a loan to France: "Loans are palliatives until inflation is corrected." The French deficit was much too large, and "as France goes, so goes Western and Central Europe." Clayton reprimanded the French for failing to attack the fiscal problem as courageously as the Belgians, who had blocked accounts and administered a severe dose of deflation to their economy after the war.

A new French approach to the World Bank after the new year proved equally disappointing. The bank would consider only $250 million of the $500 million promised in the Blum–Byrnes accords. Moreover, the interest rate was prohibitive, the restrictions placed on the use of the funds were unacceptable, and the bank was asking to interfere with French sovereignty by claiming the right to approve any future foreign loans the French planned to make. Bank officials professed to see in the French situation only a bad business proposition. Inflation was rampant, the political situation remained unstable, and the regime's future policies were in doubt. The sources of the bank's capital were, after all, private; they needed to be reassured.[92]

Despite conciliatory statements, the Ramadier government managed to resolve nothing in Franco–American relations. The contradiction remained between growing French financial need and dependence on Washington, and American dissatisfaction with France's political situation and foreign policy, which failed to take that dependence into account. On February 21, 1947 the Quai reported:

> French policy has for some time been judged in American circles as seeking excessively to satisfy the USSR, under the pretext of pursuing an even balance between East and West. It is believed that M. Ramadier has wished to fight against this impression.

A March 20, 1947 report by the Quai was still pessimistic. French–American relations remained where they had been a year earlier, in a state of "reciprocal antipathy." The French were forever finding new causes of hostility: the United States stood in the way of French designs on Germany, blocked French use of German war-prisoner labor, reconstructed the German economy, undermined French rule in Indochina, and pressed for free commerce and exchange. The debate in France, already becoming venomous over the Blum–Byrnes accords on the cinema, was a good indication of the growing hostility and resentment of American "imperialism." On the

[91]   NARA, 851.51/11-146, November 1, 1946.
[92]   NARA, 851.51/12-1046, December 10, 1946. MAE, 194, 5, April 15, 1947.

other hand, the Americans saw a Communist drive for power and influence, a French tendency to mediate between East and West that was much closer to the East than to the West, and relentless French pressure for destructive reparations from Germany. The American ambassador had warned that imports could not necessarily be continued in the same rhythm as in the past. Was his statement "a warning not empty of meaning, at a time when people are beginning to discuss, if only as a still theoretical possibility, the formation of a government without the Communists?"[93] The contradiction had sharpened to the point where it was no longer tolerable. With the coming of the cold war, it needed to be, and was, resolved.

[93]   MAE, Y 1944–9, 120, March 20, 1947.

3

L'année terrible

I   FRANCE CHOOSES THE WEST

THE TURNING POINT of the postwar era occurred in 1947, with the Truman Doctrine, the elimination of the Communists from the governments of France and Italy, the Marshall Plan, and the founding of the Cominform. These events marked the beginning of the cold war, and forced a resolution of the contradictions troubling Franco–American relations. The ties between the two countries were recast. Several steps were essential. The Truman Doctrine, although immediately concerned with Greece and Turkey, made clear Washington's intent to struggle against communism everywhere in the world. Many concluded that the normalization of relations between Paris and Washington required the elimination of the Communists from the French government. The Communists in fact departed in early May, removing the last internal French obstacle to a deepening of French economic dependence on Washington. On June 5 Secretary of State George C. Marshall launched the famous initiative that was to become known as the Marshall Plan. Loans to the Europeans were replaced by simple grants in aid, in exchange for which recipient countries accepted the direct involvement of Washington bureaucrats in their economies. The Marshall Plan had many aims. Foremost among them was the American intent to reconstruct the German economy in a way that would be palatable to other Europeans, primarily the French. Within a month of the plan's announcement, the British and Americans raised the "ceiling" on German steel production in the Ruhr which had been painstakingly negotiated in 1946. The resulting opposition in Paris revealed the fragility of France's governing coalition.

The weakened Ramadier government now faced a powerful Communist party riding the crest of genuine working-class discontent, causing Washington to rethink its relationship with de Gaulle. The founding conference of the Cominform in September 1947 was followed by a new level of Com-

munist militancy, which appeared to assume an insurrectionary character
with the strikes of November and December. The municipal elections of
October 1947 confirmed resurgent Gaullist strength, while the political crisis consequent upon the strikes appeared certain to bring the general to
power. Washington was prepared to throw its support to de Gaulle in exchange for some substantive changes in his program. But the general refused
to seek power in view of the troubled circumstances, and the Americans
turned to a new centrist coalition under the MRP leader, Robert Schuman.
To help stabilize the Schuman government, the U.S. Congress passed an
interim aid bill, in exchange for which Paris accepted the revised levels of
industry in Germany. As a consequence of the Ramadier government's
weakness and the crippling extent of French economic deprivation, Washington became deeply involved in French internal economic and political
affairs. The basis of the new Franco–American relationship was established.
In its broad outlines it remained fundamentally unchanged until 1954.

The economic catastrophe facing France in 1947 became apparent in February. A wheat shortage loomed because of severe winter frost and a shortage of seed. Minister of Agriculture Tanguy-Prigent was dispatched to
Washington in the hope of negotiating increased purchases of American
grain. But the shortage was worldwide and there were many other pur-
chasers competing on the American markets. The French were accorded
362,000 tons of wheat through June, although at least 500,000 was needed
if the bread ration was to be maintained at the already low level of 250
grams per day.[1] Meanwhile, the Blum–Byrnes credit was nearing exhaustion. Negotiations for the promised follow-up credit from the World Bank
dragged on. It was not clear how the French were to get the needed foreign
exchange to finance wheat and other purchases. There was only one source
of goods and one source of dollars.
  The United States was also the key to French hopes in Germany. There
appeared to be some encouraging development. George C. Marshall was
much more sympathetic to France than Byrnes. The new secretary of state
had fond memories and friendships from World War I, which he often recalled in conversations with French officials. As a general, he was able to
argue the French case with greater authority against his Francophobe former colleagues in the War Department, who were charged with the administration of occupied Germany. The French were aware that General Clay
and his political adviser Robert Murphy of Vichy fame were unreceptive to
their demands, and it was therefore with some joy that the Quai read Bon-
fjnet's cable of February 12: Marshall was satisfied that the French proposals
on Germany "were consistent, on many points, with American views." The

[1]   Archives Nationales (A.N.), F60, 672-73, Comité économique, January 13, 1947,
      February 25, 1947.

Americans, too, favored strong local government in Germany and a decentralized federal structure. They wanted to increase Ruhr production, but they saw the necessity of exploiting its industry in the interests of the entire continent.[2] Marshall's favorable disposition to the French was reflected in a satisfactory rate of coal deliveries from the Ruhr early in 1947. On his way to Moscow, Marshall paid a visit to President Auriol. Auriol rambled on about French distrust of Germany and needs for security. Marshall listened sympathetically.

In March the Foreign Ministers of the Four Powers convened in Moscow to discuss the the German question. On the eve of the meeting, Minister of Justice Teitgen, who with Ramadier and Bidault monopolized foreign policy decisions in the French cabinet, met with Caffery to receive the text of President Truman's remarks on the Greek and Turkish crises. "It's a bomb," the ambassador remarked of the Truman Doctrine. "From now on the situation is clear. One must choose." Caffery's concern was not internal French politics, but rather the French policy of remaining equidistant from Washington and Moscow.[3] This was clear from Teitgen's analysis of the ambassador's remark. "To lead us to this choice, the American government has two means, which are coal and the recruitment of German manual labor." The Americans had long resisted French efforts to draft German labor for their mines. But supplies of German coal were most important for France; the need was "absolute." Without it living standards must be reduced and the government perpetually reduced to begging for credits. "These perspectives appear to me to be threatening to the independence of our position in the world," Teitgen said. Unless Moscow agreed to a German settlement that ensured the French need for coal, "we may find ourselves constrained, at the outcome of the Moscow Conference, to enter into an accommodation with London and Washington." Washington was closer to the French position on German decentralization than Moscow in any case. Was it not time to examine what concessions the "Anglo-Saxons" were ready to give France in exchange for its agreement to adhere to their bizone?

Teitgen insisted, however, that Molotov be given every opportunity to meet French demands. He must understand that the French need for coal and a voice in the administration of the Ruhr could force France "to enter an agreement with the Anglo-Saxon powers." Realization that France might align itself with the West could bring the Russians to terms. If not, "it would be appropriate to ask them by what methods they could lead the Moscow Conference to take decisions concerning coal that are favorable to our demands."[4]

[2] A.N., 457 AP 80 (3), Papiers Georges Bidault, February 12, 19, March 28, 1947.
[3] Ministère des Affaires Etrangères (MAE), Y 1944–9, Internationale, CMAE, Moscou, Corréspondance, March 14, 1947.
[4] MAE, Y 1944–9, CMAE, Moscou, Corréspondance, March 14, 1947. Annie Lacroix-Riz cites the Caffery remark as meant to obtain the removal of the Communists from

Bidault did exactly as Teitgen suggested. On March 18 he explained to Stalin the advantages of a German federal structure, the French need for the Saar, and internationalization of the Ruhr. The Russian leader was not wholly negative. He apparently understood the primacy of the French need for coal.[5] Two days later Vishinsky gave Bidault the impression that Moscow's views were identical with those of France. Perhaps Caffery's menacing choice could be avoided: "In effect, the French delegation's efforts to find a common ground equidistant from Soviet exclusivism and Anglo-Saxon demogogy have permitted us to expect certain results. . . ." But a day later the Russian foreign minister dropped his own bomb. Molotov criticized projects that "have as a goal the destruction or the weakening of the German state," and he denounced federalism. The Russians had suffered more than anyone from Hitlerite aggression, but they would neither condemn the German people in their entirety, nor reduce the German state to powerlessness.[6] Molotov favored the creation of a German Provisional Government. Now it was Bidault's turn to object, and Marshall found himself playing the role of conciliator between the French and the Russians.

Molotov also refused to support French claims to the Saar. When the French Communists, in the past the most vocal supporters of Bidault's hard line on Germany, sided with Molotov, Bidault gave vent to all his pent-up anticommunism. The Saar might have been the last straw for Bidault, but the French foreign policy reorientation was much deeper, involving hopes for a decentralized German structure, assured coal supplies, and access to the Ruhr. Suddenly, the Americans seemed likely to grant these demands and not the Russians. And France, in turn, made its choice, irrevocably and firmly with the West, no matter what the price. It was in a sense ironic that Bidault's declaration to Secretary Marshall took place in Moscow. At the conclusion of the conference Bidault alerted Marshall to the serious situation in France in terms of coal, food, manpower, and credits. Bidault complained that the $500 million loan from the World Bank, promised in the Blum–Byrnes agreements, had been reduced to a first segment of $250 million and appeared encumbered with conditions that were unacceptable to a sovereign country. He then "digressed to say he knew that in the minds of some there are uncertainties regarding France and its foreign policy in the future. He felt that anyone that knew France could not doubt the ultimate choice where France would stand." America could rely on France, Bidault said; France simply needed support and time in order "to avoid civil war."[7]

Marshall appreciated the gravity of Bidault's declaration. He promised to

the French government: "L'entrée de la France dans la guerre froide (1944–1947)," *Cahiers d'histoire de l'Institut de Recherche Marxiste*, 13 (1983): 4–24.

[5] MAE, CMAE, Moscou, 185, March 18, 1947.
[6] Ibid., March 22, 23, 1947.
[7] National Archives and Records Administration (NARA,), 851.504/4-2347, April 23, 1947.

speak to John J. McCloy, head of the World Bank, about the French loan, and to look into other French problems in Germany:

> I wanted him [Bidault] to know there is every disposition by the United States to help the French Government in its present dilemmas. . . . I am impelled and motivated by a desire to assist the French government. I said that I had a general comprehension of the delicate political situation in France and take it into account in my reactions to the problems that arise. Bidault said that he realized this and was grateful.

The French had altered their foreign policy to coincide with their financial needs. Could their internal political balance long remain unchanged?

The belief persists that Washington "ordered" the French government to eliminate the Communists from the cabinet, despite the existence of only the flimsiest of evidence. Caffery's remark to Bidault, "one must choose," referred to French policy in Germany. The French ambassador to Colombia reported that his American counterpart remarked that the French situation was confused, "but one must expect that between now and August 15 some upsets will occur which will clarify the situation one way or another." Did this not mean the State Department had made a decision about French affairs?[8] But it is not clear why an American ambassador in Bogota should have known what the Paris embassy did not, and the vagueness of the remark, coming only two days before the crucial cabinet crisis in Paris, seems sufficient to render it meaningless.

French politicians hardly needed outside prodding to expel the Communists from the coalition in any case. In 1947 anticommunism was developing in France with fervor equal to if not greater than that in Washington, and French politicians intended to eliminate the Communists just as soon as they felt strong enough to do so. No sooner had the Ramadier government been formed, than Caffery reported that MRP leaders Schuman, Teitgen, Maurice Schumann, and Michelet wanted to exclude the Communists "no matter what the consequences." Bidault told the ambassador that the Ramadier government could not last because the Communist ministers were fighting the others at every step; they were a threat "to Western civilization as we know it."[9] Caffery noted that politicians of the center and left were cooperating in trying to neutralize Communist infiltration in the Interior, War, Veterans, and Industrial Production ministries. Depreux, at the Ministry of the Interior, was pressuring the Paris Prefect of Police, Luizet, who had been "playing the Communist game." General Revers had replaced de Lattre, who "flirted" with the Communists. François Mitterrand was eliminating Communists from the Ministry of War Veterans "as fast as he [could]." The French zeal in purging Communists was greatly encouraged, Caffery

8   MAE, Y 1944–9, March 1947–June 1947, dispatch of April 28, 1947. Cited by Annie Lacroix–Riz, *Cahiers d'histoire.*
9   NARA, 851.00/1-2747, January 27, 1947; 851.00/1-2847, January 28, 1947.

thought, by the Truman declaration on Greece and Turkey. Ramadier, too, Caffery was sure, was considering getting rid of the Communists in the aftermath of the Truman speech, and it was always possible that the Kremlin would itself order the Communists out of the government, although the Russian ambassador thought there would be no crisis soon.[10]

There were many signs of the coming cabinet crisis that was in a sense overdetermined. Caffery was merely a spectator, and the outcome was not at all dependent upon what he might do. In March the Indochina disagreement provided the absurd spectacle of the Communist ministers voting differently from their colleagues in the National Assembly. A final showdown was building: The Communists clearly could not oppose the war and remain in the government. Their departure now appeared only a question of time. Douglas MacArthur III wrote to Woodruff Wallner, head of the European desk, that French anti-Communist leadership was "at last showing signs of life." Needed now was a campaign to educate the population to the danger. A means must be found to neutralize or break the Communist domination of the CGT, preferably by a split, and a charismatic individual was needed to head an anti-Communist coalition, like Blum or de Gaulle. Washington expected a cabinet crisis to occur after the Moscow conference, at the earliest in mid-April, although May or June were more likely. The embassy was encouraged; the possibilities were better than at any time since the liberation. But there were even greater dangers with the Communists in opposition: It was essential that any anti-Communist coalition have "roots in the working class." The elimination of the Communists must not be the excuse for a turn to a right-wing domestic policy that would serve to alienate the workers further from the regime and strengthen the Communist party in the long run. Getting rid of the PCF was a difficult trick to accomplish, but Caffery now thought it worth a try:

> A year ago I was discouraged about the possibility of preventing the Communists from eventually taking over the country; now I have come to believe that they will not take it over; but the process of organizing the democratic forces into an effective machine will be long and tedious; and without a doubt the Communists if they don't take it over will struggle hard to keep it weak and divided.[11]

There were disquieting signs, however, reports of Communist plans for a coup, and feelers from de Gaulle to the Communist party for support. André Philip told the ambassador that before the Socialists would act to "kick the Communists out of the cabinet," economic conditions would have to improve. Teitgen said the Communists could not be removed without the promise of American aid; with it, "we would be brave enough to stick out

---

[10]   NARA, 851.00/2-1947, February 19, 1947; 851.00/3-1447, March 14, 1947; 851.00/3-2047, March 20, 1947.

[11]   NARA, 851.00B/3-2647, March 26, 1947; 851.00/3-3147, March 31, 1947.

our chins in the presence of the Communists anywhere." But the ambassador had no aid to offer. De Gaulle told Caffery that he intended to return to power in the near future, which alarmed the ambassador further. The general frightened the Socialists, throwing them into the arms of the Communists. Caffery feared the government would not fall for another six to eight weeks, and when it did, Auriol would recall Bidault, who would take back the Communists. On April 25 Jean Chauvel predicted (accurately) the crisis would occur within a week, raising American hopes. But on April 29 Caffery saw no signs of the predicted crisis and thought the "political thermometer was cooling." Nobody now appeared to want the government to fall after all.[12]

The Communists did not want to leave the government over Indochina, for fear of lending support to conservative charges of their "antinational" character. The Renault strike, which spread rapidly by May 1 and won the support of the CGT, afforded an opportunity to break with the government on a wage issue, emphasizing the party's social vocation. Caffery was unable to tell when the crisis was coming, how it would unfold, or what would be its result. On May 2, with the Communists having declared their support of the strikers against Ramadier, he complained that "it is impossible to forecast how the crisis will develop." Would Ramadier remain in power, replace the Communist ministers, or resign? After Ramadier dismissed the Communists, Caffery was unable to predict what the National Council of the Socialist party would do. The Blum–Ramadier faction wanted the party to approve the government's continuation, but the Mollet group wanted the Council to force the government to resign. Caffery turned to his regular source in the Interior Ministry, but got no prediction on how the crisis would be resolved. Ramadier told Caffery that to remain in power he needed to be assured of American wheat and coal. In their absence, the workers would flock to the Communists, de Gaulle would return to power, and the PCF and de Gaulle would struggle for control of France. The scenario of a final armageddon between the PCF and de Gaulle became a continuous refrain in the coming months, and provided the substance of several of the ambassador's dispatches to Washington. Ramadier's continued pleading for help, however, could well have had the negative effect of turning the Americans against him.[13]

The Americans had little to promise the French. The negotiations for the $250 million loan from the World Bank were concluded, and the loan made the front page of *Le Monde* on May 1. But it now seemed a paltry amount in view of the enormity of French needs now visible to everyone, and could hardly have been a factor in the cabinet crisis. Moreover, the French refused

12 NARA, 851.00/3-2447, March 24, 1947; 851.00/4-347, April 3, 1947; 851.00/4-1547, April 15, 1947; 851.00/4-947, April 9, 1947; 851.00/4-1147, April 11, 1947.
13 NARA, 851.00/5-247, May 2, 1947; 851.00/5-547, May 5, 1947.

to concede to the bank's terms concerning future trade practices; the bank granted the loan "to avoid embarrassment," but regretted that its first loan could not be a model for others as originally hoped.[14] Had Caffery been involved in the French cabinet crisis, Ramadier would not have chosen the moment of its unfolding to charge that Washington had failed to keep its commitments of wheat shipments. Nor would Caffery have replied so bluntly that the United States had kept its commitments; Ramadier had no grounds to blame the Americans for the French shortage, or to cast doubt on the good will of the American government. Caffery warned the French government of the "disappointment, not to say disillusionment" with which Ramadier's charges would be received in the United States and the negative effect they would have on future French aid requests.[15] Far from promising increased aid at the moment of the French cabinet crisis, as the French asked, Caffery was now threatening to reduce it.

On May 5 the Associated Press reported that Caffery had promised the French enormous amounts of aid if Ramadier dismissed the Communists from the government. The origins of the story remained obscure. Spreading it did not serve the PCF's interest, since the party expected to return to the government very soon in any case, and did not understand the American role in its isolation until informed of it at the Cominform conference in September by the Russians and Yugoslavs. The American reaction to the story casts doubt on its validity: Marshall sent an urgent query to Paris, to which Caffery replied that the press report was without foundation. To reporters in Paris he said it was "news to us." Off the record, he regretted the story as particularly inopportune because it was likely to have a negative effect and influence the Socialist party's National Council in favor of toppling the government, while fueling charges of American interference and "dollar imperialism." To Marshall, Caffery expressed his suspicion that the Communist party was actually the source of the rumor. They must have lacked ammunition of their own to influence the Socialist National Council, Caffery speculated.[16]

It is instructive to compare the French cabinet crisis with the Italian, where the American role was more intimate. In Italy too, the push from the Christian Democrats and internal strife remained decisive in the expulsion of the Communists. Despite rumors of a deal between de Gasperi and the Americans to eliminate the Communist party from the government during the prime minister's visit to Washington in January 1947, the evidence was to the contrary. De Gasperi wanted the Communists to remain in the cabinet to vote the peace treaty and the Lateran pacts, which occurred in March 1947. As the prime minister was leaving the United States, the Export-Import

14 *Le Monde*, May 1–2, 1947; NARA, 851.51/5-947, May 5, 1947.
15 A.N., 457 AP 80 (2), Papiers Georges Bidault, April 30, 1947.
16 NARA, 851.00/5-547, May 5, 1947; 851.00/5-647, May 6, 1947.

Bank voted a paltry $150 million loan to Italy with ill grace and unfavorable terms.[17] On March 4, 1947 Ambassador James Dunn saw "no other workable basis of govt. than coalition cabinet comprised of three mass parties," which included the Communists. He thought the government would last at least until the next elections.[18] The Italian cabinet divided seriously on a program to deal with runaway inflation in April, yet de Gasperi could get no response out of Washington on a new loan.

On April 28 the prime minister called for a government of "technicians." Marshall now cabled Rome on May 1, to ask what steps the United States could take to "strengthen democratic pro-American forces," and Dunn replied that many Italians "are begging us for a stand." Any government would need material and moral support from the United States, but American aid "should be based upon the quid pro quo of necessary changes in political orientations and policies."[19] In the midst of the cabinet crisis, however, the Italian ambassador to Washington, Tarchiani, "could not say" in response to queries, whether de Gasperi would succeed in forming a government without the Communists. On May 20 Tarchiani finally requested assurances of American support for a government of technicians. In reply Marshall promised "a public demonstration of American aid and material assistance," but he remained suspicious of the Italian crisis and demanded that any new government include the Saragat Socialists. The Ramadier government was the model Washington wished to see repeated in the other countries of Western Europe.[20] On May 28 Dunn argued that "this is the opportunity for U.S. government to indicate in bold relief its political support for the first postwar Italian government formed without the Communists."[21] By this time Marshall's Harvard speech was already composed, but it contained only a blueprint and a hope, not a promise of assistance. On June 17 Dunn warned that the "delicate balance against totalitarianism" in Italy depended upon the reality, not simply promises, of U.S. aid.[22] Washington's response to both crises was improvised, and both American ambassadors were taken by surprise. The myth of American "orders" should be laid to rest.

During the political crisis the Americans continued to receive the most alarming reports concerning future French economic prospects. Commercial attaché Ivan White warned on April 8 that the overall economic and

17 John L. Harper, *America and the Reconstruction of Italy* (New York: Cambridge University Press, 1986), pp. 110–36.

18 Foreign Relations of the United States (FRUS), 1947, III, Italy, March 4, 1947, p. 871.

19 FRUS, 1947, III, Italy, May 1, 1947, p. 889; May 3, 1947, pp. 889–92; May 7, 1947, pp. 895–902.

20 Robert Faenza and Marco Fini, *Gli Americani in Italia* (Milan: Feltrinelli, 1976).

21 FRUS, 1947, III, Italy, May 16, 1947, p. 905; May 20, 1947, pp. 908–9; May 28, 1947, p. 912.

22 FRUS, 1947, III, Italy, June 17, 1947, p. 923.

financial situation in France remained in disequilibrium, jeopardizing the Monnet Plan and focusing attention on "the politicoeconomic aspects of the continued unrest among important sections of the French population." France could have monetary stability or reconstruction and modernization, White thought, but not both at the same time. The balance of payments deficit for 1947–8 was likely to be $1.3 billion with no apparent means of financing it. On May 16 White offered a trenchant analysis of French economic problems, and he called for totally new approaches to the problem of French rehabilitation. France's potential deficits had been substantially underestimated. There was a chronic food deficit, yet a high rate of consumption by the urban rich and the farm population. The impact of the scarcity fell entirely "on the urban salaried classes. This creates an import need which would not exist in a situation of perfect distribution." White estimated that wage earners received only 70 percent of the share of the national income that was theirs before the war. With the food crisis, White said,

> the execution of the Monnet plan, with its heavy emphasis on investment, operates as a continuing disruptive force on the social and political structure of France. . . . The question arises as to whether a democratic form of government in France can be evolved and consolidated during the next few years on the basis of the foregoing situation.

White warned that financing the Monnet Plan for France would not accomplish the basic goal of weakening the hold of the Communists on the working classes and strengthening democracy, while "a France free of either Communist or extreme rightist domination is vital to the national interest of the United States." An alternate emphasis on food production and light industry was needed in French economic planning, which would demonstrate the benefits of American aid while raising living standards.[23]

Ivan White's analysis dramatized the real choice facing the French on the eve of the Marshall Plan. The problems of East–West diplomacy and the composition of the cabinet also involved questions about French social structure. American influence in the postwar era helped the French to rebuild their economy while maintaining a society based on a grossly unequal distribution of wealth. American analysts were aware of this and focused on the French tax system in their complaints about the French class structure. The Americans tried to use their aid as an inducement to get the French to abandon reliance on indirect taxation and introduce a genuinely progressive tax system that did not concentrate the burden on those least able to pay. But American aid could also have provided the reason the French were able to escape a genuine equalization of their tax burden. Those conscious of historical analogy knew that the French government of Louis XVI had

[23] NARA, 851.51/4-847, April 8, 1947; 851.51/4-2247, April 22, 1947; 851.51/5-1647, May 16, 1947.

also been faced with substantial budget deficits, a shortage of grain, and an unequal tax system. In the absence of foreign aid, it launched an attack on the tax structure, and paradoxically brought about its own destruction in the process. In light of that analogy the Marshall Plan could not help but appear to be the deus ex machina that provided the minimum needed to allow traditional elites to maintain their hold on power.

Jefferson Caffery had no reputation in Washington as a liberal, yet he was brought to support the views of the progressives at the lower echelons of the Paris embassy. On May 12, 1947 the ambassador insisted that a new analysis of the French situation was necessary given the temporary exclusion of the Communists from the government. The Ramadier government was the best that could be hoped for in the present circumstances. "Most important is the fact that the present government is essentially Socialist and headed by a Socialist." Ramadier had some labor support, success in office would bring him more, and the Communists were trying to sabotage him for that reason. Ramadier and Blum had shown "great courage" in convincing the Socialist National Council to support a government that excluded the Communists. A failure of the present government meant de Gaulle and the Communists would have to fight it out for supremacy, and a victory for either would be a disaster for democracy. American material help was critical; France still had a desperate need for wheat and coal. But Caffery was also partially convinced by Ivan White's analysis. The French must be pressed to revise the Monnet Plan to emphasize agriculture, housing, and higher living standards. That was the only way to avoid political extremism.[24]

There is no inconsistency in the numerous theories that have been adduced in order to explain the Marshall Plan. It was an act of enlightened self-interest by an American bourgeoisie concerned with creating a free-trading capitalist interdependent world under benevolent American hegemony. Convinced of its fitness to rule, nothing was more natural for the American elite than to believe it was acting in the universal interest of everyone and preserving freedom against an evil despotism. The Marshall Plan was genuinely believed to be a bulwark for Western Europe against the threat of communism. It was not merely sold as such to a recalcitrant American Congress but also so regarded by its originators. The rebuilding of German power and the integration of Germany into a revitalized Western Europe were basic underlying American aims. The Marshall Plan gave the French and other Europeans the means to buy from the Germans, reestablishing a contractual system of international trade and payments, while rejecting the post–World War I scheme of reparations financed by American loans.[25]

[24] FRUS, 1947, III, France, May 12, 1947, pp. 709–13.
[25] For the argument that the Marshall Plan expressed a newly emerging neoliberal corporate capitalism in America and a program to export that model to Europe, see Michael J. Hogan, *The Marshall Plan: America, Britain, and the reconstruction of Western Europe* (New York, Cambridge University Press, 1987). I agree with Charles

The French understood the Marshall Plan as a device to purchase their assent to German reconstruction: "It means, in effect, consent on our part to the realization, through the influence of American aid, of the fusion of the Western zones," Bonnet wrote.[26] The Marshall Plan did not respond to an economic crisis or depression but rather a shortfall in the European balance of payments. It was used to finance ambitious internal schemes of reconstruction and development, not only to pay for emergency shipments of wheat and coal. Nor did it accomplish its ambitious goals of a multilateral system of trade and payments and European integration. But these were the more long-range aspects of the plan; their absence in the short run did not mean the plan was a failure.[27] The plan also fit an agenda in terms of American internal politics. Roosevelt had long held the State Department in contempt and he used his own personal emissaries, like Harry Hopkins, to conduct diplomacy. Truman also was suspicious of the "striped pants" diplomats. The Marshall Plan was designed as a dramatic initiative that would reassert the primacy of the State Department over the making of American foreign policy.

France was the linchpin of the Marshall Plan, just as France became the centerpiece of the Mutual Defense and Assistance Pact (MDAP), which followed it. France accounted for 20 percent of the total financing involved in the Marshall Plan, and 50 percent of the MDAP funds. From the American perspective, France was the most important country of Western Europe, geographically its heart. Its economy was fragile and it faced a serious Com-

---

Maier that the Europeans had little to learn from the Americans about cooperation between government and private industry: see Charles Maier and Stanley Hoffman, eds., *The Marshall Plan: A Retrospective* (Boulder, CO: Westview Press, 1984), and Charles Maier, *In Search of Stability: Explorations in Historical Political Economy* (Cambridge: Cambridge University Press, 1988). Alan S. Milward, in *The Reconstruction of Western Europe, 1945–51* (London: Methuen, 1984) stresses the internal European drive for reconstruction and dismisses the Marshall Plan as essentially about a balance of payments crisis. John Gimbel, *The Origins of the Marshall Plan* (Stanford, CA: Stanford University Press, 1976), emphasizes the importance of the German problem. This is certainly how the Quai originally interpreted it. Joyce and Gabriel Kolko, *The Limits of Power: The World and United States Foreign Policy, 1945–54* (New York: Harper & Row, 1972), argue that anticommunism was a cynical ploy used to sell the plan to the American Congress. But American fear that without the Marshall Plan Europe would "go Communist" was very real. Pierre Melandri, *Les Etats-Unis Face à l'unification de l'Europe, 1945–1954* (Paris: A. Pedone, 1980) correctly stresses American attempts to use the plan to achieve the unification of Europe.

26 MAE, Y 1944–9, Etats Unis, 11, June 18, 1947, Bonnet to Bidault. Bonnet thought France must insist as a quid pro quo on its demands of decentralization of Germany and control of the Ruhr.

27 Milward makes this argument in *The Reconstruction of Western Europe*. Imanuel Wexler in *The Marshall Plan Revisited: The European Recovery Program in Economic Perspective* (Westport, CT: Greenwood Press, 1983) argues impressively that the Marshall Plan succeeded brilliantly in terms of the long-term goals of its originators.

munist threat. It was the principal obstacle to the reconstruction of Germany and its high tariffs, and protected internal markets provided an anti-model of the desired system of liberalized trade and payments. It was committed to a serious program of modernization, which the Americans had come to regard, despite its drawbacks in terms of consumption and housing, a model of its kind. The Americans, allergic to planning at home, hoped the Marshall Plan would become a kind of Monnet Plan for Western Europe, as well as the underpinning of the new unified Europe they were seeking.[28]

The State, War, and Navy Coordinating Committee (SWNCC), predecessor to the National Security Council, ranked France fifth among world problems facing the United States in April 1947. The first four were Greece and Turkey taken together, Iran, Italy, and Korea, ranked in that order, in terms of vulnerability to Russian subversion. William Clayton estimated on May 28 that of an initial $5 billion in aid, $1.75 billion for France represented an absolute minimum standard of living; "if it should be lowered there will be revolution." No sooner was the Marshall Plan announced than it was recognized to be too late to respond to the dimensions of the French crisis. Sixteen European nations accepted the Marshall Plan in the weeks following its announcement. The French invited them to meet in Paris to draw up a coordinated response to the American initiative. Before the invitations were issued, Ambassador Douglas cabled from London that France needed immediate temporary assistance to ensure political stability. If no action were taken, he said, quoting Bevin, "France, and with her most of Europe, would be lost." Paris should be the meeting place of the sixteen nations in order to bolster Ramadier. Marshall cabled his agreement: "We share Bevin's concern for French position, and agree as to importance of French stability." Including Italy in his recommendation, Marshall saw no alternative to an interim aid package for both countries before the Marshall Plan came into existence, given the timetable involved.[29] The enabling legislation for the Marshall Plan proper did not get through Congress until April 1948.

The initial French reaction to the Marshall Plan was skepticism combined with an attempt to twist it from the outset to their own conceptions. Bidault appeared enthusiastic. He and Bevin immediately decided to meet to coordinate a response, and the State Department was pleased to see the two competing to upstage each other. But the French had their own proposals. Without "appearing to have a plan of their own," they suggested to Wash-

---

[28] Melandri, *Les Etats-Unis*, pp. 75–128. Marshall to Embassy in France, FRUS, 1947, III, Marshall Plan, June 12, 1947, expressed the hope that his program might be "somewhat along the lines of the Monnet Plan, but on a much larger scale, involving several countries." p. 251.

[29] FRUS, 1947, III, The Marshall Plan, May 27, 1947, pp. 230–2; July 4, 1947, pp. 310–2; July 10, 1947, p. 323.

ington the formation of a series of ad hoc committees devoted to the crises in specific raw materials and industries. The French were prepared to head up the committee concerned with coal.[30] The American suggestions might permit breaking the vicious circle of French dependence on imports, but France had its own [Monnet] Plan anyway: The Marshall suggestions were "for the margins only." The ad hoc committees were designed to avoid precisely what the Americans appeared to have in mind: "We reject the idea of a huge conference which would construct a too heavy and slow machinery."

But it was just such an international machinery that Washington had in mind to achieve the European integration the Americans thought necessary for European reconstruction and prosperity. It could not be avoided, and the British and French had to concentrate later on trying to manipulate it to their own advantage. The French understood that there was no Marshall "Plan" at the moment of the secretary's Harvard speech. There was no American government commitment of any kind, nobody knew how much aid would be required, whether and how much of it Congress would appropriate, and how it would be administered. Nor was there any assurance that the American government could mobilize popular and parliamentary assent for such a commitment, without which, the French feared, "our initiatives will remain a dead letter."

Paris saw at once that the Soviet Union could have no place in such a scheme. For despite the noble motives proclaimed at Harvard on June 5, the Americans did not expect or wish the USSR to respond to their offer; if it did, as the British observed, "the enormity of their needs would absorb all available credits and destroy all possibility of success."[31] Later in the year, during a courtesy call on former Secretary of State Byrnes in Washington, Bidault permitted himself to speculate as to why the Soviet Union had not responded positively to the Marshall speech at the start, which would have been the surest way of killing the American initiative from the outset.[32] The Russians knew, if they agreed to the Marshall Plan, the Americans would find a way to exclude them – after all, "the exclusion of the Communists from the Italian government, the formation in France and Belgium of centrist cabinets, were the political conditions of American aid."[33] The invitation sent to Moscow to participate in a tripartite conference with Britain

[30]   FRUS, 1947, III, The Marshall Plan, June 16, 1947, pp. 254–6; June 18, 1947, pp. 258–60. MAE, Y 1944–9, Conférence de Paris, 128, June 24–July 4, 1947. A.N., Papiers Georges Bidault, 457 AP 20, June 10–June 30, 1947.
[31]   There was some doubt in Washington about whether the Russians would accept, and fear that if they did the program would never get through Congress. See Maier and Hoffman, eds., Marshall Plan.
[32]   A.N., 457 AP 80 (4), Papiers Georges Bidault, September 23, 1947.
[33]   A.N., 457 AP 20, Papiers Georges Bidault, July 2, 1947, memo marked Président du Conseil, trés secrète.

and France to respond to the American initiative was a propaganda ploy. Both Bidault and Bevin confided to the Americans that they hoped the Russians would refuse to cooperate, and Bidault won the plaudits of Washington by firmly rejecting Molotov's warning that the American schemes inevitably involved the interference of Washington in the internal affairs of the various European nations.[34] British Ambassador Duff Cooper found the French "surprisingly firm" with the Russians, and Washington was surprised and delighted: Bidault had resisted the Russian demands for a blank check from Washington. He had "shown great courage and had given the fullest and even surprisingly, solid support having in mind the present critical state of French internal politics." Bonnet forwarded an article from the *New York Times* depicting France at the head of an independent Europe locked in a bitter struggle for survival with the Kremlin. Finally, after a year and a half of fence-sitting, Bidault and Ramadier had defied the French Communists, and Washington had recognized and assimilated the French choice. The Americans were delighted to have France as an ally. Ironically, the French had aligned with Washington because they thought they would be better able to achieve their goals in Germany. It soon became clear, however, that the Marshall Plan was meant to induce Paris to accept the German policy it had hoped to avoid.

II AMERICA CHOOSES GERMANY – AND DE GAULLE

As always the French were a difficult ally. Bidault understood and approved Washington's agenda with regard to the Russians, but he opposed the American policy in Germany and tried to block it. Clayton was in Paris on July 9, and expressed his delight that France had taken the initiative in convening the conference of sixteen European nations to formulate a reply to Marshall's proposals. But Bidault only wanted to talk about Germany. He warned Clayton that no change in the current arrangements was possible in view of Communist arguments that the United States and Britain gave priority to German reconstruction over French. Any change in the Ruhr would put the French government in a difficult position. The March 1946 limit on Ruhr steel production of 7.5 million tons was adequate, and France could supply Europe's additional steel needs if it were given sufficient coke. Bidault demanded that the Americans support French claims in the Saar, as promised. Clayton was uncompromising in reply: Dismantling of German industries for reparations must end, and increased Ruhr production was necessary because American taxpayers would not indefinitely subsidize Germany. Bidault reacted angrily. France could not accept decisions that fore-

---

[34] MAE, Y 1944–9, Plan Marshall, 228, July 1, 1948. FRUS, III, 1947, Marshall Plan, July 1, 1947.

shadowed the creation of a central German state; by acting without consulting France, the British and Americans were renewing the error they had made at Potsdam. No French government could accept exclusion from the Anglo-American club.[35] Clayton wanted done with the conversation, but Bidault raised the level of rhetoric:

> M. Bidault warned M. Clayton again against any public declaration that could cause the French people and Europe to believe that reparations are being abandoned and priority given to raising the German economic potential. If such a declaration were made, he asserted that the conference which was to convene Saturday would be condemned to failure and there would be no Europe.

Caffery also warned against announcement of the Clay–Robertson agreement to raise the level of steel production in the bizone, lest ammunition be given to Communist efforts to discredit the French government. Bidault protested to Caffery again a few days later, but the issue had been decided; Caffery could only insist that Washington "let them know what we have in mind. . . ."[36] Averell Harriman confronted Bidault with the decision on July 16. The latter's reaction was "hysterical." Protesting "unilateral decisions against French interests," Bidault said: "We have 180 Communists [in the National Assembly] who say, the Marshall Plan means Germany first. If something permits them to say this again . . . I tell you the government will not survive." Bidault could not overcome the combined hostility of the Gaullists, the Communists, and his own political allies; he preferred to resign.[37] On July 18 Chauvel sent formal notes of protest to Cooper, Caffery, Bevin, and Marshall. The British–American decision predetermined the future of Germany and personally challenged the position of the French government and its Minister of Foreign Affairs. This was unacceptable. Bidault penned another rhetorical note: "I have burned my bridges," he wrote Marshall, "I have committed my country . . . not only has it all been done in vain, but it is all turning against the cause which I have served. I shall be personally unable to continue my work."[38]

Bidault's protests could not stop the drift of U.S. policy. Kennan put it succinctly. The French must choose: There must be a rise in the German levels of production or there could be no U.S.-financed recovery in Europe. Marshall promised he would make no further public announcements on Germany until Paris's views were considered, but he also reassured the War Department that he would support Clay–Robertson. The State Department

[35] MAE, Y 1944–9, Conférence des Seize, 129, July 9, 1947.
[36] FRUS, 1947, II, The Occupation and Control of Germany, July 11, 1947, p. 986. NARA, 851.00/7-1547, July 15, 1947.
[37] A.N., 457 AP 80 (4), Papiers Georges Bidault, July 16, 1947. FRUS, 1947, II, Germany, July 20, 1947, pp. 997–9.
[38] NARA, Main Decimal File, 711.51/7-1747, July 17, 1947.

agreed that the recovery of Germany and that of Europe were "two aspects of one problem." The British suggested London and Washington notify the French that they were prepared to consider any "representations" Paris might care to make. Matthews thought the idea arrogant and inflammatory: Was not the term "consultation" more appropriate given French sensibilities? To be sure, Bidault's warnings had some impact. Clay–Robertson would not be implemented unless there were "a threatened collapse of democracy in France." But were the French not using the Communist threat as a bogey to frighten the Americans? Clay thought so. The French government would always use the argument that their government would fall; he said, they "insist this will result and nobody can prove otherwise except by actual test." Clay thought the risk had to be taken.[39]

And Clay took the risk, without bothering to consult Marshall. On August 1, 1947 Secretary of the Army Kenneth Royall declared that he knew of no agreement to consult with the French before the level-of-industry limit was raised in the Ruhr. Bidault again protested, but this time Clay had overstepped his limits. Lovett complained in turn to Truman. The renewed French protests showed the "unworkable and dangerous nature of any such type of understanding with the War Department on matters affecting the U.S. foreign policy. . . . The War Department has no right . . . to limit . . . consultation with another government. We are unable to live up to our agreements and open to French charges of duplicity and dishonest dealing."[40] The French were momentarily cheered, but the situation from their point of view did not improve. On August 4 Cooper and Caffery simultaneously delivered notes to Bidault inviting the French to make "representations" after all. Bidault reportedly "blew up." Bonnet called on Marshall to say that the crisis in Paris was serious. Bidault wanted to come to Washington to explain the disastrous consequences of lack of consultation with France on Germany.

But how much of Bidault's histrionics were public posturing? On July 21 the Quai warned the French government that obstruction on Germany was not paying. France should agree to a higher level of industry in Germany in exchange for certain guarantees: assurance of sufficient coal for France, prohibition of strategic industries in Germany, international control of the Ruhr, and support for the French steel industry.[41] On August 2 the Quai identified three problems facing France: the need for American aid, Washington's demands in Germany, and monetary stabilization. Unfortunately, all three were connected, and the French need for assistance dictated concessions both on Germany and the adoption of a stabilization plan. The Americans, more-

---

[39] FRUS, 1947, III, The Marshall Plan, July 18, 1947, Memo by George Kennan, pp. 332–33; FRUS, 1947, II, Germany, July 21–6, 1947, pp. 1003–10. Gimbel, *The Marshall Plan*, pp. 231–41.

[40] FRUS, 1947, II, Germany, August 3, 1947, pp. 1014–6.

[41] MAE, Y 1944–9, Internationale, Conversations Anglo–Américaines, July 21, 1947.

over, would have to be pleased in other ways: ". . . it is certainly in a liberal direction and an economy giving more room to private initiative that France can recover its prosperity. The affirmation of this tendency is equally necessary to create in America the indispensable climate for the success of M. Marshall's suggestions."[42] The French were drawing the implication that their government must evolve more sharply to the right.

On August 8 Bidault told American officials that publicly he still supported the harsh terms of the Morgenthau plan, but privately, "We know that we have to join with you in the control of Germany and reorganization of Western Europe, but please don't force us to do so at the point of a gun." Clayton lunched with Bidault and Monnet in Geneva on August 7; Bidault said he would agree to the new industry levels if an international board controlled Ruhr production. Clayton advised Washington to accept internationalization of the Ruhr, for "if the French government falls the Marshall Plan may go with it." The next day the United States and Britain agreed to tripartite talks with the French to settle the German problem.[43] The French had won some sort of a victory, but it was clear the German levels of industry were not really negotiable. Marshall instructed Lewis Douglas, the American negotiator in London, to defend Clay–Robertson vigorously unless "French democracy appears threatened." But from an internal perspective, it now appeared that the Americans had already written off French democracy in any case.

With the Communists no longer in the French government, there was no longer any restraining influence at work on French labor, which had suffered severely from lagging wages in a period of inflation. From April to October 1947, prices rose by 58 percent while salaries went up only 22 percent. On June 2 the bread ration was reduced to 200 grams per day, and by August the price of bread had risen 135 percent.[44] An ominous series of strikes broke out, which the premier, trying to hold the line on wages, attributed demagogically to a "chef d'orchestre clandestin." Despite the announcement of the Marshall Plan, the situation continued to deteriorate, with no American assistance in sight. On June 24 Matthews warned that the Ramadier government "had begun to crack." There was little the American government could do except ship some emergency wheat and coal. The French must handle the crisis by themselves; fortunately, they believed that if the Communists returned to the government, their prospects for American aid would be diminished. "In the negative sense we should do nothing to discourage this belief," Matthews wrote.[45]

[42]   A.N., 457 AP 20, Papiers Georges Bidault, August 2, 1947.
[43]   FRUS, 1947, III, The Marshall Plan, August 8, 1947, pp. 345–50. FRUS, 1947, II, Germany, August 8, 1947, pp. 102–6.
[44]   Annie Lacroix-Riz, *La CGT de la liberation à la scission de 1944–1947* (Paris: Editions Sociales, 1983), pp. 235–42.
[45]   NARA, 851.00/6-2447, June 24, 1947.

Charles Bohlen took a more alarmist view. The Communists were seeking to undermine Ramadier and force him to accept their return to the government, this time with control of the "key ministries" previously denied them. If this happened, France would drift in the direction of the USSR. The French crisis was "ostensibly" internal, Bohlen observed, and the United States could not act publicly without being accused of interference in French internal affairs. On the surface the situation "is not one that is susceptible of treatment by U.S. government action."[46] But Bohlen insisted that the State Department not remain passive in the face of danger. The embassy was aware of efforts by AFL organizer Irving Brown to engineer a split in the CGT, something the moderate Socialists in France were interested in doing as well. The American government needed to help in that effort; it must devise "instrumentalities" capable of combatting Communist activities among workers on their own ground, and support those resisting Communist penetration of labor unions. Bohlen suggested the establishment of a secret fund for use by the Secretary of State at his discretion in the interest of national security. The fund was established, and small sums were allocated to Force Ouvrière tendency in the CGT by both the State Department and the AFL during 1947. More massive intervention had to await 1948, however, when the CIA and the Marshall Plan bureaucracies were organized and functioning (see Chapter 4).

In the meantime, Caffery concluded that the French government was impotent and the only solution was to return General de Gaulle to power. He was the only figure able to overcome the "incoherent, impotent" paralysis affecting the anti-Communist forces in France. Misery discredits democracy, the ambassador observed, and Ramadier was personally weak. A strong leader was needed and de Gaulle alone "stands above the crowd." Caffery's informant in the Interior Ministry told him that without immediate injections of American aid, Ramadier was doomed. De Gaulle, the Communist party, or both would come to power, and social turmoil was now "inevitable." The Communists, moreover, charged that the United States, overflowing with goods, deliberately withheld help from the French in order to force them into submission. In fact they hoped no American help would arrive before the October elections, by which time famine and the beginning of the winter cold in France would have their effect. Caffery pleaded with Washington for emergency aid, and pressed Ramadier to show some leadership, take the public into his confidence, and explain France's financial predicament.[47] Perhaps stirring speeches could convince the French to endure their deprivation a bit longer.

But neither Ramadier nor any other politician appeared capable of han-

---

[46]   NARA, 851.00/6-2847, June 28, 1947.
[47]   NARA, 851.00/8-3047, August 30, 1947; 9-747, September 7, 1947; 9-1347, September 13, 1947; 9-1647, September 16, 1947.

dling the crisis. On October 2 Caffery met with Gaston Palewski, de Gaulle's closest adviser. Caffery would not risk a personal meeting with de Gaulle, nor did the general as yet want to meet with the Americans. But Palewski and Caffery began a dialogue, if not actual negotiations, on the terms of the general's return to power with American tolerance and aid. Palewski said de Gaulle was prepared to take power, continue the Marshall Plan negotiations, and put France at the head of a European federation. Internally, he would implement a draconian fiscal program to prevent inflation. Caffery was pleased: "De Gaulle's ideas closely approximate U.S. thinking except on Germany," he reported. And from the American perspective, of course, nobody else in France was accommodating on the German question either. On October 6 Caffery reported de Gaulle's election speech at Vincennes as a "spectacular success," evidence of the general's growing popular support. At the same time, he nervously noted the activities of the venerable former premier Herriot, suspected to be negotiating with the Communists for a new popular front government based on a program of "appeasement of Russia."[48] All the more reason for Washington to look for a de Gaulle solution.

Douglas MacArthur III summed up the reversal in embassy thinking: Ramadier had failed. He had not achieved budgetary or monetary stability. His party was divided internally and unable to agree with others in the coalition. There was evidence of fatigue, lassitude, and apathy of the French people in the face of "corruption and moral disintegration." The only apparent alternative leader was de Gaulle. No successor government of the center-left could hope to stop Communist sabotage and treason without resorting to arbitrary imprisonment and infringing on civil liberties. "It is painful for me," MacArthur wrote, "whose social and political views are considerably to the left of center, to have reluctantly to confess that until France has a more authoritarian regime ... it is difficult to see how the Communists are to be prevented from preventing French recovery." A showdown between de Gaulle and the Communists seemed near, and if the general came to power the United States would have no choice but to back him. Washington must decide how to respond to expected queries from General de Gaulle.[49]

Woodruff Wallner, head of the European desk of the State Department, briefed Marshall on the embassy's conclusions in anticipation of a press conference in which the secretary feared he might be asked questions on the French situation. If France were to remain in the Western orbit, the Communists must be isolated and a large non-Communist majority united around a political program. Although such a majority existed, it had not taken the form the United States wished. Instead of a centrist coalition, anti-

---

[48] NARA, 851.00/10-247, October 2, 1947; 10-647, October 6, 1947; 10-947, October 9, 1947.
[49] NARA, 851.00/10-1047, October 10, 1947.

Communists were rallying around "an erratic, mystical, military figure whose capabilities for wise government and harmonious foreign relations we have every reason from past experience to doubt." The de Gaulle showing in the municipal elections was a "gesture of despair," and once again the French were rallying around a "man on horseback." But Wallner concluded, "It is no less true that it is vitally in the interest of the United States that non-Communist polarization around General de Gaulle succeed."[50] Once in power de Gaulle would need the support of labor, and the Americans should insist that he seek a coalition with the Socialists. In the meantime, to avoid discouraging de Gaulle's supporters and "providing by a sudden enthusiasm for the general ammunition for the Communist party machine, it is recommended that [Marshall] decline all comment for the moment on the French political situation." The de Gaulle solution was reportedly also being urged upon President Truman by Admiral Leahy, chairman of the joint chiefs of staff, who kept informed about the general through William Bullitt. Leahy had overcome his former antipathy for de Gaulle in the interest of defeating the Communists.[51]

Active exchanges of views with the general continued; on October 24 Palewski said that if de Gaulle were called by President Auriol to form a government, he would demand constitutional revision and a referendum as well as exceptional powers for a specified period "to cope with the Communists and put our house in order." If de Gaulle failed, only the Communists remained. De Gaulle would need financial aid from the United States and emergency supplies of grains and meat to stop the inflationary spiral. The Socialists must stop "straddling" and rally to de Gaulle. Caffery agreed to the need for constitutional revision, but the idea of full powers caused shivers in Washington, which wanted the general to rule democratically with the support of the moderate Socialists and non-Communist labor unions. Caffery welcomed the department's perspective, saying it "parallels our thinking here and gives me authorized backing for the things I have been saying to de Gaulle's people. I shall hammer away at them at every opportunity." The Socialists were the key. Caffery feared de Gaulle would attack and try to destroy them, which could only work to the advantage of the Communists: "this is, I think, the key question at the moment and the one on which I am exerting every particle of influence I can." A majority of the French were ready to rally around de Gaulle; the Americans must do the same, while trying to "reduce the dangers." Caffery warned, however, that the general had not changed in the last two years. He would be difficult to deal with on Germany, North Africa, and Indochina.[52]

Could de Gaulle have come to power in October 1947? The municipal

[50] NARA, 851.00/10-2247, October 22, 1947.
[51] *Le Monde,* November 4, 1947.
[52] 851.00/10-2447, October 24, 1947, 10-2947, October 29, 1947.

elections of October, which gave the RPF almost 40 percent of the vote, strengthened the general's hand, and Caffery received assurance from several influential politicians that they were prepared to back him. The ambassador's source in the Interior Ministry regarded de Gaulle's rule as inevitable, and Georges Bidault was resigned to it as well.[53] Sources in the MRP and Radical parties indicated that they would throw their support to de Gaulle. To be sure, de Gaulle had cornered himself with his declaration of October 27. He refused to take power under the constitutional mechanism of the Fourth Republic, nor would he resort to a coup d'état.[54] But some way out of this dilemma might be found if he would begin the process of contacting other politicians. Instead, de Gaulle sent word that he did not want to take power under the present circumstances. Anticipating a hard winter, even with American aid, because of the climate of civil war in the country, he would not risk failure, and preferred to hold himself in reserve.

Jacques Soustelle explained to Caffery that de Gaulle needed more time to perfect the RPF organization and consolidate left-wing support. He anticipated he would be ready to take power in May 1948, not before. In the meantime "Ramadier got his vote of confidence because we told our friends in the Assembly not to upset the apple cart." Caffery nevertheless used the opportunity to drive home the State Department's views. He suggested de Gaulle bid for Socialist support by making a statement clarifying his economic and social philosophy and endorsing a specific program. Soustelle promised that the general would do so in December. Caffery was pleased, but still deplored de Gaulle's lack of understanding of Socialist leaders, and suggested the general enter into contact with them. To Palewski, the next day, Caffery reiterated the "disastrous effect dictatorial methods would have in the U.S. . . . I told him I hoped to hear no more talk of full powers." Caffery again stressed the importance of de Gaulle gaining support from organized labor.[55] On November 6 Caffery and Palewski discussed colonial policy, on which the general proved less progressive than the present government; "I shall continue in conversations with de Gaulle's entourage, particularly Soustelle, Malraux, Palewski, and Chaban-Delmas, to stress the importance of an enlightened colonial policy."

On November 7 André Malraux told Caffery that de Gaulle wanted to work with Blum, Auriol, and Ramadier; their attitude was the obstacle. Malraux said "de Gaulle is not a dictator or he, whose views are left of center, would not support him." De Gaulle recognized he had made an error in failing to approach the trade unions in 1944, and he had rectified that omission by making the declaration on social policy that he had promised Caffery. But the general's statement backfired, and the American press saw

[53] 851.00/10-2247, October 22, 1947; 10-2547, October 25, 1947; 10-2447, October 24, 1947.

[54] Jean Lacouture, *De Gaulle*, vol. II: *Le Politique* (Paris: Seuil, 1985) pp. 321–31.

[55] 851.00/11-347, November 3, 1947; 11-447, November 4, 1947.

the suspicious specter of fascistlike corporatism in his ideas. De Gaulle said he would forbid any political role for organized labor, which could legitimately represent the workers' economic interests only. In America such pronouncements reeked of authoritarianism. Malraux complained that the *Herald Tribune* had distorted de Gaulle's ideas, but Caffery was discouraged: "We stressed the unfortunate impression created by de Gaulle's program departing from ordinary democratic forms, particularly one that would jeopardize the independent status of labor."[56] In the following weeks, Caffery continued to pressure the Gaullists to abandon corporatism.

At the height of the cabinet crisis in fall 1947 Paul Reynaud called at the embassy, announced he would form a government, and asked for American support. Caffery replied that "we support any democrat, Blum, Teitgen, or Reynaud, he no more than any other." A bit disingenuous in view of the lengthy tractations with de Gaulle's entourage, but the ambassador had become an important figure in the French political game.

De Gaulle ruled himself out as a candidate for political power before the eruption of political violence in Marseille on November 12. The Marseille events were followed by the vast strike movement, which began on November 18, and both events appeared to have insurrectionary characteristics. Minister of the Interior Jules Moch demonstrated the government's complete mastery of the situation, however, repressing the strikes with great ferocity, and he was similarly able to restore order in Marseille. In view of Moch's success, it has been argued, de Gaulle no longer thought it necessary that he take power. The deaths of General Leclerc and de Gaulle's daughter Anne have also been cited as reasons for de Gaulle's decision. But de Gaulle had told the Americans of his reluctance earlier.[57] He declined to take power because it was not a good time in view of the widespread misery, social unrest, and the necessity to depend on American support they entailed. To rule under such circumstances, de Gaulle feared, would be to lose support rapidly and leave no alternative but the Communists. Better to let the politicians of the Fourth Republic ride out the crisis and lose their popularity. The general would take power when his prospects for reform and durability had been increased.

De Gaulle's tactics were not best calculated to win American respect, however. Caffery regarded de Gaulle's maneuvering as a display of cynicism or cowardice. Moreover, the general remained inactive during the violent social crisis occasioned by the strikes. He declined to support the government or condemn the Communist threat, deeply disappointing the State Department. In the meantime, the strength of the Schuman government, which replaced Ramadier on November 24, was reassuring. Caffery was delighted;

---

56 851.00/11-647, November 6, 1947; 11-747, November 7, 1947; 11-1147, November 11, 1947.
57 These explanations are offered by Lacouture, *De Gaulle*.

in character and patriotism he thought Schuman "at the top of French political life. No one questions his honesty, integrity, or sincerity." Of Schuman's political skills, the ambassador was not as sure. But Jules Moch, the
new Socialist minister of the interior, quickly emerged as the man of the
hour in dealing with the strike wave. His firm policy of repression, but-
tressed by the mobilization of French conscripts, greatly impressed Washington. Caffery discussed precautionary military measures with the Interior
and Defense ministries in case of Communist insurrection. He was disturbed
to find how few disciplined troops the French had on hand in the metropole
in case of serious disorder, but impressed with Moch's emergency orders to
prefects and dispositions of riot troops (CRS). English translations of Moch's
emergency measures were transmitted to the State Department. Thus reassured, Washington did not panic, despite the gravity of the crisis, as it had
during the constitutional referendum eighteen months before.[58] Nobody now
believed the Communists could successfully carry out a coup.

American interim aid was legislated during the strike movement, which
greatly helped to stabilize the Schuman government. The Gaullists accused
the embassy of intervening in the French political process, putting "mor-
phine shots" into a moribund French government, artificially keeping it alive.
But Caffery was assured by others in the general's entourage that de Gaulle
really favored American aid. In December John Foster Dulles visited de Gaulle,
causing speculation that the Americans expected de Gaulle to be the next
premier. But Dulles represented a Republican administration that hoped to
be in power a year later; the State Department had lost interest in de Gaulle.
With the crisis past, Caffery noted that Schuman's prestige was enhanced
and de Gaulle's had sunk. "As everyone was aware he [de Gaulle] would
have nothing to do with the recent crisis for fear of getting his fingers burned
and was happy to let the Schuman government run all the risks. This of
course is in line with his well-known policy of not desiring to take office
during the hard winter months." On December 23 Caffery reported that
even de Gaulle's followers were "disgusted with these tactics." In the meantime, Jouhaux and the newly created Force Ouvrière, upon whom the Americans pinned their hopes for the development of a non-Communist labor
movement, condemned de Gaulle's corporatism. The Gaullists, having refused to take power themselves, were making trouble for Schuman in the
National Assembly, which did not endear them any further to Caffery.[59]

By January 1948 Caffery's impatience had turned to anger at the Gaullists. The next few months, he thought, were the most vitally important period since the Liberation. The Schuman government was making a courageous and determined effort at economic stabilization. Its unpopular measures

---

[58] NARA, 851.00/11-647, November 6, 1947; 851.00/11-2147, November 21, 1947;
851.00/11-2447, November 24, 1947.
[59] NARA, 851.00/11-1747, November 17, 1947; 851.00/12-1147, December 11, 1947.

were being opposed by not only the Communists but the Gaullists as well, who threatened to pull the rug from under the premier. De Gaulle did not want Schuman to succeed or the situation might not mature properly for his own contemplated takeover next spring. Caffery was incensed: "I am stating frankly to them [the Gaullists] that while it is an internal matter and none of my business, I am strongly of the opinion that any premeditated effort by the Gaullist machine deliberately to undermine the present government will be very damaging to de Gaulle's prestige in the United States." De Gaulle would need the support and confidence of the American people, which he would lose if he "put personal ambition ahead of national interest." Caffery sharply warned the Gaullists that any further opposition to Schuman "played the Communist game."[60]

Caffery was now very deeply involved in the French political game. On February 3, he noted that Paul Reynaud had made some "injudicious remarks" to the press about government policies:

> I let him know I was disappointed. He gave to understand he would take no part in efforts to turn out Schuman. I have taken occasion to speak very plainly with some members of the right. . . . Georges Villiers promised he would advise them to change tactics and I hear he has done so. I am continuing to give pertinent counsel to de Gaulle's friends.[61]

A new era had opened in French politics. French cabinet crises would not take place in the near future without direct American involvement, and the embassy actively tried to bolster governments that it wished to see survive.

The new American involvement in French internal politics was paradoxically furthered by de Gaulle. His presence, waiting in the wings as the potential strong man of French politics, made possible settlement of the German issue on American terms. That outcome was doubly ironic in view of de Gaulle's hostility to American influence and opposition to the reconstruction of Germany. Clay's insistence that the United States must be willing to "risk" the fall of French democracy was followed by State Department agreement that the level of industry in Germany must be raised, the perception in the embassy that Ramadier was doomed, and the overtures to de Gaulle. Washington could do as it wished in Germany, confident that the Communists could not seize power in France, and that the only real alternative to the shaky Fourth Republic was a quasi-monarchical presidency under de Gaulle. The Americans preferred centrist governments, to be sure, but they were prepared to work with de Gaulle.

From the French point of view, the German settlement of August 28, 1947, was barely face-saving. The tripartite London talks gave the French the opportunity to "consult" rather than simply make "representations,"

---

60 NARA, 851.00/1-1248, January 12, 1948.
61 NARA, 851.00/2-348, February 3, 1948. Villiers was the head of the National Confederation of French Employers.

but the result was the same. The revised level of industry for the Ruhr was announced the next day at 11 million tons of steel.[62] The Quai agreed with the *London Economist:* Clay had run "rough-shod over the French." To be sure, the British and Americans promised that no priority would be given German reconstruction over French, a final Ruhr settlement was not prejudiced by the change, and there would be continuing discussion of French needs for coal. But these were meaningless reassurances of accepted facts. The London talks were held to let the French have their say, but not to listen to them. The new ceiling on production in the Ruhr was also a "needless blow" to the French, since Germany was not likely to reach the new levels anytime soon. French acquiescence to a political settlement in Germany on American terms could not be far behind.

The financial crisis in Paris brought the French to their knees. On September 10, the Ministry of Foreign Affairs notified Washington that all imports of needed raw materials, including wheat, coal, and cotton, must cease by the end of October 1947, because French currency reserves would by then be totally exhausted.[63] With the conference of the sixteen nations under way in Paris, and an interim aid bill for France and Italy being drafted in Washington, there was no serious possibility that Washington would allow such a catastrophe to occur. Meanwhile the State Department compensated for the slow pace of congressional reaction to the French crisis by palliatives. The French were granted the second "tranche" of $250 million from the World Bank promised in the Blum–Byrnes agreements. The Export-Import Bank permitted $100 million of its loan to be used for food and raw materials purchases instead of equipment. Purchases were stepped up for American troops stationed in France, and private loans extended against expected French recuperation of gold plundered by the Germans and Japanese. Paris was prevented, however, from seizing private holdings of French citizens in the United States, estimated at several billion dollars, because the Treasury Department would permit no investigation or inventory of private foreign investment in the American economy. Paris was irritated, believing that U.S. banks might be a place of refuge for illicit profits gained from wartime black-marketeering, but it could not force the issue.[64]

In an effort to reassure the French, Marshall made the unusual gesture of calling on Bidault in the latter's Washington hotel room. Marshall said he understood the necessity of immediate emergency assistance to France and would take up the details of interim measures at once with Secretary of the Treasury Snyder. To the dependent French, it now appeared that little but American benevolence stood between them and catastrophe. The result was a rash of concessions to Washington's views, on Germany and on most of

[62] MAE, Y 1944–9, Pourparlers de Londres, 376, August 28, 1947.
[63] A.N., Papiers Georges Bidault, 457 AP 80 (4), September 10, 1947.
[64] FRUS, 1947, III, France, September 23, 1947, pp. 756–7; October 13–7, 1947, pp. 774–8. Also in A.N., Papiers Georges Bidault, 457 AP 80 (4), October 2, 3, 10, 1947.

the other outstanding differences between the two countries. On September 19 Ramadier sent a message to Clayton detailing the "tragic situation of our wheat provisions" and the impending dollar exhaustion. The French needed at least $100 million per month to live through July 1, 1948. In exchange Ramadier promised to enact "a complete program of economic and monetary stabilization," which would include an end to all inflationary advances from the Bank of France. Ramadier's promise, which was repeated by Schuman, was important in the origins of the Schuman–Mayer Plan, implemented in January 1948, which economic historians now credit for the French economic miracle of the 1950s.[65] The French government also declared that it recognized the necessity of the economic integration of Europe and was ready for negotiations with any European nations to achieve it. In Germany, Ramadier noted: "We foresee that after the November Conference the question of fusing the [German] zones will come up." France was ready to consider zonal fusion if it were accompanied by an agreement on international control of the Ruhr. On September 23 Bidault appropriately concluded that the German question had become a "lost cause" for France.[66]

The Marshall Plan came under discussion simultaneously by the sixteen nations assembled in Paris, three separate ad hoc committees established by President Truman to examine its effects on the American economy, and a number of different committees of the Senate and House of Representatives. The meetings of the sixteen European nations and the investigations of President Truman's ad hoc committees were all orchestrated so as to impress Congress, which ultimately confided administration of economic aid to a new agency directly responsible to the president, whose head enjoyed cabinet status: the Economic Cooperation Administration. Europeans were understandably confused by the different messages coming from Washington. Anxiety grew as it appeared that American aid would not be free of stringent conditions and that these might be incompatible with the national sovereignty of the recipient countries. But conditions of aid that appeared absurd or unacceptable during the early stages of planning, later seemed tolerable as viewpoints changed under ever more severe conditions of hardship, want, and internal social unrest.

Consul Francis Lacoste reported in August that the Herter Committee of the House of Representatives was only ready to grant aid "with the guarantee that the United States will have a quasicomplete control over the countries concerned, that socialization will be stopped, and free enterprise restored . . . and that the Communists will not receive a centime, directly or indirectly." The final conditions were not that onerous, but the effect of

---

65 On the benefits of the Mayer plan see François Caron, *An Economic History of Modern France* (New York: Columbia University Press, 1979), p. 275.

66 A.N., Papiers Georges Bidault, 457 AP 80 (4), September 18, 19, 23, 1947.

such reports was to soften the resistance of European politicians. When Robert Schuman met with the subcommittee for France of the House Foreign Affairs Committee, he was told bluntly that American opinion demanded that France balance its budget, raise taxes, establish a more equitable system of taxation, improve the efficiency of tax collection by means of thorough fiscal reform, impose restraint on wages, stop peasants from feeding wheat to livestock, and generally force the French to "tighten their belts." France must help itself before the United States would help it. Schuman promised the necessary reforms, admitted the inequitable nature of the French fiscal system, and allowed that whole categories of the French population escaped without paying taxes, in particular the peasants and urban middle and professional classes, a situation that he promised to rectify. La coste promised the committee that French nationalization policy would be limited to those industries considered to be public services in Europe. The French had no intention of extending nationalization to all fields or discouraging competition and free enterprise.[67] American demands frequently corresponded with the intent of French officials, many of whom desired the same reforms and welcomed American pressure to achieve them. But such discussions established a precedent for internal French fiscal, monetary, and economic policy to become the concern not only of American diplomatic and economic aid officials, but of the U.S. Congress, the press, and public opinion as well.

The idea of establishing counterpart funds in local currencies of American aid is often seen as the original genius of the Marshall Plan. Yet counterpart funds were initially denounced by the Europeans in the form in which they emerged from Congress.[68] Counterpart funds came from the transformation of receipts from the sale of American goods into national currency, which could then be made available to the recipient government for internal investment, debt retirement, or other uses. The originality of this scheme was that American aid was used twice, so to speak; it relieved the dollar shortage but also gave a stimulus to internal investment and growth while helping in the control of inflation. The issue was not the counterpart funds themselves but the question of who was to control them. Hervé Alphand noted with alarm that Congress intended the ECA to control the counterpart of U.S. aid in national currency: "These views are obviously unacceptable." The Delegation of the Committee of European Economic Cooperation, the organization created by the sixteen nations that were recipients of the Marshall Plan aid, protested the idea in Washington:

> We vehemently protested against such a solution, underlining the serious political embarrassment. . . . This would mean giving the American government

---

[67] FRUS, 1947, III, France, September 10, 1947, pp. 739–42.
[68] Harry Price, *The Marshall Plan and Its Meaning* (Ithaca, NY: Cornell University Press, 1955).

exorbitant powers infringing on the freedom of action of the assisted countries. We insisted on the necessity of giving no justification, even a superficial one, for the attacks of which American policy is the object on the European continent.[69]

These attacks came from Communist parties, among which the largest and most threatening was the French, and the concerns expressed by the committee were largely those of Paris. Lovett, in reply, tried to reassure the committee that the restrictions on counterpart funds would not threaten the economic and financial control of the recipient government. In practice the extent of American control of counterpart funds was to differ in each of the Marshall Plan nations, depending upon the relationships between the Marshall Plan bureaucrats and local officials, as well as the political and economic conditions of the countries concerned. But what seemed on its face an unacceptable procedure became a centerpiece of Marshall Plan legislation.

The Americans were unable to obtain the kind of coordinated economic plan and steps toward integration they wished, and disappointment with the failure of the Europeans to create a "United States of Europe" was to become a continuous American refrain in succeeding years. Michael Hogan has demonstrated that integration was part of American corporate capitalism's response to Europe's postwar economic dilemma.[70] But the economic unity of Europe did not necessarily have to translate into the larger free-trading block that was the object of American policy; it could just as easily result in a European protectionism against the rest of the world. In retrospect, American plans for Europe in the postwar era seem absurdly grandiose. Some congressmen hoped the ECA would evolve into the governing bureaucracy of a united Europe. Little wonder that these projects failed. But to argue, as Alan Milward does, that the Americans were manipulated by the Europeans rather than the reverse seems an exaggeration.[71]

Manipulating sixteen nations at once was too much for the Americans, to be sure. Washington received inflated requests from the sixteen recipient nations amounting to $29 billion, rather than the much smaller sum the Americans wanted to spend, and sixteen separate "shopping lists" rather than a coordinated economic plan. The Americans rejected the initial report of the sixteen nations, sought to have the conference prolonged, and pressured each of the nations individually in the hope of achieving a more constructive result. Kennan despaired: He found England "sick," Germany isolated and without influence, and France "deteriorating." No bold regional approach to European problems was to be expected from such a state of

69   A.N., Papiers Georges Bidault, 457 AP 20, Aide intérimaire, October 20, 1947, November 10, 1947.
70   Hogan, *The Marshall Plan.*
71   Milward, *The Reconstruction of Western Europe.*

affairs; the United States would have to act unilaterally.[72] The sixteen nations were informed of American objections on September 11. The United States wanted planning and production targets on a European scale, measures to achieve currency stabilization, the elimination of trade barriers, itemized capital equipment lists, and the creation of a multinational organization with genuine executive powers. But prolonging the conference for another few weeks was hardly sufficient to achieve such a full agenda. On September 20 Lovett concluded that the pressure in the various European capitals was ineffective, and Washington accepted a cosmetically altered report. British delegate Sir Oliver Franks greeted the report as proof that "a new hope" had been born, the last chance for Europe to lead a way of life relying on free institutions "broadly similar to the way of life followed and enjoyed by the people of the United States."[73]

It was not through the Organization of European Economic Cooperation (OEEC), however, that the Americans were to obtain the extraordinary influence in Europe that characterized the postwar era. Rather, the bilateral agreements, separately negotiated with each recipient nation of Marshall Plan aid, provided the latitude Washington was seeking. Bonnet became increasingly pessimistic on the prospects for French independence as he watched the interim aid legislation taking shape. On November 25, 1947 he warned that potentially unacceptable conditions would be attached to American aid. On December 13 he warned against amendments introduced by the House of Representatives calling for the president to cancel any aid if he judged the recipient nation to be "under Communist influence," and mandating that no member of the Communist party be permitted to participate in aid distribution. Bonnet protested potential "interference in our internal and external politics," and warned of embarrassment to the French government.[74] Marshall agreed that the amendments were "offensive to [French] national dignity," and gave credence to the Soviet claim that the United States was seeking to make a colony of France.[75] The amendments were dropped. But provisions were written into the final legislation prohibiting the reexport of aid commodities, requiring American approval for the expenditure of counterpart funds, and providing for mandatory publicity and facilities for American news reporting. They caused a long and tortuous process of negotiations before bilateral agreements implementing the aid program could be signed. The French pleaded that too many of the clauses of the aid bill appeared humiliating. They would much prefer agreement by private exchange of letters than by treaty, which required legislative ratifi-

[72] FRUS, 1947, III, The Marshall Plan, September 4, 1947, pp. 397–405.
[73] FRUS, 1947, III, The Marshall Plan, September 11, 1947, pp. 421–3; September 20, 1947, pp. 442–4.
[74] MAE, Y 1944–9, Plan Marshall, 229, December 9, 12, 1947. A.N., Papiers Georges Bidault, 457 AP 20, December 13, 1947.
[75] FRUS, 1947, III, France, December 10, 1947, Marshall to Lovett, pp. 814–5.

cation. Interim aid, after all, was not only in the interest of the recipient nation: "We might subscribe spontaneously to what we cannot do under pressure." In Paris the interministerial economic committee of the cabinet warned that the impression must be avoided that "all the measures that we may decide to take in the future to reestablish our economy and which, necessarily will be unpopular, are the result of American pressure."[76]

The violent strikes of November–December 1948 in France are commonly viewed as a Communist effort to wreck the Marshall Plan. The source of this interpretation was the Socialist Minister of the Interior, Jules Moch, who vigorously repressed the strikes. But the French crisis had quite the opposite effect in Washington; it served to dramatize the alleged Soviet threat to French internal security and silence potential critics of the Marshall Plan. To be sure, Bonnet was obliged to spend much time in Washington trying to calm apprehensions about the strikes, and Marshall remarked that they did not facilitate his job.[77] But Bonnet noted that the strikes elicited a wave of sympathy for France in American government circles, and observers were drawing the "necessary conclusion" that aid must not be delayed or questioned. Nobody wanted to embarrass the French government in the midst of its crisis. Even the most hostile elements in Congress, said Bonnet, appreciated the firm government response and refrained from raising the issue.[78] "One observes in all political milieux a very great desire to help us resist what is considered to be a Communist offensive directed from Moscow." When asked how the United States might help France, Bonnet emphasized the importance of the interim aid bill and concessions to French views in Germany.

American Ambassador to Britain Lewis Douglas noted that Thorez had returned from Moscow bearing promises of Soviet wheat; Douglas feared this might tip the balance in favor of Russia, and wrote Congressman John Vorys as follows:

> If we are not to run the serious risk of losing France, we should act promptly. Therefore if the House is favorable to interim aid it should approve it at once. Time is of the essence. . . . Prompt action by the Congress would so encourage and strengthen the favorable forces in France that, in our opinion, they will be able to successfully prevent what is a flagrant attempt to seize power.

Caffery also thought the strikes a result of Stalin's orders, and he characterized the strike committee as "run by NKVD agents determined to create the utmost disorder short of armed insurrection."[79]

But Caffery also remarked that the strikes were, "from an economic point

[76] A.N., Papiers Georges Bidault, 457 AP 20, December 23, 1947.
[77] MAE, Y 1944–9, 228, November 20, 29, 1947.
[78] MAE, B Amérique, 120. November 29, December 2, 1947.
[79] FRUS, 1947, III, France, December 2, 1947, pp. 807–8; November 29, 1947, pp. 804–5.

of view fully justified," and tried to impress upon the French cabinet the
need to do something about the disparity between wages and prices in France.
He met with Schuman and Finance Minister René Mayer on December 11;
both agreed the wage–price problem needed to be addressed. On December
26 Caffery "told the cabinet of the necessity of doing something constructive about the wage–price problem lest victory over the Communists be
nullified, and the next strikes be supported by Communist and non-
Communist workers as well." Schuman in turn seemed anxious that his
finance minister's projects receive the approval of the Americans: "He always asks me about Mayer," the ambassador reported, "and I told him I
have a high regard for Mayer's ability."[80] In Schuman, Mayer, and Moch
the Americans had indeed found a cabinet with which they could work. But
the Communist party found a corresponding propaganda ploy that enabled
it to emphasize the extent of alleged foreign influence in France. By continued harping on Germanic or Jewish-sounding names, the party exaggerated
the charge that France was governed by lackeys of American imperialism.

It would be an exaggeration to attribute the Mayer plan to American
influence.[81] The plan was formulated by a special committee, on which sat
Pierre Uri, himself American educated, a collaborator of Monnet, and a
crucial figure both in the process of postwar French planning and the administration of Marshall Plan aid.[82] Its most outstanding features were its
partial exchange of bank notes, determination to tax the middle classes previously able to escape taxation, and prohibition against any inflationary
advances to the State by the Bank of France. These measures won the plaudits of the Americans, who greeted the plan with warm sympathy. If it were
passed, Bonnet cabled, it would greatly help the passage of the Marshall
Plan in Washington. Caffery was equally enthusiastic:

> The determination of Premier Schuman, Finance Minister Mayer and other
> cabinet members to bring about currency stabilization and financial reform
> through parliamentary action stems in large measure from their realization
> that without it ERP cannot achieve the ends it should achieve, and that it is
> essential if long-term American aid is to be voted. I have sought every oppor-
> tunity to strengthen them in this resolve in the same manner as I have harped
> upon the necessity of arriving at adjustments of the wages and price prob-
> lem.[83]

---

80   NARA, 851.00/11-1147, November 11, 1947. FRUS, 1947, III, France, December
     20, 1947, pp. 819–20; December 26, 1947, pp. 821–2; December 29, 1947, pp.
     823–4.
81   See Gérard Bossuat, "Les risques et les espoirs du Plan Marshall pour la France,"
     Etudes et Documents (Paris: Imprimerie Nationale, 1989), pp. 218–29.
82   Interview with Pierre Uri, July 9, 1985, Paris.
83   FRUS, 1948, III, France, January 5, 1948, p. 592. The original: NARA, 851.51/1-
     548, January 5, 1948.

It was natural for Caffery to exaggerate his own role, but the Mayer Plan clearly had a large constituency behind it in France, and would have been legislated in any case. Influence cannot be measured, and historians may waste a good deal of their time in trying to answer counterfactual questions. But the American presence in France had become a potent source of pressure, which was now being directly exercised in favor of maintaining the Schuman government in power. The Americans lobbied in favor of the government's financial policies, interacting on a direct and continuous basis with government officials and members of the cabinet in the formation and passage of legislation. American influence was welcomed by those French politicians and officials who favored the same policies as Washington. The embassy enjoyed access to French documents and reports, often before these were published or otherwise made known. Financial officers in the embassy analyzed these reports and armed the ambassador and other high American officials with the kind of information needed to make their intervention more effective.[84] A symbiotic relationship was established between Americans and some French officials, who worked together toward the same ends. French internal and external politics became incomprehensible without reference to the American role.

[84] NARA, 851.51/10-2847, October 28, 1947; 11-1247, November 12, 1947. In the latter dispatch William Conkright forwarded confidential data to Washington from a "confidential source" which he warned must not be revealed lest the source be dismissed and future information be impossible to obtain.

4

Americanizing the French

I AMERICAN INFLUENCE AND FRENCH LABOR

AMERICAN POLICY toward the French labor movement until 1947 remained distinct from diplomatic questions between the two governments and Washington's attitude with regard to the internal composition of the French government. The Americans were suspicious but respectful of French neutrality, and they thought it best that the Communists remain in the French government as a guarantee of short-term social stability. But Washington wanted the power of the Communist party over the French labor movement broken. The Americans showed concern over Communist influence in the trade unions even before the end of the Second World War. The State Department maintained an elaborate network of officials in Paris to keep watch over and contact with the various trade unions and political parties of the left. The same concerns characterized American Federation of Labor (AFL), which opened a European office to combat Communist influence on European labor movements late in 1945. The American intelligence services, the OSS, and its successor the CIA, also became involved. While the State Department, AFL, and CIA all pursued their separate and independent activities in France, they tried to cooperate. A formal liaison was established between them in 1947 at the State Department through the office and staff of Raymond Murphy. A hardline anti-Communist, Murphy was a specialist on Communist affairs and an expert in weeding out internal "subversion," in which capacity he had already worked with the FBI.[1]

While concerned about Communist influence, the State Department nevertheless maintained cordial relations with the CGT from the war's end through the summer of 1947. Contact was sustained by the labor attaché,

---

[1] Martin Weil, *A Pretty Good Club: The Founding Fathers of the U.S. Foreign Service* (New York: Norton, 1978), p. 52.

Richard Eldridge, who managed to stay on cordial terms with key figures within the Communist orbit such as Pierre Le Brun, Henri Raynaud, and the general secretary of the CGT, Benoît Frachon. So greatly were Eldridge's contacts valued at the Embassy, that it refused to allow him to transfer to a post in Moscow when the State Department suggested it (see Chapter 3). Eldridge spared no efforts to alert Washington about Communist predominance within the CGT. On March 28, 1945 he reported the Communists' power and prestige were clearly hegemonic within the union, but he thought their dominant position was sufficiently tenuous so that it could be broken.[2] Léon Jouhaux, the historic leader of the CGT, told Eldridge that the balance of power would shift in favor of the reformists during 1946. Jouhaux cited the growing strength of non-Communists in the Post, Telephone, and Telegraph (PTT) unions, among the railroad workers, and in the coal fields of the north.[3]

The CGT leaders and individual Communists cultivated relations with American officials from 1945 to 1947, in accordance with the Communist party's strategy of international detente and internal political collaboration. Communist officials of the CGT kept the Americans abundantly supplied with information, most of it reassuring. CGT leaders told Eldridge that they supported a Popular Front and would not propose Benoît Frachon for general secretary out of concern for the sentiments of non-Communist members. Frachon told Eldridge that the CGT did not seek immediate transition to Socialism and supported the limited aims of the National Council of the Resistance. The CGT was the defender of small business, the battle for higher production remained the basis of Communist policy, and no strikes would occur in plants or ports "controlled by our people."[4] Eldridge was further assured that it was the Socialists who were sabotaging the Communist campaign in favor of higher productivity. Where strikes occurred they, and the Gaullists, would have to share the blame.

Frachon was not equally reassuring with regard to internal union matters, however. The forthcoming spring 1946 Congress of the CGT would see some profound changes in the functioning of the trade unions. The prohibition against union officers being active in politics would be repealed (thus enabling Frachon to serve simultaneously as secretary of the CGT and member of the Political Bureau of the Communist party). The privileged position in voting rights enjoyed by smaller (non-Communist) unions within the confederation was to be eliminated. Non-Communist labor leaders objected to these changes, but Frachon was unconcerned about the minority currents in the CGT.[5] Ambassador Jefferson Caffery was alarmed and warned Wash-

[2] National Archives and Records Administration (NARA), 851.5043/3-2845, March 28, 1945.
[3] NARA, 851.5043/7-1745, July 17, 1945.
[4] NARA, 851.5043/8-745, August 7, 1945; 8-845, August 8, 1945.
[5] NARA, 851.5043/9-2145, September 21, 1945; 11-1045, November 10, 1945; 4-

ington that the Communist party would control three-fourths of the vote at the April 1946 congress of the CGT. Caffery reminded the State Department that the CGT was an auxiliary of the French Communist party, which was in turn an instrument of the Kremlin.[6]

Caffery's fears were fully shared by the AFL representative in Europe, Irving Brown. Given the almost legendary nature of the Brown mission in Communist propaganda and its durability (he died while still on post in 1989) it is worth recalling that he was initially welcomed to France by Frachon; the Communist leader was initially delighted with the show of labor solidarity from across the Atlantic. Frachon was quickly disabused, however. The AFL was viscerally anti-Communist. The Free Trade Union Committee (FTUC), which sponsored the Brown mission, was animated by ex-Communist Jay Lovestone, anti-Communist Matthew Woll, and ex-Bundist David Dubinsky. Its specific intent was to combat the growing Communist influence within European labor.[7] Dubinsky's International Ladies Garment Workers Union (ILGWU) expended large amounts of money in refugee aid during the war and continued its foreign activities after the war. Dubinsky was also behind the Jewish Labor Committee, which sponsored a variety of overseas projects in Italy, Israel, and France. While the ILGWU was the source of much of Brown's funding, it also conducted its own overseas policy, sometimes in competition with him.

Brown arrived in Paris in the fall of 1945. In November he reported that two-thirds of the CGT was controlled by Communists; the non-Communist workers voted for Communist leaders because they were skilled unionists

---

646, April 6, 1946. Frachon's intentions were no secret; he called for changes in the CGT voting system on January 18, 1946 in *L'Humanité*; see Benoît Frachon, *Au Rythme des jours: Retrospective de vingt années de lutte de la CGT* (textes choisis), vol. 1: *1944–54* (Paris: Editions Sociales, 1967), p. 137.

[6] NARA, 851.5043/2-2046, February 20, 1946; 4-1546, April 15, 1946.
[7] See Ronald Radosh, *American Labor and United States Foreign Policy* (New York: Random House, 1969), pp. 312–24; Also Roy Godson, *American Labor and European Politics* (New York: Crane, Russak, 1976). On Lovestone see Anthony Carew, *Labour under the Marshall Plan* (Manchester: Manchester University Press, 1987), p. 61. For the relationship between the American labor movement and international organizations the older work of John Windmuller, *American Labor and the International Labor Movement 1940 to 1953* (Ithaca, NY: Cornell International Industrial and Labor Relations Reports, 1954), is still useful. For a recent critical perspective on my view of the Brown mission as presented here, see Annie Lacroix-Riz, "Autour d'Irving Brown: le Free Trade Union Committee, le Départment d'Etat et la scission syndicale française (1944–1947)," *Le Mouvement Social*, 151 (avril-juin 1990), 79–118. Working without benefit of American sources, Lacroix-Riz continues to speculate that Brown worked in close relationship to the State Department and the CIA from the outset of his mission, and that he injected huge sums of money into the non-Communist wing of the French labor movement. I have found nothing in her work to cause me to change the views presented here. A forthcoming manuscript on French labor and the cold war by Denis MacShane confirms the analysis given here.

and dynamic fighters for worker causes. The opposition lacked resources; outmaneuvered and outfinanced by the Communists, "they want help from us," Brown said."[8] Reporting to Matthew Woll in December, Brown cited Robert Bothereau's "Résistance Ouvrière" as "wanting help without being compromised." This group, later known as Force Ouvrière (FO), encapsulated the anti-Communist wing of the French labor movement, which had always maintained an autonomous presence even during the periods of French labor unity such as the Popular Front and Resistance.[9] Brown suggested an immediate grant of $5,000 from the Jewish Labor Committee. But the larger, national issue was increasingly urgent; the Communists wanted to reduce the number of general secretaries to four, isolate Jouhaux, and eliminate Bothereau. Through local maneuvers they were methodically capturing trade unions throughout the country.[10] Brown suggested a long-range program to support the non-Communist opposition. At least $100,000 would be necessary to cover expenses such as salaries of organizers, travel, and printing of propaganda. Although the amount was sizable, Brown thought it preferable to do the job completely or not attempt it at all; the stakes were too high. Recognizing that the enterprise of splitting a union movement was "not a nice way of doing business," Brown said it was necessary because only "real financial backing can reinforce the will to resist of non-Communists."

But no such funds were available in 1945–46, and nothing was done prior to the April 1946 CGT Congress, a "completely dominated Communist party affair."[11] The CGT, said Brown, had become a Stalinist organ with "no prospect of internal reform." No discussion of wages and working conditions took place; instead the orators exhibited a chauvinistic nationalism, backed antilabor practices such as speed-ups and piece work, restrained workers' legitimate economic grievances, and supported the Communist minister of labor, Ambroise Croizat, who enforced "unpopular and vicious wage practices" in the name of the battle for production. The non-Communist group under Jouhaux and Bothereau (FO) "lack central direction" and were unable to harness the opposition forces. But masses of anti-Communist workers were still ready to act if they were afforded the right leadership, Brown said. Many in the opposition were "ready and willing to accept the logic implicit in this analysis and urge the preparation for the eventual and inevitable split." The task was to identify, help, and cultivate these people, for "the future of democratic free trade unionism lies in the

8 Irving Brown to Abraham Bluestein, November 27, 1945, Archives of the State Historical Society of Wisconsin (SHSW), Florence Thorne File, Box 16. Most of the sources in the Thorne collection are cited in Radosh's account.

9 See Alain Bergounioux, *Force Ouvrière* (Paris: Seuil, 1975), pp. 30–5.

10 Brown to Matthew Woll, SHSW, Thorne File, 16, December 14, 1945.

11 Brown, "Report on CGT Convention," April 8–12, 1946, SHSW, Thorne File, 16.

eventual split which will leave the CGT as a pure, unadulterated Communist organization about which the workers can have no illusions."[12] Brown met with most of the anti-Communist leaders; the split, when it came, must appear "a logical necessity and not something that will reinforce the interests of the employers." The AFL could help in this work by providing financial aid.

The PTT strike of July 30–August 2, 1946 showed the acuity of Brown's analysis. Caffery reported that it was a wildcat strike in defiance of the Communist leadership and an impressive example of how "an alliance of non-Communist minorities can temporarily overthrow Communist control by organizing worker discontent."[13] Communist union officials told Eldridge that "this was a strike against the Communist leadership of the PTT and also of the CGT" planned by "scoundrels, Trotskyites and impractical revolutionary syndicalists," while strike leaders said that the rank and file were "heartily sick of political exploitation of the PTT and the CGT by the Communist 'old beards.' " A campaign to overthrow Communist control of the PTT was under way; Caffery hoped this would be the first of many instances in which non-Communists joined together to attack Communist control of an important union. The PTT strike had not been "spontaneous," he emphasized; through careful planning the anti-Communist alliance had prepared the discontented rank and file for action by open and clandestine propaganda. The first stage of the struggle to wrest control of an important union from the Communists had been "brilliantly completed."[14]

The Americans continued to support anti-Communist initiatives in the French trade unions through 1946. Brown and Eldridge offered the dissidents moral support, some material help, "advice and know-how" (assuming the French needed it), and assurance of further help in the future.[15] How important these promises were in the planning of French scissionists is impossible to measure. The creation of FO as an autonomous group within the CGT occurred in September 1946, as the result of a fusion of several anti-Communist tendencies, including Reformist Socialists, Anarcho-Syndicalists, and Trotskyites.[16] The Americans could not plan or orchestrate the strikes in France, nor could they anticipate the events that eventually produced the split in the French unions for which they were hoping. On the other hand French non-Communist trade unionists were reluctant to break with the parent CGT until they could be assured of the necessary

[12] SHSW, "Report on CGT Convention."
[13] NARA, 851.5045/8-546, August 5, 1946. Frachon at the time blamed the PTT strike on the Socialists; later he cited it as the first example of overt American interference in French labor affairs. *Au Rythme des jours*, p. 162.
[14] NARA, 851.5045/8-1646, August 16, 1946. See the account of the strike in Bergounioux, *Force Ouvrière* p. 47.
[15] Irving Brown, personal interview, September 6, 1985.
[16] Bergounioux, *Force Ouvrière*, p. 61.

logistical support: They needed headquarters, secretarial help, typewriters and mimeograph machines, and the money to hire people to staff a new bureaucracy. External funding began to trickle in during 1947. The AFL, through the FTUC, made about $20,000 available to non-Communist unions in France before the split of the CGT, while the ILGWU report for 1947 shows another $20,000, $15,000 for "Il Populaire" and $5,000 for "Force of Riviera (sic)" which clearly meant FO.[17] These amounts were increased in succeeding years and augmented by U.S. government funds so as to assure the non-Communist union organizations the means of survival.

The CGT continued to cultivate good relations with the U.S. embassy, however, perhaps as yet unaware of efforts by the Americans to reduce the Communist role in the unions. Frachon assured Eldridge that the CGT would not upset things during the election of May–June 1946 and criticized the Communist party for permitting irresponsible slogans during the campaign, such as "Thorez au pouvoir." On June 12 Frachon told Eldridge of his satisfaction with the election results. He condemned the CFTC (Christian unions) for irresponsibly advocating pay increases and he called for Social-ist–Communist unity. Frachon asserted that the CGT and the PCF had re-strained workers from demanding wage increases for too long; it was now necessary to reward them for their effort and discipline. But the CGT would recommend that the government declare a pause in any new nationaliza-tions or structural reforms.[18] In November 1946 CGT leaders still professed support for the Monnet Plan and welcomed the prospect of American aid, which was essential to its execution.[19] The main problem facing France was the danger of fascism; the Communists did not favor a socialist economy but rather a mixed system, consisting of state-owned, state-directed, and private sectors, all working in harmony. As late as February 1947, Thorez was still trying to legitimate the PCF in American eyes. He emphasized for Caffery the CGT's restraint on the wage issue and commitment to the con-trol of inflation; despite occasional public posturing, the Communist leader said, the union was not seeking general wage increases but would be satis-fied with the correction of certain minimum wage figures which were "ob-viously" inadequate.[20]

A different tone entered these talks after the Communists left the govern-

---

[17] Godson estimates the total amount of aid received by Force Ouvrière during 1947 at $20,000, to which the contribution of the ILGWU, whose typists obviously had dif-ficulty with French, should be added. International Ladies' Garment Workers Union, *Report and Record* (New York, 1947). In the Archives of the ILGWU, New York City.

[18] NARA, Paris Post Files, 850.4, Confidential File, Memos of Conversation dated May 28 and June 12, 1946. The Paris embassy files are housed in the annex of the Na-tional Archives in Suitland, Maryland.

[19] NARA, Paris Post Files, 850.4, November 27, 1946; reported as 851.504/11-2746, November 27, 1946.

[20] NARA, 851.5041/2-1747, February 17, 1947.

ment. On May 13, 1947 CGT leader Pierre Le Brun complained to Eldridge of "growing American influence in France." Truman appeared to be extending a Monroe doctrine to Western Europe, the CGT leader said, the result of which was to stiffen the resolve of French employers in the face of wage demands by the unions.[21] But Le Brun still reaffirmed the CGT's support of the Monnet Plan and hope for American assistance, and he assured Eldridge that nobody familiar with the present situation in France anticipated a Communist government or an attempt by the party to take power. The PCF still hoped for American toleration of the formation of a new government with Communist participation.

The crisis of the "insurrectionary" and "political" strikes of the fall of 1947 led to a coordination of the Embassy's and Brown's efforts. Caffery forwarded Brown's analysis of the strike movement to the State Department on November 27.[22] The Communist aim, said Brown, was a gradual buildup toward a general strike as an instrument for the seizure of power, and he feared the Communists would use coercion and terrorism to force the cooperation of recalcitrant workers.[23] He urged that the government provide armed protection to assure the security of men crossing the picket lines. "The present situation offers a unique opportunity to break the Communists' stranglehold in the CGT," Brown wrote, and he warned that the government must not meet the workers' wage demands. If the strikes were treated as a genuine labor dispute the Communists would emerge with their control of the labor movement intact and their prestige increased; the government must dramatize the political issue of anti-Communism in the strikes. Meanwhile Socialists, syndicalists, and Christian unionists must cooperate in a back-to-work movement with government assistance to mobilize the workers against Communist terrorism. Brown insisted that the World Federation of Trade Unions be split in order to break the Communist hold on the French and Italian labor movements.[24] As things were, the WFTU provided a "mantle of respectability" to the CGT in the eyes of the workers. Brown left for London in an effort to enlist the help of Ernest Bevin and the British Trades Union Congress in this effort. His analysis made an immediate impact in Washington; Acting Secretary of State Robert Lovett wired Paris that "We believe it might be useful for Brown to see Bevin . . . we assume you will extend Brown such assistance as you deem appropriate."[25]

---

[21] NARA, 851.00/5-1347, May 13, 1947.
[22] NARA, 851.504/11-2747, November 27, 1947.
[23] In fact the strikes can be explained by more limited goals of the workers: see Jean-Pierre Rioux, *The Fourth Republic, 1944–1958* (Cambridge: Cambridge University Press, 1987), pp. 129–31. Annie Lacroix-Rix, *La CGT de la Liberation à la scission de 1944–1947* (Paris: Editions Sociales, 1983), stresses economic explanations as do I in *French Communism in the Era of Stalin* (Westport, CT: Greenwood Press, 1983).
[24] On the WFTU split see Carew, *Labour under the Marshall Plan*, pp. 68–77.
[25] NARA, 851.504/11-2747, November 29, 1947, Marshall to Caffery.

On November 5 Frachon delivered a blistering attack on the Brown mission in France, accusing the American labor organizer of working toward the division of the French workers and functioning as a tool of the State Department.[26] The Embassy was concerned by these attacks, but the AFL nevertheless formally adopted a proposal by Brown calling upon the State Department to establish liaison with the union, and specifically asked that the State Department's anti-Communist specialist, Ray Murphy, be assigned to this task.[27] The AFL was "the focal point of the struggle for freedom all over the world," with its most critical activity now directed at France and Italy; aid to free trade unions must be stepped up in these two countries.

On the eve of the December 19, 1947 split in the CGT, the U.S. embassy feared that Bothereau and other reformist leaders were holding back for fear of lack of the necessary funds, offices, staff, and equipment. The department enlisted the support of the Congress of Industrial Organizations (CIO), which agreed to a policy of support for Jouhaux.[28] Caffery was pleased to see the development of Belgian, Dutch, and Scandinavian union support and asked that "this information be discreetly transmitted to CIO and AFL." The CIO was reluctant to act, however, unless Léon Jouhaux approved. Brown had earlier despaired of getting Jouhaux's cooperation and banked on younger, more aggressive figures taking the lead – indeed, Brown hoped to see Jouhaux replaced by such leaders as Bothereau and André Lafond. Despite his reluctance, Jouhaux rallied to the need for a split, but he spoke with "suppressed fury" of Brown: "It would be helpful if the Americans did not claim they caused the CGT split. I hear that Brown has decided I should not head the CGT-FO. . . ." It was striking, Jouhaux thought, that Brown, allegedly a Socialist, should "possess so little understanding of the French situation."[29]

The split developed from the internal dynamic process of French labor, and Brown did FO considerable damage by intemperate claims to its paternity, a theme Frachon used with great effect in CGT propaganda. Caffery recognized this: The split, he thought, resulted from a mass movement of protest against Communist policies among the rank and file of French labor, "it was the workers who voted with their feet." The division of the CGT was a reflection of the anti-Communist sentiment of the rank and file. The key question now was whether the practical questions involved (funds, of-

26 For examples of Frachon's attacks, see *Au Rythme des jours*, pp. 233–70. "Everyone knows that there are men in France charged with the distribution of dollars in order to carry out the split of the CGT. . . . [The splitters] have for a long time been in liaison with the American agent Brown, who dispenses dollars, advice, and orders under the supervision of the State Department."

27 SHSW, Thorne File, Box 17, Folder 2, Committee on International Labor Relations, November 17, 1947.

28 NARA, 851.5043/12-1747, December 17, 1947; 12-2147, December 21 and 23, 1947.

29 NARA, 851.5043/12-2647, December 26, 1947.

fices, equipment, and salaried personnel) would not present too great an obstacle for the nascent non-Communist union to survive.[30] The record of actual fund transfers from America at this point is meager, however. Brown promised $5,000 every three weeks to FO militants continuing through January 1948.[31] Later the AFL executive extended a fresh "loan" of $25,000 for which it expected no immediate repayment. The Ministry of Labor, however, granted FO 40 million francs from some frozen labor funds available since the Vichy regime, and these more likely made the difference in FO's survival.[32] These funds were insufficient, however, and quickly became a matter of concern at the Embassy. On January 7, 1948 Caffery wrote a personal and top secret letter to Under Secretary of State Robert Lovett appealing for further help: "The real key to the French political situation . . . has been the control of the French labor movement . . . by the Communist party." The recent split in the CGT must therefore be regarded as "potentially the most important political event since the Liberation of France." But a program was required to assist the new non-Communist CGT-FO "to carry out a massive, nation-wide campaign to bring about the adherence of the majority of French workers to this new organization. . . . The principal obstacle to the rapid crystallization of the opposition movement is the lack of funds."[33] In the past, Caffery noted, the Embassy had enjoyed the discretionary use of $5,000 a year through Mr. Raymond Murphy's office in the State Department.

> More recently, additional sums, bringing the total to roughly $28,000, have been secretly made available from private American business firms and the Central Intelligence Agency. I believe that Secretary Harriman has interested himself in this aspect of the matter and has greatly facilitated the collection of these funds, most of which have found their way into the French labor movement through the contacts of the European representative of the AF of L, Mr. Irving Brown, whose organization has also contributed funds. (Unfortunately, from our point of view, the AF of L funds have had to be spread over several countries.) Furthermore, I am told that Mr. Cope, the local CIO representative, intends shortly to return to the United States for the purpose of making an appeal for a very substantial contribution from his organization.
>
> Our feeling here is that the next few months will be the crucial period when financial help can be most effective and that an additional sum of say $250,000 would pay enormous dividends. Compared to the stake which we have in Europe and the amounts which we are contemplating spending for European recovery in the next few years, this is a relatively small sum. Whether the money comes from the Government or private sources, I believe that such

30   NARA, 951.5045/12-2047, December 20, 1947.
31   SHSW, Thorne File, Box 17, Minutes of the International Labor Relations Committee, October 19, 1947. Cited in Radosh, p. 320.
32   Bergounioux, *Force Ouvrière*, p. 92, estimates that 70 percent of the FO budget during its first year came from subventions.
33   NARA, 851.50/Recovery 1-748, January 7, 1948.

additional aid as we can give should reach the French preferably through American Labor organizations with whom the arrangements could no doubt be worked out through existing channels, at least with respect to the AF of L. I appreciate that this is not the type of operation which the United States Government has indulged in in the past and I appreciate that it is fraught with certain risks. I am certain, however, that so far as France is concerned there is nothing at this time which would bring more concrete and lasting benefits or which would help more in achieving the fundamental aims of our foreign policy here.

Lovett replied that he would see to the availability of some "unvouchered funds" for this purpose on an interim basis until long-term arrangements could be made.[34] There is no record of the actual transfer of these funds to the AFL from the CIA. But Thomas Braden, who was then in charge of organizing the CIA's European operations, later claimed he delivered $50,000 in cash to Irving Brown for retransfer to the French.[35] Nor is it clear whether the $28,000 that Caffery wrote had already been transferred was in addition to or the same funds received by FO from the AFL in the winter of 1947–48. The archives of the American Federation of Labor and the CIA remain closed for the period.

Many frightened French hoped for and requested American intervention, and welcomed it when it came. During the height of the strike movement the American consul in Nice reported that "conversations with government, church, and business representatives here include always their expressions of surprise that the United States Government continues its policy of non-intervention in the internal affairs of France, particularly in view of the active participation of the Communists. The feeling is strong that funds should be available to combat the Comintern financed group."[36]

But the Americans were intervening. The strikes occurred during the Embassy's conversations with General de Gaulle about the latter's return to power; Caffery told General Benouville that a Gaullist government would be as unstable as its predecessors if it did not enjoy the support of French non-Communist labor.[37] Benouville said de Gaulle was aware of the problem and was working hard to win labor support, but he would not approach the Socialists; Caffery warned against any effort to bypass or crush the Socialists. Irving Brown concurred in the Embassy's conclusion that a de Gaulle government was likely and desirable in France, and like Caffery, he did not

[34] NARA, 851.50/Recovery 1-748, January 24, 1948, Lovett to Caffery.
[35] Thomas Braden, "I'm Glad the CIA Is 'Immoral'," *Saturday Evening Post*, May 20, 1967. Braden also later transferred $50,000 to the French unions through Victor Reuther, who became CIO European representative in 1950, explaining that he had been transferring funds "for some time" through Brown. *The Brothers Reuther and the Story of the UAW. A Memoir by Victor G. Reuther* (Boston, Houghton Mifflin, 1976), p. 426.
[36] NARA, 851.5045/12-547, December 5, 1947.
[37] NARA, 851.00/12-147, December 2, 1947.

hesitate to approach the RPF directly.[38] On January 31, 1948 Brown told de Gaulle's advisor Jacques Soustelle that "de Gaulle should avoid corporatist-type statements on labor policy that smack of Vichy," because "this tends to split the anti-Communist labor front."[39] Soustelle denied there was any "fascist" content to de Gaulle's ideas.

Caffery and the ECA also payed close attention to the wage–price relationship; by mid-1948 the ambassador had concluded that price increases and the restraint on wages imposed by the Mayer Plan had eroded the meager gains labor had won following the crushing of the strike movement of 1947. Caffery feared a new social explosion and recommended to Washington that a "preventive wage increase" be granted the workers "in order to give the government a breathing spell."[40] Dire warnings also came from Irving Brown, who reported that Bothereau said prices must be held or FO would rejoin the CGT in seeking wage increases, if only because of rank and file pressure.[41] Washington took the warnings seriously: On August 27, 1948 Secretary Marshall cabled "[We] feel it important our agreement with [the] Embassy analysis [of the] wage–price situation be made known to both [the] ECA and French Government. ... You may in your discretion give [the] French to understand we would not regard some immediate wage and/or cost of living increases now as incompatible with long-run aims [of] budgetary stabilization and financial equilibrium. We agree failure of concessions to anti-Communist labor will strengthen [the] Communist party and weaken [the] economy with costly strikes."[42] But after a cabinet crisis and talk of a new Popular Front in France, the Queuille government granted only a modest increase, and France headed for a new confrontation with French labor in the form of the brutal coal strike of October–November 1948.

Despite American pressure the French government remained determined to hold the line on wages, ignoring resentment building among the miners. Caffery finally concluded that wages were not anyway the central issue in the strikes, which were about "technical and political" questions, in particular the "reconquest of the nationalized coal companies" from the domination of the CGT and the Communist party.[43] In this he was no doubt correct. But the government's opposition to any concessions was nevertheless demoralizing French labor: "There is evidence that the trend which resulted from the split between Communist and non-Communist labor unions (the capital event of post-war France) has come to a stop and may be re-

[38] Irving Brown, "From Crisis to Crisis: The Communists Keep France in Turmoil," *American Federationist*, May 1947.
[39] NARA, 851.5043/1-3148, January 31, 1948.
[40] NARA, 851.5043/8-2348, August 23, 1948.
[41] NARA, 851.5043/8-948, August 9, 1948.
[42] NARA, 851.5043/8-2348, August 27, 1948.
[43] NARA, 851.5045/9-3048, September 30, 1948.

versed and replaced by a trend toward unity, in which the superior organization of the Communists would prevail."[44] During the apogee of the strikes, Washington cabled Paris with irritation; John L. Lewis had attacked the French government and the ECA, saying the French government should stop making war on its own citizens at the expense of the U.S. taxpayer. The State Department instructed the Embassy to obtain statements from FO and the CFTC protesting Lewis's remark. Caffery called on the French labor leaders in order to elicit the requested messages. On October 28 he called on Léon Blum as well, who wired Lewis condemning the coal strikes as political, not caused by legitimate labor grievances. Blum also wrote a reply to Lewis in *Le Populaire*.[45] Meanwhile urgent American coal deliveries ensured the French sufficient stockpiles to face down the demands of the miners. The Fur and leather workers' union of New York sent $2,500 – about 700,000 francs – to the strikers, but the Soviet trade unions sent the more impressive figure of 18 million francs. Caffery denounced this "crude intervention in the internal affairs of another state by the Soviet government. . . . [It] should be labeled as such and broadcast to the whole world including the USSR."[46]

Léon Blum denounced the Communist party for the assistance it received from Moscow, but himself sought subsidies from American trade union sources for the continued publication of the Socialist newspaper, *Le Populaire*. As indicated above, the ILGWU records showed $15,000 paid to "Il Populaire" during 1947.[47] On June 16, 1948 Blum wrote David Dubinsky that, failing an immediate infusion of economic aid, the Socialist newspaper faced "catastrophe." *Le Populaire* was living from day to day, Blum wrote, at the perpetual mercy of its creditors; help from the ILGWU was indispensable and urgent. Blum appealed to Dubinsky's "profound knowledge of the European situation and workers' interests."[48] Dubinsky raised $17,000 for Le Populaire, $10,000 of which was paid in December 1947 and $7,000 more the following March, and the ILGWU became a regular source of funds for the Socialist party organ thereafter. Regular appeals were received from Socialist party dignitaries at ILGWU headquarters; Daniel Mayer, Daniel Verdier, Robert Blum, all called on Dubinsky's generosity. Dubinsky sent $15,000 in 1951 and $25,000 in 1952, while assisting Robert Blum's mission to the United States in 1950 in its efforts to raise another $75,000 for the newspaper. Irving Brown succeeded in raising 3 million francs independently for *Le Populaire* from the Rothschilds.[49] In 1953, tired of the re-

44   NARA, 851.5045/10-548, October 5, 1948.
45   NARA, 851.5045/10-2748, October 27, 1948.
46   NARA, 851.5043/11-1548, November 15, 1948.
47   See note 17.
48   Léon Blum to David Dubinsky, June 16, 1948, David Dubinsky Papers, ILGWU Archive, Box 33, Folder 6.
49   The various French Socialist appeals to Dubinsky are in the Dubinsky Papers, ILGWU,

peated appeals, Dubinsky offered to put *Le Populaire* on a regular subsidy and approached labor leaders throughout the United States to raise money for that purpose. Dubinsky arranged the $25,000 loan granted FO by the AFL in October 1948, for which he received the warm thanks of Bothereau.[50] The report of the ILGWU for 1950 shows a total of $300,000 sent both *Le Populaire* and Force Ouvrière in the preceding three years. All this did not prevent Jules Moch from making an issue of alleged Soviet aid to *L'Humanité* during the strikes of November–December 1948; in reply, Jacques Duclos challenged Moch to an investigation into the sources of funding of both *L'Humanité* and *Le Populaire*. Not surprisingly, Moch refused.

According to Thomas Braden, Lovestone received up to $2 million in CIA funds for French trade union subsidies after 1950, and the subsidies continued until the Americans became disillusioned with the meager results achieved.[51] Much of this money went into the battle of the docks. Concern for the condition of the dockers' unions in France arose from fears that the CGT-controlled unions would interfere with Marshall Plan aid shipments. These fears became critical in 1950 with the beginning of shipments under the Mutual Defense Assistance Program and the declared PCF policy of preventing the manufacture and transport of arms used in the "dirty war" in Indochina. Irving Brown and Pierre Ferri-Pisani worked together to organize dockers for FO in the violence-prone port of Marseille as well as in Bordeaux, Le Havre, and Cherbourg. The CGT was accused of harassment of workers who tried to ignore its strike calls; Brown and Ferri-Pisani, through the anti-Communist Mediterranean Port Committee, organized their own shock troops to take control of the ports, lavishly distributing funds for that purpose. In 1950 Communist dockers who tried to buck the efforts of the Ferri-Pisani organization were "chucked into the harbor," according to *Time Magazine*.[52]

Time was referring to the defeat of the CGT-led dockers' strike in Marseille in March–April 1950. But this victory for Brown became the subject of regret in the State Department, which feared that the result of Brown's antics was to strengthen the grip of the Communists on French labor. The

---

Box 229, Folder 6. Irving Brown wrote Dubinsky that he was "flabbergasted" to hear of the money going to *Le Populaire*.

[50] ILGWU, *Report and Record*, 1950.

[51] Braden, "I'm Glad the CIA Is 'Immoral'."

[52] *Time Magazine*, March 17, 1952. Ferri-Pisani had an unsavory past as a former associate of the Communist turned collaborator Simon Sabiani in Marseille. See Paul Jankowski, *Communism and Collaboration: Simon Sabiani and Politics in Marseille, 1949–1944* (New Haven, CT: Yale University Press, 1989), p. 29. Reuther says the Mediterranean Port Committee was an AFL front bankrolled by the CIA, which continued to operate for years while paid off by the agency, eventually going into the drug business in South Vietnam. *The Brothers Reuther and the Story of the UAW*, p. 412.

defeat of the dockers' union also had the effect of reinforcing the reactionary attitudes of the stevedoring companies, which refused any reasonable concessions to labor and made the CGT appear, despite its defeat, the only militant representative of the workers.[53] The influence of Ferri-Pisani's Port Committee and FO in fact declined among the dockers by 1952. Augustin Marsily, head of the reformist union in Marseille, broke with the committee, protesting Ferri-Pisani's methods to Brown. Marsily claimed that he had defeated the March–April 1950 strike in which "I threw 4400 men into the port of Marseille." But in doing so he had not consorted with thugs and gangsters, and imposed as the head of the "free" dockers' union "common criminals," tactics Marsily attributed to Brown. Marsily accused Ferri-Pisani and Brown of aiming to install an iron-handed dictatorship over the dockers, and tried to organize his own union. The result was that the FO organization among the Marseille dockers was dissolved and the CGT re-emerged supreme. "It is hard to avoid the conclusion that the Mediterranean Committee has been consistently more interested in the political struggle than in organizing a union," the American consul wrote.[54]

American assistance to FO has been vastly overemphasized in France, and on balance, given its propaganda value to the CGT, may well have done more harm to U.S. interests than good. To be sure, Bothereau acknowledged the importance of American assistance in a letter to David Dubinsky: "I must thank you today and over the long term for the generous aid received from your organization. It has permitted us to deal with the most urgent situation in which we find ourselves. . . .[55] Thomas Braden later was more categorical; Lovestone and Brown stepped into the strikes of 1947, he wrote, and "with funds from Dubinsky's union, they organized FO."[56] Irving Brown, then and later, was also prone to exaggerate his own role. But the judgment of Caffery was that the bitter political strikes of 1947 gave rise to FO, and if the Americans were midwives in its birth, they were unable to affect its subsequent growth and development. Almost at once stinging critiques appeared of FO's internal operations in American Embassy reports. The only solution, the Americans rapidly concluded, was the overturn of a sclerotic leadership by popular pressure from below, or the new union would never provide an effective antidote to Communism. In April 1949 Norris Chipman, reviewing one year of the existence of independent trade unionism in France, complained that the split in 1947 had been "unplanned, improvised, confused." The mentality of the FO leadership was insufficiently anti-Communist while its pro-government timidity in wage disputes angered the rank and file.[57] The means FO enjoyed were not "justified by the meager

53 NARA, 851.06/3-3152, March 31, 1952.
54 NARA, 851.062/5-2152, May 21, 1952; 12-153, December 1, 1953.
55 Dubinsky Papers, ILGWU, Box 249, Folder 4b, October 1, 1948.
56 Braden, "I'm Glad the CIA Is 'Immoral'."
57 NARA, 851.504/4-449, April 4, 1949.

results obtained. To permit FO leadership to vegetate in their easy-going ways is one of the best (or worst) ways of making it easy for the Communists. We should support the most active [unions] regardless of their affiliation." Chipman recommended support of the RPF unions.

David Bruce, who succeeded Caffery as ambassador, agreed that FO leadership was under attack from its left wing, leaders of which had long been seeking Jouhaux's removal with Brown's support. "These and other aspects of the labor situation are being investigated with a view to definite recommendations regarding actions that might be helpful."[58] Bruce was won over to the "autonomous" union group despite its origins among ex-Communists and revolutionary anarchosyndicalists. The report of the "autonomes," wrote Bruce, was "the most realistic, most modest, as well as the most interesting report that has issued from labor since the Liberation."[59] Bruce especially appreciated their indictment of the French tax system as a "scandal" due to its inequities, a view that dovetailed perfectly with the critique of French finances being developed by the Marshall Plan Mission.

Brown, frustrated by his inability to overturn the leadership of Jouhaux, further became impatient with FO's support of French colonialism. On a visit to North Africa, Brown complained that he was shadowed everywhere by French government agents, and in an interesting switch, "accused of playing into the hands of the Communists."[60] If France does not change its colonial policies, Brown predicted, "Communism will progress." Noting the bidonvilles, he remarked that he had only seen worse in India. Noting that FO was also pro-settler in Algeria, Brown insisted that the International Free Trade Unions retain ties to the nationalists, use their influence at the Quai to win toleration of the moderate Algerian advocates of independence, and induce FO to accept the nationalist unions as the best barrier to Communism. Although FO never broke with the International organization on the colonial question, it never abandoned its position on the issue.

Brown did not share Bruce's conclusions about the desirability of supporting unions to the left of FO, however. This suggestion seemed to Brown an example of a dangerous willingness in the State Department to flirt with left-wing forces, a reflection, perhaps, of the liberalism of Secretary of State Dean Acheson, whom Brown's boss, Matthew Woll, thought "a very bad appointment for us. He has been leaning altogether too strongly toward the Communist end."[61] Brown advocated a different approach: the suppression

58 NARA, 851.5043/6-1049, June 10, 1949.
59 NARA, 851.5043/10-1949, October 19, 1949.
60 SHSW, Thorne File, Box 14, December 13, 1950, report of Irving Brown. Force Ouvrière's differences with the AFL on the colonial question are abundantly documented in Jack Kantrowitz, "L'Influence américaine sur Force Ouvrière: mythe ou réalité?", *Revue Française de Science Politique*, 4 (August 1978): 717–40.
61 SHSW. Thorne File, Matthew Woll to Florence Thorne, Box 17, Folder marked 1949, January 7, 1949.

of the CGT by the French government and the acceptance back into the fold of trade union leaders of the interwar period, who had been compromised under Vichy. It was senseless to "condemn eternally people who out of mistaken patriotism supported the Vichy regime, although they were mortal enemies of the Nazi occupation." Only by the rehabilitation of anti-Communist trade unionists of the prewar era could the free trade unions be revitalized. Brown also called on the French government to deny the CGT representative rights in the French labor movement on the ground that it was the "agent of a foreign power."[62] His suggestions were not appreciated by everyone in the American labor movement, however. In 1952 Dubinsky received a scathingly critical report of Brown's methods, characterized as a perverse combination of police methods and amnesties for traitors: "No positive results or decline in Communist party strength have resulted from Brown's 'cloak and dagger' operations."[63]

If AFL felt increasingly frustrated in its efforts to colonize FO, the CIO had its own sort of romance with the left wing of the Catholic unions, the CFTC. It was always Brown's policy to try to bring the CFTC and FO together to form an anti-Communist front. Victor Reuther, European representative of the CIO, thought the solution to French labor problems might be the secularization of the CFTC, followed by its merger with FO. Reuther developed a close relationship with Paul Vignaux, leader of the CFTC's left wing, and some money very likely changed hands as a result of this relationship as well. While the AFL raised its funds internally or took them from the State Department and the CIA, the CIO was helped by the ECA. In November 1952 the CFTC leadership attacked Victor Reuther and the CIO for interference in its internal affairs, accusing the American union of offering bribes to those members of the CFTC who were willing to work toward unity with FO.[64] Not surprisingly CGT leader Benoît Frachon had a field day with this information, blasting American "agents" who he claimed had been installed in France for years in order to subsidize labor divisions in the interests of the capitalists and American imperialism.[65]

In fact the reality was much more complex than that. Various American agencies, the two rival unions, AFL and CIO, the two parallel American bureaucracies of the State Department and Mutual Security Agency, successor to the ECA, and the CIA, all had their own policies, with little overall coordination taking place between them. All by this time had relatively large amounts of funds to distribute. But the American unions, in their rivalries, shocked and confused French opinion. The CIO accused the AFL of being a tool of the State Department, while the CFTC majority accused the CIO

---

[62] Irving Brown, "Plain Talk on France," *American Federationist*, December 1951.
[63] William Bomberg to David Dubinsky, March 14, 1952, in David Dubinsky Papers, Box 249, Folder 4b.
[64] NARA, 851.062/11-352, November 3, 1952; 1-1253, January 12, 1953.
[65] *Au Rythme des jours*, p. 514.

of working in the interests of the MSA. In exasperation the State Department deplored the "anarchy" inherent in this situation. Was the United States fighting the Communist-controlled CGT, or the majority leaderships of both non-Communist unions, the CFTC and FO? Meanwhile the Confederation of the French *patronat* complained that the United States promoted "socialism" in France through the policies of the MSA, which promoted worker participation in the ownership of industries, although it was unknown in the United States itself.[66]

With the coming of the Republican administration in 1952, American intervention in the wage question ceased, and a healthy skepticism permeated the State Department concerning its ability to influence French trade unionism as well. The August 1953 strikes were unique among labor conflicts since the war in that they were located predominantly in the public sector and spearheaded by FO and the CFTC. American labor leaders consequently argued that the French government now had a golden opportunity to strike a blow against the CGT by making concessions to the strikers and handing a victory to the non-Communist unions. So obvious was this to the leadership of FO that when Premier Joseph Laniel failed to jump at this chance, Bothereau approached the State Department, appealing to Ambassador Douglas Dillon to pressure Laniel into granting wage increases and negotiating an end to the strikes with the non-Communist unions. Dillon, however, recommended that Washington remain "scrupulously aloof" from what was apparently a quarrel between the government and its Socialist opposition.[67] Having worked in Washington's interests for so long, FO was nevertheless unable to cash in its notes when they seemed to have fallen due.

The embassy, for its part, concluded that its intervention in French trade affairs had been a bad business. Dillon noted that the Christian unions, stubborn and fiercely independent, were the only ones able to grow in what had been recently a very poor period for French labor. These unions were proud of their ability to function "without assistance from either Western or Eastern patronage." Neglect by foreign governments otherwise interested in influencing French labor has "induced it [the CFTC] to maintain a policy of independent action in order to survive and assisted it in gaining stature in the eyes of characteristically independent French workers."[68]

The United States never ceased its intervention in French labor affairs. Indeed, as late as 1985, Force Ouvrière was reported to have received a $500,000 grant from the "National Endowment for Democracy," a conservative organ of the Reagan administration; the French union immediately declared that the money had been transferred to Solidarity in Poland.[69] But the chaotic nature of American intervention, and the Embassy's admi-

---

[66] NARA, 851.062/12-1852, December 18, 1952.
[67] NARA, 851.062/8-1553, August 15, 1953.
[68] NARA, 851.062/6-153, June 1, 1953.
[69] *The New York Times*, December 5, 1985.

ration for the success of unions that resisted such interference, invite skeptical conclusions concerning what that intervention achieved. The futile efforts of the Americans to displace the leaderships of CFTC and FO are in themselves ample proof that those organizations were always authentic emanations of French working-class traditions, never creations or puppets of Washington. The pretension of the American unions to transfer organizing skills to the French was empty of content. The French had been organizing trade unions as long as the Americans; if they had less success at it, this reflected the different traditions of the working classes of the two countries. What the Americans did have, and used in great abundance, was money. The total amounts expended by the Americans in their efforts to buy influence in French labor, as well as in the press and politics, may remain forever hidden. But they also remain of limited importance.

II   HOLLYWOOD'S IMPERIALISM AND COCA-COLONIZATION

One of the more curious aspects of the postwar period is the enormous amount of acrimony expended by both Americans and French over ostensibly superficial questions. Films and Coca-Cola, two items that in the American experience often go hand in hand, are cases in point. (A third item in this American triptych, popcorn, seems never to have caught on in France.) At a time when basic essentials of food and coal were lacking, and the Americans were lending and then giving the French billions, both these nonessential items were pressed upon the French as exports for which they were expected to pay with their very scarce dollars. There is more here than frivolity, or the political clout of the companies in question, although both the Motion Picture Association (MPA) and the Coca-Cola Company carried an unusual amount of weight in Washington. Both items carried a symbolic importance as manifestations of the superiority of the American "way of life," which magnified their importance far beyond the few millions they were expected to earn. Fitting symbols of the consumer society, both were symbols of anticommunism as well. Hollywood played the role of the repentent sinner, purged itself of radicalism under the pressure of congressional committees in search of "anti-Americanism," and turned to safer, apolitical, often mindless forms of entertainment at the same time as it sought to recapture its prewar export markets. Coca-Cola was "the most American thing in America," a product marketed by mass advertising, symbolic of high consumption, and tributary to the success of free enterprise; for its president, James Farley, a politically powerful anticommunist, it contained the "essence of capitalism" in every bottle.[70]

---

[70]   Richard Kuisel, "Coca-Cola au pays des buveurs de vin," *L'Histoire*, 94 (1986): 22–8.

The importance attributed to nonessentials in a time of great scarcity does not, in itself, require explanation. Tobacco, for example, was purchased by the French from abroad during the dollar shortage, and later with Marshall Plan funds. By today's standards more noxious than either film or Coke, tobacco was in extreme demand in the postwar period; in Germany it served for a time as currency. In France the government monopoly refused to import American cigarettes, only to deprive itself of the tax revenues it would have gained had it sold them freely, since they were available on the black market. Worse, smugglers paid higher prices for cigarettes than they would have cost the government, and converted their earnings into dollars illegally, exacerbating the currency shortage. The Ministry of Finance estimated the treasury's losses at 60 billion francs yearly through this system, while the Communists made political use of the tobacco shortage to embarrass the government.[71] The ECA shared the French government's view of tobacco and increased its dollar allocations for imports in 1948 from $500,000 to $1,925,000.[72] Marshall planners aware that Southern congressmen wanted aid funds expended on tobacco to relieve the surpluses in their states, justified the use of aid monies for a nonessential item by arguing that it was needed to bolster European working-class morale. Neither Hollywood nor Coca-Cola profited directly from Marshall Plan funds as did the tobacco companies. But the demand for diversion was just as strong as the craving for tobacco; only the desire for the sweet beverage had to be created.

Hollywood placed great importance upon reconquering a film market where it had reigned supreme since the First World War.[73] Washington politicians sought to assist the filmmakers for several reasons. The "free flow of information" and the export by image of the American way of life were attributed immense importance in the worldwide struggle against Communism. Film clips were an important source of news; instructing the American embassy to intercede with the French in favor of Loews newsreels in 1946, Secretary of State Byrnes noted that "news releases are an important cog in the Department's information program."[74] The State Department also hoped to break down French protectionism and gain a foothold for American trade in the French market. Concessions with regard to films were taken as a gauge of French willingness to be part of the free system of international

---

[71] Archives Nationales (A.N.), F 60, 672–3, February 20, 1947 and March 3, 1947, Note à M. [Robert] Schuman, Ministre des Finances.

[72] Ministère des Affairs Etrangères (MAE), Y Internationale, 1944–9, vol. 230, July 6, 1948.

[73] For a historical overview, see Victoria De Grazia, "Mass Culture and Sovereignty: The American Challenge to European Cinemas, 1920–1960," *Journal of Modern History*, 61, no. 1 (March 1989): 53–87. Also Thomas Elsasser, "Two Decades in Another Country: Hollywood and the Cinephiles," in C. W. E. Bigsby, ed., *Superculture: American Popular Culture and Europe* (London: Paul Elek, 1975), pp. 199–216.

[74] NARA, 851.4061/MP 1-1846, January 18, 1946.

trade and payments, which the State Department believed to be the basis for peace and prosperity in the postwar era. Finally, all the major film producers had franc balances accrued since before the war to which French currency restrictions blocked access; the repatriation of some $11 million was an immediate goal for the MPA on behalf of its producer-members.

For all these reasons there were several pressure groups in Washington insisting that an acceptable film agreement be a precondition for a loan to France in the spring of 1946. Part of the legend of the Blum–Byrnes agreement with regard to film relates to the inadequacy of the screen-quota device as a means of protecting the French industry. But screen quotas were a French proposal, and the Americans fought against them, fearing quotas would reduce the share of the market Hollywood enjoyed before the war. Under the 1936 agreement, Hollywood had exported 188 films per year into France. Near parity in 1946 meant the Americans were entitled to 50 percent of the French market. Byrnes warned bluntly that the whole financial negotiation would be "handicapped" by the French insistence on quotas, but Caffery reported that Paris refused to budge.[75] The MPA condemned the screen quotas as "noxious," and only agreed to accept them if at most three weeks of every thirteen were reserved for French films. The French began by demanding six weeks of thirteen and quickly came down to five, but the Americans would go no further than four, and there the negotiations stalled, with Paris on warning that the loan in its entirety might be held up until Washington thought the issue had been settled satisfactorily. Four weeks in thirteen gave the French more than 25 percent of playing time time reserved for their own films, which had been their market share before the war.[76] On that basis the French conceded and the loan was concluded.

The Blum–Byrnes agreements did appear to lead to an immediate inundation of the French market by American films; some 340 American films were licensed for showing in the first half of 1947 as compared to 40 French ones. But the French public had been blocked from Hollywood's productions during the war years and few permits had been granted since the war's end. Audiences had been starved for Hollywood productions, always very popular in France. Moreover, French film production remained artisanal, and was unable to fill the screen space available; 250 films yearly were needed to satisfy demand, but at best French production was 124 films in any given year before 1940. After the war, with capital in short supply, between 80 and 100 films per year was the best French studios could do.[77] Not all the American films licensed by the French were actually shown, either, and while

---

[75] NARA, 851.4061/MP 9-1845, September 18, 1945; 9-2745, September 27, 1945; 10-2745, October 27, 1945; 11-1745, November 17, 1945.

[76] NARA, 851.4061/MP 4-2546, April 25, 1946; 4-2946, April 29, 1946; 5-1546, May 15, 1946.

[77] See the articles by A. Brisson, "La structure artisanale du cinéma français," *Le Monde*, December 19 and 20, 22, 1948.

Hollywood was open to the charge of palming off on the French market already amortized films of poor quality, French audiences responded by rejecting many of them. Thus American films averaged much shorter showing periods and were seen by correspondingly fewer spectators, an average of 1.1 million persons versus 1.9 million per French film.

Finally, the French did not implement the Blum–Byrnes agreements in the way the Americans expected, and began to violate them "before the ink was dry." The *Direction du Cinéma* restricted the number of films more than two years old which could be dubbed in France, and by law new films could not be dubbed anywhere else than in France. The *Direction* further restricted the showing of films in their original version to no more than fifteen theaters at any one time, and limited the number of films theaters could rent from a single distributor in any given six-month period. Since there were relatively few American companies with many films to distribute, this regulation hurt American distributors but not French ones. The dubbing rule further meant that all American films had to be recopied in France, where film stock was in short supply and allocated by the government. Not surprisingly, stock went by preference to French producers, a practice galling to the Americans since most of it was produced by a subsidiary of Kodak. The embassy repeatedly protested these practices but received only lengthy explanations, excuses, or partial concessions in reply.[78] The total effect was greatly to mitigate the impact of the Blum–Byrnes agreements on the French film industry. In fact, French producers preserved most of their market share in the immediate aftermath of Blum–Byrnes, and strengthened their positions when the agreements were repudiated in 1948.

The Blum–Byrnes agreement was so short-lived in any event that it is difficult to understand how the legend of its catastrophic impact on French film got started in the first place. Caffery noted early press criticism of the agreements and warned Hollywood producers against taking immoderate advantage of them. Some 148 American films were already circulating in France in the fall of 1946 without licenses, having entered under cover of the Office of War Information. The State Department was trying to regularize them, and "the repercussions," Caffery feared, "will harm our commercial interests in France." Opposition to Blum–Byrnes was growing and the Communist "elements" in the government had been strengthened. On January 2, 1947 the Paris representative of the MPA, Harold Smith, attacked the two-year dubbing rule as the equivalent of wartime "fascist-style" censorship under Vichy, terminology which Caffery thought very unfortunate

[78] NARA, 851.4061/MP 6-2046, June 20, 1946; 8-546, August 5, 1946; 1-247, January 2, 1947; 1-1147, January 11, 1947. As a measure of the importance of this subject to the State Department, it is perhaps worth noting that the decimal series 851.4061, Motion Pictures, contains almost as much documentation as the Financial Series itself, 851.51, in which most of the correspondance concerning the Blum–Byrnes loan is to be found.

and likely to inflame the atmosphere surrounding the agreements. The Americans and French further disagreed on the terms of the repatriation of the franc balances held by Hollywood; the American producers wanted the predevaluation rate of exchange, the French argued for the rate in effect at the time of transfer of the funds. Caffery advised the producers to give in on this question, for the unstable situation in France was such that de Gaulle might come to power with American support, in which case they would get nothing. The Hollywood producers agreed, and kept secret the fact that the State Department, as early as April 1947, considered de Gaulle's return a serious possibility, for fear this information would tend to destabilize the Ramadier government.[79]

In October 1947 the *Direction du Cinéma* once again imposed its rule against the dubbing of two-year-old films, and this time the State Department instructed Caffery not to protest. It was hardly appropriate to press Hollywood's interests at a time when the French were being forced to cut off their imports of wheat and coal pending the arrival of American interim aid. The French Finance Ministry called the embassy's attention to the severe plight of the French film studios. Production of films was down to twenty to twenty-five per annum, they said, and 80 percent of the technicians and 50 percent of the actors were unemployed. These figures, however exaggerated they may have appeared to the Americans, reflected the French perception of the problem, for which the Blum–Byrnes agreements were held to be responsible. It was true that American films were cheaper to rent, and preferred by theaters whatever their quality or popularity for the increased profits they brought. But French investment in film also dried up just as the American avalanche appeared. France produced as many films in 1946 as in 1938; the downturn came in 1947–48 after Blum–Byrnes.[80] Whether the relationship was causal or accidental, the Communists made political propaganda of the issue and formed a Committee for the Defense of French Cinema that attracted many non-Communists. Communist film critic Georges Sadoul blasted the Blum–Byrnes agreements repeatedly, claiming that the French share was down to 31 percent of the total market. The Americans had dumped in excess of 300 films on French theaters, and American companies were taking away over 50 percent of the remittances collected. The Council of the Republic, sensitive both to the plight of the film industry and Communist propaganda, finally called upon the government to renegotiate the Blum–Byrnes agreement. Sensing the impending retribution to its own interests, the MPA negotiated a voluntary quota with the Direction du Cinéma, agreeing to limit its export of films to France to 145 per year.[81]

[79] NARA, 851.4061/MP 6-1846, June 18, 1946; 11-1446, November 14, 1946, 1-247, January 2, 1947, 4-1547; April 15, 1947.
[80] A.N., Papiers Georges Bidault, 457 AP80 (2), February 6 and 19, 1948.
[81] NARA, 851.4061/MP 10-847, October 8, 1947; 11-1747, November 17, 1947; 11-

This agreement came too late. Responding to outcries in the National Assembly, on February 14, 1948 Bidault formally requested Washington to renegotiate the Blum–Byrnes agreements. Half the French studios were idle, Bidault noted, and the public failed to understand the necessity for the import of films when so many essential products were lacking in France. If this were true one suspects not so many French would have gone to the movies in the first place, but Caffery was furious in any case. The French had not rescinded the two-year dubbing rule, the fifteen-theater limitation on original version films, or the rationing of film stock. Now they wanted to renegotiate an agreement they had never observed. The French submitted a report on the effects of Blum–Byrnes in support of their request for renegotiation; the Americans found it belied the French claims. According to the statistics presented, French films had occupied 45 percent of total available screen time in 1947, far in excess of the 31 percent guaranteed by Blum–Byrnes. The French complaints had nothing to do with objective conditions in the industry, but now reflected a political-psychological situation "created by Communist propaganda against American films which has gained support from non-Communists who consider that American films are threatening French films as an art form and expression of French genius."[82] The government was caving in to the Communists, feeling that the Americans would not insist.

Caffery argued against concessions. The French should be made to live up to the agreement before the United States consented to renegotiate it. Ironically, the French now wanted a limit on the total number of films imported in addition to a change in the screen quota. According to the General Agreement on Tariffs and Trade, negotiated the year before, only the screen quota was an acceptable form of protection for the cinema. Limitations on the number of films, for which the Americans had previously argued, were now unacceptable. The negotiating positions of the two countries had been reversed.

But Marshall saw the futility of forcing the film question in view of the severe French dollar shortage and the inflamed political atmosphere in Paris. On April 1948 he ordered concessions to the French point of view. To make matters worse, Caffery could not even announce American agreement to renegotiate Blum–Byrnes, because Bidault, before the National Assembly, had implied negotiations were already under way. For the United States to announce agreement to negotiate would make the foreign minister appear to be a liar. When negotiations did open, the French position hardened further; not only were there no French concessions on operating regulations, but the National Assembly passed a film production and ticket revenue tax,

2947, November 29, 1947; 12-2447, December 24, 1947; 1-2048, January 20, 1948; 12-1847, December 18, 1947.
[82] NARA, 851.4061/MP 2-1448, February 14, 1948; 2-1848, February 18, 1948; 4-948, April 9, 1948.

the proceeds of which were to go toward subsidies for the modernization of the French film industry. This was clearly discriminatory: American films were to be taxed in order to provide subsidies for French companies. Caffery protested, and the angry MPA threatened to withdraw from the French market. But the French would not be moved. The Assembly cleverly left the amount of the tax to the discretion of the government, which would clearly set the rate depending on the satisfaction the French obtained in the negotiations. But Caffery had sadly to inform the MPA that there was nothing to be done.

> The French apparently feel that the internal importance of the film problem would justify any unfavorable international consequences which might result from unilateral action. The question is psychological and political. ... By placing major blame for the present conditions of the French filmmaking industry on the Blum–Byrnes understanding the government escapes its responsibility for its lack of action in this field during the period since the Liberation.

The settlement to which both the State Department and the MPA agreed was virtually dictated by the French. The Blum–Byrnes agreements were declared to have been terminated. The screen quota was raised to five weeks minimum required screen time in each thirteen-week period for French films. The MPA accepted a numerical limit on its exports to France of 121 films per year. The French would remove neither their limitation on the dubbing of older films nor the restriction of original version films to fifteen theaters. And a tax on film production was set at 400 francs per meter of film, payable at the time of a film's appearance.[83]

Ironically, all this negotiation probably had minimal influence on the development of the French film industry, which responded rather to structural conditions created by the two world wars and less tangible issues of individual creativity and genius than to protectionist measures. French film advocates bitterly protested, for example, their virtual exclusion from the American film market during this period. But there were no formal restrictions against French films in the United States, only a surfeit of popular Hollywood productions, and in any case Italian films were popular in America, while the Italian industry, which suffered from some of the same structural problems as the French, was not in crisis. Henry Magnan reported French film production in the post Blum–Byrnes years as follows: 84 in 1947–8, 92 in 1948–9, 106 in 1949–50, and 105 in 1950–1.[84] One would expect capital for investment in films to be scarce in this period, and the Monnet Plan did not provide for the cinema any more than it did for housing. French films retained a more-or-less constant share of the domestic market, about 25 percent, through the 1950s, as compared to an American share of roughly

---

[83] NARA, 851.4061/MP 4-2048, April 20, 1948; 5-2648, May 26, 1948; 7-848, July 8, 1948; 8-348, August 3, 1948.
[84] *Le Monde*, July 14, 1951.

50 percent. The French market share fell drastically in 1947 but then leveled off. The Catholic *Repertoire Générale des Films* gave the following statistics:

	American		French	
1944–7	188	40%	211	45%
1947–50	265	50%	133	25%
1951–2	333	52%	165	26%
1952–3	180	46%	106	27%

The decline in French market share reflected the disappearance of the monopoly of French production from the Vichy period, and it was not fully accounted for by the rise in American imports. British, Italian, Russian, and other foreign films also penetrated the French market once again with the war's end.

It is perhaps of greater interest anyway to inquire about the general impact this inundation of American films had on French audiences. The anti-American press of the time leaves no doubt on this issue: Frenchmen were being corrupted by American tales of gangsterism and eroticism, "poison darts that corrupt the minds of French youth," perverse images of so-called Western civilization.[85] But the Catholic church took a rather different view. Applying its censorship guide to 637 recent films, French and foreign, available to French viewers by 1951–2, it came up with the following percentages of production in each category:

Rating category	American	French
3 (suitable for all)	70%	7%
3B (inadvisable for children)	63%	16%
4 (adults only)	56%	20%
4A (adults with reservation)	44%	30%
4B (inadvisable)	40%	43%
5 (to be prohibited)	—	95%

Of 31 films deemed suitable for children, Hollywood produced 22, France only 2. Of 22 films rated in category 5, France produced 21. The same percentages prevailed earlier and later: In 1951–2, France produced 14% of the films in category 3, the United States 72%, while in category 4B France produced 53% and Hollywood only 24%. In 1952–3 the United States produced 38 films suitable for children, France 8, while France produced 23 films judged "inadvisable," Hollywood 8. Judging French produc-

---

[85] *L'Humanité*, January 3, March 19, April 20, 1948.

tion as a whole in that year Catholic censors found that the French produced "34% of unhealthy films for 44% good films and 22% of films that
require reservations"[86] Catholic censors had only the warmest praise for
the majority of Hollywood's productions. And while one does not normally
accuse the Catholic church and the Communist party of holding similar
values, it is clear from Communist rhetoric that in the matter of film criticism they were not that far apart. Communist complaints about the perni-
cious effect of films were directed at the wrong target.

Looking at American production another way one finds that serious dra-
mas, which constituted the major part of French film production, accounted
for only between 16% and 24% of American exports to France during these
years. On the other hand westerns were 11–12%, comedies 20–34%, mu-
sicals 6–8%, police films 10–11% and war-adventure films 21–30%. French
and American films appealed to different audiences. Reeling from the blows
of political persecution Hollywood emphasized mindless entertainment and
meaningless fantasies. French producers in contrast willingly abandoned
children's audiences to the Americans, helping to condition future genera-
tions to a diet of American production, and ensuring that France would
remain, as it perhaps has always been, fascinated with American cinema.
On the other hand Hollywood's absurd fantasies, which were honed during
the grim and bitter Depression years as a much needed escape mechanism,
were equally popular in the grim circumstances of postwar France. The impact of film in the Depression era was brilliantly portrayed in Woody Allen's
The Purple Rose of Cairo, which amused French audiences as it did American ones in the 1980s, evoking for both Hollywood's mastery of the escape
mechanism amid deprivation, misery, and want.

Could the French be made to drink Coca-Cola as they watched Hollywood's productions? A note of the Ministry of Finance, August 29, 1949
observed that French fruit juice, mineral water vendors, and wineries "are
actively aroused by the introduction into France of an American drink, Coca-
Cola, which will be supported by a massive advertising effort 'à l'américaine,' of a cost and volume such that no French producer has the possibility
of following the American corporation on this level." This "colonization"
of the French market, supported by enormous financial resources, would
weigh heavily on a beverage market that could not easily be expanded, resulting in the conquest, "to the exclusive profit of Coca-Cola, of a certain
perimeter of the metropolitan territory." Advertising benefited no one but
created demand for a nonessential and harmful product, a new source of
expense certain to weigh most heavily on the tightly squeezed budgets of
the poor. A mysterious ingredient in the drink was thought to be habit-
forming. And the biggest stockholder in the company was James Farley, one
of the most powerful politicians in Washington, giving a supplementary

---

[86] *Repertoire Générale des Films,* 1944–7, 1950–1, 1951–2, 1952–3.

argument "to those who claim that the United States expects to take advantage of the aid it brings to colonize our country." And whatever the immediate material benefits of foreign investment, the impact over the long run would be a drain on French dollar holdings as the American company repatriated its profits.[87]

To a certain number of the French, Coca-Cola became a symbol of American imperialism, "Coca-colonization," but to Washington it remained indicative of something quite different. The Marshall Plan contained a provision for the ECA to guarantee the return on capital to American investors daring enough to invest in Europe, for in the postwar years few were willing to do so. The French market was particularly awesome. Currency restrictions, political instability, the threat of communism, the postwar nationalizations, the grinding postwar poverty and want, laws requiring a majority French participation in capitalist concerns partially owned abroad, all these functioned as powerful deterrents to American investment. Moreover, France and the United States did not have a treaty of commerce; business relations were governed by a consular convention dating from 1853, and while at American insistence negotiations for a commercial treaty had begun after the war, nothing had been signed by 1949. The Americans insisted on a nondiscrimination clause with regard to American capital, a provision the French were not willing to accept immediately. From the Liberation through 1949 a paltry 10 billion francs were invested in France by Americans, most of it in companies that had been there before the war. Thus $5 billion had gone into oil refineries and $3 billion into radioelectricity; for the rest France loomed as virgin territory for American investors.[88] The French government authorized the repatriation of returns on foreign investments in France after August 31, 1949; the Coca-Cola Company was one of the first American concerns to appear on the scene to take advantage of this provision. Washington wanted the company's way smoothed, not to give the French tooth decay, but in the hope that other sources of private investment for French economic growth would follow.[89]

Coca-Cola wanted to enter France as a bridgehead to Europe; it would do all bottling and distribution with French materials and labor, importing nothing but the concentrate itself. According to *Le Monde*, colored maps on the walls of Coca-Cola company headquarters outlined a strategic plan for the spread of the beverage, which Europeans were to be taught to consume in volumes analogous to the enormous quantities ingested by Americans. The Pernod company and Glacières de Paris agreed to distribute the product in Marseille and Paris. Coke had been known in France since before

[87] A.N., Papiers René Mayer 363 AP 12, August 29, 1949.

[88] See Gilles Bertin, *L'Investissement des firmes étrangères en France (1945–1962)* (Paris: Presses Universitaires de France, 1963).

[89] *Le Monde*, September 22 and 24, 1949, ran a two-part series on foreign investment in France.

the war, and it had made great inroads in North Africa, where Muslims took to it freely as a preferred alternative to wines preferred by the French colons – alcohol being proscribed by the religion of Islam. In the face of resistance the company did not hesitate to mobilize the American diplomatic corps. Ambassador David Bruce brought the company's ambitions to the attention of Finance Minister Maurice Petsche and Premier Georges Bidault in December 1949. In the spring of 1950, the French were forced to consider the matter on the level of the cabinet, which decided that the company should be allowed to market its product in France without restrictions.[90]

Coca-Cola rapidly became a major public issue, on a scale nobody could have anticipated. Not only the French beverage companies, but health groups denounced the caffeine content of the drink and warned against addiction; puritans objected to the symbol of the relaxed, leisure-oriented, American life-style; civil libertarians denounced its advertising techniques as similar to totalitarian propaganda. The Communist party accused the company of establishing its tenticular routes for the purpose of facilitating espionage on behalf of American intelligence services – had not the company hired Kenneth Pendar, assistant to Robert Murphy in North Africa during the Vichy period and admitted [former] intelligence agent, as head of its North African operations?

On February 28, 1950 the issue reached the National Assembly:

Communist Deputy: Mr. Minister, on the grand boulevards of Paris, they are selling a drink called Coca-Cola.

Minister of Health: I know it.

Deputy: What is serious is that you know it and yet you do nothing.

Minister: I have no legislative authorization to act.

Deputy: This question is not simply an economic question, or even a question of health. It is also a political question. One must know whether, for political reasons, you are going to permit French men and women to be poisoned.[91]

The French were not permitted to be poisoned. The National Assembly passed a bill authorizing the Ministry of Health to ban any vegetable-based drink it found injurious to public health. Leaving the issue to the government was a way for the assembly to act without doing anything. But the legislation alarmed the American National Trade Council, which pressured the State Department and threatened retaliation against the import of French wines and champagnes. The State Department promised that any real French government action would result in vigorous protests under GATT, but in the meantime, as in the case of film, the inflamed political atmosphere in Paris, where every economic question appeared to be capable of becoming "psy-

90 *Le Monde*, December 30, 1949.
91 Cited by Kuisel, in "Coca-Cola aux pays des buveurs de vin."

chological and political," dictated a more cautious approach. Bruce advised the President of Coca-Cola Export Company, James Curtis, to accept the limit on exports proposed by the French and refrain from protests.[92] Curtis complied.

But the matter was not allowed to rest there. In March 1950 French fruit juice producers sued to ban the drink on the ground that it violated a 1905 law requiring pharmaceutical products to list all their ingredients on their labels. A study in support of the suit by a journal with the unlikely name of *Revue des Fraudes* attacked Coca-Cola as inherently fraudulent: Its secret ingredient, "7x," either contained cocaine and was illegal, or did not, making the company guilty of false advertising. The courts ordered Coke subjected to laboratory analysis, the first of several such investigations, while the efforts of the company to bring its product in from Morocco were frustrated as well. The tariff benefits of the French Union did not apply to Coca-Cola. Bruce protested to the Quai d'Orsay, and James Farley could not be restrained; condemning the National Assembly action, he noted with pride the company had made its drink available to the troops in Europe during the war, and "Coca-Cola never harmed the health of American soldiers who liberated France from the Nazis, thus permitting the Communist Deputies to sit in the National Assembly."[93]

But not only Communists disliked the beverage and what it implied. *Témoignage Chrétien* condemned it as "the avant garde of an offensive of economic colonization against which we feel the duty to struggle here." And not everyone in America thought the company's French fortunes should be the object of State Department concern. Congressman Wilbur Mills, acting on behalf of a soft drink company in his district, challenged the recycling of Marshall Plan funds into profits for Coca-Cola. The State Department denied the charge, but clearly it was no more justifiable to breech protection of the dollar shortage for film than for Coke. The American *Catholic Transcript*, following its sister French publication, charged that Coca-Cola's plans constituted "a vast economic invasion [of France] in contradiction to the spirit of the Marshall Plan." Would not a France covered by Coke billboards be a constant reminder of Communist propaganda against trusts, corporations, and the "bulldozer promotion of American economic imperialism?"[94]

The issue died down in the press but dragged on in the courts. On December 5, 1950 Bruce again called at the Quai d'Orsay, which complained to

[92] NARA, 851.316/3-750, March 7, 1950.
[93] *Revue des Fraudes* (1949), in A.N., Papiers René Mayer, 363 AP 12, Memo from Minister of Justice to Minister of Agriculture, September 4, 1950. NARA, 851.316/3-1350, March 13, 1950, 3-1550; March 15, 1950. *Le Monde*, March 3, 1950.
[94] The *Témoignage Chrétien* article is cited by Richard Kuisel, "Coca-Cola aux pays des buveurs de vin." NARA, 851.316/5-950, May 9, 1950, has the Mills correspondance and a clipping of *The Catholic Transcript*, March 30, 1950.

the Ministry of Justice; this was not the first American protest, and the embassy in Washington had been subjected to pressure from press and public opinion in the United States "which threatens to compromise certain of our exports and could even have a harmful influence on the allocation of Marshall Plan credits." The Quai demanded a report for Ambassador Bruce, while a note to the Coca-Cola Company stated that expert analysis seemed likely to conclude that allegations of falsification or toxicity brought against the beverage were groundless. Separate analyses were going on in France and Algeria, however, and when Minister of Justice Mayer ordered them consolidated he was told it was impossible because there were different concentrations of phosphoric acid in the Algerian and French examples. Either the drink was diluted with more sugar and water in Algeria, or there were two concentrates being imported. Not to be outdone, the Coca-Cola Company sued, charging theft by persons unknown of its concentrate, which it had refused to release for independent laboratory analysis.[95]

Farley continued to pressure the State Department, which continued to pressure the Foreign Ministry. In December 1952 a lower court found no basis for prosecution of the company, but a higher court ordered a new investigation of the drink, appointing a panel of three medical experts to subject it to analysis once again. One of the experts worked for the Perrier Company and another was a member of the Communist-controlled Peace Movement. Nevertheless, the legal obstacles to Coke were eventually cleared in France. The lawsuits were dropped, and the ban authorized by the National Assembly was never invoked by the government. By 1953 enough of the French were familiar with the beverage to have an opinion about it; according to Professor Kuisel 17 percent liked it while 61 percent did not. One suspects these figures would be inverted today, although the French consume less of it per capita than do other Europeans.[96]

The Coca-Cola question went beyond taste, economics, or politics, to the heart of the growing American–French symbiosis. America was to become the source of military protection, the overriding concern in foreign policy, the source of popular culture, the symbol of economic modernization. These were realities of the postwar world, inevitable consequences of the war about which one could do very little. But America also aspired to be the shaper of French internal economic development and the arbiter of French internal politics as well. Nations, inevitably, influence each other by virtue of sharing the same planet. But there were always traditionally understood limits to be observed, and these were violated in the conditions of the postwar era. It was the sense of having passed beyond the proper norms of international relations that made the French so acutely sensitive to a range of things that

[95] A.N. 363 AP 12, Papiers René Mayer, December 5, 1950, March 22 and 24, 1951.
[96] NARA, 851.316/1-2152, January 21, 1952; 12-1852, December 18, 1952. Kuisel, "Coca-cola aux pays des buveurs de vin."

otherwise might have gone unperceived. Coke and films were symbols of something much deeper, a penetration of America into the national psyche, an awakening to the new reality of French weakness and America power, and a resentment against the brutal ways in which the United States often appeared to want to use its power. Perhaps it was also because France was so much less Americanized in those years that it had that much greater a complex about becoming so. It was to become easier to accept American cultural and consumer influences when the national power had been restored and the independence of the nation no longer seemed in question. From 1945 to 1954 this was not yet the case.

5

Building an alliance

I NATO, ANTICOMMUNISM, AND FRENCH STABILITY

AMERICAN-FRENCH RELATIONS from 1948 through 1950 involved three distinct aspects: a conventional diplomatic relationship, an American role in directing and planning the growth of the French economy, and activity by U.S. government and private agencies on the internal French political scene. All of these were integrally related. From the diplomatic standpoint, the major development was the construction of the North Atlantic Alliance. The traditional historiographical view of NATO interpreted it as a response to a perceived military threat to the West by superior Soviet forces. Revisionist historians took the opposite tack, stressing an alleged American offensive designed at once to consolidate Washington's sphere of influence in the west and pursue an aggressive policy designed to loosen the Soviet grip on its area of hegemony in the East. Gabriel Kolko argues that NATO responded at once to an economic recession in the United States and Europe, which necessitated a military buildup to alleviate the pressure, and an American desire to stabilize its European allies while the ECA forced them to adopt conservative and deflationary economic policies that restricted consumption. Having discovered that the United States did not perceive a real danger of Soviet military aggression during the construction of the alliance, historians have cast about for other American motives. Melvyn Leffler stresses a general postwar Pentagon strategic plan to keep any unfriendly power from dominating the Eurasian land mass, and the desire to bolster the internal politics of the nations of Europe against internal subversion. Thomas Paterson says NATO was established to give the Europeans a "psychological boost" or "will to resist." Timothy Ireland places NATO in the context of the Marshall Plan; it was designed to reestablish the European balance of power by rebuilding Germany as its economic and strategic center and inducing France to accept German recon-struction.[1]

But whatever Washington's motives, the diplomatic record reveals a re-luctance on the part of the Americans to part with a centuries old policy of hostility to alliances with the old world, and a determined effort by the Europeans, spearheaded by the British and French, to involve the United States militarily in Europe on a permanent basis.[2] The American Congress and public opinion were historically opposed to involvement in Europe. The Europeans concentrated their efforts on the U.S. State Department, which finally rallied to the support of a North Atlantic Treaty and carried it through Congress while winning over public opinion. American and French views on the alliance differed seriously, and the result diverged from what each had envisaged. But the building of an Atlantic alliance was nevertheless a fundamental French foreign policy objective. Two important French consid-erations were met in the treaty as it took shape in 1949. The common de-fense strategy provided for a military effort to stop the Russians as far to the east as possible, in Germany. The United States abandoned the "periph-eral strategy," which would have established the defense line at the Pyrenees and English Channel. And the treaty was supplemented by a Military Assis-tance Act; Congress authorized a major effort to rearm America's European allies. France became the principal recipient of American military assistance, which made the signing of the Atlantic Pact a major success for French diplomacy.

The North Atlantic Treaty was meant by the Americans and the French to be a barrier to internal Communist subversion as well as a response to Russian military aggression. It supplemented a political and economic effort by Washington to stabilize the European polity and society. The Marshall Plan, separately administered by the ECA, gave the Americans an unprece-dented degree of leverage with which to influence internal French and Eu-

---

[1]   Joyce and Gabriel Kolko, *The Limits of Power: The World and United States Foreign Policy 1945–54* (New York: Harper & Row, 1972), pp. 455–6; Melvyn P. Leffler, "The American Conception of National Security and the Beginnings of the Cold War, 1945–48," *American Historical Review*, 89, no. 2 (April 1984): 346–81; Thomas Paterson, *Meeting the Communist Threat: Truman to Reagan* (New York: Oxford University Press, 1988), p. 47; Timothy P. Ireland, *Creating the Entangling Alliance: The Origins of NATO* (Westport, CT: Greenwood Press, 1981).

[2]   See Lawrence Kaplan, *The United States and NATO: The Formative Years* (Lexing-ton: University Press of Kentucky, 1984). Kaplan sees Bevin and Bidault manipulating the New World on behalf of the old. Also Escott Reid, *Time of Fear and Hope: The Making of the North Atlantic Treaty, 1947–49* (Toronto: McClelland and Stewart, 1987), and Alfred Grosser, *The Western Alliance: European–American Relations since 1945* (New York: Continuum, 1980). The revisionists' emphasis on the American role in the creation of the alliance seems to me misplaced. Kolko appears simply wrong; the recession hit the United States in 1949, as the NATO negotiations were being concluded, and the ECA, at least in France, was trying to encourage expenditures on consumer goods and housing.

ropean economic development. It will bear separate analysis in the next chapter. In the sphere of French internal politics, the Americans were active in two critical ways among others. The Embassy tried to stabilize the French government by pressuring opposition politicians not to vote against it and admonishing members of the cabinet not to desert the coalition and bring it down. The Embassy conducted continued, direct relations and exchanges of views with influential members and leaders of all the major non-Communist French political parties, including the Reassemblement du Peuple Français (RPF) of General de Gaulle. Second, the United States embarked on a major effort to turn French public opinion away from its apparent infatuation with communism. Washington's internal anti-Communist offensive in France involved both overt and covert aspects, the former the sphere of the State Department, the latter of the CIA. Apart from the continuing effort to influence French workers to abandon the CGT in favor of non-Communist trade unions, the United States covertly sponsored two major anti-Communist extravaganzas during this period aimed principally at French public opinion, the non-Communist "Peace Movement" headed by the Radical Deputy Jean-Paul David, and the Kravchenko affair.

Coordinating the multifaceted American policy was not easy; often the major goals came into conflict. The emphasis on political stability, for example, often militated against placing too much pressure on the French government diplomatically, lest the cabinet fall. The French could find strength in external affairs flowing from their internal weakness. This was evident during the devaluation of the franc of January 1948. Washington desired a French devaluation to increase the purchasing power of its aid dollars and force the French to develop their exports and tourism so as to earn, rather than simply receive, their dollars. But the French did not adopt a simple devaluation as the Americans and British wished. Paris created a two-tiered system for the franc: a free market for dollars and gold internally, but a higher rate for international exchange, which pleased neither the British nor the International Monetary Fund (IMF). Paris, aware of international opposition to its policies, requested Washington to instruct American representatives on the Fund to support the French measures, and to pressure the British to accept them. Schuman wrote Secretary of the Treasury Snyder that the complex devaluation was part of a French fiscal effort "without parallel in the nation's history," while René Mayer cleverly stressed the American official's role in the origins of the French stabilization program.[3]

Angered by the French move, the British Labour government appealed to

---

[3] Archives Nationales (A.N.), Papiers Georges Bidault, 457 AP 21, January 18 and 19, 1948. Papiers René Mayer, 363 AP 7, January 18, 1948. Mayer wrote: "I have decided in this difficult moment to appeal to you directly, Dear Mr. Secretary, since you have been familiar with our program since the moment it was conceived, to ask you urgently to give directives to American representatives on the International Monetary Fund favorable to our plan."

Léon Blum to combat the devaluation in the name of international Socialist solidarity. The Socialist leader was not loathe to do this, since he regarded the Schuman–Mayer deflation plan as calling for a disproportionate level of sacrifice from the working class. But the State Department feared that a negative decision by the IMF on the French devaluation would bring a revival of nationalism and be used by the political opposition against the Third Force. The French people would lose faith in the prospect of European economic cooperation and the ERP. Should Schuman fall the result would be catastrophic: internal turmoil, inflation, a probable succession by de Gaulle, failure of ERP, dictatorship, revived strength of Communism, and the possibility of civil war. Marshall therefore reacted with caution to the devaluation, while at the American Embassy in Paris Caffery lectured Blum on the necessity of support for Schuman. It was "incomprehensible," the ambassador said, that Blum would put Socialist doctrine above the survival of the Third Force and thus play into the hands of both de Gaulle and Communism. Blum affected "pained surprise," at Caffery's intervention. He complained that the Mayer plan was unfair to the workers and the devaluation violated international socialist solidarity. Moreover, the Socialists could not accept a free market in gold. Caffery retorted angrily: Did not Blum realize that the fall of Schuman would lead to the coming of de Gaulle, which could mean a dictatorship and the elimination of the Socialist party itself? Blum, according to Caffery's report, reluctantly agreed, and acted to avert the crisis; the Socialists accepted the Mayer Plan. Marshall cabled Caffery his appreciation: "Do not hesitate [to] approach Blum again or other leaders whose parties show signs of bolting whenever you feel this action would be salutary."[4] Schuman survived, and so did the two-tiered devaluation.

The paternity of the NATO alliance probably belongs to Ernest Bevin, who, following the failure of the London Conference of Foreign Ministers in December 1947, first proposed to Marshall a military alliance between the United States and Western Europe to contain Soviet aggression. Marshall was initially noncommittal, and told Bevin that the initiative was premature. The ERP was not yet voted, and Congress was not ready for an alliance. The Europeans had best go ahead by themselves, and then propose to Washington how it might be of assistance.[5] The same tactic had worked well in the origins of the ERP: Washington preferred that the initiative come from the Europeans. Bevin issued his appeal for a West European Union in January 1948, which brought France, Belgium, the Netherlands, Luxem-

---

[4] National Archives and Records Administration (NARA), 851.00/1-2348, January 23, 1948; A.N., Papiers Georges Bidault, 457 AP 21, January 28, 1948. Foreign Relations of the United States (FRUS), 1948, III, Western Europe, January 29, 1948, 614–8.

[5] Reid, *Time of Fear and Hope;* John W. Young, *Britain, France and the Unity of Europe, 1945–1951* (Leicester: Leicester University Press, 1984).

burg, and Great Britain together in a military pact signed in Brussels on March 18.

But since 1947 the French had been pressing Washington for an alliance on their own. In October 1947 General Revers, who was appreciated by the Americans for his anticommunism, told the American military attaché, General Tate, that France could supply up to one million men and between twenty and forty divisions for the defense of the West if given the necessary arms. The American response was standoffish, and the CIA recommended against an invitation to Revers to visit America. But the Pentagon decided to send General Bull on a mission of inquiry to France, not for conversation, but to listen and learn. In the interim American military intelligence digested the lesson of the successful French mobilization against the October–November strikes. The French army had mobilized in good order and would fire on Communist workers if ordered to do so. Clearly, a strong, democratic, and independent France was very much in the American interest. If France fell, not only would Europe go with it, but much of the French colonial empire might follow as well. The United States should consequently support France economically, combat Communist propaganda there, and equip French forces, now of proven loyalty and competence, to enable them to oppose the threat of internal Communist subversion. Moreover, should a Communist government come to power illegally in France, the United States must be prepared to recognize and support a legal democratic government in opposition to it, and commit American forces to the defense of a non-Communist government if so requested.[6]

American plans involved three possible scenarios for a European war: "Broiler" was the code name for war in 1949 or earlier, in which case it was not anticipated that Western Europe could be successfully defended. Nor could the Russians be stopped in the case of "Bushwhacker," the term used to denote war occurring after June 30, 1949. But both these possibilities were thought unlikely owing to the American nuclear monopoly. The NATO alliance was not born due to the fear of immediate war.[7] It was the third case, "Charioteer," meaning war in 1955 or 1956, that most concerned the American military. In this event, a powerful France would be expected to help resist the Soviet onslaught and protect the essential basing areas in North Africa for supply of the continent. It was worth the effort to strengthen France as much as possible, perhaps even in time for "Bushwhacker" in 1949. France began to loom in the American mind as the key to Western Europe and the center of its defense. The military leaders thought the present French government the strongest France had enjoyed since the

6 NARA, Military Branch, Plans and Operations, 091, France, Box 12, 1946–8, October 21 and 27, 1947; December 31, 1947, Intelligence Digest, France.
7 Reid, *Time of Fear and Hope*, pp. 16–18.

war. Unlike the State Department, they did not fear de Gaulle, whom they regarded as "the strongest anti-Communist force in France, today or in the future."[8] For these reasons they advocated the equipping of France as soon as practicable with material to support an army of one million men.

Bidault and Teitgen met with Douglas MacArthur III and General Bull on January 29, 1948, and told the Americans of the fear and "psychosis" existing in France over the belief that the United States did not plan to defend Europe in case of Soviet aggression but would rather establish a defensive perimeter at the Pyrenees and England. Bidault and Teitgen asked the Americans to prepare to fight farther to the east, in Germany, even in the event of immediate Russian aggression. France had rejected Communism and made its "final choice" to join the United States against Russia, Teitgen said. The government was now stable; it had mobilized 290,000 men during the insurrectionary strikes with perfect order and discipline. The Communists counted on two things, Teitgen warned, misery and fear. The Marshall Plan had dealt with the first; a corresponding military alliance was necessary to eliminate the second. The United States needed Europe, the French ministers said, or it would find itself left with "only Asiatics and African and colonial natives" to defend when the Russian steamroller descended upon the continent. Teitgen wanted immediate staff conversations with the Americans and equipment sufficient to put forty French divisions in the field.[9]

French Ambassador Henri Bonnet was well informed on American planning. On April 8, 1948 he reported that the "highest military authorities" did not believe that the Russian army could be stopped short of the Pyrenees in the event of war. The United States, in response to an invasion, would attack the vital centers of Russia directly, while planning to reconquer the continent as in the last war. Hence, the Americans were placing great importance on the acquisition of bases in North Africa such as Port Lyautey and Casablanca. Bonnet thought this order of planning frightening: France was to be left to languish under Soviet military occupation, and the Americans did not see how Europe could be defended without a military contribution from the Germans: "It is possible that, given this kind of thinking, we will one day have to oppose a project that can only aggravate an already dangerous situation, the rearmament of Germany."[10] The seeds of future tension and conflict were thus present even as the Atlantic alliance was first being constructed.

The Brussels treaty had as a major purpose drawing Washington into an alliance in Europe. Its military planning was premised upon the arrival of

[8] NARA, Military Branch, Plans and Operations, 091, France, Intelligence Digest, December 31, 1947.
[9] Foreign Relations of the United States (FRUS), 1948, III, Western Europe, January 29, 1948, pp. 617–22.
[10] A.N., Papiers Georges Bidault, 457 AP 24, April 8, 1948. See also Kaplan, *United States and NATO*, p. 4.

American assistance from the onset of hostilities. The pact was designed as a first step "on the way toward a tight association with the government in Washington, with a view to organizing, with its cooperation, the defense of Western Europe, and to obtain immediate support in that effort."[11] The French ambassador to London, René Massigli, noted American "tutelage" in the negotiation of the pact, when its emphasis shifted from Germany to the Soviet Union as the potential aggressor.[12] Belgian Foreign Minister Paul Henri Spaak noted Bidault's acceptance of the Russian danger, and thanked Washington, assuming that American influence was responsible.[13] But Bidault had told Marshall earlier that his continued demonstration of concern for security against Germany was purely for domestic political reasons. By now everyone knew who was the real enemy.

If there was any doubt, it was eliminated by the Czech coup d'état of February 1948. This event more than any other touched off panic in Paris. Bidault's message to Secretary Marshall of March 4, 1948 eloquently expressed this anxiety and deserves stature as a landmark of the cold war, as surely as Churchill's "Iron Curtain" speech and the Truman Doctrine. Bidault dramatically noted the descent of the iron curtain over Hungary, Bulgaria, Rumania, Poland, and now Czechoslovakia. An entire "intermediate, autonomous zone of Europe" had disappeared in the last year, and the Soviet *gleichschaltung* (coordination, a term used by the Nazis) now threatened Vienna, Rome, and Berlin, all in countries where "internal [subversive] action can at any moment be supported by action from outside."[14] The French government wanted to construct the last bulwark of freedom against this onslaught but was unequal to the task "which destiny confers upon it." Personally appealing to Marshall to consider the seriousness of the danger, Bidault insisted that the European Recovery Program must at once be supplemented by a military alliance. Staff discussions must begin at once between France, England, and the United States. The attempt by the French to become part of a kind of "directorate" of the West, made up of these three powers, became a leitmotif of the postwar period which continued through the return to power of de Gaulle in 1958.

Bidault had the MAE's full support in his quest for an American alliance. Jean Chauvel thought the Soviets had carried off the Czech coup in preparation for launching a European war. "Under these conditions it is clear that the measures foreseen by the Marshall Plan are radically insufficient to

---

11 A.N., Papiers Georges Bidault, 457 AP 25, Pacte de Bruxelles, Négociations de Washington, Pact de l'Atlantique, internal analysis dated September 4, 1948. Kaplan quotes Jean Chauvel as stating that the purpose was to obtain American assistance: *United States and NATO*, p. 62.

12 René Massigli, *Une comédie des erreurs: Souvenirs et réflexions sur une étape de la construction européene* (Paris: Plon, 1978), p. 134.

13 FRUS, 1948, III, Europe, March 4, 1948, p. 38.

14 A.N., Papiers Georges Bidault, 457 AP 25, March 4, 1948.

deal with the situation." Building European wealth only tempted Moscow further by making the West a more attractive prize. The emphasis of the Marshall Plan needed to be reversed; military defense should be put ahead of economic recovery to compensate for a Russian military superiority that Chauvel calculated at 16 to 1.[15] Like Bidault, Chauvel thought the Russians enjoyed an additional advantage from their fifth column in the west: "In addition, given the strength of the PCF, the beginning of hostilities could be for us the signal for serious internal difficulties, while an invasion could take the form of an insurrectional government."

Marshall was impressed by the French fears. He told Truman that American talks with the Europeans on defense were necessary "to stiffen their morale." On March 12, 1948 he cabled Bidault that 'we share your views and ... appreciate fully, I think, the dangers facing France and the other free countries of Europe.'[16] But the American secretary of state did not have the same appreciation of those dangers; according to him, Bidault's message reflected a "case of the jitters" and the French were unduly alarmed and pessimistic. The Americans had no real fear of war. They calmly withdrew their ambassador from Prague and went ahead with plans to construct a unified government in West Germany. The French were shocked. To Chauvel, the Americans were acting from a position of weakness and inviting Russian reprisal. The "dangerous period opened by the Truman Doctrine," he thought, would not be closed until sufficient American-backed military strength existed in Europe to make Moscow hesitate. The West must prepare militarily, not wave a red flag in front of the Russian bull ... "the American administration must also be conscious of the fact that incendiary declarations are susceptible of having different consequences, that there is a relationship of cause and effect between the Truman Doctrine of March 1947 and the subsequent absorption of five countries by the Soviets." Guarantees without teeth, which was what Washington offered the Europeans, only invited more trouble. "There also our experience suggests some reflections that it would be useful to knock into the heads of the Americans." Chauvel's categorical imperative was a package including a military pact of the United States and the sixteen Marshall Plan countries, American troops stationed in Europe, and a plan of defense on the Rhine, or even better, the Elbe.[17]

Marshall put off the French, telling them to see to the defenses of the Brussels pact. The United States would act once it had seen what the Europeans were prepared to do for themselves. Meanwhile, the military conversations requested by Bidault were held, but Paris was excluded. On March

---

[15] Ministère des Affaires Etrangères (MAE), Fonds nominatifs Henri Bonnet, March 12, 1948.

[16] FRUS, 1948, III, Western Europe, March 4 and 12, 1948. pp. 38, 50. MAE, Fonds Henri Bonnet, March 13, 1948.

[17] MAE, Fonds Henri Bonnet, March 18, 1948.

22, 1948 American, British, and Canadian representatives secretly convened in Washington in what became the first phase of the negotiations leading to the Atlantic Alliance. The French were always made to feel that they were knocking at the door of a closed Anglo-Saxon club. To be sure, the question of French participation in the talks arose, but the British were still fearful of Communist influence in Paris, while the Americans regarded the French as a "security risk." Moreover, to admit the French was to put up with their immediate and tiresome appeals for weapons, while the United States wanted to discuss what to do over the long term.[18] In the dark about the talks, Paris fretted over American provocations and Russian responses in Germany. France aligned its German policy with the Americans and British for lack of an alternative, but worried about the wisdom of doing so. The Soviets were easily capable of forcing the West out of Berlin, the French thought, and the creation of a West German government might be regarded as a provocation sufficient to goad the Russians into war.[19] "The French government considers it as evident that the danger of conflict resides precisely in this disparity between the direction of the German policy of the Western powers and the forces which they dispose of to support that policy." Should not Washington refrain from provocative acts so long as France lay totally at the mercy of an invader? France needed a military alliance and immediate arms assistance. Unfortunately, Bonnet wrote, "Respect for logic, as you know, is not always a determining element in the policies of the Anglo-Saxons."[20]

By April 1, 1948 a virtual draft of the North Atlantic Treaty had been secretly concluded between the British, Canadian, and American representatives in Washington. The next step was for the North Americans to approach the signatories of the Brussels pact. But first, Congress had to consent to the necessity of ending the American historic objection to alliances and proclaim a new internationalism. The Vandenberg resolution, which on June 11, 1948 received a very large majority in the Senate, endorsed American association with regional and collective arrangements affecting the national security. The State Department interpreted it as authorization to open "exploratory talks" with the Brussels powers, in July 1948.[21] The ERP was voted by Congress in April 1948, and bilateral treaties regularizing its implementation were being negotiated with the sixteen members of the OEEC at the same time as the preparations for NATO were completed. ERP began formal operations in France at the beginning of July. An illusory optimism thus pervaded Washington during the first half of 1948, as Washington pursued its three-pronged policy: the North Atlantic Treaty, the Marshall Plan, and the bolstering of the Schuman government in France, which appeared to have finally achieved a precarious equilibrium.

[18] FRUS, 1948, III, Western Europe, March 22 and April 13, 1948, pp. 59–62.
[19] A.N., Papiers Georges Bidault, 457 AP 25, May 10, 1948.
[20] A.N., Papiers Georges Bidault, 457 AP 24, April 17, 1948.
[21] Kaplan, *United States and NATO*, 74.

In his efforts to shore up the Schuman government, Jefferson Caffery freely pressured opposition and government politicians of the right and left. The Americans retained their ties with de Gaulle, who still loomed as a major force in French politics and appeared certain to come to power should Schuman fail. Hickerson instructed Caffery to assure the existence of channels of communication with the general and explore the possibility of seeing him personally; it was important that de Gaulle be informed about American views, in the event that "we may have something definite and immediate to impart to the General."[22] Caffery did quietly try to arrange a meeting, waiting a suitable time after the death of de Gaulle's daughter in January 1948, but being sure to inform Schuman, Blum, and Bidault of what he was doing. De Gaulle, for his part, sent word on March 17 that he would welcome a meeting, but not immediately. He did not wish to embarrass Schuman, with whom he still hoped for an agreement. But on March 22, Schuman told Caffery he thought it preferable that the American ambassador not see de Gaulle after all, although he did not of course "wish to dictate whom I (Caffery) can and cannot see."[23] The prescription against American ambassadors seeing de Gaulle was to last into the mid-1950s, when it was broken by Ambassador Douglas Dillon, but contact through intermediaries continued without interruption.

Bolstering Schuman took second place among American concerns in Europe in 1948; the precarious situation of Alcide de Gasperi, prime minister of Italy, raised serious fears in Washington of a Communist triumph in that country. The Italian elections of April 18, 1948, resulted in a major U.S. effort to shape the internal politics of Italy. The Americans were encouraged by the French to intervene in Italy. Bidault sent Marshall a message urging an immediate announcement of American aid for Rome. Marshall assured Bidault the United States would not sit idly by while the Communists came to power in Italy, legally or otherwise, and offered to coordinate American action with the British and French.[24] George Kennan wanted de Gasperi to outlaw the Communist party. Kennan was able to galvanize the CIA into action in a massive effort to defeat the Communists, with the sum of $10 million becoming a benchmark for such election efforts in Italy and France thereafter. Ambassador James Dunn warned publicly that Marshall Plan aid would cease if the Communists won the elections, while the Vatican announced that a vote for the Communist party was a sin. Italian-Americans undertook an orchestrated letter-writing campaign to friends and relatives in Italy warning against the consequences of a Communist victory. The United States declared its support for Italian control of Trieste, sent arms to strengthen Italian security forces, flooded Italy with propaganda showing the benefits

[22] FRUS, 1948, III, France, February 3, 1948, p. 624.
[23] FRUS, 1948, III, France, February 13, 1948, March 17 and 22, 1948, pp. 630–4.
[24] A.N., Papiers Georges Bidault, 457 AP 21, Feburary 13, 1948. FRUS, 1948, III, France, March 2, 1948, pp. 629–30.

of American aid, and sponsored the showing of everything from newsreels to the antibolshevik satire, *Ninotchka,* with Greta Garbo. The defeat of the Italian Communists in the elections of April 18, 1948 was regarded as one of the earliest major successes of American intelligence operations and a model for many other efforts to come.[25]

Following the Italian election victory the Americans enjoyed a short period of optimism. Like their Italian comrades, the French Communists appeared to be in check. The American consul in Marseille reported that the Soviets and the PCF were preparing an armed uprising in the south of France to coincide with an Italian Communist election victory, but Caffery conferred with the highest French prefectoral and military officials, all of whom assured him that French security forces were adequate to prevent serious trouble.[26] Congress passed the ERP while the Brussels and germinating Atlantic pacts promised a new sense of military security. Industrial production in France reached a level 12 percent higher than 1938 and a successful tax reform act was passed. The CGT had been badly hurt by the defection of Force Ouvrière, the strikes had been defeated, and several meager Communist efforts to mobilize demonstrations against Schuman appeared to have failed.[27]

But in May 1948 Schuman again appeared to be in trouble. Caffery immediately sent a warning to de Gaulle through General Benouville: If de Gaulle tried to undermine or destroy the Schuman government "it could not fail to create the most adverse reaction in the United States." De Gaulle's willingness to interfere with the success of economic stabilization constituted proof for Caffery that the general placed personal ambition above the national interest. On May 28 Caffery again focused on Léon Blum, in an effort to quash Socialist murmurings of rebellion in the government coalition. Caffery thought British Labour could now be urged to approach the SFIO through Blum to gain support for Schuman. When the British had approached Blum on devaluation of the franc, they had "nearly upset the apple cart," but in this case the ambassador thought their intervention might be useful. In London, America's Ambassador Douglas approached Bevin the next day about pressuring Blum to support Schuman.[28] Caffery meanwhile approached other French politicians in an effort to bolster Schuman.

[25] James E. Miller, "Taking Off the Gloves: The United States and the Italian Elections of 1948," *Diplomatic History,* 7, no. 1 (Winter 1983): 35–57. See also William R. Corson, *The Armies of Ignorance: The Rise of the American Intelligence Empire* (New York: Dial Press, 1977), pp. 295–7, and U.S. Congress, Senate, "Final Report of the Select Committee to Study Government Operations with Respect to Intelligence Activities" (Washington, DC: Government Printing Office, 1976), popularly known as the Church Committee, vols. I and VI.

[26] NARA, 851.00/3-1348, 4-1648, March 13 and April 16, 1948.

[27] NARA, 851.00/4-2248, April 22, 1948.

[28] NARA, 851.00/5-1248, May 12, 1948; 5-2848, May 28, 1948; 5-2948, May 29, 1948.

The French chafed under the London accords on Germany and remained resentful of American steps toward the creation of a West German State. Opposition to Bidault consequently grew, even within the cabinet. The foreign minister had become the symbol of the French capitulation to the United States over Germany. Undeterred, Caffery pressured the French cabinet ministers: "I pointed out the frivolity and gravity of mixing personal dislikes with a serious issue. . . . We know Bidault's weakness but must support him now for the sake of the London accords. It would be nice to have the accords and dump Bidault, but alas!"[29] But Caffery's efforts were to little avail. On June 18 he reported that the government was weak and likely to fall. Disagreement had emerged over the wage–price ratio and the coal subsidy. René Mayer wanted to eliminate the subsidy, but the others feared the effect of a rise in the price of coal on other key sectors of the economy, and several ministers approached David Bruce about the use of Marshall Plan funds to continue supporting the industry. Bruce and William Tomlinson rejected this idea as an inappropriate use of Marshall Plan funds, and refused pending a Mission review of the whole French economy. Meanwhile the government fell.

Even as Caffery tried to bolster Schuman, American policy appeared to undermine him. The wage–price disparity grew, yet the ECA adamantly opposed any increases in pay, and rejected French plans to use counterpart funds to maintain the price of bread as well as coal. The negotiation of the bilateral agreements implementing the ERP proved much more difficult than anticipated, and only last minute threats by Washington of a cessation of aid produced agreement (see next chapter for details). In the Atlantic pact talks, French demands for immediate arms assistance clashed with American insistence on a long-term alliance. And Washington rudely pressured Schuman to seek National Assembly ratification of the Baie d'Along agreements with Emperor Bao Dai of Vietnam, as a means of satisfying Vietnamese aspirations for sovereignty while keeping the country out of the Communist orbit (see Chapter 8). Given all these contradictory pressures, one wonders if Schuman did not resign at least in part to get Washington off his back.

The treaty negotiations became stalled because of a difference between American and French conceptions of the alliance, which was aggravated by French awareness that initial discussions between the Anglo-Saxons had taken place without them. Henri Bonnet protested to Washington that he had been informed of a revival of the Anglo–American "combined chiefs of staff" of World War II, and demanded that Paris be admitted. The Americans replied that the "combined chiefs" no longer existed and no private Anglo–American talks were taking place. When Bonnet again pressed the issue on August 20, Theodore Achilles reported: "Believing that anything

---

[29]   NARA, 851.00/6-248, June 2, 1948; 6-748, June 7, 1948; 6-1848, June 18, 1948.

less than a categorical negative would throw the French Government into a 'complete tizzy,' I gave him a categorical negative."[30] But again the Americans were being somewhat disingenuous. The British had in fact requested such talks, which were under active consideration until they were finally rejected by the American joint chiefs of staff.

At the "exploratory talks" on the North Atlantic Treaty in Washington, the French demanded immediate, large-scale military assistance to meet what they regarded as an imminent Soviet threat. Paris showed more interest in weapons than the treaty. The Americans rejected the French "piecemeal" approach to rearmament, as they had with respect to economic aid, and pushed instead their conception of a long-term treaty with a coordinated approach to rearmament to follow. At the meeting of August 20, Bonnet protested that France had pressing problems which a long-term pact simply would not solve, and he demanded military equipment and assurances at once, "today."[31] The ambassador "went on in this vein for an hour," and when told that surplus American military equipment simply did not exist, he rejected this and again asserted France's immediate needs. Bonnet also insisted upon a "forward" military strategy to meet the Soviet threat in Germany. If a Russian military occupation of France occurred as a result of the American strategy of defense at the Pyrenees, the entire economic and social elite of the nation would be exterminated. It would be worse than the Nazi occupation. Bonnet told Marshall that the French had three conditions before they would sign a pact: unity of command, immediate shipments of materiel, and the prompt dispatch of American troops to France. Marshall was reportedly so irritated that he wanted to break off the negotiations.[32]

On October 24 Assistant Secretary of State Lovett wrote to Caffery, "The French are in our hair," and told the ambassador to inform Paris that its demands were "fantastic." The United States, not France, after all, was doing the favors by signing a treaty in the first place. The Canadians saw in this American behavior the same lack of sympathy and understanding for France that had permeated the White House and State Department since 1940. But in Washington, Canadian Foreign Minister Lester Pearson had to agree that the French attitude was causing increasing impatience and was "incomprehensible to everybody." The combined pressure of the United States, Great Britain, and Canada was finally necessary to get the French to agree to the alliance. There was a pay-off, however. The United States agreed immediately to equip three French divisions in Germany.[33] Supplies suddenly materialized that Bonnet had just been assured did not exist. A similar pattern

---

30 NARA, Military Branch, Record Group 319, OPD, 334, Combined Chiefs of Staff, TS, August 17, 19, 20, September 7, 1948.
31 FRUS, 1948, III, Western Europe, August 6 and 20, 1948, pp. 200–19.
32 Reid, *Time of Fear and Hope*, 117.
33 NARA, Military Branch, Plans and Operations, 091 France, Box 12, Section 2, Case 10, August 28, 1948, September 13 and 16, 1948.

was to characterize the whole tortured history of American military aid to France in the postwar period. The French would make panicky requests, which the Americans rejected with explanations that supplies or funds were not available. Under further pressure, or to win French agreement on another issue, the Americans would then grant the aid, demonstrating their disingenuousness and convincing Paris that there were always more supplies in American warehouses, or dollars in the treasury.[34]

While these negotiations continued, France underwent one of the most prolonged cabinet crises of the postwar era. Schuman fell on July 18 in a negative vote over the military budget; but the difficulty he had in forcing the National Assembly to accept the June 1948 London accords for the restoration of German sovereignty indicates that the deputies were taking out their frustrations on both Bidault and him personally.[35] In the London accords France finally accepted Washington's German policy in exchange for Marshall Plan aid. Bonnet reported the usual "vif regret" in Washington upon Schuman's fall.[36] Caffery held the Socialists responsible for the crisis, but he could not blame them. Despite all the ambassador's pleading the government had failed to hold prices to the ratio achieved following the October–November strikes of 1947. Moreover, the fortunes of Force Ouvrière had been compromised by its willingness to cooperate in holding wages down. As the crisis dragged on, the French watched Washington's reaction with increasing concern. The government had fallen at a moment of high international tension (the Berlin blockade), French finances were once again in dissarray, and "The American public is beginning to ask if it has not invested its money in an enterprise without hope and whether the Marshall Plan credits are not being poured down the bottomless pit of European political and economic disorder." American hopes were somewhat reestablished with the Marie government and the plenary powers given Paul Reynaud as minister of finance. Schuman remained in the government, moving to the Ministry of Foreign Affairs, where he was to remain until 1953. But Reynaud proved unyielding on the wage question despite an intervention by Secretary Marshall, who made it quite clear the Americans now regarded some increases in wages justified despite their concern for French financial stability.[37] (See Chapter 4.) Caffery noted that the key to French politics remained the wage–price problem "even if Communist demagogy were not present to fan the flames." Marie fell in turn, in September; the Socialists had refused to accept his policies, which clearly would have hurt labor most.[38]

---

[34] Truman Library, National Security Council Meetings, NSC/21, September 16, 1948. See Chapter 7 for further examples. Also Kaplan, *United States and NATO*, p. 81.
[35] Raymond Poidevin, *Robert Schuman, homme d'Etat, 1886–1963* (Paris: Imprimerie Nationale, 1986), pp. 173–90.
[36] MAE, B Amérique, 120, July 26, 1948.
[37] MAE, B Amérique, 167, August 27, 1948.
[38] NARA, 851.00/8-1948, August 19, 1948; 8-2848, August 28, 1948.

President Auriol, himself a Socialist, reported that Ambassador Caffery quite understood the Socialist position, and supported it.[39]

Caffery's concerns on the fall of Marie soon became quite different, however, for during the prolonged crisis of early September there was renewed talk of a new Popular Front government, perhaps under Herriot. The Communists announced that they would not necessarily oppose American aid, on condition that any restrictions prejudicial to French sovereignty were removed, and, for the occasion, they dusted off Thorez's 1946 speech about a separate French road to socialism.[40] Caffery was alarmed. He immediately informed leaders of the Radical party that "bringing Communists back into the government would not be understood in the USA and that it would have most unfortunate effects on American aid to France." Upon hearing that trade union leader Léon Jouhaux might be favorable to Communist participation, the ambassador "took steps to have him informed that if the Communist party were included it would probably not be possible for us to continue our substantial aid to France."[41] The rumors continued after the formation of the Queuille government on September 15. Communist participation in the government, it was said, might be a guarantee of social peace. Caffery was "still hopeful that this tempest will blow itself out," and attributed the persistent rumors to wishful thinking and the French sense of defenselessness in the face of a possible Soviet invasion.

But talk continued, and on October 2, Paul Devinat, who was secretary of state in the prime minister's office, officially inquired of Caffery about American reactions should the Communists return to the government. Caffery told Devinat that it would unquestionably mean the cessation of American aid to France. Devinat promised to tell President Auriol, among others, and later phoned Caffery to say that the matter had been raised at the cabinet meeting and settled. One wonders whether Queuille's threat to return the Communists to power was not meant as an implicit warning to the Americans to relax their pressures. Caffery's opposition to the threat of the Communist party's return moderated his attitude toward the Gaullists. During the crisis rumors abounded of the general's imminent return, and the embassy was constantly queried about this possibility: "We continue to take the line that it is a matter for the French themselves. . . . While the United States could not assist financially or militarily a government with Communists (who seek to wreck ERP and refuse to fight the USSR) the U.S. wishes [the] success of any French government not containing these elements and responsive to the wishes of the majority."[42]

39 Vincent Auriol, *Journal du Septennat, 1947–1954*, vol. II (Paris: Armand Colin, 1977), September 1948, p. 416.

40 NARA, 851.00/9-1048, September 10, 1948; *L'Humanité*, September 8, 1948.

41 NARA, 851.00/9-448, September 4, 1948; 9-1048, September 10, 1948; 9-3048, September 30, 1948; 10-248, October 2, 1948.

42 NARA, 851.00/10-248, 851.00/10-948, October 2 and 9, 1948.

It was at just this juncture that the bitter coal strike, precipitated by wage demands, the government's decrees modifying the nationalization statute in the mines, and Queuille's announced price increases, was scheduled to begin. Queuille's contemplated invitation to the PCF to participate in the government, blocked by Caffery, was probably the only means of averting the imminent labor unrest. Queuille reacted to the strikes with almost unprecedented ferocity. Nonetheless, the Americans still thought the situation called for pay increases and a more moderate stance toward labor. During the strike, Washington made extra efforts to assure the French coal supply, and Caffery condemned the strikes as a "commando operation," observing with approval that the government was engaged in an all-out, open and declared war with the Communist party. But observers in the Embassy were equally critical of Queuille, who too easily allowed his struggle against the Communists to appear to be a struggle against the working class itself. At the strike's end, the embassy noted, Queuille had failed to provide any new leadership to the working class, Force Ouvrière appeared doomed to failure, and the Communist party's hold on the workers was undented. If French workers were left defenseless and at the absolute mercy of a selfish bourgeoisie, it would be a hollow victory over the Communists indeed.[43]

De Gaulle was the only realistic alternative, and he remained unacceptable to Washington. John Hickerson warned that de Gaulle, more than Queuille, failed to understand the elements of a modern industrial state, and was blind with regard to Labor. De Gaulle had the mystical, illusory notion that France was still a great power, and talked about economics "as a woman talks about carburetors." His advisers were ill-assorted, incompetent, self-seeking, and unstable, and he would no doubt be welcomed by the Communists. American support for him would be interpreted as interference in French affairs, and the United States would be held responsible if he failed. There was no real alternative to Queuille, but he must be warned to produce a stable, workable regime, or American aid would be reduced.[44] Meanwhile, in evaluating Queuille's prospects, Caffery sounded a familiar refrain. Queuille's success depended upon his ability to do something about the disparity between wages and prices; repressive measures against the Communists were not enough. "I never lose an occasion to bring this situation to the attention of the government and particularly the Radical Socialists."[45] As the French government moved more and more to the right, criticism of its apparent unconcern about Communism became a repeated American refrain. But as Queuille appeared to achieve a measure of stability in 1949, the Americans soft-pedaled their concern with labor. In 1949 Washington seemed finally to be at the point of achieving the kind of stable, compliant, and anticommunist France it had so earnestly been seeking.

[43] NARA, 851.00/10-2348, 12-2248, October 23, 1948, December 12, 1948.
[44] FRUS, 1948, III, France, October 5 and 12, 1948, pp. 662–7.
[45] NARA, 851.00/1-1149, January 11, 1949.

II THE COLD WAR IN FRANCE

Secretary of State Marshall visited Président du Conseil Henri Queuille in Paris on October 18, 1948, and received the most encouraging report on the French situation that the Americans had heard since the Liberation. The back of the strike movement had been broken, Queuille asserted proudly, and a thorough purge of the Communists in the nationalized enterprises and the state administrations was under way. The CGT had been defeated and a majority for the government parties appeared certain in the forthcoming elections to the Council of the Republic. The prime minister promised to rehabilitate the economy and balance the budget; a legislative package of fiscal measures would be voted by parliament by the beginning of the new year. These would include a law of the "maxima," placing a ceiling on advances to the government from the Bank of France to control inflation. The fiscal measures had been developed in consultation with the Marshall Plan Mission (see Chapter 6). Queuille again asked for direct military staff talks with the United States. Marshall did not reply to his request but advised the French to build their ground forces, leaving the heavy expense of weaponry for naval and air power to the Americans. The secretary pleaded with Queuille for early passage of the promised fiscal measures so as to strengthen his arguments with the American Congress, which was always eager to hear about what the Europeans were doing to achieve financial stability when deciding on ECA appropriations.[46]

The formation of the Queuille government was the occasion for a fresh American policy statement on France. The United States would continue its efforts to ensure the stability of the present non-Communist government in France or a successor of the same general complexion. De Gaulle remained unacceptable because of, among other things, his "stubbornness, disregard for economic, financial, and social considerations, and mysticism." A middle-of-the-road government relying on the non-Communist left was the best solution, which Washington would pursue actively through economic aid, contacts with political leaders of government and opposition, and influence in the trade unions. The United States would continue to press for liberal reform in the French empire and the conclusion of a treaty of commerce to open the country to the benefits of American investment. A central problem remained the wage–price relationship, which threatened social and political stability: "The real difficulties of the working class gave the Communists a powerful leverage over the non-Communist left."[47]

Central to the American analysis was the stabilization of an anticommunist France that could take its place as the mainstay of the Atlantic alliance. The United States would support any noncommunist government in France "by all means short of direct interference in the internal affairs of the coun-

---

[46] NARA, 851.00/11-1848, November 18, 1948.
[47] FRUS, 1948, III, France, September 20, 1948, pp. 651–9.

try. . . . The goal of ERP is fundamentally political and France is the keystone of continental Western Europe." The effect on Western Europe should France succumb to communism "needs no comment." The French must be made to realize the need for a strong, cooperative, noncommunist government, although there were "definite limitations on the pressures the United States can exert to this end." Washington would continue to press Paris to put its economic house in order: Increase taxes, reduce government expenditures, impose credit controls, and force the commercial and agricultural classes to contribute their fair share of the fiscal burden. More generous social policies would especially need to be pressed in the event de Gaulle succeeded in coming to power. Finally, Under Secretary of State Lovett insisted on the coordination of the different operations in which the Americans were engaged in France: diplomatic efforts, the ECA, military aid, and "covert political warfare operations," being conducted by the CIA.[48]

The Americans had a positive opinion of the personnel of the Queuille government and gave it high marks for accomplishment during 1949. The CIA regarded Queuille as an "old-type conservative," and praised him for his experience, moderation, well-ordered mind, honesty, and character as an elder statesman. Jules Moch, the interior minister who had twice bested the CGT in bitter strike movements, was characterized as one of the most capable figures in the Socialist party, although occasionally inflexible and "lacking in realism." Moch was insufficiently popular with his own party, however, and too anti-German, the CIA wrote, because his son had been murdered by the Gestapo along with the "thousands of his race who had perished at the hands of the Germans." As anticipated, Moch was to become a bitter foe of German rearmament. Schuman, though financially orthodox, was sincere, sound, hard working, mild, honest, the prototype of the true democratic leader, highly respected in the democratic world. The conservative business man, René Mayer, was Washington's favorite; his intelligence and energy made him an excellent choice for prime minister. Taking advantage of Mayer's presence in New York as a U.N. Delegate, Washington undertook to "discreetly forward such of [his activities] as would serve U.S. interests now or in the future." The only negative star in this firmament was the minister of information in the Queuille government, François Mitterrand. He was regarded as "incapable, inefficient, vain, totally lacking the drive and imagination necessary in the post which he occupies."[49] However, the CIA thought well of the French military. General Juin was "extremely pro-American," General de Lattre brilliant, fearless, and gifted intellectually, if also ambitious and opportunistic. Madame la Générale, who was said to dominate him, was strongly anticommunist. De

[48] FRUS, 1948, III, Western Europe, December 3, 1948, pp. 300–10.
[49] NARA, 851.00/3-1649, March 16, 1949; 4-449, April 4, 1949.

Gaulle, of course, was a self-proclaimed "national messiah" and a chauvinist mystic who caused either hatred or adulation.[50]

It was therefore not surprising that on February 18, 1949, Bonnet found Secretary of State Acheson very encouraging with regard to the Queuille government, with which he looked forward to the closest cooperation. Acheson praised Queuille's financial policies, and told Bonnet that France was the key to Europe, the restoration of its economy the key to the prosperity of the whole continent. Bonnet thought American military aid to France likely, because Acheson had said the economy "overshadowed any other consideration and that it must not, in his opinion, be hampered by an increase in military costs." The elections to the Council of the Republic produced a majority for the government, which greatly encouraged Washington in its hopes for French political and economic stability. And as France loomed more and more as a stable, reliable, anti-Communist partner of the United States, the expectations of what role it might play in the Atlantic community grew apace.[51] The road to the signing of the treaty was anything but smooth, however.

In September 1948 the French accepted the American and British conceptions of a long-term treaty, but they still insisted upon immediate military aid and a strategy of defense east of the Rhine, as elaborated by the Brussels treaty powers. The questions of membership in the proposed treaty and the areas of its geographical coverage occasioned further disagreement. As originally drawn the treaty excluded colonial dependencies of the European powers and was to be limited in membership to countries bordering on the North Atlantic. This excluded Italy and French North Africa. In the summer of 1948, the French had not wanted the treaty extended to any other European nations than the Brussels powers, in Washington's view because "they do not want others to share in the U.S. arms pie."[52] But in the State Department, there was interest in Italian membership in the Atlantic pact; John Hickerson feared that without participation in the alliance Italy might succumb to communism. American interest in Italian membership stimulated the French to ask that their North African possessions be included in the area to be covered by the treaty. As a minimum, Paris sought treaty guarantees for Algeria, which it administered as three French departments, as much a part of the metropole, the French insisted, as Alaska and Florida were part of the United States.[53]

The French switched to the support of Italian membership with Algeria in mind, and in January 1949, Rome applied for formal membership. But

50 Central Intelligence Agency, Research Reports, University Publications of America Microfilm Reel 1, March 17, 1950.
51 MAE, B Amérique, 120, February 18, 1949, March 22, 29, 30, 1949.
52 Reid, *Time of Fear and Hope*, p. 203.
53 FRUS, 1948, III, Western Europe, December 22, 1948, pp. 324–32; 1949, IV, Western Europe, February 8, 1949, pp. 73–88.

when Dean Acheson took over as secretary of state, he withdrew American support of the Italians. This left the French alone, for all the other nations either opposed Italian membership or were indifferent. Queuille, fortified by the knowledge that the Americans saw no alternative to his leadership, only hardened the French arguments in favor of both Italy and Algeria. In February 1949 the French insisted upon Italian membership with a stridency unseen in the negotiations up to that point. Noting the application of Norway for membership, Bonnet said he did not see how the French could accept Norway in the alliance if Italy were excluded. This outburst greatly angered Washington; although the French could not have known it, Russian pressures on Norway had been one of the original reasons for the beginning of negotiations of the United States, Canada, and Great Britain the previous March. Acheson warned the French that if they persisted in this position he could not be responsible for the consequences.[54]

But Queuille persisted anyway. Paris was additionally frustrated in another bid for full membership in the Anglo-Saxon club: on February 14, 1949, Bonnet again insisted on France's inclusion in combined chiefs-of-staff talks between England and the United States, but Washington again refused. The joint chiefs regarded France as at best a European power that lacked the strength to be considered in relation to a broad global strategy. Without French participation in staff talks, or the inclusion of Algeria, the idea of the treaty itself began to appear less desirable to the French. On March 1 Bonnet escalated French rhetoric yet again. If Norway were included, but not Italy or Algeria, he said, France would have to reconsider its own participation in the treaty. He did not see how the National Assembly could be brought to ratify the pact under such conditions. Within the State Department Hickerson had continued to argue in favor of Italian participation, and the French attitude strenthened his position. Nevertheless, the Americans put up five weeks of stubborn argument before conceding the issue.

On March 2, 1949 Acheson told Truman France was emphatic on the Italian (and Algerian) question, and had threatened to reconsider its membership; "We had to believe them." Truman regarded the Italians as ineffective and undependable, and the inclusion of a former enemy state seemed to him an unnecessary affront to the USSR. These arguments were later to be used by the French in an equally futile struggle to prevent German membership. But the president gave in. The French obtained treaty coverage for Algeria, membership for Italy, and the promise of the Military Assistance Pact just a day later. Schuman was elated. The terms were exactly what the French had hoped to derive from the negotiations in the first place. Acheson further declared that the extension of military aid was an indication of the

[54] FRUS, 1949, IV, Western Europe, February 25, 1949, pp. 122–4.

great confidence America now had in France.[55] Be that as it may, the French had faced down Washington and won a diplomatic victory.

The treaty was signed in April 1949, and during the summer it was brought before the French National Assembly for ratification. Schuman and Queuille now sought to make public the assurances they had received from Washington earlier. An aide-memoire by the French Foreign Minister asked "clarification" of U.S. intentions to defend Western Europe in case of Soviet attack. Without such guarantees, Schuman warned, the National Assembly might not ratify the treaty. Acheson replied on June 21 that American policy was, as often stated, "containment," which meant that Washington would not permit the occupation of Western Europe by Soviet forces.[56] On July 8 Acheson also formally promised the French they would be included on any military executive body established within the framework of the treaty organisation. On July 24 *Le Monde* proudly announced that France would be the principal beneficiary of American military aid. The State Department declared that Paris would receive up to 50 percent of the entire military aid package, almost $1 billion in real dollar value. France was already receiving 20 percent of total Marshall Plan aid, the total of which, *Le Monde* announced, amounted to $1,313 million since the ERP's inception.[57] The announcement of American munificence was clearly part of a cleverly orchestrated press campaign designed to secure ratification of the North Atlantic Treaty.

But the French government trumpeted its guarantees too loudly for Washington's taste, perhaps seeking through the press promises it could not get in writing. Schuman wanted to introduce the treaty with a public declaration concerning eventual French membership on an executive body of NATO and the promised arms package, but Acheson objected. Congress was certain to resent any appearance of conditions placed on treaty ratification or pressure coming from abroad. In a curt note, Acheson warned the French that these tactics served neither American interests nor their own, and he instructed the embassy to warn the French of the "deplorable reaction" in the United States to any reservations that might be placed by the French government on its treaty commitments.[58]

With the Marshall Plan, NATO, and the signing of a Military Assistance Pact, American policy to shore up France as the focal point of its European strategy was almost complete. But all these efforts would eventually be without effect if Washington failed to win the battle for French opinion or keep the government stable. The embassy repeatedly tried to strengthen the French

[55] FRUS, 1949, IV, Western Europe, March 1, 1949, pp. 126–35; March 2, 1949, pp. 141–5; March 3, 1949, 146–50.
[56] FRUS, 1949, IV, Western Europe, June 16, 1949, p. 306; June 21, 1949, pp. 307–9.
[57] *Le Monde*, July 24–5, 1949, August 6 and 12, 1949.
[58] FRUS, 1949, IV, Western Europe, August 10, 1949, p. 318; August 17, 1949, p. 321.

government and anchor it firmly in the center-left of the political spectrum. Queuille was defended from political attack, but also reminded that Washington deeply cared about his government's complexion. Caffery did not wish the conservative trend evident in the municipal elections of March 1949 to be reflected in national politics, and he warned Queuille that the Socialists must remain part of his coalition. The French must keep their conservative tendencies under control so as not to alienate the working class. In a parallel effort Caffery met with Mollet and other Socialist leaders to seek their continued support for Queuille. The ambassador was greatly disappointed with the Socialists, whom he found preoccupied with the irrelevant clerical issue and unhappy in alliance with the Catholic MRP. For the ambassador the question of lay education was simply a diversion from crucial economic and political questions. Worse, the Socialists appeared to support Queuille only out of "defeatism and self-sacrifice"; they feared the Communists and de Gaulle but could not see the importance of "formulating an imaginative program of political education and action to become again a workers' party while remaining in the government."[59] The tragedy of French politics lay in the Socialists' apparent willingness to abandon the role of defenders of the working class to the Communists.

In April 1949 Paul Reynaud attacked the government for excessive zeal in its deflationary policies and attributed this to pressure from the United States. Privately, Reynaud assured Caffery that he did not wish to unseat Queuille, but rather to force some liberalization of his policies. But Caffery suspected that Reynaud was acting out of personal ambition rather than patriotism, and recommended to Washington that the conservative politician not be shown too much consideration during his forthcoming trip to the USA. Hickerson agreed; the former premier had shown not only "distressing weakness" in 1940 during the fall of France, but also a total lack of vision and foresight in August 1948, when he had opposed even token wage increases that were clearly inevitable. Reynaud returned to France in May and showed signs of opposing Queuille once again amid debates in the National Assembly on the nationalizations and social security system. This angered Caffery, who summoned Reynaud to the embassy and told him to back down. It was simply irresponsible, Caffery said, to threaten a government crisis when the prospects for French economic recovery were the brightest since the Liberation. The State Department approved Caffery's action and suggested the embassy similarly "impress on [other] political leaders [the] danger in political maneuvers having adverse effect [on] French–European stability and recovery." Reynaud was contrite, protesting he did not want a crisis, but only to shake the government out of its complacency. Caffery warned him the embassy feared adverse

[59]   NARA, 851.00/4-2049, April 20, 1049; 851.00/5-2049, May 20, 1949.

effects would result from a cabinet crisis or a dissolution of the National Assembly.[60]

The Americans' main concern, however, was defending the government against Communist attack and finding ways to take the offensive against the Communists in the eyes of public opinion. The Embassy was particularly concerned by the Peace Movement, which it interpreted as the device chosen by the Soviets to wreck the North Atlantic Treaty, just as the strikes of 1947–8 had been masterminded by the Kremlin in an effort to destroy the Marshall Plan. The Peace Movement was regarded with the utmost serious-ness in Washington, and its origins traced to high Soviet policy.[61] By early 1949 it had become "a powerful propaganda vehicle as it coincides with the deep and instinctive aspirations of the [French] masses." It was a desperate attempt to block the Atlantic Pact and nullify its effectiveness through psy-chological and social sabotage. The Peace Movement had opened a new phase in the East–West struggle which "oblige[d] the French government to break Communist subversive power in order to survive." The question was how to break the hold of the Communist party on such a large segment of French opinion. The Embassy agreed with the French that repression of the Communist party would only serve to strengthen its appeal. Moreover, following Thorez's February 28, 1949 statement that French workers would never make war on the USSR, Queuille ruled out petty persecution of the party; he would judge the party by what it did, rather than by what it said, and assured the Americans that he could handle any Communist threat. "I know you Americans are disturbed at the prospect of French labor sabotag-ing the manufacture of military supplies." Any such attempt, Queuille said, would be dealt with sternly. Washington never hesitated to urge stronger measures against the party on French governments that did not share its sense of urgency about the Communist threat. But it also sought to find different ways of attacking the problem. What was needed to counter the Peace Movement, Caffery concluded, was an equally effective anti-Communist propaganda campaign devoted to similar themes.[62]

On March 3, 1949 Caffery called on Queuille to discuss the Communist peace campaign and pressed him to take measures to counteract it in order to "put the French government on the offensive."The *Président du Conseil* agreed on the need to do something, but he pleaded that the French admin-istration was poorly equipped for this sort of operation. Moreover, the min-ister of information, François Mitterrand, "could not be counted on to or-ganize and carry out such a campaign effectively." Queuille would not create a new bureaucracy to circumvent Mitterrand, but he appointed a high offi-

---

60 NARA, 851.00/4-1149, April 11, 1949; 851.00/4-2049, April 20, 1949; 851.00/5-2649, May 26, 1949.
61 NARA, 851.00B/4-2648, April 26, 1948.
62 NARA, 851.00/2-2849, February 28, 1949.

cial in his own office to take responsibility for the countercampaign. Caffery was promised that action could be expected soon, and he was gratified by Queuille's assurances, but he nevertheless repeated how seriously Washington regarded the question. He stressed the highly unsettling effect on French opinion of the Peace Movement, its reverberations in the United States, and the dangerous implications it held for the success of the Atlantic Pact, military aid, and American foreign policy in general.[63]

Queuille was quick to respond. On March 16 Caffery received word that the "Union démocratique pour la paix et la liberté" had been created by the government to carry on peace propaganda. Queuille himself drafted the texts for the initial posters that were placarded all over Paris the next day. The cabinet, according to Caffery, was astonished, but accepted without a mur mur. The posters, of which the abassador approved, carried different texts, the general message of which was that the Communist party was really against peace and that Stalinism would lead to a Soviet military occupation of France. Caffery was extremely pleased: "without undue immodesty the Embassy believes that this accomplishment is in no small part due to its efforts in driving home to Queuille and entourage as well as the [government] coalition the necessity for concerned action against Commie [sic] propaganda, particularly the phony peace campaign."[64]

Queuille eventually turned over responsibility for the effort to Jean-Paul David, an anti-Communist leader of the Rassemblement des Gauches républicaines. *Paix et liberté* was ostensibly a mass movement of concerned citizens interested in a "genuine" peace as opposed to the Communist propaganda campaign. In reality its council of administration included representatives of the state bureaucracy, the major government parties, and the Paris prefecture of police as well as the Sureté. Its funding came largely through the French *patronat,* but these sources were in turn without doubt transmitting funds from the American CIA. Along with Force Ouvrière, *Paix et liberté* accounted for the major part of the CIA's effort to promote mass non-Communist organizations in France during the 1950s. Other forms of CIA activity existed as well that were oriented toward influencing public opinion. These included subsidies to the established political parties, friendly media, and certain cover organizations of intellectuals. A well-known example of the latter was the Congress for Cultural Freedom, which published such prestigious anti-Communist revues as *Encounter* in England and *Preuves* in France. The dynamism of *Paix et liberté,* however, came from its leader, Jean-Paul David. It put out innumerable posters, some very cleverly done; one of the best known depicted Picasso's famous dove of peace deformed into the shape of an atomic bomb. *Paix et liberté* sponsored a radio pro-

---

63 NARA, 851.00/3-449, March 4, 1949; 851.00B/3-349, March 3, 1949.
64 NARA, 851.00B/3-1849, March 18, 1949; 851.00/3-1649, March 16, 1949; 3-1849, March 18, 1949.

gram, published a great deal of printed material, and organized occasional demonstrations. It supported several groups of ex-Communists, including the Italian ex-Communist Angelo Tasca, who was otherwise employed by the American embassy as an analyst of the Communist party. *Paix et liberté* enjoyed a good deal of notoriety and some propaganda success during the cold war until 1954. In that year its network of informants in the Communist party, according to Paul-Marie de la Gorce, was compromised in the "Affaire des Fuites," a sordid scandal involving the transmission of national defense secrets to the Communists. Allegedly, in that affair, *Paix et liberté* was trying to damage both the Communist party and the Mendès France government at the same time, an objective that also conformed to the goals of American policy (see Chapter 9).[65]

The major anti-Communist publicity extravaganza mounted by the State Department and the CIA in France in 1949 was the Kravchenko affair. The Russian defector's account of his experiences during the Stalin years, titled *I Chose Freedom,* sold 400,000 copies in France. Coming on the heels of another successful anti-Communist work, Authur Koestler's *Darkness at Noon,* it caused great anguish in the Communist world. A review in the Communist literary periodical, *Les Lettres Françaises,* tried to discredit Kravchenko's book as a CIA fabrication. There was at least a half-truth in this charge. *I Chose Freedom* was in fact rewritten by an ex-Communist journalist for the *New York Post,* Eugene Lyons, from an "unreadable" text 1,500 pages in length provided by the Russian exile, but with more or less respect for the facts as told by Kravchenko.[66] The decision to bring suit against *Les Lettres Françaises* for its denunciation of the book was deliberate and political: Kravchenko accompanied publication of his book by a campaign of public appearances designed to further anti-Communist sentiment. His sponsors chose France for strategic, cold war reasons because of its vibrant intellectual life and the prominent role played there by Communists. "In France I was in the midst of a political battlefield, in which blows for and against Communism could be dealt with real effect . . . where the CP constituted a present political power which might . . . grow in strength or decline."[67] Kravchenko sued *Les Lettres Françaises,* its editor, and the

---

[65] Paul-Marie de la Gorce, *L'Après-Guerre: Naissance de la France moderne* (Paris: Grasset, 1978), pp. 400–2. De la Gorce places the origins of *Paix et Liberté* during the Pleven government in 1950 and makes no reference to its American origins and funding. The poster description is his. On *Preuves* see Pierre Gremion, "Preuves dans le Paris de Guerre froide," *Vingtième Siècle,* 13 (January–March 1987): 63–81. On American attempts to make life difficult for Mendès France, see Chapter 9, II. Also René Sommer, "Paix et Liberté?: La Quatrième République contre le PC," *L'Histoire,* 40 (December 1981): 26–35.

[66] Guillaume Malaurie with Emmanuel Terré, *L'Affaire Kravchenko, Paris 1949: Le Goulag en correctionnelle* (Paris: Robert Laffont, 1982), pp. 37–44.

[67] Victor Kravchenko, *I Chose Justice* (New York: Scribner's, 1950), pp. 422–3.

alleged author of the review, "Sim Thomas," for slander. The subsequent trial created a sensation.

To verify his allegations about life in interwar Russia, Kravchenko combed the displaced persons camps of Germany in search of witnesses. The American Military Government assisted his search and expedited exit visas for all the witnesses requested by Kravchenko's lawyer, Maitre Georges Izard. Secretary of State Marshall was personally involved, cabling Caffery to inform Izard of the availability of the witnesses. The head of the State Department's East European desk, Lewellyan Thompson, monitored the trial on a daily basis. In December 1948 the French police advised the Embassy that security measures would be eased if Kravchenko could visit Paris under an assumed name. Thompson made the necessary arrangements and cabled the Embassy in reply that "Paul Kedrin" would be arriving at Orly at 12 noon on January 8, 1949, via Air France. Maitre Izard and the French authorities were notified. However, an Air France employee leaked the Russian's cover to the Paris press, resulting in a field day for the Communists, who repeatedly denounced "American Secret Agent" Paul Kedrin during the trial.[68] As his case required, Kravchenko routinely sent requests through the Embassy to Washington for documentation, which he asked to be forwarded by diplomatic pouch. For the most part, the Embassy complied. But it refused Kravchenko's request for a public declaration concerning the conditions of his defection, for nothing "must imply that the Department was involved in the preparation of the case."[69]

The trial was followed very closely by the Embassy, which forwarded a weekly summary of the proceedings to Washington. Caffery reported enthusiastically that "no trial since that of Pétain has provoked so much journalistic excitement here." The Gaullist press was as eager as the rest to make propaganda of the Communists' embarrassment. The plaintiffs were easily able to demonstrate that the alleged author of the incriminating review, Sim Thomas, did not exist, but was an invention of *Les Lettres Françaises*. Caffery was delighted by the testimony of the British Labour politician Zilliacus, a fellow-traveler who nonetheless freely referred to the Soviet "police-state apparatus." Margrete Buber Neumann's testimony was able to shake up even some devoted Communists. A survivor of the Gulag, she had been turned over to the Nazis by Stalin in 1939 as an accompaniment to the Nazi-Soviet pact along with some other German Communists, and her comparison of Nazi and Soviet camps was not flattering to the Russians. Caffery noted that the moderate and right-wing publications were daily getting new material to use in the service of the anti-Communist cause. The "humorous lightness" of their coverage, he wrote, contrasted vividly with the "deadly

[68] NARA, 351.1114 Kravchenko, Victor/7-2748, July 27, 1948; 7-3048, July 30, 1948; 12-2748, December 27, 1948.
[69] NARA, 351.1114 Kravchenko, Victor/1-2849, January 28, 1949; 2-249, February 2, 1949; 2-349, February 3, 1949.

earnestness" of the left, which behaved like "a heavy better who can't enjoy the game for fear of the bankroll he stands to lose."[70]

There were some difficult moments for the Kravchenko camp, however. The defector, for obvious reasons, could not produce a Russian-language version of his manuscript until late in the trial, and then Communist experts exposed its apparent adaptation from the American idiom. In the meantime, a Belgian newspaper published revelations of the role of Eugene Lyons in the manuscript's composition. Kravchenko himself behaved in an immoderate and foolish manner during the trial, frequently interrupting testimony loudly in Russian or bad French, lending a burlesque note to the proceedings. The verdict went in Kravchenko's favor, but he was awarded only one franc in damages as opposed to the 20–5 million spent in staging the trial. But the court did rule that he authored the manuscript, and indirectly the authenticity of the purges and the collectivization of agriculture in the USSR, as related by his witnesses, were verified in the eyes of public opinion. Caffery treated the result as a splendid propaganda victory, second in importance only to the signing of the Atlantic Pact. It was, in the ambassador's words, a victory for the West as well as a personal victory for Kravchenko. Public opinion polls bore the ambassador out, showing 35 percent of the French in favor of Kravchenko, 15 percent for *Les Lettres Françaises,* and 24 percent with no opinion. But the State Department was less enthusiastic. Acheson saw no purpose in sponsoring a visit by Kravchenko to Germany, and when Caffery suggested that the Russian be sent to lecture in Italy, Ambassador James Dunn demurred, fearing disturbances there and that the Department would reap negative publicity from any association with the case.[71]

The Kravchenko case fit into the strategy adumbrated by George Kennan a year earlier of driving home to the French the discrepancy between Communist propaganda and the Soviet reality. It was followed up by a similar suit filed in November 1949, against *Les Lettres Françaises* by the ex-Trotskyite and contributor to Jean Paul Sartre's *Les Temps Modernes,* David Rousset. A frequent caller at the American Embassy in 1949, Rousset sought support for his efforts to build a new party of the non-Communist left. In December 1949 the Embassy facilitated a visa for him, and put him in touch with the anti-Stalinist New York intellectuals who regularly contributed to *Commentary* and *Partisan Review.*[72] It is impossible to measure the impact

---

[70] NARA, 351.1114 Kravchenko, Victor/1-2649, January 26, 1949; 1-2749, January 27, 1949; 2-249, February 2, 1949; 2-449, February 4, 1949. See also the published stenographic account, *Le Procès Kravchenko, Comte rendu sténographique,* 2 vols. (Paris: Albin Michel, 1949).

[71] Malaurie and Terré, *L'Affaire Kravchenko,* 204. NARA, 351.1114 Kravchenko, Victor/4-549, April 5, 1949; 032 Kravchenko, Victor/4-749, April 7, 1949; 4-949, April 9, 1949.

[72] NARA, 751.001/1-2550, January 25, 1950.

of extravaganzas like the Kravchenko case on public opinion. Partisan publications preached to the already converted. But there were exceptions, particularly among the intellectuals. Dominique Desanti covered the trial for *L'Humanité*. Listening to the testimony of Margrete Buber Neumann, who told of Stalin turning over German Jews to Hitler, she was both horrified and unable to disbelieve; her faith was shaken. Of course, the Kravchenko case was one incident among many that led to her eventual break with the Communist party. But it could well have affected others similarly, and in this sense fulfilled in some measure the hopes of its sponsors.[73]

Caffery's naive enthusiasm for the Kravchenko case could have played a role in his replacement by David Bruce in 1949. Bruce had already been carrying out ambassadorial functions as head of the Marshall Plan Mission and had acquired extraordinary influence among French politicians. On June 6, 1949, as the new American ambassador, he lunched with Premier Queuille. Bruce, like most top Marshall Plan officials, was a wealthy member of the American industrial and business elite, and in terms of fiscal policy quite conservative. He was a Democrat, however, and did not lack a sense of compassion and concern for social justice. Bruce approved the thrust of American policy toward the non-Communist left, but remained vehemently anti-Communist. Perhaps most important, as President Auriol sensed at once, Bruce was a Francophile. According to the secretary of state, Dean Acheson, "not since Benjamin Franklin had anyone been closer to or more understanding of the French situation than David Bruce."[74]

Bruce found Queuille relaxed and confident and counting on remaining in power until the year's end. The Americans had much to be pleased with in Queuille's stewardship. The Marshall Plan was under way and the economy seemed to be on an even course. The NATO alliance had been signed and the French were looking forward to carrying out their part of the military burden. Queuille had given free rein to the Americans in carrying the cold war into France domestically by sponsoring *Paix et liberté* and the Kravchenko trial. Bruce made known his satisfaction: "I expressed my hope that Queuille would not underestimate the prestige he had acquired in American eyes in the last few months." Bruce told Queuille that the premier's position and personal authority were "integral elements in French recovery and stability"; Queuille was obviously pleased to hear this.[75]

In August, with the minor flap over the conditions of French ratification of NATO out of the way, Bonnet reported to Queuille the further favorable evolution of American opinion with regard to France in recent months. The Third Force was now seen in Washington as relatively stable and France

[73] Domenique Desanti, *Les Staliniens (1944–1956): Une expérience politique* (Paris: Fayard, 1975).
[74] Auriol, *Journal*, vol. 3, 1949, January 17, 1949, p. 24. Dean Acheson, *Present at the Creation: My Years in the State Department* (New York: Norton, 1969), 294.
[75] FRUS, 1949, IV, Western Europe, June 6, 1949, p. 646.

no longer thought to be wavering between social revolution and conservative dictatorship. Most important, as the French perceived, "it cannot be denied . . . that the reinforcement of liberal policies in France and the concommitant weakening of *dirigiste* tendencies enters, in appreciable part, into the motifs of optimism in American opinion toward us." In September 1949 the French liberalized their policy with regard to foreign investment, allowing the transfer of profits out of the country. Washington regarded the step as a clear sign of the return of French economic health. The *New York Herald Tribune* saluted the convergence of the American and French economies, while the *New York Times* welcomed the most liberal economic step taken yet by any country of Western Europe. Even the *Wall Street Journal* was pleased. The French position had been immeasurably strengthened in Washington.[76]

But idyllic moments in French–American relations had a way of rapidly disintegrating into bitterness and discord. In the summer Queuille ran into some unexpected budgetary difficulty and requested an "advance" in the release of counterpart funds. Although contrary to ECA policy, the advance was granted; but financial problems had a nasty way of degenerating into political ones. The pound was in trouble and the French did not want a substantial British devaluation. They counted on the United States to exercise a restraining influence in London. Instead of consulting Paris, the Americans, Canadians, and British held private talks that set the new level of the pound at $2.80. The French were furious both at the sharp extent of the devaluation (from $4.00) and their apparent exclusion, once again, from the Anglo-Saxon club. On September 22 Queuille called on Bruce to express his irritation and warned that his own position was now weakened and the government likely to fall.[77]

Queuille further received a report from Bonnet asserting that a historic shift in American policy was taking place away from the European continent and France in favor of the special relationship with Britain and the Commonwealth. There was some substance to Bonnet's belief. The State Department had adopted a fundamental policy change, recognizing finally that Britain could not be coaxed into joining Europe. France was to be left alone on the continent to deal with the Germans.[78] Acheson was, moreover, clearly an Anglophile. He and the British ambassador, Sir Oliver Franks, enjoyed a relationship of mutual friendship and held weekly lunches during which international affairs were frequently discussed. Schuman had noticed that the British foreign minister, Ernest Bevin, rapidly became "Ernie" to the austere American secretary of state, while the French minister remained "M. le Président" or simply "M. Schuman." Finally Bonnet had perhaps

[76] MAE, B Amérique, 167, August 29, September 9, 1949.
[77] FRUS, 1949, IV, Western Europe, September 22, 1949, p. 663.
[78] Michael Hogan, *The Marshall Plan: America, Britain, and the Reconstruction of Western Europe, 1947–52* (New York: Cambridge University Press, 1987), p. 267.

been informed of a British attempt to put their "special relationship" with America in writing, an idea the American secretary thought misguided. Was the relationship not special precisely because it did not need to be stated?[79] Queuille was once again jealous at French exclusion and disquieted at the prospect of dealing with the Germans in Europe without the power of Britain as a balance. Bruce cabled Washington for a correction of Queuille's "misimpression," and warned that the government could fall. The State Department reacted quickly. Bonnet had apparently misheard or misunderstood something said to him, or worse, engaged in "interpretive speculation." Acheson insisted that American policy was precisely the reverse of Bonnet's report, relying primarily on France as the linchpin of Europe. The United States meant to continue the closest possible relationship with the continent and counted on France to exercise leadership in that connection.[80]

Queuille fell anyway shortly thereafter. Bonnet now reported the American reaction to be "measured and comprehensive." After a year of stable government the Americans were not so concerned over every crisis as had been the case earlier.[81] Or perhaps Washington had concluded, with George Kennan, that the French were simply paranoid on the subject of Anglo-Saxon conspiracy. "I don't see that there is anything we can do for the French," Kennan observed. They were not amenable to rational argument.[82] As the crisis dragged on, however, American impatience grew. It was resolved on October 28, 1949 by formation of a second government under the ambitious and distrusted Georges Bidault. Despite Bonnet's report of "profound satisfaction" in Washington, the Americans were not especially sanguine. Bruce characterized Bidault as a "left-center leader with a concern for social justice," in that sense perhaps an improvement over Queuille. The cabinet included all the prestigious figures in French politics, including Queuille, Moch, Mayer, Schuman, and Pleven. Teitgen at the Ministry of Information was bound to be an improvement; he was more imaginative, energetic, and conscientious than Mitterrand. But the cabinet was more fragile than before and the economic situation unresolved. The deflationary measures applied by Queuille appeared to be in the process of erosion. More seriously, a working relationship had been established between the Queuille government, Maurice Petsche, the minister of finance, and the ECA. With Queuille's fall that relationship collapsed.[83]

France seemed to Washington now once again in the throes of a basic political realignment. Interparty resentments were rife, and it was difficult to see how a new crisis could be averted, with the construction of yet an-

[79] Acheson, *Present at the Creation*, p. 325; Truman Library, Acheson Papers, "Princeton Seminars," Microfilm Reel 3, Track 2.
[80] FRUS, 1949, IV, Western Europe, September 23, 1949, pp. 663–5.
[81] MAE, B Amérique, 120, October 18, 25, 28, 1949.
[82] Kaplan, *United States and NATO*, 137.
[83] NARA, 851.00/10-2849, October 28, 1949; 851.00/11-549, November 5, 1949.

other cabinet even more difficult than the last. The atmosphere was preelectoral, the government stopgap, and a succession of bourgeois–peasant governments seemed each one more likely to leave the interests of the workers unrepresented than the last. The choices appeared to be between even more instability or more Gaullist influence. Despairing of the prospects, the Embassy began to wonder whether a dissolution of parliament and early elections, given the apparent diminution of Communist influence, might not be a preferable alternative after all. The Embassy concluded it should work toward the implementation of a changed electoral system that would later permit the construction of a stable majority.[84] There is no evidence that the French electoral law of 1951 resulted from American pressure. It nevertheless neatly corresponded to American desires. It reduced proportional representation from the national to the departmental level, and by encouraging *apparentements,* or electoral alliances, contrived to reduce both Communist and Gaullist influence in the National Assembly, if not in the country. But that triumph lay in the future. For the moment, after eighteen months of ERP, NATO, MDAP, and a variety of schemes emphasizing internal covert political action and psychological warfare, Washington still found itself in search of a suitable France. French political instability, moreover, threatened the success of the Marshall Plan, to the implementation of which we must now turn.

[84] NARA, 851.00/12-2149, December 21, 1949.

6

The Marshall Plan

I WASHINGTON AND FRENCH FISCAL STABILITY

THE IMPLEMENTATION OF THE MARSHALL PLAN, and the establishment of NATO, opened new phases in the diplomatic relations between the United States and Western Europe. Both initiatives institutionalized an American role in the internal politics and economics of the European nations. In the case of the Marshall Plan, the new American role took the form of a "Mission" to each recipient nation, which had as its function the supervision of the expenditure of counterpart funds in local currency accrued as a result of American dollar assistance. In France, as elsewhere, francs in the counterpart fund could not be expended without the express approval of the Marshall Plan Mission, although they were for all intents and purposes French treasury funds. Similarly, the Mutual Defense and Assistance Pact, which followed upon the establishment of NATO, involved a Military Advisory and Assistance Group, which took up residence in Paris to oversee the use of American armaments. This in itself might have been less onerous, but the French soon began to press Washington for actual subsidies to their military budget. The subsidies involved the Americans in the direct influence, if not supervision of, the entire French budgeting process, civilian and military.

To be sure, the French had their own agenda for the uses of American aid. Despite the heavy-handed American presence during the Marshall Plan years, the contours of French economic development took shape within the bounds of the Monnet Plan; American pressure was limited to the problem of fiscal stabilization. The French also had their own military agenda. They succeeded in directing the Americans toward financing of the Indochina War and the creation of their own arms industry. It is impossible to say, therefore, that the France that emerged from this unprecedented American role in its internal economic and military policy was different from the one French planners had in mind. Moreover, the Americans never recognized in the end product the France they had been trying to create. Yet the tension of American pressure and French resistance and manipulation of that pressure left a permanent and bitter residue in terms of diplomatic relations between the two nations. The later questions of the European Defense Community and the achievement of peace in Indochina appeared linked specifically to American economic and military aid, and France had to experience its process of decision making on these questions as a virtual declaration of independence from the United States. This in turn contributed to the troubled relations with the United States of Mendès France and de Gaulle.

The ECA was created to administer Marshall Plan aid programs in the recipient nations. It became a parallel, sometimes rival service to the State Department, and intruded itself into the conduct of American economic foreign relations. Headed by an administrator enjoying cabinet rank, the ECA also had a European "Office of the Special Representative (OSR)," headquartered in Paris, to interact with the OEEC. In addition, each of the Marshall Plan countries had to accept an American Mission, the head of which became as important to American diplomacy as the ambassador. In Paris the OSR grew to encompass 600 American employees plus a much larger number of French workers; its headquarters, the Hotel Talleyrand, became a second major center, alongside the embassy, of the American colony. The French Mission, with its own quarters and staff, located in the Embassy annex, became still a third. The ECA was headed in Washington by Paul Hoffman, formerly president of the Studebaker Corporation. The special representative in Paris was Averell Harriman, a multimillionaire from New York who had become a practitioner of personal diplomacy under Roosevelt. The first head of the Marshall Plan Mission in Paris was David Bruce, who subsequently replaced Jefferson Caffery as ambassador. All three were representatives of the American business world. Hoffman, Harriman, and Bruce joined Caffery in assuming great importance in the internal life of France.[1]

The ECA missions dealt directly with the economic ministries of the host countries, and frequently forced the creation of a separate agency in the bureaucracy of the host country to deal with them. In France this took the form of an "Interministerial Committee for Questions of European Economic Cooperation," headed by a secretary general attached to the premier's office. The Missions assumed varying degrees of importance in the countries in which they operated. The greatest American influence was ex-

---

[1] Harry Bayard Price, *The Marshall Plan and Its Meaning* (Ithaca, NY: Cornell University Press, 1955). See also Hadley Arkes, *Bureaucracy, the Marshall Plan, and the National Interst* (Princeton: Princeton University Press, 1972).

ercised in Greece, where the Mission actually ran the economy in a manner very close, even in Washington's view, to a colonial relationship.[2] Much influence was exercised by the ECA in Italy and a minimal amount in Great Britain. France fell somewhere in between. Much argument took place in France about whether ECA Mission infringed upon French sovereignty. But the Mission never made decisions for the French; rather, it became a critically important pressure group in the making of French economic policy, just as the Embassy had become a focal point of French internal politics. The policies advocated by the Mission were in many cases also pursued by powerful interests in the French society and bureaucracy. Thus François Bloch-Lainé wrote that American aid "[was] not experienced either as domination or subordination vis-à-vis the lender."[3] Other French bureaucrats and politicians felt differently, however, when they found the Mission's influence being used against them. The Mission could not help but exercise political influence as well, which it did not always succeed in coordinating with the embassy.

The Americans had two fundamental economic goals in France: financial stabilization and the creation of a consumer economy. Washington regarded the inflationary cycle as the source of French political instability.[4] Many of the French agreed; to quote again François Bloch-Lainé, "rigor has no country." But the Americans also wanted to participate in decisions with regard to the level and priorities of French investment. Here their influence was limited by the prior existence of the Monnet Plan, which spelled out carefully the target sectors of the economy to which funds were to be allocated. The Monnet Plan enjoyed a national consensus. Moreover, the Americans had accepted it in outline during the negotiations leading to the Blum–Byrnes agreements in 1946. A further pattern of noninterference with the objectives of the Monnet Plan was set during the period of interim aid early in 1948. Georges Bidault then insisted that pursuit of the objectives already set in the Monnet Plan could not be interrupted without causing severe

---

[2] National Archives and Records Administration (NARA) (Suitland annex, Maryland), Agency for International Development (successor to the ECA), Economic Cooperation Aministration Files, Record Group 286, Office of the Special Representative in Europe, Confidential Incoming Cables, Box 1, July 17, 1951. Hereinafter cited as AID RG286. The Greek mission reported that "direct intervention in Greek affairs was unavoidable." William Foster, successor to Hoffman as head of the ECA, warned against the establishment of a colonial relationship with Greece "wholly contrary to American objectives." Memo of July 6, 1951.

[3] François Bloch-Lainé and Jean Bouvier, *La France Restaurée, 1944–54: Dialogue sur les choix d'une modernisation* (Paris: Fayard, 1986), pp. 90 and passim.

[4] For a detailed and somewhat different treatment of the material covered in this chapter see the excellent work by Chiarella Esposito, "The Marshall Plan in France and Italy, 1948–1950: Counterpart Fund Negotiations" (Unpublished PhD dissertation, State University of New York at Stony Brook, 1985), which has the additional merit of comparing the French and Italian cases.

problems of social dislocation, unrest, and wastage. Washington agreed, in exchange for a promise to achieve fiscal stabilization.[5]

Acceptance of the Monnet Plan inhibited American attempts to exercise influence over French fiscal policy, however. Washington attributed the French inflation to irresponsibility and a regressive tax structure that placed the heaviest burden on those least able to pay and permitted large-scale fraud. The Americans also criticized the low standard of living of the working class, which they blamed on a selfish French bourgeoisie who kept wages low and ignored essential social expenditures such as housing. To deal with inflation, the Mission wanted some of the counterpart funds used to retire government debt to the Bank of France, as was being done in Great Britain. But the Mission was unable to urge a corresponding cut in French expenditure for reconstruction and development without being blamed for blockage of the Monnet Plan and interference in French internal affairs. Richard Bissel, head of the ECA Mission in December 1948, noted that "the size of reconstruction and modernization expenditure is in excess of the amount which French economy can support at the present time without inflation and that careful review would reveal the possibility of very substantial reductions without endangering the achievement of French self-support in 1952–53 at adequate consumption levels."[6] Washington never succeeded in obtaining such reductions.

Control over the release of counterpart funds was the weapon Washington hoped to use to achieve fiscal stability. The French were pressured to use only noninflationary sources of income for government expenditure, improve tax collections and their distribution among different groups in the population, restrict credit, and maintain an equitable price–wages equilibrium. In April 1948 the first real instance of a release of 25 billion francs of counterpart funds arose. The Embassy thought that the Mayer Plan, with its forced reconversion of 5,000 franc notes and increased taxes, had reached the limit of politically tolerable deflation. No further tax increases were possible for the moment. A significant budget deficit remained, however, due to the expenses of the Monnet Plan, which could not be reduced. The result was that "in the absence of resources from counterpart the French Government would have to resort to inflationary financing through central bank advances with all the undesirable political, psychological, as well as economic consequences of such an action." To avoid that outcome the Em-

---

[5] NARA, AID RG286, ECA, Office of the Special Representative, France, Box 18 of 92, Report on Interim Aid, July 1948.

[6] NARA, AID RG286, ECA, Office of the Administrator, Country Subject Files, France, Report of December 31, 1948; Office of the Special Representative, Country Subject Files, France, Box 18, Counterpart, December 28, 1948. The best treatment of this question of the uses of counterpart is in Imanuel Wexler, *The Marshall Plan Revisited: The European Recovery Program in Economic Perspective* (Westport, CT: Greenwood Press, 1983).

bassy agreed to release the 25 billion francs in exchange for further French promises to refrain from inflationary forms of financing. But Washington remained skeptical "whether the French Government financial and fiscal program was really calculated to bring inflationary financing to an end."[7] It could not really be so calculated as long as the expenditure in the Monnet Plan remained untouchable.

Nor could the ERP officials avoid the political implications of their actions, as equally became apparent during the period of interim aid. On April 7, 1948 the French government proposed that an additional 26 billion francs of counterpart funds be allocated to continue subsidies necessary to maintain coal and wheat prices at their current low levels.[8] The Embassy refused on the grounds that this was not an appropriate use for counterpart funds. But the government could neither borrow nor increase taxes to make up the difference, and had promised the Americans not to resort to inflationary advances from the Bank of France. The delicate structure of Third Force coalition cabinets, moreover, meant that any shortfall in government funds was likely to be the occasion of a cabinet crisis. True to form, an emergency deficit occurred in July 1948, and Finance Minister René Mayer, unable to use the counterpart funds, called for new taxes in a futile effort to maintain the coal and wheat subsidies. The government then collapsed.

Schuman resigned on the pretext of a disagreement about the military budget. The Socialists nonetheless overthrew the government because they were generally dissatisfied about rising prices and lagging wages, while Washington remained critical of Schuman's failure to do anything about the wage–price disparity. Caffery and Marshall hoped for an increase in salaries to strengthen and reward Force Ouvrière for its cooperation during the Mayer Plan, but the ECA backed the government in its determination to hold the line on wages. Price increases followed in the fall, occasioned by the refusal to release counterpart for subsidies, and helped precipitate the confrontation between the government and the coal miners over wages. Failure to release counterpart funds, the Americans quickly demonstrated, was as pregnant with consequences or more so than quick agreement to unblock them.

Mission control of counterpart expenditure became a part of all the bilateral agreements Washington negotiated with the sixteen Marshall Plan nations by July 1948. These agreements were concluded with the greatest of difficulty. Conscious of the possible erosion of its sovereignty, and sensitive to Gaullist and Communist attacks on this ground, the French government was further motivated to resist American demands than it might otherwise have been. The principle of counterpart funds was not really negotiable,

[7] NARA, AID RG286, ECA, Office of the Special Representative, Country Subject Files, France, Box 18, Report on Interim Aid, July 1948.
[8] Ibid. The embassy administered the interim aid program. The mission took up its functions in July 1948.

having already been written into the interim aid bill, but other aspects of the draft bilateral agreement appeared to threaten sovereignty, to the extent that the Quai doubted whether it could obtain ratification: "In its present state this draft is often shocking in its form and raises numerous basic difficulties." It was dominated by "the double disdain" of the State Department and the American Congress with regard to the recipients of Marshall Plan aid, and risked providing fuel for every malicious criticism of the Marshall Plan coming from the extreme left. Averell Harriman, chief American negotiator for the ECA, cabled the State Department that the bilateral agreements were unacceptable; French and British negotiators said they could not present them to their parliaments, and Bidault, Reynaud, and other friendly politicians warned that signing the agreement was "suicidal." The treaties played into the hands of the Communists and contained conditions that "no free country could accept."[9]

Two of these conditions had to be withdrawn by Washington: most-favored-nation treatment in international trade for occupied Germany and Japan, and arbitration of currency exchange rates by the International Monetary Fund. In the first the Europeans saw a humiliating demand for equal treatment of the enemy; the second demand raised once again the symbol of national control over currency which had so agitated de Gaulle at the time of the Normandy invasion. American preponderance on the IMF meant the United States would be able to impose its will on international exchange rates. Further objections were raised to the American demand that a portion of counterpart funds be reserved for the development of strategic materials lacking in the continental United States, the arbitration and period of application clauses of the treaty, and its general tenor and style. Bidault demanded that such offending phrases as "at the request of the American government," and "the French government declares it is ready," be edited out of the text wherever they appeared. Nor could the French government legally bind itself to the provisions of an American piece of legislation, or accept the control over the OEEC that would be exercised by the ECA.[10]

On June 18 Bonnet reported from Washington that having withdrawn its demand regarding exchange rates, Washington was now taking a hard line in the negotiations. Failure to ratify by July 4 would mean termination of

9 Archives Nationales (A.N.), F60 ter 391, Textes. The F60 ter series contains the records of the French interministerial committee charged with implementation of the Marshall Plan. See, in carton 391, the text of the agreement as signed, and comments on earlier drafts in "Note pour le Ministre des Finances et des Affaires Economiques," June 7, 1948, and "Examen du Projet," June 27, 1948. Also Foreign Relations of the United States (FRUS), 1948, III, Western Europe, European Recovery Program, June 4, 1948, pp. 446–7, June 21, 1948, pp. 454–5.

10 A.N., Papiers Georges Bidault, 457 AP 22, June 18, 21, 1948. Pierre Melandri argues that the American Congress actually intended the ECA to become the administrative framework for the construction of a united Europe *Les Etats-Unis face à l'unification de l'Europe, 1945–54* (Paris: A Pedone, 1980).

aid on that date. Bidault replied that at least five clauses in the treaty as written were still unacceptable and the French government was joining its opposition to the British. Bidault would risk the aid cutoff. "Whatever the economic problems that a suspension of aid would create, the government cannot, in the present state of the negotiations, reject that possibility." In the face of such resolve the Americans made further concessions, limiting their demands for strategic materials to a determination by the recipient country that sufficient supplies were available, and giving in on arbitration and length of the treaty. The French were in turn ready to make some accommodation on most-favored-nation status for Germany and Japan, but the British rejected that clause, and Paris could not afford to appear to accept less than the British. By June 28 the French were ready to sign: "the Government believes that the terms of this agreement fully respect the necessities of French sovereignty." But nothing happened in French–American relations without a crisis: In Germany, General Clay lost patience on the most-favored-nation question and pushed Hoffman into threatening to cut off aid to all nonsignatories of the bilateral agreements: France, the United Kingdom, Belgium, and Sweden. London still refused to bend, however, and five days later the Americans agreed to withdraw their demands. The treaty was signed.[11]

The French put the best possible light on the signing of the treaty, stressing the numerous concessions obtained from Washington. These were not negligible. The exchange-rate clause was now only a repetition of Bretton Woods, which everyone had lived with for years, and the arbitration agreement was fully reciprocal. The accord terminated on June 30, 1953, as the French demanded. Strategic materials of interest to Washington would be made available only "whenever possible." Even the clause stipulating that the French government "will make every effort" to accomplish higher production, free exchange, and currency stabilization was so phrased as to "exclude all American interference in our economic, budgetary, financial, and monetary policies. It is not a question, as the Communists write, of making France an American colony, but on the contrary, of liberating it economically and financially." The French government had not sold its birthright for a plate of beans, as the Communists charged.[12] The essentials had been won. Bonnet met with Hoffman and Bruce on June 25, and was told that American objectives in France were no different from those spelled out in the Monnet Plan.[13]

Privately, however, the French feared they had opened a Pandora's box. The Quai feared that the bilateral agreement had aggravated feelings of

[11] A.N., Papiers Georges Bidault, AP 457 22, June 18, 21, 23, 1948, 28, 1948; 457 AP 21, July 2, 3, 8, 1948.
[12] A.N., Papiers Georges Bidault, 457 AP 22, June 29, 1948, "Schéma pour un exposé du Président du Conseil," and accompanying "Historique."
[13] A.N., Papiers Georges Bidault, 457 AP 22, Bonnet to Bidault, June 25, 1948.

suspicion and contempt for the United States in France. The Europeans had an inferiority complex already; it would not be helped by the appearance that instead of *associés* in a common enterprise the French were *assistés* in need of charity, a humiliating idea in contradiction with their national pride. The French must be taught the message that American counterpart funds meant fulfillment of the objectives of the Monnet Plan, which would lead in turn to the reestablishment of French independence.[14] Jean Monnet himself did not put the question much differently in a revealing letter to Georges Bidault:

> We are to a great extent going to depend on this country [the United States] as much for the maintenance of our economic life as for our national security. This situation cannot continue without great danger. We are today [for the United States] "the stake" *[l'enjeu]*. We must transform this situation quickly into one of independence and collaboration.[15]

Monnet rejected charges that the United States was reactionary, imperialist, and wanted to control France. That might be the ultimate outcome, however, unless the French were strong enough to take up the challenge and use the Marshall Plan to reclaim their independence. For Monnet, as for Washington, this meant attaining financial stability.

Shortly after the signing of the bilateral agreement a joint American–French conference was held at the Bank of France. American treasury representative William Tomlinson immediately demanded an end to expansionist policies; the Bank must impose tight controls on credit. Was this Washington's way of reducing the Monnet Plan expenditure after all, which the Americans had otherwise agreed was untouchable? The ensuring argument was a kind of dialogue of the deaf: The French insisted that credit had expanded only to keep up with increased levels of industrial production, the Americans argued that increased credit was a source of inflation. Tomlinson tried to rule out any further expansion of credit during 1948, but backed off after a furious argument. The Americans were not there to dictate policy, he said, but sought only "improved understanding." But continued American pressure was applied in collusion with officials within the French bureaucracy who agreed with American policies, and the bank did significantly tighten credit for the remainder of 1948.[16]

Dissatisfied, Washington directed its attention to the premier's office and turned for pressure to the threat to withhold counterpart funds. Bruce thought it very important "to disabuse certain French officials of the impression that one way or another the counterpart will be available to them irrespective of the actions they take. . . . It is difficult to say how effective our influence

14 Ibid., June 28, 1948.
15 A.N., Papiers Georges Bidault, 457 AP 21, Monnet to Bidault, April 18, 1948.
16 NARA, AID, RG286, ECA, Office of the Special Representative, Country Subject Files, Box 70, France, August 20, 1948.

can be on the present political and economic situation in France but our role clearly is to continue to exercise such influence as we can." [17] The prolonged cabinet crises of the summer and fall of 1948 interfered with any effort to apply pressure, and it was not until the formation of the Queuille government on September 15, 1948 that counterpart negotiations could begin in earnest. The crises had severely limited American economic influence, moreover. Caffery was too busy warning French politicians away from the temptation of a renewed alliance with the Communists, and had to threaten to suspend U.S. aid altogether. In the face of political questions of such seriousness, freezing counterpart funds seemed of little moment.

On September 13 Queuille requested assurance of the release of counterpart funds through November 15, 1948, prior to the submission of his program to the National Assembly, or he would seek further advances from the Bank of France. Bruce was alarmed: Rising prices, labor unrest, retention of grain by peasants, and deteriorating confidence in the currency were all aggravated by a fragile and ineffective political coalition. Government authority was vitiated by a weak constitution and an irresponsible parliament, its only cement the fears of Gaullism and Communism. There was one frail reed: "Prime Minister Queuille [is a] man of character and determination, skilled in [the] political arts. Program suggested by him . . . is from fiscal viewpoint most courageous and satisfactory proposed to meet present difficulties." Bruce warned that refusal of Queuille's request presented a "particularly grave risk if demand is tied to U.S. refusal to accept program as satisfactory." The result, Bruce warned, would be financial chaos, a crisis no successor government would be likely to be able to solve, and even collapse of the Republic. [18] At the National Advisory Council in Washington several officials regarded his telegram as "virtual blackmail." The United States was being told it must release counterpart funds or bear the responsibility for renewed inflation and a possible collapse of the Fourth Republic. There seemed little choice though; support for Queuille would enable him to emphasize American understanding and cooperation in French recovery efforts, while refusal would "serve no useful purpose and might aggravate the inflationary situation." [19] Queuille was assured that counterpart funds would be released, and as a consequence was able to tell the National Assembly that France's friends would stand by her in her hour of need: "I have some reason to hope that the aid of our allies will not be refused us if Parliament makes the necessary effort. We have personal assur-

[17] NARA, AID, RG286, ECA, OSR, Central Secretariat, Country Subject Files, France, Box 2, June 3, 1948.
[18] NARA, AID, RG286, ECA, Office of the Administrator, Country Subject Files, France, Box 2.
[19] NARA, AID, RG286, ECA, Administrator's Country Subject Files, Box 2, National Advisory Council Document No. 742, September 15, 1948.

ances that we will be able to unblock 120 billions if we put our house in order."[20]

Queuille was obliged to make several commitments to the Americans in return with the aim of achieving financial stability, including new taxes, budgetary savings, and streamlining the administration of the nationalized enterprises.[21] Queuille also announced salary increases of 15 percent, thus belatedly satisfying an American demand since the summer. But combined with price increases in transportation, postage, and tobacco, the pay increases looked insufficient to workers, and the government's efforts to rationalize the nationalized coal industry led directly to the bitter strike in that industry which began on September 29, 1948.

The Americans were not fully satisfied with Queuille's efforts, however. On October 19 Foreign Minister Robert Schuman asked Averell Harriman whether the French might make as large an aid request for 1949 as they had received in 1948. Harriman's reply was discouraging. He advised Schuman to reduce the French request by at least 10 percent, not only because Congress expected its aid appropriations to lessen as recovery advanced, but also because of the feeling in Washington that France had received much more than it deserved for "political reasons." Harriman also cited the American perception of an unequal tax burden in France that adversely affected the working class, and he urged the prime minister to reduce the consumption of the wealthy by means of increased taxes.[22]

The Americans were deeply concerned by the ugly sabotage of the coal fields that accompanied the strikes of October and November 1948. Washington blamed the Communists and supplied emergency shipments of coal so as to enable the government to withstand the miners. But these events led to despair about the French, and expressions of concern that they were beyond help. Henry Labouisse noted that France was receiving more aid than was economically justified, yet the trend toward economic improvement now appeared to have been reversed. The reduction of aid would no doubt help the Communists. What was Washington to do, turn to de Gaulle, continue aid indefinitely notwithstanding French instability, or cut off aid and wash its hands of the whole business? Political instability was the major obstacle to French economic recovery, yet only crises seemed to bring decisions in France. The current strikes were aimed at the defeat of the Marshall Plan, but the Communists were also exploiting the government's failure to deal with inflation and low real wages. Queuille's pay increases were too

20 NARA, AID, RG286, ECA, Administrator's Services Division, Country Files, France, Box 16, September 17, 1948.
21 NARA, AID, RG286, ECA, Office of the Special Representative, France, Counterpart, September 25, 1948. Queuille asked his letter be kept secret because its contents might prove "embarrassing" if revealed.
22 NARA, AID, RG286, ECA, Office of the Deputy Administrator, Country Subject Files, France, Box 1, October 19, 1948.

little and too late, and his government refused to force sacrifices on the agricultural and entrepreneurial classes. The non-Communist unions, CFTC and FO, despite American support, had been undermined. The Americans concluded that at a minimum, a complete overhaul of the tax system was necessary. To some nothing less than a complete overhaul of French society in general would suffice.[23]

These questions were discussed in an internal paper titled "The French Crisis," which circulated in the ECA in November 1948. France was now designated the major obstacle to the success of the entire European Recovery Program. Could the United States continue to throw money down the drain given French refusal to straighten out their mess? De Gaulle was not a viable option, but economic assistance to the French without the imposition of conditions appeared useless as well. The French must be told that their political instability was unacceptable. The remedy, to be sure, was in their hands: "We have neither the right nor the intention to interfere in such domestic matters." But American economic assistance must depend on the French ability to master their internal situation. Clearly American policy had reached a turning point.[24]

Word of this internal American debate leaked, greatly worrying the French. In London the *Economist* reported that the United States was considering cutting off aid to France; the Americans were allegedly hoping that an anticorruption government, including both Blum and Reynaud, would emerge as a result of their pressure.[25] In Paris, Harriman, Caffery, and Bruce objected to the conclusions of "The French Crisis." The timing was all wrong, and the effect of its release could be disastrous. Marshall agreed, settling the debate for the moment; it was not yet the time to apply severe pressure on the French.[26] Bruce argued that economics, not politics, were the problem, and finances only must be the focus of policies of the Marshall Plan Mission. Washington's task was not to speculate about or try to dictate "vague political solutions," but rather to pay attention to the real current situation. The problem was the French government's "irresponsibility verging on dishonesty in hiding from the French people the inflationary consequences of failing to provide adequate financial resources." It was not clear why Bruce regarded this as an economic rather than a political problem, but he did agree on the future solution. Only the imposition of the most severe condi-

[23] FRUS, 1948, III, Western Europe, France, October 13, 1948, p. 668. NARA, AID, RG286, ECA, European Programs Division, Mediterranean Branch, Country Subject Files, France, October 19, 19, 1948, Memo of the Finance Division.
[24] NARA, AID, RG286, ECA, European Programs Division, Mediterranean Branch, Country Subject Files, France, "The French Crisis," and Memo of November 15, 1948.
[25] A.N., F60 ter, 378, October 28, 1948.
[26] FRUS, 1948, III, Western Europe, France, October 27, 1948, pp. 670–2.

tions on the release of counterpart funds "may influence the government to make additional efforts on compressing expenditure or increased taxation and to follow the sustained application of the necessary fiscal and financial policies."[27]

The outcome of the internal debate resulted in an unprecedented American effort to coerce the French into adopting "responsible" fiscal policies. On November 15, 1948 Tomlinson and Bruce met with Queuille and Minister of Finance Maurice Petsche. The Americans were frank. Congress must be convinced of the existence of a genuine French effort to achieve financial stability or the future of the ERP would be in doubt. There were two ways open to the French to avoid price rises. "Either by increasing fiscal charges ... or by obliging the French people to restrain growth in income, profits, and borrowing." The French must undertake radical measures of fiscal reform, or American taxpayers would not consent to having their own tax monies used to assist France. Bruce told Queuille that France must do more to increase its exports and halt the flow of capital out of the country. Concern about the French situation even overcame Washington's traditional repugnance to currency restrictions. Queuille appeared reluctant to talk about reforms, however. He warned that fiscal reform could be achieved only gradually, and seemed eager to vaunt his anticommunism, bragging about his success against the Communists in the recent strikes and his ability to "pluck the petals from the Communist artichoke." Bruce complained in turn that the government was not taking sufficient advantage of negative publicity surrounding the PCF as a result of the strikes.[28] Queuille apparently understood the gravity of Bruce's remarks. On November 24 he informed Bruce that he would undertake the necessary reforms.

On November 28, 1948 Bruce reported that Queuille and Petsche had submitted a "surprisingly drastic" budget and investment program to the inner cabinet. It appeared to be a serious and realistic effort to achieve financial stability and, therefore, deserved full ECA support. The ECA decided that it was necessary to strengthen Queuille's resolve. The effort took the form of a letter from Bruce to Queuille which, despite its gentlemanly tone, had the hallmark of an ultimatum. The letter was in some respects unprecedented, coming from neither the head of the ECA, nor from the ambassador, but simply from the head of the aid Mission. The American terms were simple. Bruce noted the concern in Washington about "justifying aid to France on the basis of performance in France during the first year of the Marshall Plan." Despite "admirable efforts," and important progress, "events have proved that immediate and greater efforts must be forthcom-

27 FRUS, 1949, IV, Economic Recovery of Western Europe, January 8–9, 1949, pp. 367–70.

28 A.N., F60 ter, 378, November 15, November 24, 1948. NARA, AID, RG286, ECA, European Programs Division, Mediterranean Branch, Country Subject Files, Box 4, report of November 18, 1948.

ing to create internal financial stabilization and to restore confidence in the French franc."[29] Bruce went on with extraordinary frankness.

> Not to press forward to an early achievement of these goals would, in our opinion, seriously jeopardize the success of the recovery of Western Europe. Accordingly, we are strongly of the opinion that the chances of France obtaining adequate appropriations from the next American Congress are distinctly poor unless a realistic fiscal and financial program for 1949 is adopted by the French Assembly. From the viewpoint of our own legislative deadlines it is of first importance that basic legislation in this regard be enacted before Congress meets next year to act upon further appropriations for the Marshall Plan.

Bruce then listed the conditions under which releases of counterpart funds for 1949 would be continued: (1) a fiscal effort sufficient to cover all government expenditure without recourse to the Bank of France; (2) utilization of counterpart only for the investment program; (3) the continuation of recently announced credit controls; and (4) reform of the fiscal system eliminating "obvious inequities" in the tax burden, which would require "drastic shifts" in the incidence of taxation. French failure would mean not only the loss of counterpart funds, but severe overall reduction of American aid and "diminished cooperation from other European nations in French recovery efforts."

Bruce's letter was designed to insert itself neatly into an internal dispute that the Americans were acutely aware was taking place inside the French government. It was combined with other forms of pressure; warnings to Bonnet, in Washington, and representations in Paris by the British. The cabinet was already on notice from French sources: the Quai warned that Congress would focus on France when the time came to appropriate Marshall Plan funds for the next year, and the risk of an aid reduction was serious: "Certain Americans could be wondering in effect whether the only result of aid given to France is not to maintain artificially its level of consumption." Without a severe fiscal effort "Europe will be made without France." The French had shown no real will to reform, but only made transparent their "present malaise." The ECA's critique struck a responsive chord: The Quai warned that with all the other European nations making extensive fiscal efforts, France appeared to be the weak point in the system and the point of convergence of adversaries of the Marshall Plan on a world scale.[30]

Yet it was by no means clear that the Bruce letter was having its desired effect. Word of its existence leaked, and the Americans were forced to deny that they had issued an ultimatum to the French to balance their budget or

[29] NARA, AID, RG286, ECA, Office of the Deputy Administrator, Country Subject Files, France, 1948–9, Box 1. Also in A.N., F60 ter, 378 in French translation, and published in Bloch-Lainé and Bouvier, *La France Restaurée.*

[30] A.N., Papiers Georges Bidault, 457 AP 21, October 11, 1948.

lose their economic aid. Washington feared the letter would backfire, and Queuille be forced to make a demonstration of his independence. The ECA, while approving the letter as "interestingly and excellently put," tried to minimize its importance.[31] Queuille, if he was not the source of the leak, used it to request an immediate release of counterpart funds because "very real political dangers of current leaks about American conditions" were playing into the hands of Communist propagandists and had "unfortunate effects" in other circles who were jealous of French sovereignty.[32] On December 7 Chauvel wrote to Bonnet that he was "quite worried about the state of mind of the Government with regard to fiscal measures which are expected of us as much by the Americans as by the English." Monnet was pushing for the reforms but was "in a bitter confrontation with Finances, and in general poorly thought of by the Government."

Chauvel feared Queuille's fiscal program would not be adopted, France would lose Marshall Plan aid, the Germans would benefit, and the result would be the permanent loss of French preponderance and leadership in Europe. Bonnet was summoned to Paris to explain the seriousness of the issue: France's failure to put its house in order would work to the advantage of Germany. The Americans counted on France to lead the movement toward European unity that was expected to come from successful implementation of the Marshall Plan. Congress, in its hearings, had France "under the glare of spotlights," and one heard everywhere that French bankruptcy could not indefinitely be bailed out by the American taxpayer.[33] The same fears were expressed by President Auriol, to whom Bonnet wrote in a similar vein. Personalities as diverse as President Auriol, Pierre Mendés France, Guillaume Guindey, Bloch-Lainé, Hervé Alphand, and Jean Monnet were all bringing pressure on Queuille and Petsche to introduce fiscal reforms in the direction desired by the Americans – and themselves.[34]

Were the Americans responsible, then, for the famous *loi des maxima*, introduced on December 13, 1948, which finally put the French government's finances on a stable footing for the following year? The question is counterfactual and unanswerable. American influence was a principal component of the internal French decision-making process, without consideration of which virtually no important aspect of the early Fourth Republic can be explained adequately. The *loi des maxima* denied the French government access to inflationary sources of income for the financing of the 1949 bud-

[31] NARA, AID, RG286, ECA, Deputy Administrator, Country Subject Files, December 14, 1948, Howard Bruce to David Bruce.
[32] NARA, AID, RG286, ECA, Office of the Deputy Aministrator, Country Subject Files, December 9, 1948.
[33] Ministère des Affaires Etrangères (MAE), Fonds nominatifs Henri Bonnet, December 7 and 18, 1948.
[34] Gérard Bossuat, "Le Poids de l'aide américaine sur la politique économique et financière de la France en 1948," *Relations Internationales,* 37 (Spring 1984): 17–36.

get. Every government expense would be financed by increased receipts or economies. The Americans certainly welcomed it as a "most unusual and favorable development in French public finance"; if applied it would magnify the importance of counterpart funds and greatly increase American leverage on the French economy. France would now fully play its part in the economic recovery of Europe. The ECA Mission deliberately understated its role in the passage of the law; it had simply made its views known. The rest was up to the French, although French officials had welcomed American input into their decision making. The Mission assumed no responsibility and did not interfere. It had, moreover, refrained from recommending to the French a reduction in their investment goals as established in the Monnet Plan.[35]

On December 27, 1948, in a letter to David Bruce, Queuille pridefully outlined the *loi des maxima* and asked, as a measure of the seriousness of the French government, that 25 billion francs of counterpart funds be released in order to lower the ceiling of advances from the Bank of France from 200 to 175 billion francs. The request was quickly granted, and as the New Year began, the outlook for France was considerably brighter. The strikes had been defeated, a promising fiscal program of stabilization was in place, and French–American relations had never been better. But the French still had an uphill struggle. In February 1949, the French Embassy in Washington forwarded a typical example of the difficulties facing the French in American opinion. An article in *Fortune* magazine indicted France as "the most flagrant example of what is wrong with Europe," and "the prize tax evaders of the Western world. . . . the cancer of Communism has rarely found a more hospitable body," said *Fortune,* because the "better" citizens would not make, in conditions of freedom, even a fraction of the sacrifice they would have to make if the Communists were actually to take over.[36] It is remarkable how socially conscious American business circles were capable of being when looking at any other society than their own.

II THE USES OF AMERICAN AID

By 1949 the ECA Mission, the American Embassy in Paris, and the French government had worked out their respective roles, and there seemed every reason to expect that the path to French economic recovery would be smooth. But French–American relations seemed to thrive on crises. In April 1949 after Congress had made its aid appropriations, the French approached the Mission with a new request for the release of counterpart funds. The French wanted to avoid the humiliation involved in monthly requests, and Queuille,

[35] NARA, AID, RG286, ECA, European Programs Devision, Mediterranean Branch, Country Subjects Files, France, 1948–9, Internal Finance, January 4, 1949.
[36] A.N., F60 ter, 388, February 5, 1949.

citing the great success of the *loi des maxima,* submitted a program of expenditure covering the whole of 238 billion francs France would receive through December 1949. Queuille proposed to designate 122 billion francs for the nationalized enterprises targeted for priority in the Monnet Plan, especially coal, electricity, and the railroads, 96 billion for the private sector, mainly for the reconstruction of war damage and agriculture, and the remaining 20 billion for the Saar and French overseas territories.

Bruce was sympathetic, but knew better than to ask Washington for blanket release of the year's counterpart funds. The French expected routine release of funds while they gave minimal information to the ECA and avoided further policy commitments. They expected to finance current treasury operations with counterpart funds and justify the expenditures to the Mission by the bookkeeping device of retroactive application of the funds to past investments that had been funded from other sources. This sleight of hand was firmly rejected by the Mission. Instead of endorsing the French request, therefore, Bruce asked Washington for autonomy for the Mission in Paris to decide upon counterpart releases. Bruce praised the Queuille government's policy as the "soundest in a decade," however, and argued that Queuille deserved all the assistance he could get. The denial of counterpart could cause a government crisis, and no successor was likely to do better than Queuille, while the political situation was in delicate balance; the Mission needed the greatest flexibility because parliament could be "tactfully led but not driven." [37]

Paul Hoffman, however, intended to keep control over counterpart funds in Washington, especially where the French were concerned. He did not believe that the French had mastered their fiscal problems. The December program had not been as effective as hoped, and the government showed signs once again of giving in to pressures to expand credit. Hoffman agreed to a release of 25 billion francs for the month of April but deferred a decision on May pending a review of French finances, and he reserved all decision-making authority to Washington. [38]

The French found Washington's obstinacy upsetting; they continued to press for routinized releases and tried to avoid providing enormous amounts of documentation, but failed repeatedly on both counts. The Americans insisted on weekly summaries of French treasury operations, which drove the French to despair. Paris withheld information, kept Washington at bay with excuses, and insisted that monthly reports were more than adequate. On March 17, 1949 Bruce returned to Schweitzer a list of projects for which he had inadequate documentation to evaluate worthiness for ECA assistance. Included was a French request to purchase locomotives, which Bruce insisted be justified by estimates of the expected volume of traffic on the lines

[37] A.N., F60 ter, 498 (1949), April 6, 1949; FRUS, IV, 1949, France, April 4, 1949, 638.
[38] FRUS, 1949, IV, France, April 6 and 22, 1949, pp. 638–40.

on which they were to be used. Railway officials thought themselves perfectly qualified to judge their own equipment needs; and since all internal investment came from one source in the treasury in any case, the French could underwrite themselves what Washington refused to finance.[39] The whole process seemed to them an exercise in futility.

Most galling were American demands for publicity. Congress wanted to finance individual, spectacular projects in full, believing public displays of American generosity were the most effective way to combat Communism and anti-American sentiment. The French sought to be as discreet as possible about the source of financing, regarding it as something of a humiliation that they could not provide for all their investment themselves.[40] The ECA was caught between conflicting pressures in Paris and Washington, while Congress became increasingly impatient with accounts of French "ingratitude." There was little question as to which of these pressures would prove to be more important. On August 17, 1949 Barry Bingham, successor to Bruce as head of the French Mission, asked Schweitzer for a list of proposed projects with "broad human interest and public appeal," suitable for the widest publicity. By the year's end, he had extracted a promise that in 1950 all reconstruction, as opposed to investment, would be financed with ECA funds. Bingham demanded a breakdown on all expenses for ECA-financed projects and noted that Congress was especially interested in housing, hospitals, and schools. The French were instructed to give particular attention to means of publicity: Each project must be prominently labeled to identify the funding source. The absence of such labeling was unfavorably commented upon in Washington.[41] These demands were sarcastically referred to within the Mission as reflecting the policy of the "bronze plaque."

In its first program review of French investments, the Mission tried to propose projects itself, rather than simply approve or reject those submitted by Paris, which went beyond the procedure informally agreed upon at the time of the bilateral accords. Thus an April 29 Mission review of the French program criticized the coal industry for paying too little attention to safety in the mines, thereby supporting the position of the Communist unions against the administration of the *Charbonnages de France*. The Americans also suggested more be spent on housing for miners. With regard to electricity, the Mission criticized the French emphasis on hydroelectric power as excessive. The Americans thought French investment in the railways too heavy and their electrification too extensive; one suspects the Mission imagined a France like California today, laced with polluting freeways. Washington never ceased to hammer away at one area in particular; the French noted, "Finally it appears to [the Americans] that social concerns should have occupied a larger

[39]   A.N., F60 ter, 388, March 17, 1949.
[40]   A.N., F60 ter, 357, April 19, 21, 26, 30, 1949.
[41]   A.N., F60 ter, 499, December 5, 1949.

place in the program."[42] They wanted the construction of housing, hospitals, and schools to show that the Marshall Plan and American generosity could deliver these things rather than the Communists. Instead, the Monnet Plan gave them almost a Stalinist model: emphasis on heavy industry and transportation to the exclusion of consumer goods and light industry.

The largest part of interaction between the two governments continued to be in the area of fiscal policy. The Americans pressed for tight credit and a balanced budget with prohibitions against any inflationary financing. The French were constantly led into temptation and called back to the virtuous path by their American paymasters. Acheson himself instructed the Mission that the principle of withholding release of counterpart must be upheld if French government operations exceeded resources available from tax revenues and noninflationary borrowing. If the French were unwilling to raise taxes they would have to cut expenses. Hoffman, from his side, insisted on tight credit. It was left to the Mission to deal with French reactions. In April 1949 Bruce noted that credit restrictions were the heaviest in the history of French banking. Further tightening, he thought, would encourage strong resistance. But Hoffman would not relent. Paul Reynaud attacked the government's credit policies, and received a lecture from the ambassador on political responsibility. *Le Monde* reported that tight credit was being imposed by the Americans as a condition for the April release of counterpart funds, and *Combat* told its readers that Queuille wanted to ease credit but had run into an ECA veto. Acting Mission chief Horace Reed cabled that the "press campaign bears every earmark of being inspired by certain French authorities, particularly in view of accurate references to insistence on our part on continued credit restriction in connection with last week's counterpart release." Reed warned that if a recession developed the United States must be ready to bear the blame.[43] Still the American pressure continued.

In May Reed noticed distinct improvement in the French economic situation, and Hoffman approved the monthly counterpart release while asking for better treasury information. In June the ECA made a public announcement that 20 billion francs of counterpart was being applied to debt retirement, proof that the goals of the Marshall Plan were well on their way to fulfillment. But in July, the whole edifice once again appeared to be a house of cards. The French treasury was again bankrupt, and Finance Minister Petsche declared that if he could not obtain an emergency release of counterpart the financial crisis would result in the collapse of the Queuille government. Once again, the ECA found itself trapped by its insistence on the tight control of counterpart funds. The fate of the French government had a way of becoming entangled with every minor shortfall in the treasury's

[42] A.N. F60 ter 499, April 29, 1949.
[43] NARA, AID, RG286, ECA, OSR, Administrative Services Division, Country Files, France, Box 16, April 11, 1949.

cash flow. Petsche insisted that the current crisis was due to "special difficulties," but the reality was that the French government could not borrow, because the public lacked confidence in its ability to repay, nor could Queuille approach parliament for new sources of revenue. If the *loi des maxima* was to be observed, the Americans must come to the rescue, or Petsche would resort to the inevitable inflationary advances from the Bank of France. Petsche coupled his appeal with a promise to liberalize French import policies and push for a generally more lenient trade policy. The Americans were not impressed, however; they could not release counterpart funds to meet an emergency in regular government operations. They needed a long-run purpose and a justification. Washington did not wish to be seen as bearing the responsibility for Queuille's fall, though. The solution chosen was to release the August allotment of funds for unspecified investment and then to allow the French treasury to tap the monies immediately for other purposes, repaying the debt later in the year. On July 27 Hoffman released 30 billion francs, and the Queuille government received a new lease on life.[44]

Bingham tried to put the best possible light on the situation. Queuille's progress until the summer had been little short of startling. Without the ECA, he claimed, France would have gone Communist the previous winter, and much of Western Europe very possibly along with it. Petsche was trying to observe the prohibition on recourse to the Bank of France, hence his perpetual fear of budgetary crisis. The ECA must hold firm in its support for Queuille; it could not abandon him now.[45] There was to be no postponement of the inevitable, however. On October 9, 1949 Queuille resigned. The issue was again his disagreement with the Socialists over pay increases, but he was bitter over the devaluation of the pound and an alleged Anglo–American arrangement to exclude France from discussions of the new rate of exchange. Before resigning, Queuille satisfied his domestic political supporters, letting credit expand once more. The Mission was furious. The French had used the cabinet crisis to reneg on their anti-inflationary commitments. Queuille was told in his capacity as head of the caretaker government that there could be no October release of counterpart funds. The Mission thought it better to act at once; to wait until a new government was formed and then refuse to release counterpart would be interpreted as American dissatisfaction with the new government and interference in French internal affairs. But Queuille argued precisely the opposite. He had already been violently criticized for doing American bidding, he said. He had persisted in deflationary policies as long as possible and no further measures

[44] NARA, AID, RG286, ECA, Office of the Special Representative, France, Counterpart, Box 18, May 23, 25, 1949; Country Files 1949–50, France, Box 70, July 22, 27, 29, 1949. Some of the same documents are in A.N., F60 ter 498 (1949).
[45] NARA, AID, RG286, ECA, Office of the Administrator, Country Subject Files, France, August 13, 1949.

were possible. If counterpart funds were withheld from him now, he warned, it would make it that much harder to form a new government. Washington was damned either way. A few days later Queuille offered a way out of the impasse. The American government could withhold counterpart funds, but it would be announced that this was to regularize the advance granted the French in August. The disagreement could in that way be papered over without Washington committing itself.

Washington was not pleased. The August debt could be considered settled only if the French submitted a list of projects to which the 30 billion francs were now being applied. Throwing up its hands in the face of this tangle, Washington passed the responsibility for a solution back to the Mission in Paris. "We believe this is a political decision which can only be made by Mission on basis your appraisal best time for enforcing anti-inflationary commitments, [and the] best means of using our bargaining position." Bruce now had at least a part of the autonomy he had been seeking. The Mission decided to offer the French the opportunity to regularize the August advance. But now it was the French government's turn to decline. Paris preferred not to receive the funds rather than submit to a detailed discussion with Washington of the entire financial situation, at least until the political crisis was settled.[46]

The Bidault government was formed on October 28, 1949. Petsche remained at the Ministry of Finance, but Bidault was less tractable in dealing with the Americans. The impasse continued, the first real confrontation between Washington and Paris since a year earlier. On November 17, Tomlinson wrote Petsche that the ECA could not unblock the 35 billion francs due in view of the French relaxation of anti-inflationary measures and failure to move forward on trade liberalization. But Petsche called the American bluff with threats of his own. On November 21 he wrote an impassioned appeal to Harriman, Bruce, and Bingham for the release of counterpart funds, failing which, he warned, he would be forced to have recourse to the Bank of France. Once again the Americans were threatened with responsibility for causing even more inflation, which their policies were supposed to prevent. And Petsche warned again that refusal of the release was certain to be seen as a lack of American confidence in the Bidault government. Bingham replied that the ECA could not afford to be identified with the deterioration of the French economic situation, lest the entire ERP be jeopardized in Congress. He asked for renewed commitments by the French government against inflation and in favor of trade liberalization. At the same time Bingham told Washington that to refuse the release of counterpart funds would seem pu-

---

[46] NARA, AID, RG286, ECA, Office of the Aministrator, Country Files, France, Box 70, Counterpart, October 14, 24, 27, 1949. A.N., F60 ter, 498 (1949), November 9, 1949.

nitive, and do more harm than good. Bingham could only promise that if counterpart funds were released, he would continue strong representations with both Schuman and Bidault to insist on American views.

The dilemma remained. The ECA undertook a new review of the French situation, and in the meantime, told Paris that in exchange for reinforced credit controls, November counterpart would be released. The National Advisory Council would decide on release for December, regularization of the August advance, and the policy governing counterpart release in 1950. But when the Mission asked the Bank of France to raise the rediscount rate, the bank refused; suddenly it could not impose deflationary policies because the French government remained committed to full employment. As expected, the Bidault government was turning out to be much more resistant to Washington than its predecessor. On December 2 Tomlinson told Schweitzer that the French would have to impose 300 billion francs of new taxes at a minimum, or the ECA would be unable to get a renewed allocation from Congress for the continuation of counterpart and financing of the Monnet plan. The alternative was the continuation, of the existing freeze on counterpart and reduced American aid levels in the future, with conditions imposed by Congress that the French might really find it impossible to meet. Tomlinson was somber. If France failed to make the necessary effort, it would compromise the whole future of European recovery and cooperation.[47]

In arguing for the release of counterpart funds, the French attempted to paint a rosy picture of their internal situation. Industrial production was 31 percent higher than in 1938, prices had been stable through June 1949, and the trade deficit had been reduced to about one billion dollars in 1949. The dollar, which had traded at 517 francs on the free market in January, was down to 400 francs. To be sure, the French government remained under severe constraints. The investment program, Indochina war, deficit in the SNCF, and balance of payments deficit, all admittedly had caused in the past a resort to "certain methods of financing of an inflationary character." Inflation had been aggravated by the September 1949 devaluation of the pound, a rise in wages, and price increases. But Petsche and Bidault promised a new effort at rigor in 1950. Taxes would be increased by 20 percent, there would be full integrity in the handling of special accounts, a limit on borrowing by the nationalized enterprises, and the government would abolish quotas and trade restrictions while imposing new controls on credit. Bidault and Petsche appeared to be capitulating to American views.[48]

The Americans had heard all these promises before. Tomlinson was depressed by the whole recent history of French–American negotiations over finances, despite the stern warning he had just given Schweitzer. The refusal to release counterpart, he now saw, "involves headaches we were not will-

[47] NARA, AID, RG286, ECA, Office of the Special Representative, Country Subject Files, Box 70, Counterpart, November 10, 17, 21, 30, 1949. A.N., F60 ter, 378, Tomlinson to Schweitzer, December 2, 1949.

[48] NARA, AID, RG286, ECA, OSR, Box 70, Counterpart, November 30, 1949.

ing to deal with in Britain." There counterpart funds had simply been used to retire government debt, and the Americans were not involved in approving government expenses. The greater measure of influence Washington enjoyed in France had become an undesirable burden. In August Tomlinson had thought the French would be more realistic about their finances if the Americans pressured them by blocking release of counterpart funds, and the threat of doing so had undoubtedly kept government expenses down. But there always remained the possibility that the French would lift the credit ceilings at the Bank of France: "Santa-Claus is popular with everyone in France." The same problem had occurred the year before, and the ECA had then released counterpart funds. "This reasoning raises the question of whether the ECA Mission to France should continue to play the role which should be played by the Bank of France and the Parliament," Tomlinson wrote. As a matter of principle, the desire to avoid doing so was obvious. But the Bank of France would not perform its function, Baumgartner, the governor, was an accomplice of Petsche in the tricks of inflation, and the presses would continue to roll if not for the undertakings the finance minister had been obliged to make to the ECA. Tomlinson thought the French did their best "with their backs to the wall." But the counterpart funds belonged to them and could not be released "at the whim of well-meaning Americans for red, white, and blue drinking fountains in public squares." The ECA wanted low-cost housing, but it was unlikely to get it as long as the French refused to make it part of their own program.[49]

Echoing Tomlinson's pessimism, the NAC approved the release of counterpart funds on December 13, including the regularization of the August advance. It was the Americans who gave in after all. The NAC acted despite its clearly expressed dissatisfaction with the French performance, but with the recognition that failure to release the funds was unlikely to lead to any improvement in the situation and that the "adverse repercussions outweighed the possible benefits" of withholding release. The Americans could not afford to be held responsible for yet another cabinet crisis in France. The August advance was settled by a simple bookkeeping transaction. The Americans continued to be concerned about the inflationary trend in France, and noted that the reluctant release of funds "does not indicate satisfaction with the manner in which the French government has fulfilled assurances to us on the subject of achieving international stability." For the 250 billion francs of counterpart anticipated in 1950 the NAC thought it necessary for the ECA to reexamine the whole question of counterpart fund releases. Withholding counterpart was at best a "delicate and fragile weapon," the efficacy of which depended entirely on the degree of reluctance the French showed in going to the Bank of France for inflationary means of financing. Washington did not want the French to believe that counterpart would never,

---

[49] Ibid., December 2, 1949, Tomlinson to V. Abramson, U.S. Treasury.

under any circumstances, be withheld. But the new head of the ECA, William Foster, concluded that monthly confrontation over the release of counterpart weakened the American negotiating position, and he decided that in 1950 the releases would be on a quarterly basis.[50]

In a survey review of the second year of Marshall Plan aid in France, the ECA painted a mixed picture of its relative degree of success in influencing the internal French economic situation. On the positive side, GNP had increased by 9 percent, exports were up 40 percent, finances were relatively stable, and the rate of investment was 16 percent. The new stability and confidence in France, the ECA was certain, was a direct result of its intervention. But the Queuille measures had in the end been the result of a constant struggle between "economic imperatives and political and social exigencies." On the negative side, real wages were 28 percent below 1938 levels (although equal if social benefits were added in), productivity was a mere 25 percent of the estimated American level, and external assistance covered 13 percent of French government expenditure. The Americans also thought the government role in the economy was too large in France, accounting for 37 percent of GNP, with fiscal receipts at 31 percent of national income. No further increase in taxes was possible or desirable, although the distribution of the tax burden needed to be improved. Given the French threat to resort to inflation, the Mission had agreed to release counterpart funds in December, "notwithstanding its dissatisfaction with the French performance." But refusal to release the funds clearly would not have helped the situation, and the adverse repercussions in French internal politics were certain to outweigh the possible benefits.[51] The Americans had learned the limits of their influence in view of French political instability.

The ECA consequently decided that its emphasis in 1950 must be on productivity and social benefits, with the latter the issue of priority: "France has not yet developed the strong labor movement that is both a means and an objective of the Marshall Plan." No labor organization in France believed that the government really wanted to improve labor's economic position, and both FO and the CFTC had suffered from identification with the government's policy of holding wages down. As a result labor had not received an appropriate share of the national income. This must be remedied in the year to come. The Mission continued to support the Monnet Plan, but recommended changes in its emphasis. The French should postpone modernization of their railroads, increase investment in agriculture, and encourage the shift to private investment. They must do more to stimulate exports to the dollar zone, but Washington recognized it could help here less by criticizing than by lowering its own tariffs. The Americans were not

---

[50] FRUS, 1949, IV, France, December 6, 1949, pp. 654–6; NARA, AID, RG286, ECA, OSR, Country Files, Box 70, France, Counterpart, December 13, 1949.

[51] NARA, AID, RG286, ECA, European Programs, Mediterranean Branch, Country Subject Files, France, February 1, 1950.

above self-criticism. The ECA wanted the French government to admit frankly its dependence on the United States, and take the lead in fighting for reforms, the expansion of European trade, liberalization of commerce, and European integration.

The ECA did not criticize excessive "statism" or social expenditure on the part of the French. The Americans wanted "debudgetization" of investment, but this was also the aim of the Monnet Plan.[52] The Americans praised the infrastructure of the French welfare state, and found the social security system well designed and administered, fully accomplishing the goals for which it was intended. Washington did not object to the bulk of its aid being channeled into the public sector, despite occasional murmurs in Congress. On the contrary, in approving a loan from counterpart funds to the French steel project, Sollac, which was a private enterprise, the ECA Mission insisted on demonstration of the usefulness of the project as an integral part of the French economy. Tomlinson noted that before the war, French private investment had more often sought outlets abroad than in France, and was not to be trusted. Transport and energy loans, in contrast, were almost never questioned by the ECA, precisely because these were made to nationalized enterprises in conjunction with the goals of the Monnet Plan. The Mission did strive, however, "to influence the French government to create again the conditions for the normal [private] functioning of the savings and investment mechanism."[53]

In 1950 the Mission remained frustrated in its efforts to achieve its goals in France. Bidault's government was fragile and unable to propose a budget, so Parliament passed provisional "twelfths" to allow the government to function for the months of January and February. The Mission could not, therefore, approach the French with regard to their commitments to avoid inflationary financing, let alone change the emphasis in their investment policy. The same dilemma remained concerning counterpart funds, moreover: without releases they would go to the Bank of France to finance the continued high levels of their investment program. By refusing release, De Margerie wrote to Schweitzer, the Americans force us to resort to inflation "against which they never ceased to warn us last year." Tomlinson hurried off to Washington to argue the French case, again successfully – releases were approved for January and February 1950, on the argument that to withhold the funds would fuel inflation rather than end it.[54]

In April the government ended wage and price controls, permitted a return to collective bargaining, and passed a budget. The ECA could now resume negotiations, and pursue its new emphasis on increased social expenditure, particularly housing. The Mission also wanted more trade liber-

[52] Bloch-Lainé and Bouvier, *La France Restaurée*.
[53] A.N., F60 ter, 358, 1950, Tomlinson to Foster, May 5, 1949.
[54] A.N., F60 ter, 500, January 13, 28, 1950.

alization, labor retraining, productivity, agricultural investment, dollar exports, and tourism. The French alone had the right to propose expenditures; they must be convinced of the necessity of these programs, which should be "French programs" in every sense and minimize the appearance of American dictates. The ECA provisionally authorized the commitment of 230 billion of the available 250 billion francs of counterpart funds for the Monnet plan, but reserved 20 billion frances for expenditures "not included in the French investment program as presently constituted."[55]

As Bingham had foreseen, the French resisted the ECA decision as "undue interference" in matters that were their own responsibility. They were keenly aware, however, that the proposal was the result of long discussions within the Mission and between it and Washington, during which some American officials had advocated that as much as 100 billion francs be reserved for the so-called critical sectors, especially housing. The French therefore decided that the path of wisdom was to agree to the consecration of 20 billion francs for special uses desired by the Americans, under the subterfuge of rejecting Washington's proposal and then proposing the same thing themselves. While insisting that Parliament alone was qualified to legislate in this matter, Petsche suggested that 12 billion of the reserved 20 billion francs be designated for housing expenditure, and lists of proposed projects were duly prepared for presentation to the Mission. Henry Parkman, of the American Mission, was delighted, and left no doubt, in his reply, of American aims: "I have noted with pleasure your statement that the French government intends, in the greatest possible measure, to select for counterpart financing those expenditures in the investment and reconstruction budget whose execution will most effectively contribute to the fight against Communism. . . . We consider that any amelioration of the housing conditions of working groups would be a direct contribution to the solution of labor unrest in France."[56]

But the French refused to earmark the 12 billion francs for new housing as the Americans wished. Parliament had authorized 37 billion francs for housing the previous year, but appropriated only 21 billion. The 12 billion francs might make up this shortfall, or perhaps serve to convince the deputies to increase the appropriation for the following year.[57] For the present, however, the French thought actual expenditure of the 12 billion francs unrealistic and simply held the funds without spending them. The Americans continued to apply pressure, but to little effect. On November 16, 1950 Washington complained that the Paris Mission was getting nowhere on the question of housing, and Parkman pointedly warned the French that they must show progress on this question. Failure might result in the whole of 1951 counterpart funds being earmarked for housing and nothing else. The

55 NARA, AID, RG286, ECA, OSR, Central Secretariat, Country Subject Files, France, Box 2, Bingham to Katz, April 11, 1950.
56 A.N., F60 ter, 500 April 13, 1950; 501, April 19, 1950.
57 A.N., F60 ter, 358, Petsche to Timmons, July 11, 1950.

French were not amused. "Such insistence that we modify our budget is manifestly inadmissible. It constitutes interference in French affairs." In desperation the Mission proposed a compromise: the funds would be granted by Washington for housing, but the pace of construction would be left to the French. The housing could be built over a period of years, and the funds meanwhile allocated to other purposes. But the French rejected this scheme too: The obligation would remain for Parliament to appropriate the funds for housing at some point, the Americans were bound to claim the credit and the government would be embarrassed. The Quai recommended that France refuse in view of the need for rearmament and threaten recourse to the Bank of France.[58]

It did not come to that; the issue was again compromised, and Paris agreed to put 14 billion francs for housing in its 1951 budget. Meanwhile the ECA began to change its mind once again about what the French should be doing. Expenditure for housing was meant to reduce the appeal of communism and anti-American sentiment in France. But in light of the Korean conflict, did not the external threat of communism deserve priority over that from within? The French must rearm before they rebuild. Some senators were already calling for the complete devotion of counterpart funds to military expenses. In October 1950 Parkman again wondered whether it was worthwhile to induce the French to spend one billion francs to promote tourism, when they could not cover their burgeoning military expenses.[59] In any case the housing was never built, and the 12 billion francs set aside for it did not supplement what the French would have spent in any case.[60] In all no more than 3.1 percent of total counterpart funds went to housing, and no more money was spent on dwellings than the French wanted to build. The failure to influence the French to build housing as an antidote to communism was a constant regret among Mission personnel. Jules Moch later remarked that housing had been the French government's last priority, reconstruction and modernization always first, but later giving ground to the military buildup. The government had firmly resisted American pressure in its determination: "We were absolute in our decision to do this, even if it was cruel to the population."[61]

Along with housing, the Mission placed its emphasis on productivity and technical assistance in 1950, with equally disappointing results. Michael

58 NARA, AID, RG286, ECA, Office of the Deputy Administrator, November 16, 1950. A.N., F60 ter, 358, September 30, 1950, November 1950.
59 NARA, AID, RG286, ECA, Central Secretariat, Box 1, October 11, 1950, Lane Timmons to Henry Parkman, Box 2, July 20, 1950, memo by Parkman.
60 A.N., F60 ter, 500, December 27, 1950.
61 Truman Library, Price Interviews, see in particular those of Robert J. Myers and Lane B. Timmons, and the separate Oral History interview with Jules Moch. The general question of counterpart negotiations is well covered in Esposito, "The Marshall Plan in France and Italy, 1948–1950: Counterpart Fund Negotiations."

Hogan argues that the message of productivity was the centerpiece of the Marshall Plan, which involved an American attempt to reconstruct Europe on the model of a newly emerging American neocapitalism.[62] Labor officials were recruited from the United States to teach productivity as an alternative to Marxism; rising living standards mitigated class conflict. The ECA provided technical experts throughout Europe, and set aside funding for productivity training in the United States for European cadres and workers. In May 1949 the French requested $2.9 million to finance 1,280 visits by French employers and workers to American factories. The Mission scaled down this initial request, but included funds for publications stressing productivity, films, and various kinds of publicity and services.[63] Under the Mission's impetus the French established a *Comité syndical consultif* and a national committee on productivity.[64] Most of the Marshall Plan countries did the same.

It is difficult to evaluate the concrete influence of these committees. But the amounts expended on them were small in comparison to the totality of Marshall Plan aid, and the Mission's reaction was most often frustration. The French understood American methods, but showed no eagerness to adapt them to factories at home.[65] Crude American attempts at a kind of stimulus–response mechanism (the offer of free soap, for example, in the coal-mining regions as a reward for reduced absenteeism) brought derision from the workers and sabotage from the CGT. Mission experts deplored the attachment of the French to their "decayed" economic system and the protection of marginal producers, on top of which they had superimposed a huge and expensive welfare state. Efforts to produce more under such circumstances simply made no sense. The State Department warned that the productivity missions to the United States must be carefully screened so as to keep out Communists, an almost impossible task.[66]

Washington was equally dissatisfied with the failure of Paris to reduce trade barriers and pursue economic integration with sufficient resolve. The OEEC never developed into the supranational entity for which the Americans hoped. The major impediment was London, which fought all supranational schemes, but Paris, which was willing to strengthen the OEEC,

62 Michael J. Hogan, "American Marshall Planners and the Search for a European Neocapitalism," *American Historical Review*, 90, no. 1 (February 1985): 44–72. Also Charles Maier, *In Search of Stability: Explorations in Historical Political Economy* (New York: Cambridge University Press, 1987).

63 NARA, AID, RG286, ECA, Office of the Special Representative, Country Subject Files, France, Box 22, May 13, 1949.

64 A.N., F60 ter, 357, May 19, 1949. See also Richard Kuisel, "L'American Way of Life et les mission françaises de productivité," *Vingtième Siècle* (January–March 1988).

65 NARA, AID, RG286, ECA, Office of the Deputy Administrator, Country Subject Files, France, October 2, 1950.

66 Truman Library, Price Interviews, Irving Swerdlow. NARA, RG59, 840.50 Recovery/11-2648, November 26, 1948.

preferred to push for a smaller Europe. The more restrained French ambitions gave rise to the initiatives that had such uninventive names as "Fritalux" and "Finebel," and finally culminated in the Schuman Plan, forebear
of the EEC. But Washington was distinctly displeased with the French reluctance to reduce customs barriers. Despite repeated expressions of American irritation and threats to apply pressure, little of a concrete nature was
accomplished until the Schuman Plan. In November 1950 the Americans
noted 300 charges of excessive tariffs brought against the French by the
OEEC, 60 percent of all the complaints brought by that organization. Even
when the French tried to act, lower-level negotiators seemed intent on frustrating the designs of policy makers at the top of the French bureaucracy.
The result was a "snarled up logjam, for which anything short of dynamite
would be useless." American officials observed that "the French are past
masters at the art of telling the Americans what they think we want to
hear." European integration for Paris, Washington correctly perceived, was
primarily political, not economic.[67]

Washington complained after more than a year of operation of the Marshall Plan that even the guarantee of American business access to "strategic
materials" available in the French Union remained a dead letter. Only one
deal had been concluded by October 1949, and American concerns were
frustrated in their efforts to secure concessions in the mining of New Cale-
donian nickel and Moroccan lead.[68] Some of these obstacles were later overcome, but the program never achieved the dimensions for which the Americans had hoped. Nor did the French take kindly to American efforts to
publicize Marshall Plan aid in the colonies, which they saw as a blatant
attempt to undermine their sovereignty there.

Yet American influence remained more extensive in French economic development than it appeared. The Americans were effective by supporting
bureaucrats and pressure groups who shared their goals. In seeking greater
French emphasis on agricultural investment, Bingham suggested "finding or
creating through persuasion influential groups in the French government
who want to see instituted the type of dynamic agricultural program we
have in mind." Similar tactics explained the Mission's success in obtaining
credit controls, limits on inflationary financing, and such steps as were made
toward the liberalization of trade. Two weeks after Bingham's suggestion,
Foster expressed his satisfaction that the French had agreed to increase agricultural investment, despite "the difficult problem the Mission faces in

---

67 NARA, AID, RG286, ECA, Office of the Deputy Administrator, Country Subject
    Files, France, November 2 and 16, 1950.
68 On European integration see Melandri *Les Etats–Unis Face à l'unification de l'Europe*,
    and Alan Milward, *The Reconstruction of Western Europe 1945–51* (London: Me-
    thuen, 1984). Also Wexler, *The Marshall Plan Revisited*. On strategic materials, NARA,
    AID, RG286, ECA, Office of the Administrator, Country Subject Files, France, Oc-
    tober 10, 1949.

bringing influence to bear on the French government in this direction."[69] In October 1949, despite French frustration with the results of the British devaluation, Tomlinson recommended that the Mission be "turned loose in counterpart negotiations to see whether we cannot help Guindey, Schweitzer, Fillipi, Monnet, and the others to beat down the opposition from the patronat, the FO and CFTC, the CGA, and the technical ministries," in the effort to secure trade liberalization. In that case the array of forces against the Mission and its French bureaucratic allies was simply too great. But a month later the Mission saw a greater opening in its effort to get some movement toward European integration. The views of the Finance Ministry on European unity were close to those of the Mission; Guindey, Schweitzer, De Margerie, Bloch-Lainé, Monnet, and Petsche all were favorable. The Mission concluded it would be worthwhile to threaten "punitive" action, on the use of which the French themselves appeared to agree: ". . . nearly all the key officials, except those in the technical ministries, seem to agree in principle to the desirability of the action we propose . . . we should put all the pressure we can or we won't get action at all or soon enough for Congressional presentation."[70] It was not uncommon for these French high bureaucrats to request American pressure, through the withholding of counterpart funds or other means, to help them achieve their own agendas.[71]

The Americans were most effective when their goals were specific and their pressure indirect, exercised in alliance with factions of the French who wanted the same ends. The ECA, the Mission, the French interministerial committee, and most of all money gave Washington a vast amount of influence in the outcome of decisions that made and unmade governments and charted the direction of French policy for years to come. Despite the relative failure to achieve the broad goals of European unity the Americans set for themselves, the progress made in so short a time was striking. The ECA may well have laid the foundations of the movement for European unity and integration, although that movement took a form and a direction the Americans could not predict. It is impossible to say, moreover, how integration would have developed had Washington been able to devote to it the kind of concentrated energy and expense that was ultimately to be mobilized in another domain, the military. By 1949 it was clear that the ECA would have to make way for the Mutual Defense and Assistance Program. Eventually both were to be merged into the Mutual Security Agency, which expressed Washington's aim of directing not so much the European economy as its collective military policy. Here again, France was to play the key role in American calculations. From 1950 to 1952 the military reconstruction of France brought American influence, tutelage, and commanding physical

[69]   FRUS, 1949, IV, France, September 1 and 15, 1949, 652–7.
[70]   NARA, AID, RG286, ECA, Central Secretariat, Box 2, October 19, 1949, December 8, 1949.
[71]   Interview with Pierre Uri, July 9, 1985.

presence in France to their greatest and most extreme point of the postwar period. But once France rearmed, it sought emancipation from American tutelage, ultimately rejecting American plans to win the Indochina war and to build a supranational European army in the European Defense Community. Under the government of Pierre Mendès France in 1954, France finally declared its independence of Washington. It is to that story that we must now turn.

7

Military aid and French independence

I THE UNITED STATES, THE SCHUMAN AND PLEVEN PLANS, AND THE FRENCH MILITARY BUDGET

BETWEEN 1950 AND 1952 French–American relations were once again transformed as the major concern of Paris and Washington shifted from French economic recovery to military preparedness. The Marshall Plan was only in its third year when it was eclipsed by the Mutual Defense and Assistance Pact (MDAP), under the terms of which "end items" of American military equipment began pouring into France in unprecedented and staggering amounts, dwarfing in dollar value the remaining grants and counterpart funds in the province of the Economic Cooperation Administration. France was a major recipient of Marshall Plan aid, accounting for about 21 percent of the total dollar aid disbursed; it was the single largest target of MDAP, which could as easily have been named the French Military Assistance Program. France accounted for more than 50 percent of the military equipment distributed among the Europeans, receiving about $500 million in military hardware in 1950 and like amounts in the two successive years. There was logic in this largesse. The defense of Western Europe depended upon American strategic bombing, the Royal Navy's control of the seas, and European ground troops, the vast majority of which, until the question of a German contribution could be broached, would have to be French. Paris rejected the role of provider of infantry, however, and struggled to reestablish itself as a major military power on land and sea, and in the air. Paradoxically, these efforts, rather than leading to greater independence from Washington as they were designed to do, only further dramatized French dependence on American generosity.

The price of continuing American assistance was demonstrated European progress toward the goal of unity. American geopoliticians thought in continental terms. They could see neither economic growth nor West European security without political organization on an all-European scale. But by 1950 the Europeans had made very little progress. There was good reason. Both the British and the French still thought in imperial terms. Their colonial empires fostered the illusion of continuing world power. Neither wished to be thought of as another Belgium. The British simply rejected Washington's pressure while the French, in much greater economic and military need, tried to twist American efforts to serve their own purposes. French diplomacy was shaped by Washington's determination to restore the economic and military strength of Germany. The French were unable to prevent German recovery, and tried to use the European unity movement as a means of maintaining a measure of control over that process; hence the Schuman Plan and the European Defense Community (EDC). Both were French initiatives, and each reflected the genuine enthusiasm for European unity of the man who dreamed them up, Jean Monnet. But each bore clearly as well the imprint of Washington. Paris pursued both plans with a zeal proportionate only to the extent that it thought its interests were served. In the case of the Schuman Plan, the foundations of what later became the European Economic Community were established. In the case of the EDC, after tortuous negotiations and endless delay, the result was rejection of the plan by the National Assembly and a crisis in French–American relations.

While EDC was in the planning stages, Paris turned its attention to the task of extracting from Washington the economic means of reestablishing itself as a military and diplomatic power of world rank. France simultaneously tried to convince Washington to help it retain its crumbling colonial empire, without which Paris feared eclipse by a stronger Germany in Europe. The French proposed that the military burden of all the NATO powers be shared equally according to the presumed ability of each to pay, with the contribution of each measured in terms of comparative national income. Washington would agree only to bilateral negotiations with each European power, thus making itself the arbiter of what constituted an adequate defense contribution and dispensing its funds accordingly. The result from the French perspective was a policy that French politicians themselves perceived as little better than begging. The repeated trips to Washington of French politicians, hat in hand, would have provided an almost comic leitmotif to the period, had they not involved an incessant series of humiliations, bitterness, and recrimination.

Washington was drawn into the Indochina conflict as well. The American perceptions of how the war should be won and the political settlement to follow victory differed substantially from those of Paris, the Americans stressing Vietnamese independence with an option to withdraw from the French Union. The level of American aid, at least in the early stage of U.S. involvement, was never enough from the French perspective. As for the French colonization, or *"mission civilatrice"* in North Africa, there the Americans

showed no comprehension at all. Late in 1952, as a consequence of disagreements over economic and military aid, Indochina, and North Africa,
a wave of anti-Americanism and nationalism swept France, with the
result that under the conservative government of Antoine Pinay, whose anti-
Communist measures Washington had both stimulated and approved,
French–American relations declined to their lowest point since the war. Only
once more during the history of the Fourth Republic were relations with
Washington to decline so precipitously – under the most powerful and popular leader of that regime, Pierre Mendès France, when Paris finally declared
its independence of Washington.

The bilateral agreement implementing the Mutual Defense and Assistance
Program was signed on January 27, 1950. Minister of Defense René Pleven
and Ambassador David Bruce were in a hurry to see American arms deliveries begin. Many in Washington feared that France, with its huge Communist party, lacked the will as well as the means to defend itself. Bruce
was anxious to prove to Washington that France would prove a viable ally,
and counted on the "psychological effect" of the arms deliveries: "I believe
Pleven to be absolutely sincere in his desire to get France satisfactorily rearmed
and to instill in the people the determination to fight any aggression." It was
most important for Bruce that the arms shipments coincide with concerted
action against "Commie" propaganda. On February 2, 1950 American military aid officials and representatives of the French ministries of Defense,
Information, and Foreign Affairs met to plan the anti-Communist effort.
Bruce wanted the French to spearhead the propaganda effort themselves, so
as to make the best impression in Washington. The Communists had begun
a noisy campaign against the "dirty war" in Vietnam, and they began a
campaign to prevent the unloading of American ships carrying equipment
destined for Indochina. Bruce and Pleven both wanted a rapid arrival of the
equipment to demonstrate the government's control of the situation: "the
sooner a confrontation takes place with the CP the better."[1] The ambassador seemed most eager to confront the party in the ports, where Irving Brown's
organizing efforts were presumably having their effect.

  Pleven had his own concerns, however; he wanted the deliveries to be
routed through Cherbourg, where the dockers were both unemployed and
anti-Communist. Nor was he as eager as Bruce for a confrontation with the
PCF. Because of the interval between releases and new conscriptions, the
French army was at half troop strength in the event that it had to deal with
any major disturbances, and Pleven needed to move 37-millimeter ammunition, in extremely short supply, to Indochina, to expedite prosecution of

[1] National Archives and Records Administration, (NARA) 751.5MAP/1-450, January
4, 1950; 1-2150, January 21, 1950; 1-2550, January 25, 1950; 2-350, February 3,
1950; 2-1050, February 10, 1950.

the war there. On April 13 the U.S. ship *Importer* arrived at Cherbourg with the first cargo of arms and ammunition. Pleven was on hand for a dockside ceremony, and Bruce noted the smooth unloading of the ship. Communist demonstrators were nowhere in evidence. In May the U.S. Military Assistance Advisory Group (MAAG) set up its headquarters at 58 rue de la Boetie, adding another twenty persons to the burgeoning American bureaucratic presence in France. The French aircraft carrier, the Dixmude, picked up forty-four aircraft in Norfolk, Virginia, and French pilots and officers departed for the United States for training. On the surface MDAP was off to a successful start.[2]

But nothing undertaken by French and Americans together ever seemed to go off smoothly. Pleven and Schuman protested the slow pace of deliveries, and complained when shipments went to ports other than Cherbourg, leaving the dockers there idle and receptive to Communist propaganda. Acheson was annoyed, but directed the ECA to route its shipments to Cherbourg, and convinced Jay Lovestone to direct AFL-CIO Care packages there as an act of international solidarity with fellow unemployed workers. Lovestone was irritated in turn, however, because Brown and Ferri-Pisani, like Bruce, wanted AFL assistance concentrated on the Mediterranean ports, where the Communists could be confronted on their own ground. The French protested that they could not pay 50 percent of the cost of MDAP shipping, as required by Congress; it was illogical to make them pay for an aid program. To the Americans this was just another example of French small-mindedness. MDAP deliveries accelerated rapidly in the latter part of the year, however, and were a continuing backdrop of French–American relations through 1952. Yet they rapidly became obscured in subsequent aid negotiations. Taken for granted by the French, who regarded arms assistance as their due, the Americans repeatedly pointed to the weapons shipments as examples of their munificence when the French were complaining of shortfalls in other forms of promised aid.[3]

The immediate effect of the arms deliveries was to restore France to definitive military supremacy over Germany; this in turn could have played a role in the proposal for the Schuman Plan. But intense American pressure for progress in European unification began in October 1949, when ECA Administer Paul Hoffman, in a blunt speech, warned that future American assistance would be tied to demonstrable progress toward integration. The Americans pushed the candidacy of Belgian Foreign Minister Paul Henri Spaak for head of the OEEC in the hope of bringing more prestige to that organization, forced the acceptance by its members of a 50 percent reduction in internal tariffs, and pushed through the establishment of the Euro-

---

[2] NARA, 751.MAP/1-1350, January 13, 1950; 1-1750, January 17, 1950; 3-2250, March 22, 1950; 4-1850, April 18, 1950; 4-2750, April 27, 1950; 5-1250, May 12, 1950.

[3] NARA, 751.5MAP/5-1750, May 17, 1950; 5-2350, May 23, 1950; 6-950, June 9, 1950; 6-1050, June 10, 1950; 6-2050, June 20, 1950; 6-2250, June 22, 1950.

pean Payments Union, earmarking 25 percent of Marshall Plan Assistance in 1950 for the subsidization of inter-European trade. The French responded by pushing plans for the establishment of customs unions with the Italians and Benelux countries. Such amusing names as Fritalux and Finebel captured the headlines briefly early in 1950, but as schemes for European unity they rapidly failed when Washington declined to support them, ostensibly because they were insufficiently supranational, but largely because they ignored Germany.[4] Washington was uninterested in European unity unless it offered a solution of the German problem. Meanwhile, German steel production bypassed French totals for the first time, and the new West German state applied for membership in the International Authority for the Ruhr. Unable to respond adequately to Washington's pressure, France faced another crisis in terms of its relations with the new German Federal Republic.[5]

From the French perspective German coke and Lorraine ore were an obvious economic unit, but while the French desperately needed German coke, the Germans could easily dispense with French ore, a lesson the French had painfully learned after World War I. The Americans, eager to eliminate any vestige of limitation on German sovereignty, suggested to the French that the Ruhr authority could attain legitimacy only if the coal and steel industries of France and the Benelux were brought under its purview as well. This suggestion was first aired by the American high commissioner for Germany, John J. McCloy, a close friend and associate of Jean Monnet. It was also proposed by Lewis Douglas, the Francophile American ambassador to Great Britain, and George Ball, then an attorney for the French government in the United States. Ball became close to Monnet during his work at the French Supply Council, and later became instrumental in the creation of the institutions of the Community, which owed much to American ingenuity and precedent. Monnet was familiar with American antitrust legislation, which he used as a model, with American support, to force the deconcentration of the Ruhr steel industry and its partial divestiture of ownership of coal. The very notion of a "High Authority," so named because no such institution existed in European practice, further owed much to the example provided by American regulatory agencies such as the Federal Trade Commission. Ball wrote a report for Monnet on American agencies during the elaboration of the Community's institutional framework.[6]

[4] Annie Lacroix-Riz, "Crédits américains et coopération européenne (1949–1954)," in Patrick Fridenson and André Straus, *Le Capitalisme français, 19e–20e siècle: Blocages et dynamismes d'une croissance* (Paris: Fayard, 1987), pp. 327–53; Alan Milward, *The Reconstruction of Western Europe, 1945–51* (London: Methuen, 1984), p. 391. Imanuel Wexler, *The Marshall Plan Revisited* (Westport, CT: Greenwood Press, 1983), pp. 234–5.
[5] See Raymond Poidevin, *Robert Schuman, homme d'état, 1886–1963* (Paris: Imprimerie Nationale, 1986), pp. 220–39.
[6] Milward, *Reconstruction of Western Europe*; René Massigli, *Une comédie des erreurs: Souvenirs et réflexions sur une étape de la construction européene* (Paris: Plon,

The French were not prepared to enter into a relationship with Germany until their claim to be a world power, as much as a European power, was recognized. Two weeks before the proposal of the Schuman Plan, Georges Bidault, who succeeded Henri Queuille as premier in October 1949, proposed an Atlantic High Council for Peace. Bidault's grandiose scheme provided for an executive organ of the NATO alliance, on which the United States, Britain, and France would have permanent seats; in short, a three-power directorate for NATO that would institutionalize France's claim to be a world power. A similar plan had been proposed by the French during the founding of the alliance, and it would be proposed again, ad nauseum, by every French government that remained within NATO, including that of General de Gaulle. Bruce saw in the plan a transparent effort by the French leader to strengthen his personal political position; and given Bidault's ambition, it could not be excluded that he was proposing himself as the third great figure in the movement toward Atlantic unity after Churchill and Marshall. Nevertheless, Bruce advised Acheson that there was some advantage to supporting Bidault: Allowing the French to appear as the originators of Atlantic unity "might well afford us the opportunity of attempting a serious step toward the integration of Germany within the Atlantic community." Acheson had earlier proposed to Schuman that the French take the responsibility of offering a solution to the German problem. But this was not the answer the American secretary of state was looking for: The creation of a directorate in the alliance would only alienate the smaller European powers, while no mechanism for a solution to the German problem was evident in Bidault's proposal.[7]

Bidault's proposal for the Atlantic High Council was put to Bruce before the prime minister made it public. Schuman similarly put the European coal and steel pool to Acheson during the American secretary's visit to Paris on May 9, swearing him to secrecy with respect to both the British and the French cabinet, neither of whom were to hear the plan presumably unless the American secretary could be brought to offer his support. Acheson was not at first entirely disposed to cooperate. "Here I was closeted on Sunday morning with the Schuman plan, damndest cartel I had ever heard of in my life, I couldn't tell anyone." Acheson recognized, however, that American pressure might well work to eliminate whatever monopolistic or restrictive trade practices were implicit in the proposal. The essential thing was that it offered a mechanism for the integration of Germany into Western Europe

1978), pp. 226–31; Pierre Melandri, *Les Etats–Unis face à l'unification de l'Europe, 1945–54* (Paris: A. Pedone, 1980), pp. 222–63; George Ball, *The Past Has Another Pattern: Memoirs* (New York: Norton, 1982); Jean Monnet, *Memoires* (Paris: Fayard, 1976), 280–345; Fondation Jean Monnet (Lausanne) Papiers Jean Monnet, Dossier G. W. Ball, AMG 10/6.

7 Foreign Relations of the United States, FRUS, 1950, III, North Atlantic Treaty Organization, April 15, 1950, pp. 54–5; April 20, 1950, p. 58.

and accepted the reconstruction of Germany as a major economic, if not yet military power. Acheson cabled Washington of the "deep impression" made on him by the proposal, but thought it too early to approve fully, pending the clarification of its cartel aspects and French aims in the Ruhr. But in Washington policymakers were much more enthusiastic. John Foster Dulles, then an adviser to the State Department, who was close to both McCloy and Monnet, called it "brilliantly creative." Averell Harriman thought it "the most important step toward economic progress and peace since the original Marshall Plan speech on European Recovery." Bruce, for his part, waxed eloquent: France, the natural leader of the continent, had emerged from her lethargy and spirit of defeatism, and once again stood erect "as a standard to which her neighbors might rally." Lewis Douglas saw in it a tribute to French creative leadership, and not surprisingly, thought the political benefits of the plan "tremendous." [8]

Washington's enthusiasm for the Schuman Plan was not lessened by British opposition. Acheson thought he had blundered in agreeing not to tell the British, and as a consequence, in London, Bevin gave Schuman "absolute, unshirted, hell." But it had long been clear in Washington that European unity would have to be made without the British. On June 2 the State Department and ECA issued joint instructions to American diplomats that the United States must avoid the appearance of direct involvement; the initiative was to remain with the Europeans. But the situation might develop so as to require the exertion of "strong U.S. influence to avoid watering down the proposal," and to assure "retention of the favorable aspects of the original scheme." From the beginning American pressure was used to oppose any proposal that would nullify the supranational character of the High Authority "which the United States considers to be of key importance." The American role in bringing about successful negotiation and ratification of the Schuman Plan was critical at every stage of the process. [9]

The Schuman Plan marked the beginning of a new era in European unity, but it also closed an old. It was the culmination of the period of European economic recovery and revealed the extent and the limits of what American pressures for European unity might achieve. In June 1950, North Korea invaded the South, Truman decided to intervene with American troops, the United Nations Security Council endorsed the American decision, and the universal concern of the Atlantic nations became military strength as opposed to economic recovery. Charles Bohlen was present when Bruce in-

[8]   FRUS, 1950, III, Economic Recovery of Western Europe, May 10, 1950, pp. 694–5; May 11, 1950, pp. 696–7; May 20, 1950, pp. 702–4; June 6, 1950, pp. 720–4. Truman Library, Acheson Papers, Princeton Seminars, Reel 3, Track 2, Page 10. Also Dean Acheson, *Present at the Creation: My Years in the State Department* (New York: Norton, 1969), p. 382.

[9]   FRUS, 1950, III, The Economic Recovery of Western Europe, June 2, 1950, pp. 714–5; July 25, 1950, pp. 741–2. Poidevin, *Robert Schuman*, 260–72.

formed Schuman of the American decision to intervene in Korea. The Frenchman's eyes filled with tears, Bohlen wrote, as he exclaimed: "Thank God this will not be a repetition of the past," apparently thinking of the failure to stand up to Hitler in the 1930s.[10]

There seems ample evidence of genuine panic in Western Europe over Soviet intentions in the summer of 1950, and it was universally believed that NATO conventional forces could not stand up to Soviet power. The condition of the French army, which would have to serve as the backbone in any fighting in Germany, now became a source of universal concern. At a NATO meeting on July 26, Marshal Montgomery blasted "the inadequate state of training of French troops." General Jean de Lattre could only agree that this was so, while Jules Moch pleaded for understanding of French political problems: the need to maintain a satisfactory standard of living lest Communism grow, and the bleeding to which the French were subject in Indochina. Lewis Douglas thought NATO action was necessary to correct the "grievous deficiencies in command and general setup of the French armed forces, on which all NATO planning depends." Douglas thought the only solution would have to involve utilization of the military potential of Germany, but first "We must persuade the French to put their military house in order." Only then could German rearmament be considered. Paris was on the defensive, already under pressure to increase massively its own military contribution and to accept some rearmament of Germany, when on July 22, 1950, Acheson issued his query to all the NATO allies on the nature and extent of the increased defense effort they proposed to undertake. The Americans wanted an answer by August 5.[11]

The French immediately threw the challenge back to the allies, proposing that NATO agree to establish a common defense fund, along with an international war cabinet and an executive authority with guaranteed membership of France, Great Britain, and the United States. The three-power directorate now reappeared under the guise of a collective rearmament plan. Sacrifices must be borne equally by all, the French argued. Separate national rearmament alone, under present political conditions, made German participation impossible, while a collective, federated defense effort "permits the full utilization and cooperation of the Atlantic community without rearming Germany independently." France was inadequately armed, the price of its reconstruction and modernization, while the Indochina War was draining the life blood of the nation, and could not be dealt with in the future by French resources alone. An "internal fifth column" threatened that an excessive French financial effort would lead to internal disintegration. Rearmament must be a collective enterprise, the French argued. In anticipation

[10] Charles Bohlen, *Witness to History* (New York: Norton, 1973), p. 292.
[11] FRUS, 1950, III, Western Europe, NATO, July 12, 1950, p. 132; July 22, 1950, pp. 138–41; July 26, 1950, pp. 141–4.

of such an agreement, Paris announced it was prepared to undertake a three-year military program to mount fifteen new divisions at a total cost of 2,000 billion francs.[12]

Washington was not impressed with the French proposals. Bruce noted that the French wanted to "spread the inflation" resulting from their rearmament expense, and they offered the Germans the opportunity only to contribute soldiers, not military units. The plan was also a transparent attempt to collectivize the cost of the Indochina War, and to make the United States underwrite the military budgets of all the European states. The Americans were disappointed with the scale of the French military contribution, moreover, and regarded the French as capable of greater sacrifice.[13] The inequities of the French fiscal system, which allegedly allowed whole segments of the population to escape paying taxes, were still an article of faith in Washington. The American mode of analysis found an echo in Paris. In *Le Monde*, Jean Jacques Servan–Schreiber used the argument in support of the growing neutralist sentiment. France, he wrote, was already practicing a policy of neutralism through its heavy social expenditure and purely symbolic level of military expense. Why not proclaim openly what one practiced privately anyway?[14] Such opinions alarmed the Americans. Lewis Douglas wondered whether France had the will to fight, or the capacity to build a national army able to carry the brunt of Western defense. On August 1 Bruce told Pleven and Petsche that the United States would not cooperate in any attempt to establish a common fund for military expenses, nor would it transfer MDAP aid to any such organism. Pleven was disappointed. France could not, he said, support the burden of a land war in Europe for the third time unless assured of the massive mutual support of her allies. Petsche warned that autarchy in defense was as bad as autarchy in economics. These arguments were to no avail. Washington would not listen.[15]

Douglas had a solution to offer, however. While a German army, he agreed, would be a "tragic mistake," a European defense force including the Germans should be pushed with a greatest urgency within NATO. This idea was not new. It was proposed in various quarters during the summer of 1950, among others by Paul Reynaud, André Philip, and Winston Churchill. The proposal was actively considered in the U.S. State Department in August. Bruce and McCloy endorsed the idea, McCloy suggesting that the French idea of a common budget might be incorporated in some way to make the plan more palatable in Paris. Matthews wrote a position paper

12   Archives Nationales, (A.N.), F60 ter 415 (1), "Note sur le financement du réarmement," July 31, 1950; also memos of August 16 and 19, 1950.
13   FRUS, 1950, III, Western Europe, NATO, July 28, 1950, pp. 148–59; July 31, 1950, p. 165.
14   *Le Monde*, July 28, 1950.
15   *Le Monde*, August 1, 1950. FRUS, 1950, III, Western Europe, NATO, August 1, 1950, pp. 168–75; August 2, 1950, p. 179.

arguing for British and American participation, and on August 21, impressed by the unanimity within the department, Acheson announced that the idea might become U.S. policy and merited an approach to European governments. On September 2 Acheson instructed Bruce to broach the idea to Schuman. But the French rejected the plan as another scheme for German rearmament and membership in NATO, without even a gesture in favor of French ideas for shared costs.[16]

Internal developments in France helped Washington in its decision to apply the pressure necessary to bring the French into line. The replacement of Bidault by Pleven as premier in July 1950 was regarded favorably by the State Department. The Socialists reentered the government, bringing it more stability; despite the demands for wage increases and "controlled inflation" they represented, "one cannot govern against the Socialists, however difficult it is to govern with them." Bruce particularly mourned the death of Léon Blum in March 1950. The elder statesman's passing had created a "void" in the Socialist party, presenting the difficult problem of "with whom in the PS one can talk in order to exercise real influence or effect decisions that could be carried out." No other leader of the non-Communist left enjoyed the same contacts as Blum across the Atlantic. Jules Moch appeared to Bruce to be the new party strong man. Moch was intelligent, anti-Communist, and ambitious, but he was bitterly anti-German, rejected the Schuman Plan, made no apology for the alacrity with which the Socialists overturned cabinets, and was quick to resort to charges of American "interference" in internal French affairs. Bruce still thought that with Moch as defense minister and Pleven as *Président du Conseil,* the government was stabler and better able to deal with military issues. If anyone could sell German rearmament to the PS, Moch could.[17] The trick was to sell it first to Moch.

Schuman parried the new American pressure by demanding a reply to French proposals of August; the French were prepared to increase their military budget for 1951 from 420 to 500 billion francs and undertake a three-year rearmament program of 2,000 billion, on condition that a common defense budget were established. France was prepared to field fifteen divisions in Europe and to pursue its effort in Indochina in the interest of the defense of the entire West against Communist aggression. But help was needed, because the French deficit was as large as the military budget. The French thus began a policy that was subsequently to characterize their relations with Washington: They sold their military commitments as a means of solving their budgetary and balance of payments problems. War, cold in Europe, and hot in Indochina, was to become France's major dollar export.

16   FRUS, 1950, III, Western Europe, NATO, August 3, 1950, pp. 180–2; August 8, 1950, pp. 194–5; August 11, 1950, pp. 205–7; August 16, 1950, pp. 211–9; August 21, 1950, p. 231; September 2, 1950, p. 261.
17   NARA, 751.00/3-3150, March 31, 1950; 7-750, July 7, 1950; 7-1850, July 18, 1950; 9-150, September 1, 1950.

Pleven, Schuman, and Petsche met with Bruce on September 7, 1950 to underline the importance of external financing for the ambitious French military plans. Again the French tried to use their political instability as a source of negotiating strength. If the United States did not agree to financial aid, they warned, the cabinet would come under attack for making commitments it could not keep. On September 12 Acheson told Schuman that the United States was willing to discuss the question of aid to the supplementary French arms effort. But Washington wanted an end to proposals for a common budget and insisted that France accept a German contribution to a European Defense Force.[18]

Schuman remained obstinately against any idea of German rearmament. The notion was premature, he pleaded, the French were not nearly ready to accept it, and it might provoke Moscow into declaring war. But Acheson would not be deterred. On September 14 he broached it to a meeting of the foreign ministers of the Big Three, winning British support. On September 16 he brought it before the Council of NATO. All the allies rallied to the support of Washington and France was quickly isolated. But it remained vital that French acquiescence be obtained. Bruce was told to impress upon Moch and Pleven the "extreme gravity with which continued [French] refusal will be viewed here." The French defense minister was coming to the United States to negotiate the amount of American aid. The Americans mobilized an all-out effort to change Moch's mind. British Labourite Emmanuel Shinwell, who had influence with Moch, was brought to Washington to pressure the Frenchman. Care must be taken: "We should press the French very hard in private and be as moderate as possible in public." Bruce suggested that Acheson propose to Schuman, who had developed the admirable Coal and Steel Pool, that the latter come up with his own proposal as to how German manpower might be used in the West European defense. Let the leadership come from France. "If Schuman can relay to his cabinet a course of conduct inspired by us but giving the French Government the opportunity to assert continental leadership we might obtain happy and even unexpected results." This was not a bad description of what had occurred earlier with the development of the Schuman Plan. Perhaps it could work again. Moch was sure to be difficult and dogmatic, Bruce wrote, but he was susceptible to appeals to national pride and personal vanity.[19]

The French got the message: The Americans were exerting very strong pressure for the creation of a German military force of ten divisions, and the Quai feared that a totally negative position on the part of France created the risk that "German rearmament will be accomplished despite us, almost

---

[18]   A.N., F60 ter 415 (1), September 9, 1950. FRUS, 1950, III, Western Europe, NATO, September 7, 1950, p. 269; September 12, 1950, pp. 285–8.

[19]   FRUS, 1950, III, Western Europe, NATO, September 14, 1950, p. 301; September 16, 1950, p. 310; September 17, 1950, p. 314; September 20, 1950, pp. 336–7; September 22, 1950, p. 338.

against us." France therefore should not challenge the principle of German rearmament, but rather prepare "modalities permitting the retention of sufficient control on the part of the French government over German rearmament." The model existed already in the proposal for a European coal and steel pool; France could obtain this control "in the framework of a collective organization in which France would participate and play, by the nature of things, a determining role." American pressure must again be turned to serve French interests. The Schuman Plan was designed to save the Monnet Plan, which in turn had been meant to establish French industrial dominance in Europe. The European Defense Community, as the French proposal was subsequently to be called, was designed to preserve a preponderance of French military power in the face of the inevitable rearmament of Germany.[20]

On September 23 Acheson told Bevin that if the French were pressed as much as possible, they would come through. If not he would have to consider going ahead with German rearmament anyway. This idea was enough to frighten Schuman. On September 26 he told Acheson that France would take the initiative, but he pleaded that his country could not "be dragged on the end of a chain." Schuman was willing to consider a Franco–German agreement, or possibly a common defense pool of the six European nations, France, Italy, Germany, and the Benelux. The EDC was present in embryo. The Americans were immediately suspicious of the idea, however. Under Secretary Webb warned that the French might be seeking merely a delaying tactic. Lovett advised that "we should keep the heat on the French," while Marshall and Acheson agreed that the financial problem was probably the heart of the matter. The French attitude toward German rearmament might well depend on what they could come up with as a result of the forthcoming negotiations in Washington on their military budget.[21]

On October 5 a high-level meeting took place between representatives of the State and Treasury departments about what the United States should do to assist Paris in its rearmament program. Treasury Secretary Snyder insisted that Washington could not become involved in financing the budget deficits of other nations. American aid had previously been directed toward meeting shortfalls in the balance of payments of the Europeans, quite a different thing. Unfortunately the distinction was not that well grasped in Europe, where the counterpart of American aid found its way into the treasuries of the European nations and became part of budgetary receipts nonetheless. Snyder said the French should raise the ceiling on their national debt, precisely what the ECA had been fighting with the French for two years to prevent. Harriman was alarmed. If inflation reappeared in France,

20 A.N., F60 ter 415 (1), September 18, 1950, Note.
21 FRUS, 1950, III, Western Europe, NATO, September 23, 1950, pp. 343–4; September 26, 1950, p. 353; October 3, 1950, pp. 357–8; October 9, 1950, pp. 364–6; October 10, 1950, p. 368.

he said, it could threaten national stability. But Snyder was undeterred; someone had convinced the French that they could "put us in a position to finance their entire military expenditure." They must be made to understand that this was out of the question. Acheson suggested the French add a supplementary budget for which the financing would be worked out. He was told that this was impossible under the French system. Snyder, expressing American frustration with the French, exclaimed: "Perhaps they [the French] would have to develop the type of leadership which could make it possible." But the secretary had to admit that it was much cheaper to help France rearm than to finance the equivalent numbers of American troops in Europe.[22]

Petsche had in fact outlined French budgetary proposals to Snyder in September and provided detailed breakdowns of projected state expenditures. France proposed to raise its military budget to 850 billion francs, from the adjusted figure of 580 billion earlier planned. But the earlier figure was based on an expected deficit of 600 billion, which would be met through economies and inflationary borrowing. The new increase of 270 billion francs could only be met by aid from the United States. Exclusive of existing ECA aid and the MDAP program, the French were requesting about $800 million, which would enable them to finance and deploy ten additional divisions by the end of 1951. These figures were presented to a joint United States–French Financial Committee in Washington on October 10, 1950, where the French quickly discovered a major disadvantage in their negotiating tactics. By allowing their projected military expense to depend on an undisclosed amount of American aid, the French invited the Americans to scrutinize every category of their budget to find the funds necessary for defense. The alternative, as critics later pointed out, would have been to set hard and fast levels of French forces within an autonomously and previously prepared French budget, and then negotiate with the Americans anything additional to those amounts. This would have avoided the humiliation and recrimination that became regular features of talks between the two countries. As it was, the Americans could not help but jump at the loopholes provided them. Why did the French not transfer funds from their reconstruction costs to more critical areas of military expense? Paris had a long-held policy of repairing war damage and compensating private victims, or *sinistrés*. William Tomlinson rejected that explanation; the *sinistrés*, he said, were mostly small property owners and "supporters of parties composing the present regime." The French were spending huge sums on political patronage for the middle class. Reconstruction funds could be freed for military use and low-cost housing for the workers, which the ECA had long been arguing was the key to reducing the dangerous Communist vote in France. Tomlinson saw no reason under such circumstances for the Americans to finance a budget of

[22] FRUS, 1950, III, Western Europe, NATO, October 5, 1950, pp. 358–61.

850 billion francs. The result, he warned the French, would be higher deficits, further borrowing, and inflation.[23]

Just as serious as American prying into French budgeting was the danger of misunderstanding inherent in the French negotiating process. Acheson later complained, "We just seem to be crossed up before we start in dealing with the French on finances." Moch laid out an 850 billion franc budget that "they cannot finance," said he could not accept responsibility unless it was done, and "threw it up to us." This was not in fact far from what occurred. The meetings between Moch, Petsche, Marshall, and Acheson began amicably enough on October 13. Moch requested B-26 bomber aircraft for use in Indochina, and Marshall managed to free twenty of them for the French despite high-priority needs in Korea. Marshall also promised that as fast as the French could set priorities in Indochina the United States would provide supplies. The difficulty began with presentation of the military budget, 850 billion francs, of which the United States was to provide 270 billion. Snyder and Acheson immediately attacked French plans for the production of military equipment, the totals for which approximated the amount the French wanted in aid. Moch defended French plans to produce their own planes and tanks, but Acheson insisted these programs be reduced. If Washington was to finance French arms production, the Americans demanded the right to determine what was produced. Such controversies were to become a staple of relations between the two countries during the next few years.[24]

On October 16, Acheson offered the French $200 million in aid until June 1951, with the likelihood of a similar amount in July. Washington could make no commitment beyond the end of the current fiscal year (June 30, 1951), however. Anything beyond that date depended on congressional appropriations. The failure of the American fiscal year to coincide with the French calendar year budgeting introduced yet another source of misunderstanding. Paris could somehow never believe that the American appropriations process was anything more than a formality. Moch immediately complained that the American offer was only half the French request of $800 million. Petsch noted that a 370 billion franc deficit remained, and if this were financed by inflation "he feared for the future of France." Moch warned that for France to economize even 130 billion would mean the evacuation of the Tonkin Delta, and he noted that, if French conscripts were paid as much as the Anglo-Saxons, France would have only three divisions instead of ten. But Acheson was unmoved. He saw no "immutable principle why the total deficit should be saved from the defense budget." Let the French find their budgetary savings from sacrosanct civilian expenditures like re-

[23] A.N., F60 ter 415 (1), September 9, 15, 1950, October 10, 1950; 415 (2), September 19, 28, 1950.

[24] Truman Library, Acheson Papers, Princeton Seminars, October 12–18, 1950, talks with the French.

construction and investment. But Moch and Petsche would not discuss such proposals. On October 17 Petsche resorted to the ultimate weapon in the French arsenal. He had been on the phone to Pleven in Paris, he said, and the French government was now in difficulty because of the inadequate American aid figure. But Acheson would spend no additional funds to save the French cabinet, if he believed it was in danger. The most he would offer was a communiqué stating the Americans' unflagging moral support for France. As a final indignity the Americans buried once and for all the French common NATO budget idea, citing constitutional barriers to any such surrender of sovereignty.[25]

During the aid negotiations Charles Bohlen was summoned to the French Foreign Ministry in Paris and told of a new French initiative involving the creation of a European continental army. Moch and Petsche, still negotiating the French military budget in Washington, were not to be told. Pleven wanted to know the American attitude before bringing the proposal for a European Defense Community to the French cabinet on October 18. Unlike the Schuman Plan, which the French had handled similarly, the "Pleven Plan" did not elicit enthusiasm from the Americans. Acheson complained on October 17 that the idea seemed a delaying tactic that "postponed German participation for many months," whereas Washington wanted progress on German rearmament by October 28. On October 25 Bonnet gave the proposal to Acheson, who immediately recognized in it a scheme for French dominance and permanent "second class status" for Germany.[26]

In the NATO Council only Belgium and Luxembourg offered some hesitant support to the French proposal, which was rapidly rejected. Moch became indignant, but Acheson was by now annoyed with the French defense minister's unwillingness to bend on German rearmament in any case. Pleven and Schuman must be asked whether Moch's "quasi-dictatorial intransigence accurately reflects the French government's attitude." The Pleven Plan was unsound militarily and unacceptable to NATO. The French must be pressed for a realistic proposal without which "we will be obliged to review our entire policy toward the defense of Western Europe." This was the first of several American threats to reevaluate relations with France, for which Acheson's successor, John Foster Dulles, was to become much more well known. The French were already receiving the lion's share of military aid, Acheson warned, and he could not go to Congress for more on the basis of Moch's attitude.[27]

25 NARA, 611.51/10-2050, October 20, 1950, Minutes of United States–French talks, October 13–9, 1950.
26 Edward Fursdon, *The European Defense Community: A History* (New York: St. Martin's Press, 1980), pp. 80–92. FRUS, 1950, III, Western Europe, NATO, October 15, 1950, pp. 377–80; October 17, 1950, pp. 384–5; October 25, 1950, pp. 403–4.
27 FRUS, 1950, III, Western Europe, NATO, October 27, 1950, pp. 410–2; October

Acheson tried to mobilize European socialists to convince their French colleagues that their position was "injurious to France and their party." Bevin was approached, also the Dutch, Belgian, and Scandinavian socialists. Bevin tried his luck with Guy Mollet but "got nowhere." Pleven meanwhile reassured Acheson that he could handle Moch. On November 12, Bruce cabled that the French government had still another proposal to make; if the Americans found this one unacceptable, the government would fall. France could not agree to the formation of German military divisions, but Paris might accept the establishment of "regimental combat teams," while all anti-German discrimination would be eliminated from the EDC plan. Acheson did not much like this idea either, but found to his dissatisfaction that Moch's views were shared within the French administration, while it was best to avoid a resignation of Moch and the departure of the Socialist party from the government. On November 25 moreover, Bruce cabled that Schuman had made a "historic" speech and won Assembly support for the Pleven Plan. Charles Spofford, the American NATO representative, thought perhaps that the time had come "to exert maximum pressure on the French," but on November 30, the United States and France struck a compromise. The Americans agreed not to stand in the way of French efforts to create a European Defense Community including Germany on condition that it be organized within the framework of NATO.[28]

Washington's dissatisfaction with the French attitude toward German rearmament was reflected in the economic and military aid "understanding" negotiated by Moch and Petsche. The agreement was open to conflicting interpretation, and each side did, as Acheson later reflected, hear essentially what it wanted to from the other. Washington reluctantly approved a French plan to spend 850 billion francs, but offered only $200 million in military aid for the first half of 1951, with the possibility of another $200 million later. But the French had requested $800 million. Did the failure of the French to get everything they wanted mean that Paris could lower its military expenditure? The French thought so, and the National Assembly proceeded to pass a military budget at year's end of 740 billion francs. But the State Department immediately objected that the French military budget was in violation of the plan of 850 billion presented in Washington on October 5. Did this mean in turn that Washington could reneg on its commitment of $400 million? The French thought not, but the State Department was not sure. Moreover, Washington had presumably made it clear that its assistance was not budgetary but for balance of payments purposes. In the event

30, 1950, pp. 418–23; October 31, 1950, pp. 423–5; November 3, 1950, pp. 426–31.

28   FRUS, 1950, III, Western Europe, NATO, November 3, 1950, pp. 431–2, November 4, 1950, pp. 433–4; November 8, 1950, pp. 435–6; November 12, 1950, pp. 445; November 14, 1950, pp. 450–2; November 16, 1950, pp. 460–1; November 25, 1950, pp. 485–8; November 28, 1950, p. 495; November 30, 1950, pp. 501–6.

of a short-term improvement in the French foreign exchange situation, then, would military aid be reduced anyway? As it turned out, Washington was to reduce the aid for this reason, amid bitter French recrimination. A related question: Military aid was presumably exclusive of ECA assistance and MDAP, but was it not most unlikely that these could be kept separate from one another? Finally, the reduced French military budget raised the question of where the cuts were to be made. Paris hoped to slow the pace of achieving combat readiness, but the Americans had already identified the ambitious French plans to rebuild a national arms industry as impractical and wasteful.

Obscured from view in all this haggling over francs and dollars was a broader political question. The symbol of the national sovereignty of any modern state was its army. Yet, on the one hand, as a response to American pressure to achieve European unity and the rearmament of Germany, Paris agreed to merge its military, or at least significant segments thereof, in an as yet vague scheme for a supranational army. On the other hand, the French government, in its quest for dollars, willingly subordinated the question of the level of its military commitment, and the nature of that commitment in terms of weaponry, to the intervention and arbitration of a foreign power. The Americans consequently became even more intimately involved in the internal French political and budgetary process than before. And to complicate matters further, Washington was invited to take on more and more of the French military burden in Indochina, raising even more sharply the question of the goals and objectives of the French commitment there as viewed from the two shores of the Atlantic. Historically, certainly, the involvement of one state in the sovereign affairs of another to this degree appeared unprecedented outside the sorry story of colonial relationships. As they surveyed the contemporary scene, the French could perhaps take solace in the fact that there were few nations of the so-called Free World in which the United States was not similarly involved.

II FIGHTING COMMUNISM: THE EXTERNAL AND INTERNAL FRONTS

In January 1951 Premier René Pleven sought an invitation to visit the United States in an apparent effort to bolster his prestige. Washington thought the idea inopportune, but Pleven would not be dissuaded and the visit was duly scheduled for January 29–31. Pleven was concerned by the American reaction to the cuts in the French military budget and eager to try to win American support for the scheme to create a European army. In addition, the crossing of the thirty-eighth parallel by advancing American armies in Korea was disapproved by much of French public opinion. There was malaise in the French government due to the disappointing offer from Washington of only $200 million of economic assistance. The French thought their military effort among the highest in NATO and their tax burden the maximum bearable; they rejected American criticism along these lines.[29]

The Americans had their own agenda with regard to the French. Washington was gratified that France had sent a battalion to Korea, but wanted French support for its policy of nonrecognition of mainland China. The Americans were now prepared to offer the French limited support in Indochina, so long as all means were used to defeat the "Communist Fifth Column." In Europe Washington wanted the Schuman Plan negotiations concluded quickly and was prepared to use pressure to bring about that end. The Americans still had reservations about the plan for a European army, though; they preferred German divisions to "regimental combat teams" and insisted that a "sound and practical" plan be negotiated by the participating countries without undue delay. In the meantime Washington would not pressure any nation to join the French scheme, but neither would it try to prevent them from doing so. The ultimate American aim was the integration of a rearmed West Germany into NATO. In addition, Washington had extensive requirements in terms of military bases in France, to which it planned to move the headquarters of air force operations in Europe and North Africa. And it expected full support from the French for its policy of firmness toward the USSR.[30]

Bilateral relations were rapidly reduced to wrangling over American support levels for the French military budget. Washington regarded the French retreat from the 850 billion franc level promised in October 1950 as "most unwise." The French argued that the reduced level of 740 billion francs would enable them to field the same numbers of troops as originally promised, and they demanded the full $200 million promised by Washington for the first half of 1951. But the Americans thought the French could afford a larger military effort, and they intended to make further economic aid dependent upon what Paris was prepared to do. Finally, the Americans wanted a treaty of Friendship, Commerce, and Navigation with France and an end to discrimination against American investors. The Americans thought well of the French negotiating team, which did not include Jules Moch. Pleven, although economically very conservative, was regarded as the best Defense Minister France had since the Liberation, and Washington wanted to "assist the French Prime Minister in his efforts to combat the psychological depression that exists in France by strengthening the French morale and the will to resist aggression."[31]

The talks themselves were not particularly successful from the French point of view. Pleven requested financial aid of $70 million for the building of a Vietnamese national army. This was an area of assistance that was to

[29] NARA, 751.00/12-1250, 12-1350, December 12, 13, 1950.
[30] NARA, 611.51, Truman–Pleven Talks, Briefing Book, January 29–31, 1950. Also FRUS, 1951, IV, France, January 23, 1951, pp. 291–2; January 24, 1951, p. 300.
[31] NARA, 611.51, Truman–Pleven Talks, Briefing Book, January 29–31, 1951.

appear increasingly attractive to Washington in coming months, but for the moment it still fell victim to the taboo on financial aid, Acheson noting, "We had told them before that we would not finance their budget deficits." Pleven wanted assurance of immediate American help in case of a Soviet attack and asked how and when the Americans would respond with nuclear weapons, but Washington declined to discuss its nuclear strategy. Pleven complained that too often NATO appeared to be an "Anglo-Saxon show" from which the French were excluded: "We are very nervous when it seems to be a private club we can't get in." The French were upset by Anglo–American talks on the Middle East taking place at Malta. Truman, Acheson, and Marshall professed to know nothing of these talks, which were in any case, they said, of no importance. In a hurried conference between the State Department and the joint chiefs of staff it was then decided that the United States and Britain must feel free to conduct bilateral relations that concerned them; French prestige in the Middle East had declined to the point that they could no longer make a useful contribution. If Bonnet asked about the talks again, he was bluntly to be told "so what?" Pleven asked that the Americans cooperate with France in establishing international controls on raw materials prices that the French held responsible for a part of their inflation. In return he received a lecture from President Truman on the evils of French protectionism, somewhat ironic in view of French complaints about the levels of American tariffs. Pleven asked for an aircraft carrier for Indochina and was told that none were available.[32]

The premier made his expected request for American financial aid and was again told that the United States financed balance of payments shortfalls but not budgetary deficits. The economic issues between the two countries were discussed in a separate meeting of the U.S.–French Economic Working Group. The French negotiators submitted a list of projects on which they proposed to spend the $200 million Washington had agreed to provide, but the Americans wanted further assurances that the assistance, in view of the reduced military budget, was really required. The Americans pointed to an increase in French gold and dollar reserves, which was not the purpose of American aid: "The United States could not adopt a policy of financing internal French budgetary outlays associated with the rearmament effort." Finally the Americans again rejected French proposals for a common defense budget and an international effort against inflation, and criticized French protectionism. In fact the Truman–Pleven talks served no purpose other than to put the French on notice that the Americans no longer regarded their $200 million promise of assistance as binding.[33]

---

[32] Ibid., also FRUS, 1951, IV, France, Truman–Pleven Talks, January 29–31, 1951, pp. 304–34. There are some minor discrepancies between quotes as they appear in the minutes in the National Archives and the published version in FRUS.

[33] A.N., F60 ter 435, January 29–31, 1951, Minutes of the United States–France Economic Working Group.

The frustrations in the talks remained secret, and Pleven was able to use them to bolster his political position at home. *Le Monde* trumpeted the talks as a "triumph" for the French.[34] The same discrepancy appeared during the visit of President Auriol to Washington two months later. The visit was not predominantly ceremonial. Auriol was an activist president with strong personal views, the Pleven government had just fallen, which served to accentuate Auriol's role as the guarantor of the continuity of the French state, and he was accompanied by Foreign Minister Robert Schuman, who the Americans knew would remain in that post in any successor government. Auriol enjoyed respect and admiration in America. Truman's briefing book described him as a "patient and skilled arbiter," gregarious, warm-hearted, and demonstrative, with a sense of humor. He was said to do everything "with gusto" yet remain dignified and popular. Madame Auriol was described as tall, distinguished, gracious, charming, tactful, serious, with "exquisite taste in clothes." Robert Schuman was austere, shy, devout, ascetic, "saintly," and a mystic, but endowed with common sense; he remained a friend of the United States.[35]

Auriol was to be bluntly told of American dissatisfaction with the French military effort, and warned that the United States planned to review the French military program and "suggest changes we believe to be desirable." Paris would reap the results of having drawn the Americans into its budgeting process. In the event the talks went differently than planned, and the French president emphasized general questions. He spent much time reassuring the Americans of the continuity in French policy despite the cabinet crisis, and lecturing them on the perfidiousness of Germany, a subject that did not go over very well in Washington. He stressed an improved moral climate in France vis-à-vis the Communist party, French loyalty to the Atlantic alliance, and the will of his countrymen to defend themselves, their liberty, and their independence, no matter what France's detractors were saying. The Americans stressed their enthusiasm for the Schuman Plan. John Foster Dulles, then still only an adviser to the State Department, told Auriol that French policy in Europe "was that which best responded to American aspirations," and he was eloquent about the possibility of a new departure in French–American relations. Personally, on his travels in the United States, Auriol won much goodwill. Bonnet saw the visit as an outstanding success: "never has an official visit had equal significance."[36]

Yet the disagreements between the two countries were not long in resurfacing. On April 2, 1951 representatives of the Embassy, the ECA, and MAAG met with French economic and military officials, and told the latter bluntly that their military program was unsatisfactory. French plans for the produc-

34 *Le Monde*, February 1, 1951.
35 NARA, 611.51, Truman–Auriol Talks, Briefing Book, March 1951.
36 FRUS, 1951, IV, France, Background Memo for Auriol visit, March 1951, pp. 349–62; MAE, B Amérique, Vol. 122, Bonnet to Paris, April 2, 13, 1951.

tion of tanks and planes were "uneconomical"; the manufacture of heavy equipment should be left to the British and the Americans. France should concentrate on the manufacture of spare parts and ammunition, increase its capacity for fuel storage, and improve its military training. The French protested that they could not renounce their defense production programs in aviation or armored vehicles. Paris's original military budget had been predicated on an anticipated 270 billion francs ($800 million) of American aid, instead of which the United States offered only 70 billion francs ($200 million) in the first half of the year and the possibility of another 70 billion later. The Americans had accepted the whole of the French military program as sound in October 1950; they could not go back on their word now. Angry officials at the Quai wired Bonnet to warn the Americans of the consequences of their recommendations. Decisions about the manufacture of military equipment were a French responsibility. The American request was clearly of a "political character" if not humiliating, and it was received with "surprise mixed with regret." France would not now cancel work in progress, and accept the closure of aircraft and tank factories with resulting unemployment. Nor were the French willing to be relegated to the status of a second-class power. Washington was to be told only that its proposals were "hard to accept"; Bonnet was not to sound categorically negative because the ECA was threatening a reduction of $115 million in economic aid unless France agreed. Nevertheless the American position was privately regarded as "entirely unacceptable"; the French government would stand firm.[37]

The French government stood firm and the ECA announced on May 12, 1951 that it was reducing the French economic aid allotment by $115 million. The French understood this as an expression of Washington's dissatisfaction with their military program; but Washington never made its position clear, citing the improved French position in dollar and gold reserves as justification for its action. France would accept American suggestions concerning its military program, but not orders; Washington had promised $200 million of military aid in addition to the ECA allotment of $155 million. Now it was giving with one hand in order to take away with the other. But Paris had to recognize that it had reduced its original military budget once the American aid figure became known. Thus did the consequences of the ill-considered French negotiating tactics come home to roost. Paris had to give Washington a full accounting of its military expenditure, which Congress had to have in order to legislate its aid figure. Paris used the projected aid figure to plan its budget, but then the Americans took the French figure as a commitment no matter how much aid they decided to grant. The Americans had managed permanently to place the French "in the painful position of [always] having to justify their behavior."[38]

Within weeks of Auriol's visit Bruce reported that tension between the

37 A.N., F60 ter 415 (2), April 2, 1951; F60 ter 418, April 12, 1951.
38 A.N., F60 ter 418, April 12, 1951, May 12, 1951; F60 ter 417, April 5, 1951.

two countries over American assistance to French rearmament threatened "a very damaging crisis in French–American relations." The American "change in method of financing" was interpreted in Paris as dissatisfaction with France's military program. Bruce deplored the misunderstanding; the Americans objected to the French manner of presenting their requests, and the French resisted American demands for information. Paris was unhappy that its proposal for a common military budget had been rejected, its efforts in Indochina were unappreciated, and its military program was subject to unwarranted scrutiny. Bruce warned that the United States needed French support and confidence, and recommended that an outstanding balance of ECA aid amounting to $129 million be released to France without conditions. On April 30 Acheson agreed to release the $129 million "despite the French failure to meet commitments," and the ECA followed suit.[39]

On May 15 French and American military aid talks resumed. Washington dropped its insistence on changes in the French military program in exchange for some French concessions. The French promised to modernize their tanks with American cannons and turn out 1,000 yearly in 1953. They agreed to augment their fuel storage capacity and manufacture more uniforms and spare parts. Washington in turn promised not to stand in the way of production of French aircraft, and agreed to supply machine tools for them. The French were grateful; without the aircraft production Dassault would go out of business, while the tanks were a matter of national prestige. But having retained its military projects Paris at once returned to the question of its promised aid. In a stiff note on May 30, 1951 Paris protested the ECA reduction, and warned of the "nasty repercussions" imposed by excessive civil and military expenditures without the requisite aid. The French remained confused about the aims of American policy. The Americans reduced their aid but never made their reasons clear. Was it dissatisfaction with the French arms program or the balance of payments situation as the Americans insisted? Was Paris being punished or pressured? Or was there simply a lack of coordination between different American services that created contradictions in American policy? In either case the Americans failed to see that French commitments were already beyond the nation's means. France could not reconstruct and modernize, fight a war in Indochina, build a large European army, and participate in expensive public works, a NATO "infrastructure," on its territory, all at the same time. The United States rejected multilateral sharing of the burden of rearmament in favor of bilateral agreements, thus perpetuating the unequal relationship between beggar and donor. In the meantime France faced a 1952 budget deficit of 600–700 billion francs that threatened "to overturn the economic, social, and political structure of the country and to compromise any rearmament effort."[40]

[39] FRUS, 1951, IV, France, April 18, 1951, pp. 383–7; April 30, 1951, p. 388; May 12, 1951, pp. 389–90.
[40] A.N., F60 ter 418, May 15, 29 and 30, 1951, June 25, 29, 1951.

Bruce fully agreed with this analysis. The French wanted to start talks on their 1952 military budget, but he doubted that American policies were "sufficiently defined to begin." The security of the United States and NATO required an open-ended French commitment in Indochina, the building of a NATO infrastructure in France, and a one-million-man French army by 1953. The French needed to spend $4 billion (1,400 billion francs) on their military in 1952, but could not do so because American fiscal aid in 1951–2 amounted thus far to a paltry $290 million. Meanwhile other American officials (clearly MAAG and the ECA) urged the French to increase troop pay, raise wages, increase overseas investment, and expand low-cost housing. American policy was clearly contradictory, as Paris complained. Bruce pleaded for a consistent program based on the realization that the French defense effort was central to Europe. The United States had no defined priorities and "the marginal amount of our economic assistance is not the appropriate weapon for the United States to use as pressure to influence France in this regard." The United States should extend an additional $400 million credit, giving the French the $800 million they had asked, and end the doubt, mistrust, and uncertainty plaguing American–French relations. But it was not to be. In a curt note on July 3 the United States once again informed France that Washington financed dollar deficits, not budgetary needs. French gold and dollar reserves had increased in 1950–1, hence the French were entitled to no more than $240 million from January through June 1951 and $395 million for the entire year.[41]

Despite French concerns that U.S. aid reductions would have a negative impact in the June 1951 elections, the United States remained unworried, having at last concluded that France had achieved a measure of stability, its internal politics no longer a major source of fear. On a fact-finding trip in March 1951, State Department officials found France vital to Western security and apparently stable. American postwar policies had been "conspicuously successful" there. The Communist party was in decline, "squirming" under the "get tough" policy of the government. The French government's insufficient anti-Communist resolve had long been a matter of concern in Washington, but Pleven had assured Truman that the French would take firm measures. It now appeared that American pressure was bearing fruit. Washington approved the election law, noting with satisfaction that the new system of *apparentements* (electoral coalitions) was likely to result in the election of no more than 100 Communist deputies.[42] Bruce remained

[41] FRUS, 1951, IV, France, June 28, 1951, pp. 397–404; July 3, 1951, pp. 406–8.
[42] Under this law, parties that formed alliances prior to the balloting and received a majority in a department would receive all its parliamentary seats. This clearly favored the government coalition parties against the Gaullists and Communists, neither of which could form alliances nor was likely to get a majority on its own. See Jean-Pierre Rioux, *The Fourth Republic, 1944–1951*, trans. Godfrey Rogers (Cambridge: Cambridge University Press, 1987). pp. 163–9.

concerned, however, lest the law effectively disenfranchise the working class and leave it as alienated as it was before. A tripartite working group of American, British, and French intelligence services was formed in April 1951 for the purpose of concluding an agreement for the elimination of "antinational" and "subversive" elements from sensitive government jobs. The French government refused to designate Communists specifically as the targets of this agreement as the Americans wished, but otherwise it appeared willing to adhere to the American policy outline. The working group produced a report to harmonize French, British, and American security procedures in July 1951, which the Americans found satisfactory. Unfortunately its work was transmitted to Moscow by the British spies, Philby, Burgess, and Maclean.[43]

Nor were the Gaullists any longer a major object of concern in Washington. On the contrary, despite disagreements between Washington and the French government, the embassy was "particularly struck by the fact that de Gaulle is emerging virtually as the self-constituted French spokesman for certain important American concepts." De Gaulle advocated a higher defense budget, condemned the Pleven Plan, called for a German army integrated with NATO, and wanted Spain allied firmly with the West. "It seems clear that the repeated expression of these views are made with the American as well as the French audience in mind." General Billotte was off to the United States in search of support, and de Gaulle had sent a copy of his January 1951 speech in Nimes to Eisenhower before it was released to the press. But the Americans still distrusted the Rassemblement du Peuple Français as "a political party with a military chain of command." It had never guaranteed the freedom of other political parties, and it was not clear that de Gaulle as president in a new regime would ever allow himself to be voted out of power. In any event, the future government would be a coalition as before, and the RPF was likely to find itself participating in government much like the other parties.[44]

The results of the June 17, 1951 elections confirmed the State Department's confidence. The Third Force majority gained 54.7 percent of the vote and a large majority in the National Assembly. The French people had shown their desire "to cooperate wholeheartedly with the west," and share in its defense. Neutralism, much talked of in the press, had not even been an issue. The Communists had been defeated, losing 70 parliamentary seats if only 450,000 votes, and the PCF vote declined in 91 of 103 districts. Most significantly, where American military installations were beginning to appear noticeable and GIs were a regular presence, the Communist vote had never-

---

[43] NARA, 751.00/3-2451, March 24, 1951; 4-1251, April 12, 1951; 5-3151, May 31, 1951. See also, Trevor Barnes, "The Secret Cold War: The CIA and American Foreign Policy in Europe, 1946–56. Part II," *Hitorical Journal*, 25, no. 3 (1982): 661–2.

[44] NARA, 751.00/1-2951, January 29, 1951; 751.00/5-1551, May 15, 1951.

theless declined. There had been a marked nationalist trend, and the strong representation of the Gaullists was sure to make the government especially touchy about questions of abandoning national sovereignty. But Gaston Palewski appeared at the embassy on the morrow of the vote to assure Bruce that the RPF was in fact "the best defender of American interests in France." Its nationalist propaganda should be understood in the United States as primarily directed against the Communists.[45]

A few months after the elections American analysts remained guardedly optimistic. Non-Communist public opinion in France accepted the "soundness" of American foreign policy. The government was showing a firm attitude toward the Communists although still "far short of what is desirable." The French remained impressed by the American showing in Korea, gratified at U.S. support of the Schuman and Pleven plans (the Americans rallied to the revised version of the EDC during the summer of 1951), and appreciative of American assistance in Indochina. There were still problems, however. The United States was still seen as impetuous and occasionally reckless, the French wanted a bigger voice in the councils of the West, and they remained jealous of the special relationship between Britain and the United States. The French still resented American demands for a larger defense establishment and were increasingly unhappy with U.S. unwillingness to support their policies in North Africa. But as the Pleven government began to unravel in the fall of 1951, Americans remained gratified that his problems were entirely internal and related to the intractable issue of government aid to clerical schools. If he fell, a government of the center-right would very likely succeed him. Foreign policy was not a concern.[46]

Washington remained puzzled and bothered by the internal strength of the Communist parties in France and Italy, however. Whereas the PCF had declined modestly, the Italian party nevertheless seemed to be gaining in strength. In neither case had facile assumptions about the equivalence of Communist support and working-class material deprivation proved true. Washington analysts no longer considered the PCF a serious claimant for power, but this situation could still be reversed, and the Italian Communists remained a worry; the NSC developed plans for aid to a non-Communist government and possible intervention in the event of a coup by the *Partito Comunista Italiano* (PCI). Even failing such catastrophic scenarios, Communist strength in both countries remained debilitating; the French were always fearful of antagonizing the Kremlin as much for reasons of internal as external criticism. The French bureaucracy remained permeated enough with Communists so as to preclude the sharing of state secrets, and the U.S. army opposed giving the French new weapons designs, despite costly dupli-

45 NARA, 751.00/6-1951, June 19, 1951; 751.00/6-2951, June 29, 1951.
46 NARA, 751.00/6-1951, June 19, 1951; 6-2051, June 20, 1951; 6-2951, June 21, 1951; 6-2951, June 29, 1951; 9-2551, September 25, 1951; 10-351, October 3, 1951.

cation in their arms industry. Finally, both Paris and Moscow kept an uneasy eye on the Peace Movement, through which the Communist world showed an uncanny ability to communicate with non-Communists of a wide range of political opinions and viewpoints. Measures to counter the Peace Movement, and anti-Communist propaganda by the French and American governments, whether through the counterpeace campaign of Jean Paul David, or public show trials like the Kravchenko case and the efforts of David Rousset, appeared to have very limited effect.[47]

It was in this context that in April 1951 President Truman created the Psychological Strategy Board (PSB), a subcommittee of the National Security Council, to develop a better strategy for a coordinated anti-Communist offensive "to influence men's minds and wills." The Board consisted of the under secretary of state, the deputy secretary of defense, and the director of the CIA. Its aims were to block the expansion of Soviet power, induce the "retraction of Kremlin control and influence," and "foster the seeds of destruction within the Soviet system."[48] It worked closely with the United States Information Services (USIS) and its propagandistic orientation was emphasized by the appointment of Gordon Gray, president of the University of North Carolina, as its first director. The PSB was in one sense simply another version of an intelligence oversight committee or advisory board. But as its name indicates it was designed to bring a new dimension to the anti-Communist effort and to recognize that the cold war was a struggle for public opinion above all else; in an era of nuclear stalemate the ideological battle was perhaps more important than the military one. And it was apparent that the Americans would have to develop "novel weapons" in this battle, which thus far, it appeared, the Communist world was winning. For the most part the plans and efforts of the PSB remain shrouded in secrecy. During its two-year existence it organized about forty-four different projects.[49]

Late in 1951 special task forces of the board developed "Plans for the Reduction of Communist Power" in France and Italy, and a special "Psychological Operations Plan for the Reduction of Communist Power in France." Numerous meetings of the PSB were devoted to the implementation of the French plan in the fall of 1951, which was first given the code name "Project Cloven," later "Midiron." On November 17, 1951 the plan was ready. A

---

[47] On the limited effects of *Paix et liberté* see René Sommer, " 'Paix et Liberté?': la Quatrième République contre le PC," *L'Histoire*, 40 (December 1981): 26–35.

[48] Dwight D. Eisenhower Library, National Security Council, "Status of United States Programs for National Security as of December 31, 1952," no. 6, The Psychological Program. Report presented to the National Security Council, February 10, 1953.

[49] On the general operations of the Psychological Strategy Board, see Edward P. Lilly, "The Psychological Strategy Board and Its Predecessors: Foreign Policy Coordination, 1938–1953," in Gaetano L. Vincitorio, ed., *Studies in Modern History* (New York: St. John's University Press, 1968), pp. 363–70.

meeting of PSB agreed that "the type of operations in this plan are of such delicate character and have such a high potential for helping or damaging our relations with the countries involved that [we] believe Europe and CIA are right in insisting the Ambassador be given responsibility and authority to 'direct and control' operations." Bruce took responsibility and brought the plan to Pleven on November 30, 1951. When told of what the Americans had in mind, Pleven said he personally would take charge.[50]

We can do little more than surmise about the content of Project Cloven and the various plans for the reduction of Communist power in France. A "Psychological Operations Plan for the Reduction of Communist Power in France" was approved by the board on January 31, 1952. It noted that the PCF was "a potential fifth column" and "constitutes a serious threat to American foreign policy and to NATO plans for the defense of Western Europe." The plan reviewed previous French government steps designed to remedy this situation: the electoral law of 1951, removal of Communists from key offices, and the banning of certain demonstrations, organizations, and publications. But these were deemed insufficient, and the Communist party "continues to do France tremendous harm. In wartime their parliamentary force could conduct serious guerrilla activity." The report believed the party "vulnerable to stronger use of existing government powers and to new legislation," and argued that it could be affected by a more equitable share for labor of the French national income. The report warned against "identifying the U.S. government with any particular measures whose short-term effects may be considered harmful to entrenched [French] interests," but noted that "on the other hand, we must recognize the necessity of using U.S. influence and power for the preservation of its own security by helping to remedy a situation in France which adversely affects the security of the entire Atlantic Community. . . . It is equally essential that the details of measures and programs should be of French conception and execution." Twelve pages of "desired actions by the French government" follow, all of which remain exempt from declassification in the continued interested, in 1989–90, of American national security.[51]

---

50 NARA, 751.001/11-1751, November 17, 1951; 11-3051, November 30, 1951. Truman Library, 091, Psychological Strategy Board, 5, Folders 1 and 2. More than forty documents relating to the operations of the Psychological Strategy Board have been withdrawn from the NARA 751.001 series. The contents of the various plans for the reduction of Communist influence in France and Italy likewise remain classified at the Truman and Eisenhower libraries. Thus far the State Department has denied Freedom of Information appeals for release of any of these materials under clauses in the Freedom of Information Act that permit it to keep confidential items the release of which, in its judgment, would be harmful to the national security. A "sanitized" text of the 1952 plan for the reduction of Communist power in France was released to this writer in 1989, and two further texts of "Project Midiron" in 1990. All have most of the content excised.

51 DDE Library, National Security Council, "Psychological Operations Plan for the Reduction of Communist Power in France," dated January 31, 1952.

The files at the Truman and Eisenhower libraries permit further glimpses of the possible results of the plan, if it was implemented: a "checklist" of anti-Communist measures taken by the French government from 1950 through 1952, and an essay by political scientist Charles Micaud on the "Organization and Leadership of the PCF." A declassified report to the NSC of February 10, 1953 offers some further information. None of these contain materials that cannot be obtained from public sources. The checklist mentions the various suspensions of Communist mayors by prefects, the elimination of Pierre Joliot-Curie as head of the French Atomic Energy Commission, the banning of Communist demonstrations, raids on Communist headquarters, seizures of documents, and the arrest of Communist leader Jacques Duclos during the alleged "Complot des Pigeons" on May 28, 1952. In effect one finds a catalog of the petty anti-Communist measures undertaken by the Pinay government in 1952, all of which were approved in Washington, and the stimulus for which, if the homegrown anticommunism of M. Pinay were not sufficient, could have come from there. The NSC report contains the following observation:

> In France, the Pinay government made considerable progress toward the reduction of the power of the Communist Party in France. Its campaign to expose the foreign and subversive nature of the party, combined with the increasingly nationalistic sentiment in France, served to create an atmosphere particularly appropriate for such a policy. Success of the current legal proceedings against the communist leaders would crystallize this situation. With respect to this situation, the Embassy in Paris reports its conviction that the U.S. government should and will continue to utilize every opportune occasion to reiterate concern with the problem and to make suggestions that are discreet and appropriate. However, the Embassy continues to feel that it still behooves the U.S. Government to remain as invisible as possible and to let the French proceed on their own.[52]

The American FBI reprinted and circulated for its own internal purposes the French government's materials used in the attempt to lift the parliamentary immunity of five members of the PCF Political Bureau in late 1952.[53]

Micaud's essay indicates an evolution in thought among the American governing elite about the nature of communism. Micaud thought the ERP-induced economic improvement in France was a necessary but not sufficient accomplishment to "roll back" Communist influence. The PCF remained strong because it was able to capitalize on the French revolutionary tradition, the disappointment due to the *révolution manquée* of the Liberation, the alienation of the working class, and the disappearance of liberalism.

---

[52] DDE Library, NSC, No. 6, "The Psychological Program," February 18, 1953.
[53] Truman Library, PSB, 5, 1. Federal Bureau of Investigation, Memorandum from D. Ladd to the Director, November 17, 1952, with attachments, coded 64-200-231. These materials were released to the author pursuant to a Freedom of Information Act request. The summary of the request to lift the immunity of the Communist deputies was signed by René Pleven, then in his capacity as minister of defense.

Communists had created a closed society with a self-contained system of values and managed to harmonize their pro-Sovietism with a fierce French nationalism. The choice of methods to reduce their influence was not exciting; repression would work to their advantage in the long run and was repugnant to democratic values. Nevertheless the authority of the State, Micaud cautioned, must be forcefully asserted at every appearance of a challenge from PCF ranks. In addition it was important to maintain a propaganda campaign, support manifestations of anti-Soviet Titoism, and vigorously pursue the option of creating a French left-wing reformism, or *travaillisme*. All of these options were pursued, including the support by French police for a small band of Titoists who claimed to be working within the PCF against the leadership, centered around the review, *Unir*. The last alternative was the most promising, and in this respect the failure of Force Ouvrière was no less than a disaster, for which Micaud offered a number of explanations.

The PSB tried to stimulate a vast propaganda offensive around the world in favor of American values. In Germany it sought an ideological banner around which to rally youth; reunification was the most obvious, but it was frought with dangers, not the least of which were due to "French vulnerabilities." The French desk of the State Department feared German unification would bring a neutralist regime or worse to power in France; at best it merited lip-service. In contrast European integration could rally both German and French youth around the same banner, and became the rallying cry of PSB in both countries. The campaign in its favor tied in with the private efforts of the American Committee for a United States of Europe, headed by William Donovan, former head of OSS during the war, and which included others from the intelligence establishment, including Allen Dulles, head of the CIA under Eisenhower. The CIA during this period began its active sponsorship of American and non-Communist youth and student groups, within which it favored those who supported the goal of European integration.[54]

The United States Information and Education (USIE) Official Country Plan for France in 1952 lists a wide variety of activities that need not be recounted in detail. Its psychological objectives were to help explode the "Soviet Myth," promote international cooperation, portray the United States as seeking peace and freedom, promote the acceptance of American troops in France, convince the French that U.S. policy respected French national independence, and "encourage local channels to serve as a vehicle for U.S. psychological objectives." Under this heading came the activities of the Congress for Cultural Freedom, which targeted European intellectuals, financing the reviews *Encounter* in England, and *Preuves* in France. Subsidies to the press, such as *Franc-Tireur*, and *Le Combat*, also fell under this head-

---

[54] Truman Library, PSB, 091, Germany, February 7, 1952.

ing.[55] The United States sought to enlighten French management as to the benefits of higher productivity and workers' wages, promote free trade unions, and promote visiting teams to the United States to study productivity, technology, labor relations, education, and the arts. "Target groups" in France for American propaganda were labor, opinion leaders, youth, the armed forces, and religious organizations. The fiscal program of USIE for 1952 allowed for the employment of 289 persons, American and French, a budget of close to $500,000, and the maintenance of offices in the largest cities. The Americans considered all this investment to be only a partial response to a "wealthy and aggressive, perpetually in motion" Communist propaganda machine subsidized by Moscow and capable of much greater dynamism. The activities of USIE involved the close cooperation with French armed forces, including "troop training and indoctrination courses through the local military's own psychological warfare units."[56]

The semiannual USIE report for December 1, 1951 to May 31, 1952 detailed a dramatic expansion of American propaganda activity in France to coincide with the establishment of the large-scale troop presence. Interestingly the report praised the measures of Pinay, whose "imagination and determination" had brought the French a new sense of stability, confidence, self-reliance, and initiative. Pinay had defeated PCF violence and protected USIE offices in several parts of France. The USIE sponsored a variety of publications and tried to place information items and features in the French press. It promoted a large number of films promoting the "American Way of Life"; in six months 34,000 nontheatrical programs were presented to no less than 4,760,000 persons throughout France. The association *France–Etats–Unis* alone showed to 1.6 million persons a documentary covering President Auriol's visit to the United States. In addition to the USIE radio program, "Ici New York," was heard daily on twenty stations by an estimated 1–1.5 million persons. In 1952, fifty-six French leaders received American "Leader Grants" which enabled them to visit the United States, French universities received thirty-eight Fulbright lecturers, and another thirty French teachers of English and philosophy received grants to study in the United States. USIE and MSA jointly sponsored many translations of American works, winning the cooperation of many French publishers.[57]

Reviewing efforts of the USIS in France late in 1952, Ambassador James Dunn concluded that its effectiveness varied in proportion to its "unobtrusiveness"; the French did not like to be "told" anything. The most valuable part of the program, he thought, were the exchanges of persons. The key figures in the French government's vigorous "anti-Commie" drive, Dunn noted, had participated in the program. The United States would always

55 Barnes, "The Secret Cold war," p. 667.
56 NARA, 511.51/1-1552, January 15, 1952; 2-1252, February 12, 1952.
57 NARA, 511.51/7-1552, July 15, 1952.

lack the Soviet propaganda advantage, Dunn said: moral irresponsibility, an indigenous Communist party, unlimited funds, popular resentment over low living standards, the revolutionary tradition, and the Frenchman's perennial search for novelty.[58] Dunn's rather pessimistic analysis was echoed by a report of the PSB: The French would always remain resentful of the United States, which is "the symbol of the modern economic world. This world disturbs them, as manifestations of anti-Americanism indicate, but they must adjust to it and know that they must." In addition to the understandable embarrassment of the poor recipient indebted to a rich donor, the French remained fundamentally hostile to American values. "The French mind rebels at pragmatism and subordinates economic considerations to political ones. . . . French 'realism' is more reverence for logic than care for reality." Since the French evaluated power in terms of historical experience and influence rather than economic strength, they were able to remain under the illusion that they were still a great power, and that the United States was as dependent upon them as they on it. And most important, "French understanding and feelings of the immediate Russian danger are many degrees below our own."[59]

Whatever the validity of these analyses, the Americans had mounted an enormous propaganda machine of their own in France, and the American presence was visible to the whole nation after 1951–2, as much because of the presence of more than 40,000 American military personnel as because of the information services that tried to make the French adjust happily to the U.S. presence. The several Pleven governments, and Pinay afterward, had all cooperated with American "psychological warfare" objectives. Yet beneath the surface the Americans were building up negative resistance. As irritation mounted due to continued squabbles over American military and financial aid, this resentment exploded into popular consciousness, creating yet another crisis in Franco–American relations in 1952.

III   AMERICAN AID AND THE PINAY CRISIS

Controversy over American economic aid and Off-Shore Procurement (OSP) aid continued to trouble Franco–American relations through 1952. The offshore formula helped meet the French balance of payments crisis by means of direct American government expenditures in France in dollars. Such expenditure came from several sources. During 1951 the American military buildup proceeded, coupled with the construction of a NATO "infrastructure": twenty-eight airports and a communications line, rail, telegraph, road, and so forth from La Pallice-Bordeaux, the entrepot for American military

58   NARA, 511.51/9-852, September 8, 1952.
59   DDE Library, Psychological Strategy Board, "Evaluation of the Psychological Impact of U.S. Foreign Economic Policies and Programs in France," February 9, 1953. Declassified at the request of the author in January 1989.

shipments to France, to the German border. The expenditures for these items eventually mounted to the hundreds of millions of dollars. Indochina aid became a second source, as Washington agreed to finance the production of military equipment in France for use there. Finally the Americans occasionally placed their own military contracts in France. OSP constituted recognition that the Marshall Plan had failed to solve the endemic French balance of payments crisis of the postwar years. It marked the definitive transition of American aid from a peacetime mode of economic assistance to almost exclusive concentration on the military. It also contained within it a recipe for further misunderstanding and recrimination.

The advantage of OSP was that it could be disguised as "trade, not aid"; the Americans received services and products for their dollars. It also provided flexibility, for it did not necessarily require congressional authorization. The Pentagon had many billions to spend on procurement and some discretion permitting it to place military contracts abroad. This was also a disadvantage, however, since the French tended to measure the amounts expended in their country against the totality of the Pentagon's budget, and always interpreted their allotment as demonstrative of American parsimony. Like the Marshall Plan, which preceded it, OSP lubricated the system of international trade and payments that was the foundation of the American postwar world order. It permitted the continued growth of the American export industry while allowing Washington to maintain its curbs on imports. By the early 1950s Europe had recovered, but the American market remained largely closed to its manufactures because of tariffs and a variety of structural impediments (unreasonable technical or safety requirements among them).[60] The French, therefore, came to regard OSP as their due once the Marshall Plan was terminated in 1952. OSP was additional to military aid, however, for which it was still necessary to go to Congress.

Congress was becoming increasingly recalcitrant toward the administration's requests for foreign aid, and critical of the French, who absorbed the most assistance, yet epitomized what, in the American view, was most wrong with foreign nations. The text of the Mutual Security Act of 1952 asserted that French labor conditions were worse than before the war, free enterprise had failed to take root, and non-Communist trade unions were languishing. The Mission in Paris of the Mutual Security Agency (MSA), successor to the ECA, was instructed to take action to remedy this situation. On the Senate floor Paul Douglas declared that economic aid in France and Italy had mainly served to exacerbate social inequalities in both countries. Senator Moody characterized the French fiscal system as just as much a danger to the defense of the West as insufficient military expenditure. At a State Department–joint chiefs of staff conference General Bradley asked: "Shouldn't we

---

[60] For an excellent analysis of the OSP system and resultant problems, see *Le Monde*, July 23, 27, 30, 1952, August 1, 1952.

step in and demand changes in France so that the problem [deficits] will not arise year after year?" But Paul Nitze thought that based on experience "it would not be effective to try to get a commitment out of France on cleaning up its internal situation."[61]

It was therefore with resignation that American officials informed the French that they would receive the second $200 million promised them for the second half of 1951. Washington also understood that it could not "bargain its small amount of aid for French performance involving many times that amount. Frank discussion is more availing than the carrot and stick approach." Congress being slow to act, France got no aid at all from July through October 1951, its gold and dollar reserves disappeared, and a new crisis in the French import program loomed. The French deplored their situation. No formula existed for American aid since the phasing out of the Marshall Plan and the beginning of American military assistance as an inferior substitute. The continued necessity of bilateral negotiations since July 1, 1950 kept France in a permanent condition of inferiority and uncertainty. For six months the French had been in the dark about their total allocation for 1951, which was only half the $800 million originally requested, and upon which depended the French effort in Indochina and participation in EDC. The Americans had further used the increased French dollar reserves as an excuse to reduce their ECA aid; Washington appeared to be deliberately causing the depletion of French reserves so as to keep Paris in a position of inferiority. De Margerie thought the American attitude "undignified." France should decide on the level of its reserves and its military expenditure irrespective of the American aid.[62]

It was not to be. René Mayer, minister of finance, warned Marshall of the French economic crisis at the NATO meetings in Ottawa in September 1951. In October he wrote to Harriman directly: "I believe I am justified in recalling the promises made to the French government, on the basis of which it has solicited and obtained from Parliament the vote of large and important credits and fiscal resources for the French military budget of 1951." Nothing had been received, and the depletion of French reserves threatened to force cessation of all imports. Mayer thus underlined French dependence on Washington for the level of its military preparedness and budgetary equilibrium. Harriman responded with encouragement, but the funds were still not forthcoming, and Mayer prepared a reduced import plan and ordered steps to reimpose rationing. French financial officials suspected Washington of maneuvering "to exercise ultimately new pressures on us for sacrifices in the interest of rearmament." Paris maneuvered in turn; the rationing was

---

61 A.N., F60 ter 432 (1), Financial Attaché Report on MSA of June 26, 1952; FRUS, 1952–54, VI, Part 2, France, January 28, 1952, p. 1149.
62 FRUS, 1951, IV, France, August 8, 1951, p. 413. A.N., 363 AP 19, Papiers René Mayer, Dr. 1, August 13, 1951. A.N., F60 ter 359, May 4, 1951, De Margerie to Schweitzer.

hardly necessary, and "The whole problem is to impress Washington without spreading panic in France."[63] Neither side appeared very dignified.

Mayer met with ECA officials on September 11, 1951 and informed them of an expected dollar shortfall of $650 million. The Americans seemed to promise that OSP would make up the difference between that figure and the congressional appropriation. Marshall further promised aid for the war in Indochina, allowed the French to see an American analysis placing the cost of the war at 1,000 billion francs, and admitted France could not continue its Indochina effort and European rearmament without American help. "Our position is now perfectly understood," Mayer cabled Pleven. But the United States thought a tax increase was also necessary, and Mayer asserted, "I am only more obligated to maintain my formal opposition to any formula for automatic adjustment of the minimum wage." American aid assumed French monetary stability, a high level of imports, productivity, and an adequate arms budget. All this was true, but the Americans said nothing about wages; Mayer used the American negotiations to support his traditional hard line on the issue.[64]

The American bureaucracy still moved slowly. When reduced imports and the threat of rationing failed to move the Americans, Pleven used the ultimate weapon; his government was fragile, he warned, and behind him lurked the growing strength of Mendè's France in the French Assembly. Bruce, for his part, seconded the French appeals and added his annoyance that his previous warnings of impending disaster were unheeded. On November 17 the $200 million promised for the second half of 1951 was finally released, and the French were told they could expect $650 million in 1952, to meet their defense burdens in Indochina and Europe. The French had meanwhile reduced their projected 1952 military budget to 1,070 billion francs, an amount Washington quickly rejected as entirely inadequate. On November 29, following an emergency injection of short-term assistance in view of the collapse of French dollar reserves, Bruce told Guillaume Guindey that Washington expected the French defense budget to be in the neighborhood of 1,250 billion francs. Guindey appeared doubtful, but he did tell Bruce that he thought the French would make an effort to go above the 1,070 billion franc figure.[65]

The Americans were able to keep the pressure on Paris for an expanded military budget through the Temporary Council Committee (TCC) of NATO, otherwise known in France as the Comité des Sages (the wise men). The

[63] A.N., 363 AP 19, Papiers René Mayer, Dr. 6, October 22, 25, 1951, November 1, 2, 13, 1951.

[64] A.N., 363 AP 19, Papiers René Mayer, Dr. 2, September 11, 13, 14, 1951. A.N., F60 ter 436 (1), September 10, 1951.

[65] FRUS, 1951, IV, France, November 10, 1951, pp. 437–9; November 13, 1951, pp. 439–41; November 17, 1951, pp. 442–4; November 23, 1951, pp. 449–51; November 29, 1951, pp. 453–5.

committee consisted of Averell Harriman, Lord Plowden, and Jean Monnet. The appearance of this committee, with supervisory powers over the national military budgets of alliance members, represented something of a new departure in the postwar history of Western Europe. It enshrined the system of cost-accounting of military expenses in relation to gross national product, set a norm for high levels of military expenditure as the counterpart to systems of social security and welfare in the remaking of the modern state, and potentially constituted a step forward in European integration.[66] If Paris initially agreed to this system it was because it partially met French demands for the restructuring of NATO. Although a far cry from a common defense budget, the TCC recognized the principle that each member of the alliance should offer a military contribution consonant with its ability to pay. And it elevated the French, British, and Americans to a kind of directorate to deal with the problem.

The results for the French were disappointing, however, in part because of the choice of Monnet, whose close relations with the Anglo-Saxons and internationalism seemed to work against French interests. The French response to the TCC questionnaire pleaded inability to maintain the level of expense originally foreseen due to deficits in the budget and balance of payments. Paris also expressed its displeasure at inadequate American aid during 1951. The French 1952 budget figure, 1,072 billion francs, was significantly above the 740 billion spent in 1951, allowed for the deployment of ten divisions in Europe, and included an Indochina expense of 400 billion francs. Paris further promised 20 percent yearly increases in spending until fifteen divisions were fielded in 1954. More was not possible without compromising the high investment budget, essential for economic strength, and efforts to meet the housing crisis, essential for social stability.[67]

The TCC found the French budget inadequate and set the contribution expected of France at 1,400 billion francs. Paris held to its figure of 1,190 billion. Lord Plowden cross-examined the French delegation, doubting that the French balance of payments deficit was "externally caused" and insisting that France must consume less and pay more taxes. In December Monnet pointed out to Pleven the French lag behind the expected level of forces: France would have only fifteen divisions by 1954 instead of the expected twenty-eight. Monnet could not help but express his concern for the future, moreover:

> Finally, I do not think that we can allow to go by without response the recommendations that are addressed to us concerning reforms to implement in our fiscal system. As delicate as this subject is, especially in the present politi-

[66] Charles S. Maier, "Finance and Defense: Implications of Military Integration 1950–1," Paper presented at the Truman Library Conference on NATO, September 21–3, 1989.

[67] Papiers Jean Monnet, Fondation Jean Monnet, AMI 10/4/2, December 1951. A.N., F60 ter 419 (1), December 1951.

cal atmosphere, we must not dissimulate the importance attached to it by the government of the United States, and it would be, in my view, a serious error to appear to neglect this question.[68]

Paris rejected the TCC conclusions despite Monnet; Guindey complained that the Americans were heard under entirely different conditions than the French, who had not been permitted to bring financial experts into the committee room. Washington's figures, of course, as always went unchallenged: "There was certainly no parallel between the manner in which our program was scrutinized by the American and British experts and the attitude taken on the French side with regard to the American program." The final report was written by the British and Americans, lacked any critical analysis of the American budget, and accepted unquestioningly huge outlays for luxuries, such as posh officer clubs with golf courses. All this counted as a percentage of GNP. The United Kingdom had also received velvet-glove treatment as compared with France, and the two Anglo-Saxon nations were the only ones not asked for increased outlays. The treatment of the French case in contrast, Guindey thought, had been "particularly unpleasant."[69]

The French government succeeded in bringing the TCC recommendation of a military budget down to 1,190 billion francs, but it remained dissatisfied. Pleven told Eisenhower on December 17 that the TCC report was still in excess of what the French were able to do. He had to find an additional 100 billion francs now or "his government will fall over this problem." And even that would not ensure the continuation of the French arms industry, which was necessary if his government were to survive. Pleven could offer only one solution; the Americans must take over the financing of French military production. Perhaps an additional $100 million could be transferred from OSP to Indochina, relieving the drain on the French budget from that direction. Pleven repeated that Washington did not understand the dimensions of the tragedy in Indochina and added that his government was about to fall. Bruce could make no promises, but tried to shore up the premier. He approached Paul Reynaud, asking that no "precipitous action" be taken in the National Assembly that might upset the government, and he tried to prevent Georges Bidault from resigning as minister of defense. In the meantime Pleven presented a 1,190 billion franc budget to the Assembly, with more said to be contingent on further negotiations with the Americans at the forthcoming NATO meetings in February at Lisbon.[70]

Bruce knew Pleven was beyond help, however. Embassy analysts pointed out his government was based on a minority in the Assembly and its problems were structural, reflecting the deeper unsolved dilemmas of French so-

[68] A.N., F60 ter 419 (1), December 22, 1951, Monnet to Pleven.
[69] A.N., 363 AP 20, Papiers René Mayer, Dr. 1, November 12, December 19, 1951.
[70] FRUS, 1951, IV, France, December 17, 1951, pp. 455–9; December 19, 1951, pp. 461–2.

ciety. Neither democratic processes nor "enlightened employer self-interest" were powerful enough in France to achieve the reduction of Communist power; selfishness prevailed, based on a miserly peasantry in alliance with a backward petite bourgeoisie. The Gaullists were "pseudofascist," and their opposition combined with that of the Communists forced the government to rely on an unnatural center coalition, itself divided between economic conservatives and socialist welfare-state advocates. It did appear possible that the RPF would break away from de Gaulle and join a conservative government; this would allow the Socialists to return to the opposition, where they might more successfully compete with the Communists for working-class support. But the present government was "straining at the limits" in trying to balance its various commitments on defense, EDC, and Indochina. Already one powerful voice had appeared that was ready to jettison the Indochina problem, Pierre Mendès France, and the danger existed that the Socialists, once in the opposition, would join him.[71]

Pleven fell as predicted on January 7, 1952. Edgar Faure quickly was able to form a government on January 20, however, and tried to accomplish what Pleven could not: to fill the gap between French means and the demands of Indochina and NATO with increased American aid. On January 25 Bidault, still minister of defense, told Bruce that the 1,190 billion franc budget was insufficient; in reality France would be able to field only seven divisions, and the duration of military service would have to be cut back to twelve months. Nor could France be expected to ratify the EDC treaty if its forces in Europe were not superior to those of the Germans. Again the French were throwing their problems to the Americans, as Moch and Petsche had done in 1950. Nor did Acheson like it much better this time than on the earlier occasion. Bidault's message was "explosive," he said. No further funds beyond the $600 million already promised were available. If the French kept trying to put their situation in the worst possible light, he warned, the issue might "boomerang." But the State Department PPS did not agree; in its view the French needed $1 billion in aid rather than $600 million, and it recommended an approach to Congress. Congress might come up with the money if the request were focused on the war in Indochina, which the French were arguing was part of a common front with Korea in the struggle against communism in Asia. The Americans were eventually to take over the costs of the Indochina struggle as the means of solving the French balance of payments difficulties, in effect purchasing the war. For the moment, however, this was premature. French and American negotiators met yet again in an effort to straighten out the French mess.[72]

Washington recognized the "justifications for the French evaluations,"

[71] NARA, 751.00/12-2051, December 20, 1951, this very astute analysis was authored by Martin Herz.
[72] FRUS, 1952–4, VI, Part 2, France, January 25, 1952, pp. 1140–1; January 28, 1952, pp. 1142–3; February 11, 1952, pp. 1150–3.

and a higher French budget of 1,400 billion francs was agreed upon, to which the Americans would contribute an additional $200 million (70 billion francs). The French agreed to raise their own contribution another 140 billion francs, but Secretary of the Interministerial Economic Committee Clermont-Tonnerre warned that the additional $200 million was not enough, and "nothing would be more dangerous than to allow them [the United States] to think France is ready to carry out a supplementary financial effort." Certainly anything beyond 1,400 billion francs, he said, "is purely a French question which there is no justification, in my opinion, for allowing to come up in the negotiations."[73] But everything in the French budget was already within the purview of Washington. Worse, the Americans were not really promising any additional aid in exchange for the greater French contribution. Instead they transferred $200 million from OSP to direct French budgetary aid, leaving the total aid package at $600 million. Still, the French had won a victory: Washington accepted the principle of financing the French deficit after all. Lovett, for his part, was disgusted with the arrangement. He thought it "futile to talk with the French along the lines of what we would do for them in return for what they would do." Ridgeway Knight was resigned. The French negotiating tactics created ill will, he recognized, but the United States enjoyed few options. To fall back on Germany alone was to create a defensive "arc with no depth"; the United States needed a strong France. To revert to a peripheral strategy was to leave France to neutralism, or worse, invite a Czech-style coup there. The Americans must simply make up their minds: How important is France, how many divisions do they need, and how much does it cost? The French fiscal system would not change for years, and in any case, however unequal it was, the total tax burden in France was higher than in the United States. That was all Washington really had the right to judge. Knight agreed that the best tactic to get the French sufficient aid from Congress was to focus on Indochina.[74]

French and American negotiators had a charged agenda in Lisbon. The United States was intent upon restoring full sovereignty to Germany by means of "contractual" agreements between the German government and the former occupation authorities, for which French ratification was necessary. The restoration of German sovereignty required a solution to the problem of German rearmament, which was to be accomplished through the EDC. Washington therefore increased pressure on the French to conclude the lagging negotiations, finally pushing the participants to accept a May 1952 deadline for signature of the treaty establishing a European army. The NATO–TCC recommendations for the level of French military forces in Europe constituted a third major item, which led logically and inexorably

[73] A.N., F60 ter 419 (2), February 12, 1952, "Note pour le Président."
[74] FRUS, 1952–4, VI, 2, France, February 12, 1952, pp. 1154–6; February 24, 1952, pp. 1176–9.

to the fourth, upon which, it soon became clear, everything else depended – the French budget. For if France could not balance its Indochina commitment and its European level of forces, it would not feel strong enough to agree to either the European army or the restoration of German sovereignty. The French were never really in a position to refuse German rearmament, and they feared that the Americans were prepared to go ahead without their agreement if necessary. But Paris could trade its agreement for an American commitment to make France a first-class military power. The National Assembly would never accept a German army that was stronger than the French, and Paris was sure that "such an argument cannot be rejected by the Americans."[75]

Faure was thus uninhibited in asking for even more money at Lisbon. Even the 1,400 billion franc budget did not provide sufficiently for the French arms industry: France needed an additional commitment from Off Shore Procurement beyond the $200 million that had been added to the budgetary assistance. If this additional OSP aid were not granted, the French would be forced to cancel some very expensive contracts, at very great penalties to the government, with resulting unemployment. Rather than face this result, Faure said, the French government would have to reconsider its commitment in Indochina. Washington was impressed. Bruce had warned often enough that France was overextended: Between the competing demands of Indochina, European rearmament, and economic modernization, something would have to give. But again the Americans would make no commitments, citing the limited availability of funds and the need for congressional authorization. The final memo of understanding at Lisbon promised the French $600 million in aid: $500 million of budgetary assistance and $100 million from American troop expenses in France. Additional OSP aid beyond $600 million was "not excluded," however, and Washington would study French requests.[76] That was enough for the French. In evaluating French negotiating tactics it is impossible to know whether they actually believed that vague American promises amounted to genuine commitments, or whether they thought acting as if they had a commitment would force Washington to recognize it as such. In the end it probably made no difference.

In March 1952 Bidault insisted on the importance of OSP aid and warned Lovett that its absence would force cuts in the French arms industry. To close plants, create unemployment, and relegate France to supplying human cannon fodder for NATO would be unacceptable to public opinion, and

> would lead to serious repercussions on the military, industrial, social, and political levels. . . . I ask you immediately to examine, given the dramatic immediate situation . . . whether an equitable division of tasks and resources

[75] A.N., F60 ter 421, February 4, 1952.
[76] FRUS, 1952–4, V, Part I, West European Security, February 23, 1952, pp. 146–54.

within the Atlantic Community would not necessarily lead us to rely upon France for large industrial manufactures for the French army as much as for the other nations of NATO.

France, Bidault concluded, which had been invaded three times in the past seventy-five years, had to have its own arms industry.[77]

Faure's government was short-lived, succeeded on March 9 by a conservative coalition under Antoine Pinay, who quickly became one of the most popular and stable leaders of the Fourth Republic. Pinay's secure base made him even bolder in dealing with the Americans. On May 7 Ambassador James Dunn received the French supplementary request for $616 million in OSP to be scaled over a period of three years. The request included the purchase, for France, of French-made jet and cargo planes, armored cars, and tanks. To strengthen this request, Pleven, now defense minister in Pinay's government, told Acheson of the crisis in the French armaments industry, "the social, economic and financial consequences of which cannot be exaggerated." Two of four major nationalized aviation firms were threatened with closure. Parliament would undoubtedly shift funding from the NATO infrastructure to arms production unless the government could refer to American orders. Germany was just beginning a military construction program, so France could hardly be expected to stop its own. Acheson was understanding and said he would do his best. On July 2, 1952 Pleven warned that the French commitment to twelve divisions and 1,400 billions of military expense depended upon its ability to keep the arms plants open. The French were encouraged when Jean Letourneau, minister of overseas territories, returned from Washington with an American promise of an additional $150 million in Indochina aid.[78] But the United States had previously demonstrated it could give with one hand and take back with the other.

On July 12, 1952 Dunn informed Pinay of the American reply: Washington would fund the MD-452 fighter plane to the amount of $86 million and purchase $100 million worth of ammunition produced in France. The Americans declined to finance any of the rest of the contemplated arms production, however. This decision should not in itself have been surprising to Paris. The Americans had made known their opposition to these ambitious French arms production programs the previous year, and reduced their aid commitment then in part to show their displeasure. Yet one year later Paris was requesting Washington to finance those same programs. Pleven expressed his extreme disappointment and escalated his threats. He feared he would have no choice but to resign, thus causing the fall of Pinay, a friend of the United States and the most stable leader France had in some time. Pinay called Dunn to ask reconsideration of the decision, also warning

---

[77] A.N., F60 ter 419 (2), March 6, 1952.
[78] FRUS, 1952–4, VI, 2, France, May 8, 1952, pp. 1203–5; June 10, 1952, pp. 1207–14; June 14, 1952, pp. 1215–7; July 2, 1952, pp. 1218–20.

that the government might fall. In an aide-memoire to the American government he warned of plant closures that would lead to unemployment for 25,000 workers who might rally to the Communists; he also warned of potential for rupture of the equilibrium between France and Germany. EDC had been signed with much fanfare on May 27, 1952, but this decision now threatened its ratification. For France to depend upon the Anglo-Saxon arms industries would feed "antinational" propaganda. In Washington Bonnet charged that the United States had reneged on the Lisbon agreement; he became almost hysterical: "This means the end of the French cabinet, EDC, everything." The Americans had been careful to warn that they were making no commitments in Lisbon, but the French cared little. His request for reconsideration turned down, Pinay said the American decision was a "disastrous blow to the entire French economy, programs, and policies of the Government in domestic affairs and the international defense situation." It struck at the heart of his program to stabilize the economy and fight communism. This was a matter of the "gravest character" and he was "shaken and disturbed." Dunn got the message, and became convinced that the crisis was the most critical and delicate in French–American relations since the beginning of NATO.[79]

The crisis was to get worse before it got better. But in the meantime it caused some soul-searching on both the French and the American sides. A note for Pinay from the Ministry of Foreign Affairs concluded that OSP talks with the Americans were unlikely to yield anything until the new, post-Truman administration was in place in Washington in 1953. In the meantime,

> the continued assumption of burdens too heavy for our economy and budget, in the hope that our partners will, on account of this fact, give us greater assistance, puts the French government in the relatively humiliating position of never being able to meet its commitments by its own means, and always, everywhere, on any occasion, asking for larger amounts of aid.

The French government would be best advised to close negotiations, set its own budget for 1953 within its means, and notify NATO and the United States of its decision. A 1953 military budget of 1,225 billion francs was under discussion. It would have to depend upon the Americans carrying forward their 1952 promises, however: $500 million direct budgetary assistance promised at Lisbon, $150 million additional committed to Letourneau for Indochina, and $186 million, disappointing as it was, of OSP just announced. The ministry was as yet unaware that Washington was to carry out further reductions in those supposed 1953 commitments in coming weeks.[80]

---

[79] FRUS, 1952–4, VI, 2, France, July 12, 1952, pp. 1220–3; July 13, 1952, pp. 1223–5; July 22, 1952, pp. 1225–6; July 21, 1952, pp. 1227–30; July 24, 1952, pp. 1232–3; July 25, 1952, pp. 1233–5.
[80] A.N., F60 ter 419 (2), July 25, 1952, "Note pour le Président."

Within the embassy similar reflections were occasioned by the growing influence of Pierre Mendès France, whom the Americans were to watch with admiration mixed with unease during the next two years. An embassy report noted that although Mendès France was a vocal opponent of the Indochina War, few in France questioned either his patriotism or his logic. The RPF, although supporting the government, had applauded his attack on French submissiveness to the United States in aid negotiations. Mendès condemned the government for negotiating the level of French forces with Washington, rather than the aid amount, thus "placing decisions in the hands of allied authorities," and humiliating France. The writer, probably Martin Herz, found merit in this position. The French government, instead of stating what it could do alone, "has consistently come forward with plans that were conditioned upon specific assistance furnished by the United States." Mendès argued that France could cut its military budget and improve its negotiating posture by acting with dignity. He was "basically pro-American, approves of Western collective security arrangements, and has never been known to suspect the United States of aggressive intentions." Profoundly devoted to European integration, he would, of course withdraw from Indochina, but the net effect he was likely to have was positive. All this was forgotten or ignored by John Foster Dulles, who had to deal with a Mendès France government two years later.[81]

Despite the cautioning about French humiliation, Pinay compounded the error. On August 8 he noted "with regret" the American attitude on additional OSP aid, but repeated to Washington his understanding that the 1953 French military budget depended upon Paris receiving $500 million in budgetary assistance, $150 million promised Letourneau for Indochina, and $186 million in supplementary OSP. Pinay's note caused a new crisis in the Embassy. Theodore Achilles noted that "the French think the $186 million are not included in the $650 million," but Washington was not sure. The aid negotiations had become so complex that neither side understood them fully. The French insisted that it was understood at Lisbon that they were demanding additional OSP funds for their arms industry. Now that they had it, the original amounts promised by Washington were being called into question. The misunderstanding arose again from the different fiscal years; the State Department now faced the likelihood that Congress would make cuts in the 1952–3 budget. The Embassy and MSA argued for maintenance of the integral amount of $650 million promised the French, exclusive of the $186 million, but in vain.[82]

On October 3, 1952 Acheson sent Pinay a letter through Ambassador Dunn explaining that the United States would not be able to maintain the promised $650 million in aid for the French calendar year budget of 1953.

81 NARA, 751.00/5-652, May 6, 1952.
82 A.N., F60 ter 419 (2), August 8, 1952. FRUS, 1952–4, VI, 2, France, August 9, 1952, pp. 1235–6; August 14, 1952, pp. 1238–40; August 28, 1952, pp. 1240–1; September 11, 1952, pp. 1241–4.

Reduced appropriations put the maximum available amount at $525 million. This figure included the Indochina aid promised Letourneau, but not the additional OSP commitment for the manufacture of French munitions. Acheson called Pinay's attention to the continued high level of American MDAP aid and the heavy American expenditures in France due to military installations and the NATO infrastructure, all of which were not counted in these totals. In an oral addendum to the letter, Dunn was instructed to tell Pinay that the United States expected France to maintain the level of budgetary expense for the military established at Lisbon (1,400 billion francs) but that, based upon the MSA annual review of the French financial situation, an increase in the French military budget to 1,500 billion francs might be considered appropriate.

Pinay's reaction expressed the pent-up anger in the French government over the humiliating posture in which it had placed itself. There was nothing in Acheson's note that had not been the common stuff of Franco–American relations since 1947. The Americans had acquired the habit, and took it as their right, to pass judgment on French budgetary practice, taxation, and the like. Nor was Pinay's reaction spontaneous. He had been briefed by the Quai to tell the Americans that the French were spending more on the military, per capita, than the British or the Germans, all in the interest of the common defense of the West. In view of this, "the French Government cannot accept that the use of credits voted by Parliament be submitted to the unilateral decision of a foreign government." The Americans had come to exercise "an almost complete tutelage over the implementation of the French military budget."[83] This intolerable situation must end; Pinay told Dunn of his indignation at such treatment by the most important member of the Atlantic Community. France was always ready for discussions, but "does not take orders from anyone."[84]

Pinay went on to reject Acheson's message as "offensive in tone," and warned that public knowledge of its contents would have "the most serious consequences on French–U.S. relations." The Americans had no right to lay down "expectations" with regard to the 1953 budget; French taxation and the use of revenues derived therefrom were an entirely French affair. Pinay even rejected the right of Washington to examine the use of counterpart funds derived from its direct economic assistance. Common practice for years suddenly appeared as an infringement of national sovereignty. Pinay kept Acheson's message confidential, announcing to the press that he had rejected an American note as interference in internal French affairs. The news still caused a sensation. A wave of popularity for the beleaguered *Président du Conseil* was the result. French resentment of the United States had been building over the German question, pressure for the ratification of

---

[83] A.N., F60 ter 419 (2), October 8, 1952, "Note."
[84] FRUS, 1952–4, VI, 2, France, October 3, 1952, pp. 1248–51.

EDC, and the growing American military establishment in France. To make matters worse, French repression of the nationalist movement in Tunisia came before the United Nations, where the Americans abstained rather than vote to keep the question off the agenda. France regarded the North African question as an internal affair, and the United States had the greatest difficulty in balancing its need to support France with its desire to placate the nationalists in Tunisia and Morocco and maintain good relations with the Arab world.[85]

Pinay announced the next day that the incident was closed, but its aftermath caused a rethinking of relations between the two countries. Dunn, on second thought, decided that "Our latest communication to Pinay is the stiffest we have given the French since the beginning of post-war U.S. aid. There is a line beyond which conditions may be considered as encroaching upon national sovereignty and become counter-productive." Acheson pretended to be unconcerned and said the French government was making "domestic political capital" out of the issue. But reports now came in of Russian overtures to the French, despite Pinay's ferocious domestic anticommunism, arrests, and harassment of the Communist party, which continued during his disagreements with Washington. Douglas MacArthur III warned of the need for more tact in handling the French. They believed, he said, that Washington regarded them as "fumbling and incompetent" and was therefore forever telling them what to do. Indeed, Pleven told MacArthur that he thought the United States "lacked confidence" in France and failed to recognize the importance of the French effort in Indochina.

Pinay had Dunn to lunch in an effort to mend relations. The premier was still interested in the aid figure; France faced ruin, yet the reduction in American aid was still more important than the amount. Impressed, Dunn recommended to Washington that the $650 million be integrally restored with the balance earmarked for Indochina. Dunn was concerned by President Auriol's bitter speech on October 27, 1952 at Donzère-Mondragon. The president was usually "above politics," but now criticized the Americans. Auriol claimed that the cost to France of defending the freedom of the West in Indochina had been twice the amount received in Marshall Plan aid, and he expressed his "grief" to see France, "the nation of the rights of man, put on trial in the United Nations." Bruce, now Under Secretary of State, disagreed. Until 1952, Indochina had cost half of Marshall Plan aid, but Bruce thought it useless to issue a public correction. Meanwhile attacks mounted on Foreign Minister Schuman, now regarded in the National Assembly as too pro-American and weak on the North African question, and Edouard Herriot issued a blistering attack on the concept of the European Defense

[85] FRUS, 1952–4, VI, 2, France, October 8, 1952, pp. 1251–2; October 10, 1952, pp. 1253–6. *Le Monde*, October 10, 1952. See also Annie Lacroix-Riz, *Les protectorats d'Afrique du Nord entre la France te Washington* (Paris: Editions L'Harmattan, 1988).

Community. Dunn concluded in November that relations between France
and America were worse than at any time since de Gaulle resigned in 1946.[86]

Dunn argued that restoring the $125 million in aid would yield far more
in return than the amount involved, and the United States should support
France in North Africa because "our interests lie in keeping them there."
Acheson refused Dunn's request. We support the French 90 percent, he said,
but they became upset because we could not go the other 10 percent. The
restoration of the full $650 million was not possible, and the French were
selfishly disregarding the extensive end-item assistance they received under
MDAP. In North Africa they refused internal reform or negotiations, and
would not "give us the minimum means of supporting them." The French
presented their military budget to the National Assembly on November 7,
1952. It was set at 1,420 billion francs with an additional *tranche* of 44
billion to be dependent on restoration of the shortfall of $125 million in
American aid. This amount was well within the parameters of Acheson's
memo but had the merit of meeting the criticism of previous negotiating
methods. The French had finally said what they would do themselves, leaving anything beyond that up to Washington. But Washington was losing
interest in budgetary battles with the French in any case. From Washington,
the Embassy, and Congress, pressure for the same solution emerged. Future
American aid for France should be directed to the Indochina War. In 1953
Washington was to grant the French the billion dollars in aid that State
Department policy planners had said was necessary. But virtually all of it
was directed to the Indochina struggle, and the new transaction quickly
revealed itself to be no solution. France could not sell the United States a
"dirty war" indefinitely as a means of solving its balance of payments problems.[87]

---

[86] *Le Monde*, October 11, 1952. FRUS, 1952–4, VI, 2, France, October 19, 1952, pp.
     1259–60; October 21, 1952, pp. 1266–7; October 24, 1952, pp. 1268–70; Novem-
     ber 3, 1952, pp. 1270–2. NARA, 751.00/10-2752, October 27, 1952; 10-2952, Oc-
     tober 29, 1952.

[87] FRUS, 1952–4, VI, 2, France, November 4, 1952, pp. 1273–4; November 7, 1952,
     pp. 1274–5; November 8, 1952, pp. 1276–8.

8

The United States and French
Indochina

I THE ORIGINS OF AMERICAN INTERVENTION

THE INDOCHINA DRAMA became the central concern of American–French relations in the 1950s, virtually dominating every other issue in bilateral relations by 1953–4. It was also the issue over which Paris finally declared its independence of Washington in 1954, under the government of Pierre Mendès France. Among other questions only the European Defense Community could again cause the two nations so much mutual recrimination, bitterness, and grief, and its fate was tied to the Indochina War as well. It was perhaps appropriate that Indochina, rather than the EDC, should have been the main bone of contention between the two countries. For while the latter is now a minor footnote to history, Vietnam emerged as the central problem of American life in the 1960s and 1970s.

There were three periods in the evolution of American policy toward Indochina: 1945–9, during which the Americans remained anticolonial; 1950–2, when anticommunism and the Korean War led to deeper involvement in Indochina alongside the French; and 1953–4, when the new Republican administration in Washington seized direction of the war. From 1945 to 1949 American policy was the most liberal, but also the least effective in terms of exercising real influence over Paris. American policymakers regarded the old colonial systems as moribund and slated to disappear. The central question for Washington was whether the newly emerging states of Asia and Africa would be non-Communist and open to American commercial penetration, or whether they would adopt closed economies and fall under the strategic hegemony of Moscow.

In North Africa, Washington pressed Paris for a progressive program ultimately leading to self-government, while it maintained contact with leaders of the nationalist movement, trying to reconcile French and nationalist interests along progressive lines. The American dilemma in Vietnam was that the nationalist movement was led by a known Communist, Ho Chi Minh, although the Vietminh claimed to be a broad coalition. Washington could not, therefore, identify with the nationalists in the way it did in North Africa, Indonesia, or Palestine. As a consequence American policy in Indochina from 1946–9 remained in a state of paralysis, unhappy with either visible alternative, French colonial rule or communism. As the cold war deepened, however, the French succeeded in portraying the French Union as a free association of states, the functional equivalent of the British Commonwealth of Nations. In North Africa, Washington concluded that the area could best advance under French tutelage, because disorders in the region were an invitation to Communist exploitation. In Indochina, the Americans rallied to the alternative of a nominally independent Vietnam within the French Union under the traditional emperor originally installed by the Japanese, Bao Dai.

With formal recognition by Washington of Bao Dai's regime in February 1950 came the rapid extension of American military and economic aid. This in turn brought the presence in Indochina of American bureaucratic entities with which the French were already familiar in the metropole: USIA, ECA, and MAAG. There were also some agencies with which the French were not previously acquainted, such as the "Point Four" program of aid to underdeveloped nations, launched in 1949 as a Marshall Plan for the Third World, and embodied in Vietnam in the U.S. Special Technical and Economic Mission (STEM). In time these agencies expanded to encompass hundreds of American personnel, greatly to the discomfort of the French. American aid was greatly accelerated under the impact of the Korean War, which broke out in June 1950. Washington quickly accepted the French argument that the Indochina struggle was not about the continuation of a colonial regime, but rather part of a single global anti-Communist effort of which Korea and Indochina constituted the two active components. Washington tried to shore up the Bao Dai regime, help it win popular support, and increase its autonomy and independence from the French, while bolstering the French Expeditionary Corps as the spearhead of the anti-Communist military effort. There was clearly a basic contradiction in this policy, since the French were not fighting in Indochina for the ultimate purpose of leaving it. Washington was unable to place ground troops in Indochina itself in view of its Korean involvement. American policy was to convince the French to stay on even as it weakened their motivation for doing so.

In January 1953 the third and final phase of American involvement began. Under the Eisenhower administration the American role increased dramatically in terms of financial support and direct influence over the course of the struggle. Paris sought to retreat to a holding operation, hoping for a negotiated settlement along the lines of the truce being concluded in Korea. But the Americans put increasing pressure on the French to win, holding out the promise of economic reward for doing so. By 1954 American financing accounted for at least 80 percent of the war's cost, in exchange for which Washington insisted on a greater say in military operations and planning, and the French became increasingly susceptible to American prodding, as the war became the solution to their dollar shortage. Consequently Paris reluctantly consented to a new military effort, the Navarre Plan, which was drawn up at American insistence and which gained further U.S. financial support for the French effort.

Meanwhile, in metropolitan France, the fate of Indochina became linked to the battle over the EDC. Indochina and EDC became the two poles of American policy in France, each dependent upon the other; for only French success in Indochina could allow a restrengthened France in Europe, able to take a confident place in the integrated European army alongside a militarily restored Germany. It was thus American policy as much as French that collapsed at Dien Bien Phu. Washington greeted the Menlès France government with alarm, which proved fully justified when the new premier took France out of Indochina and then allowed the defeat of the EDC. In desperation Washington tried direct pressure, international sanction, and even internal political scheming in France to salvage something of the ruin of its policy that Mendès came to symbolize, despite his efforts to placate the Americans. It was all in vain. For Mendès France demonstrated that France could pursue an independent policy in world affairs once shorn of its Great Power illusions. Mendès France thus prepared the way for de Gaulle while integrating the Communist party, which initially supported him, into the political game. In neither pole of France of the Fifth Republic, Gaullism or Socialist-Communist opposition, could Washington find the centrist France amenable to its influence, the creation of which was the goal of its postwar policy.

Just before his death in April 1945 Franklin Roosevelt recognized that he would have to accept the return of French rule in Indochina. On May 9, 1945, the United States informed France that it did not question French sovereignty, "even by implication;" the Americans believed, however, that without liberalization of the French colonial regime the French were condemned to a fruitless and bloody struggle against Asian nationalism that could last for many years. Consequently, Washington refused to assist the French in reestablishing their control, and "assumed" that French claims to have popular support among the population "would be borne out by future events."[1]

---

[1] *United States Vietnam Relations, 1945–1967* (hereinafter USVNR), Study Prepared by the Department of Defense, 12 vols. (Washington, DC: U.S. Government Printing Office, 1971), vol. 8, May 9, 23, 1945; vol. 1, pp. A20–33. This series comprises the famous "Pentagon Papers," which were released to the American government's great displeasure during the Vietnam War. With the extensive documentary record of FRUS, which contains two volumes of over 1,000 pages each for 1952–4, it is possible to reconstruct a virtually complete record of American policy and French reaction from

From the outset American policy was torn between the Asia experts and the European desk, the major concern of which was the restoration of a strong non-Communist France in Europe. Ho Chi Minh's proclamation of an independent Republic of Vietnam in Hanoi in 1945 was witnessed by a sympathetic OSS agent from whose shaky memory the Vietnamese leader elicited some phrases of the American declaration of independence to use in his own pronouncements.[2] The OSS reported that the Vietminh were hoping for American protection and susceptible to American influence. Ho Chi Minh sent no less than eight separate messages to President Truman during 1945 and 1946, pleading for American support and economic assistance and professing his friendliness to the United States. None of them were acknowledged by Washington for fear of offending the French. On March 6, 1946 Ho was promised independence for Vietnam within the French Union by Paris, and he immediately won the support of American consuls in Hanoi and Saigon; the Southeast Asia desk thought it likely that he was not "a full-fledged doctrinaire Communist." Following the breakdown of the Fontainbleau conference with the French in September 1946, Ho Chi Minh called at the American embassy, assured Ambassador Caffery that he was not a Communist, requested help from the United States, and strongly implied that he favored an activist American role in the region after the war. Caffery was suspicious, but Washington continued to support the March 6 agreement as the basis of American policy in the area.[3]

But Ho Chi Minh could do nothing to change the historical record; on the basis of information provided by the French, Acheson concluded that Ho had a "clear record as an agent of International Communism," and the United States must regard the domination of Vietnam by Moscow as the "least desirable" of possible outcomes of the difficulties there. But neither could the French regime of arbitrary arrest, torture, and graft be reimposed in Vietnam.[4] With this debate unresolved American policy remained paralyzed. When the war broke out, the United States counseled the French against attempting reconquest, prohibited the sale of American arms for use in the war, and urged caution and nonviolence on the Vietminh. Secretary of State Marshall saw two sides to the issue, colonialism versus communism, in the face of which he had "no solution to suggest." The two parties would have to work the problem out for themselves, the French hopefully conducting

published sources. These records have been supplemented by materials from the recently opened archives of the Quai d'Orsay.

[2] Lisle A. Rose, *Roots of Tragedy: The United States and the Struggle for Asia, 1945–53* (Westport, CT: Greenwood Press, 1976), pp. 64–8.

[3] U.S. Vietnam Relations (USVNR), I, Pt. 1, B36, C42-67; vol. 8, January 30, April 18, June 5, September 11, October 25, 1946, pp. 75–82.

[4] USVNR, vol. 8, November 29, December 3, 5, 1946. FRUS, 1947, vol. 6, Southeast Asia, Indochina, July 19, 21, 1947, pp. 121–3.

themselves in as liberal a spirit as possible.[5] Former ambassador Bullitt carried out a mission of inquiry in China and Indochina late in 1947; for him, the Vietminh were the "Maquisards," and the French were cast in the role of the Germans, a "black tragedy," since the leadership of the fight for independence had been captured by the Communists. But Bullitt said Washington would have no choice, failing negotiations, but to support France.[6]

In this fluid American policy the French clearly saw an opening for the Bao Dai solution, which they now began to pursue in earnest and sell to Washington. The Baie d'Along agreement of December 1947 provided for the establishment of an autonomous and united Vietnam within the French Union under Imperial rule.[7] Washington was partially satisfied, but it would not trust the agreement until it was ratified by the French National Assembly, and began to press the French government on the issue. Marshall was convinced the war was accomplishing Moscow's objectives by pinning down French troops, weakening the French economy, and denying the Vietnamese rice basket to the rest of Asia. The secretary insisted in July 1948 that the matter be put to Schuman starkly. The alternatives were to grant the independence and unity of Vietnam or lose all of Indochina to Communism. In the Paris embassy, however, Woodruff Wallner protested the tone of Marshall's message. The Schuman government was already under American pressure to raise wages and control inflation. It could not accommodate another explosive issue; discretion must be exercised in applying pressure "to avoid the charge of giving tactical advice or becoming identified with maneuvers that may imperil the government." Marshall agreed the embassy must only "apply such pressure as is best calculated to produce the desired result," but avoid causing the government to fall. Schuman was promised American support and material assistance in Indochina once the Baie d'Along agreements were ratified.[8] But the premier did nothing. Once again French governmental instability proved helpful in fending off American pressure.

Washington was aware of the popular support of Ho Chi Minh and suspected that Bao Dai was only a puppet of the French, yet the Americans moved inexorably toward support for the Bao Dai solution. Neither the absence of anti-American propaganda among the Vietminh nor the argument that Ho Chi Minh was a candidate to become an Asian Tito, made any difference. The Queuille government finally adopted legislation unifying the three provinces of Vietnam and renegotiated an agreement with Bao Dai at the Elysée palace on March 8, 1949. Vietnam, Laos, and Cambodia offi-

5   USVNR, vol. 8, February 3, 1947.
6   William Bullitt, "The Saddest War," *Life Magazine*, December 29, 1947, 64–70.
7   R. E. M. Irving, *The First Indochina War* (London: Croom Helm, 1975), pp. 49–68.
8   Archives Nationales (A.N.), 457 AP 80 (2), Papiers Georges Bidault, March 17, April 5, 1948. USVNR, vol. 8, July 2, 3, 10, 14, 1948. FRUS, 1948, VI, Indochina, July 2, 3, 10, 14, 1948, pp. 28–33.

cially became Associated States, presumably autonomous, within the French Union. Queuille and the Vietnamese Premier Tran Van Huu immediately requested economic aid from Washington. Acheson remained suspicious, however, and warned against any "premature" endorsement of the Bao Dai regime. But when Saigon officials "assumed the department desired the success of the Bao Dai experiment," Acheson wired back: "Your assumption is correct." Further pressure on the French might miscarry, and Ho was a "Commie," whether or not he might become an Asian Tito: "All Stalinists in colonial areas are nationalists," the secretary observed. The Americans held off full support for Bao Dai, however, until he could demonstrate popular support. Acheson was chastened by the failed U.S. policy of supporting the Chinese Kuomintang.[9]

Bruce now began to lobby for support of Bao Dai. The French recognition of the Associated States of Indochina was as far as Paris could go and a "milestone" in the creation of the French Union. From Saigon, officials warned that the alternative was "continued costly colonial warfare or French withdrawal and a Communist Vietnam." But other diplomats realized that support of Bao Dai would avert neither of these. The Southeast Asia desk proposed that the United States warn the French bluntly that it was necessary to accommodate Asian nationalism and grant complete sovereignty to the Associated States; otherwise no economic assistance would be forthcoming. But Bruce exploded in anger at this suggestion, as did the European desk, and the message was never sent, although Acheson said it represented department views.[10]

Acheson proposed that the U.S. demand from the French a "timetable" for independence and an international control mechanism to monitor the process. Bruce rejected these as impractical and suggested instead that Washington content itself with transfer of Indochinese affairs to the Foreign Affairs Ministry, and a public statement by Paris promising that the Elysée agreements were only one step in an "evolutionary" process toward full and complete independence within the French Union. Acheson agreed, Bruce pressed Paris for both, and got neither. Acheson got no further with Ambassador Bonnet in Washington. In the meantime the appearance of Communist Chinese troops on the borders of Tonkin, and the recognition of Ho Chi Minh as the legitimate ruler of Vietnam by both the USSR and China, proved determining in terms of American policy in the region. On February 3, 1950 the United States extended formal recognition to the Associated States of Indochina, Vietnam, Laos, and Cambodia.[11]

Paris lost no time requesting military assistance in Indochina. The Na-

[9] Foreign Relations of the United States (FRUS), 1949, VII, Indochina, March 16, 18, 1949, pp. 12–5; April 13, 1949, pp. 19–20; May 2, 6, 10, 20, 1949, pp. 21–30.
[10] USVNR, 8, June 6, 1949, 215.
[11] FRUS, 1949, VII, Indochina, December 22, 1949, pp. 112–3. FRUS, 1950, VI, Indochina, January 13, 1950, pp. 694–5; February 1, 3, 1950, pp. 715–20.

tional Defense Committee met on February 17 and prepared three lists of military needs; Bonnet presented the first in Washington on February 23, and the next two on March 1. On February 23, 1950 an American mission of inquiry departed for Indochina; it rapidly concluded that an assistance program of $23 million was about what the country could successfully absorb. The Griffin Mission, as it was known, recommended that American aid be distributed directly to the Associate States (AS) in order to build their prestige, and that France should not be given control. The ECA also favored this policy, but Paris violently objected, and when Bao Dai submitted a list of Vietnamese demands on Washington of his own, Acheson instructed that the monarch be told to route his requests through the French, for reasons of urgency and practicality.[12] He might have added politics as well. On March 9, 1950 the State and Defense departments agreed on a program of military assistance for Thailand and Indochina "to deal with Communist aggression from without and subversive activities from within." An allocation of $15 million was made by President Truman in May 1950.[13]

The outbreak of the Korean War brought an end to American ambiguity about supporting the French in Indochina. President Truman promised an immediate acceleration of aid, and linked Indochina with Korea in his decision to intervene. Paris took this as "an implicit guarantee of American intervention" in Indochina as well as Korea if necessary. The United States now regarded France as a "brother in arms" in the anti-Communist effort rather than the defender of an obsolete colonialism.[14] Tonkin rapidly assumed a central place in American strategic thinking; its loss, according to the "domino theory" rapidly coming into acceptance, would inevitably lead to the loss of Thailand and Burma as well as Indochina, then perhaps Malaysia and the Philippines, with India and even Australia sometimes thrown in for good measure. Fears arose about French resolve, however. Bonnet hinted in Washington that with Communist China on the borders of Vietnam, Paris might do well to seek diplomatic contacts with the new Chinese regime. Alexandre Parodi rejected American pressure toward further autonomy for the Associated States and warned that in the absence of sufficient motivation to stay, Paris might be prompted to consider withdrawal from Indochina altogether. Washington's reaction was immediate. Bruce sought assurances from the French of their determination to stay in Indochina,

---

12 Ministère des Affaires Etrangères (MAE), Asie 1944–55, Indochine, Dossier 263, Note, October–November 1950, "Historique de l'aide américaine." See also "Note" of September 20, 1950 on the controversy over allocating U.S. aid directly to the Indochinese governments.
13 Truman Library, Papers of John F. Melby, S.E. Asia File, 1950–2, Box 9, "Report of the Griffin Mission, May 1950"; Truman Library, Confidential File, Mutual Defense, Folder 2, March 9, 1950, April 28, 1950.
14 MAE, Asie 1944–55, Indochine, 259, "Note" by Alexandre Parodi, July 1, 1950, Bonnet to Schuman, July 5, 11, 1950.

without which American aid would be rendered meaningless, and he cautioned against overtures from Paris to the Beijing regime. On August 16, 1950, after a long talk with Pleven about recognition of China, Bruce was finally able to report that the issue was dormant.[15]

The Korean War also brought another study mission to Indochina, under John F. Melby; predictably, it concluded that failure of the West in Indochina would mean the spread of communism throughout Asia. Melby listened to a detailed lecture from High Commissioner Pignon demonstrating that Vietnam was now a fully independent state within the French Union. But the American remained unconvinced; he reported that no military solution was possible without "the application of political and economic techniques to the problem." The Communists had effectively harnessed the forces of nationalism in the area, and the French could not convince the natives of their sincerity given "the long-standing suspicion and deep seated hatred with which the Indochinese regard the French." Without a political solution, Melby thought, "the French will, in time, find themselves eliminated from the scene." Melby concluded by recommending that the French proceed rapidly with the creation of a Vietnamese national army. French forces were at the limit of their capacity, and insufficient to deal with the Vietminh and a Chinese intervention, should one occur, at the same time. Moreover, the Associated States gave priority to getting rid of the French before defending themselves against the threat of Communism, while the French showed no desire to relinquish control. "The political interests of France and the Associated States are not only different but mutually exclusive."[16]

Despite these negative conclusions Melby recommended that the United States meet in full French requests for military aid.[17] The joint chiefs of staff concurred, setting a figure of $100 million, but demanding that U.S. agreement be a prerequisite to all French operational plans. The joint chiefs also "regarded with strong disfavor the desires and continued attempts of France to settle, on the political level, the military and internal security problems of Indochina in Paris." The State Department Policy Planning Staff also warned that France must grant immediate independence and take the war to the United Nations, for "without a bolder political approach we are headed for a debacle." But Bruce, as usual, put a damper on all this chorus of complaint to Paris. Approaches to the French to change further the nature

[15] Truman Library, PSF, National Security Council Meetings Box 204, February 27, 1950, Report to the NSC by the Department of State on the Position of the United States with Respect to Indochina. FRUS, 1950, VI, Indochina, February 16, 1950, pp. 734–5; May 4, 1950, pp. 793–4; August 12, 16, 1950, pp. 851–6.
[16] MAE, Asie 1944–55, Indochine, 259, July 17, 1950; Truman Library, Melby Papers, Box 10, August 16–31, 1950, Report on Indochina dated August 24, 1950.
[17] On September 6, 1950 Bonnet reported to Paris that the Melby report went beyond expectations in its generosity: MAE, Asie 1944–55, Indochine, 263.

of their Vietnamese relations, he said, were a waste of time.[18] The CIA also doubted that any aid "short of unlimited U.S. resources could enable Bao Dai to establish a firm regime backed by the non-Communist French." Even with U.S. help it was doubtful that the French could hold on for more than 18 months; only direct American intervention could save Indochina. The most trenchant critique of American policy came from the South East Asia desk; Charlton Ogburn condemned Bruce, the West European desk, and U.S. personnel in Indochina for suppressing repeated suggested warnings to Paris to face up to its responsibilities. The Paris embassy regarded Asian nationalism as little more than "the patter of naked brown feet" in the jungles. It had been entirely duped by the French, whose folly now left Washington with the choice of accepting communism in Indochina or "pouring treasure in a hopeless cause." George Kennan, outgoing chairman of the policy staff, warned against backing the French in an undertaking which "neither they, nor we, nor both of us together, can win."[19]

Paris and Washington were able to agree that the American role in Vietnam should focus on constructing the new Vietnamese state around its nascent army. The new American ambassador in Vietnam, Donald Heath, actively championed the project; he insisted the United States must participate in the organization, planning, training of officers, promotion of cadres, and intelligence. Acheson proposed that the Vietnamese army be declared formally to exist, its personnel to consist of those Vietnamese already serving with French Union forces who would be designated as on loan to the French. Bruce blocked this idea on the grounds that the French would never accept it. But the NSC rallied to the national armies concept and it became the basis of American policy in subsequent years. American aid was now assured on condition that the French not reduce their own military contribution, and that they maintain or increase the level of their financial support, carry out full consultation with the American legation and MAAG, and faithfully implement the March 8 and December 30, 1949 agreements with Bao Dai establishing the independence of Vietnam within the French Union.[20]

The United States immediately showed impatience with the French prosecution of the war, and American and French military were to show increasing contempt for each other during the next four years.[21] Following reverses

[18]   FRUS, 1950, VI, Indochina, August 16, 1950, pp. 857–8.
[19]   Truman Library, PSF, Intelligence File, February 1950, CIA Reports, March 1950, November 1950. FRUS, 1950, VI, Indochina, August 18, 1950, p. 863.
[20]   FRUS, 1950, VI, Indochina, August 23, 1950, pp. 864–7; September 1, 5, 1950, pp. 868–76; October 11, 1950, pp. 886–90.
[21]   See George Herring in Denise Artaud and Lawrence Kaplan, eds., *Dien Bien Phu: L'Alliance atlantique et la défense du Sud-Est asiatique* (Lyon: Editions de la manufacture, 1989), pp. 61–87. This joint effort by French and American scholars is the best available treatment of the U.S.–French war in Indochina through 1955. None

the French suffered near the Chinese frontier late in 1950, the Americans demanded that General Carpentier be dismissed. After the defeat at Cao Bang, Heath blamed poor French generalship, lack of adequate military intelligence, and "squeamishness" about fighting near the China border. But Carpentier's greatest sin was apparently his failure to inform Heath of his plans. On October 15, 1950 Truman met General MacArthur on Midway island in the Pacific in order to discuss the Korean War. Indochina naturally came up for discussion as well. MacArthur said he could not understand "why the French do not clean it up." Their capacity and caliber seemed to be in doubt, a particularly unhappy situation since the essential role in the defense of Western Europe remained with French forces. Truman could not understand the French failures either. Admiral Radford thought the United States must "stiffen the backbone of the French." Averell Harriman recalled that the Free French had fought well in Italy during the war; he thought they must simply "change their attitude relative to Indochina." But General Omar Bradley said the wartime effort had been that of a select group; the ordinary French forces could not be judged by their example. Truman concluded the conversation by deploring French stubbornness. If their prime minister came to Washington, the President said, "I am going to talk cold turkey to him. If you don't want him to hear that kind of talk, you had better keep him away from me." MacArthur thought the French only needed a more aggressive general.[22]

The American military recommended that these concerns be directly put to the French, who were trying "too little, too late, and not very hard" in Vietnam. They had shown neither "vigorous leadership nor enlightened capacity," and must be "stunned" into action by speaking "frankly and bluntly" to them in staff talks. On October 24, 1950 the French generals and high commissioner in Vietnam met with the U.S. legation. The American concerns were communicated to the French, who promised to grant full independence to Vietnam, and assured Washington that some airplanes, landing craft, and napalm would be enough to turn the tide of battle. On November 15 Heath noted that liaison had improved, and the ECA's European formula of "constant subtle and effective influence" was at work in Indochina, accomplishing there what the MSA Mission in Paris had been able to do with the French budget and the NATO-TCC Committee with the French Army. On November 24 Bruce noted that Minister of Overseas Territories Jean Letourneau had made the most generous speech yet in the National Assembly, virtually promising Vietnam complete independence, a consider-

of the contributors, however, appears to have researched archives on both sides of the Atlantic.

22 FRUS, 1950, VI, Indochina, September 8, 1950, pp. 876–7; October 13, 15, 1950, pp. 890–4; FRUS, 1950, VII, Korea, October 15, 1950, pp. 948–60. This conversation was leaked to the press, and Bonnet reported its content to Paris with great distress on April 21, 1951, in MAE, Asie 1944–55, Indochine, 260.

able step toward American views. But the joint chiefs tempered this optimism with a stinging critique of French generalship and a demand for an overall plan, American-approved, for Indochina operations. On December 29, 1950 the CIA questioned whether the French had the will to stay in Vietnam and predicted they would be driven out in six to nine months. Concessions to Bao Dai were too slow, the creation of a national army was still a year away, the officer casualty toll on French forces was prohibitive, and the war consumed 37 percent of the French military budget. The Americans thought the French needed a miracle. It came in the person of General de Lattre de Tassigny.[23]

Only the pressures of the war and desperation over the possibility of losing in both Korea and Vietnam can explain the American infatuation with the general, who had previously been highly regarded by Washington, but also suspected for his alleged flirtation with Communism. De Lattre was no American toady; he was suspicious of the Marshall Plan, which he regarded as threatening the American "satellisation" of France. He was appointed to Indochina in December 1950, as both high commissioner and commander in chief of French forces with the mandate to create a Vietnamese national army. From the outset his aggressive style raised hopes that the war could be turned around. On January 23, 1951 Heath reported that de Lattre has "restored confidence and his personality overshadows Asia at the moment." The general proved adept at handling the American press, which soon portrayed him in the image of the traditional French swashbuckling hero, a latter day d'Artagnan. Heath thought his military qualities to "border on genius"; although irascible and prejudiced, he was a "modern-day Lyautey." On his visit to Washington in September 1951, de Lattre was described as a general of "extreme personal courage and ability, but whose strong sense of mission and dignity makes for occasional incidents of explosive friction with his associates and superiors." The Americans credited him with having "transformed an army beset by defeatism into a force which has won every major engagement against Communist forces." Visiting Vietnam in November 1951, General Lawton Collins found "a General de Lattre show. His personality, drive, energy, and integrity dominate all. If anything should happen to him there could well be a collapse in Indochina." Something did, of course, and there was.[24]

If the war did appear to take a turn for the better in 1951, all was not

23 USVNR, 8, October 13, 1950, pp. 350–70. FRUS, 1950, VI, Indochina, October 24, 1950, pp. 906–9; November 15, 1950, pp. 921–3; November 24, 1950, pp. 936–7; December 29, 1950, pp. 958–63.
24 Simonne de Lattre, *Jean de Lattre, mon mari* (Paris: Presse de la Cité, 1971), pp. 110, 332–46. Maréchal Jean de Lattre, *Ne pas subir: écrits, 1914–52* (Paris: Plon, 1984), pp. 467–90. FRUS, 1951, VI, Pt. 1, Indochina, January 23, 1951, p. 358; June 29, 1951, pp. 432–9; August 7, 1951, pp. 477–9; September 12, 13, 1951, pp. 494–7; November 13, 1951, p. 545.

smooth between the Americans and General de Lattre. The general took immediate exception to the activities of the ECA in Vietnam. In March 1951 de Lattre described Heath as " a dupe, presenting an honest face while all sorts of American machinations were transpiring behind our backs." In May Heath complained that de Lattre kept the Americans out of every aspect of French–Vietnamese relations, resented the ECA and the technical mission, STEM, and declined to find housing for additional personnel in MAAG. De Lattre complained that ECA officials schemed with the Vietnamese against the French and failed to consult with the French before undertaking projects. The Quai agreed, accusing the STEM mission under the zealous Robert Blum of seeking to eliminate the French from Indochina. Bonnet was instructed to protest in Washington. De Lattre claimed American economic assistance was useless and had been forced upon Paris; Acheson retorted that de Lattre was either the victim of a "monumental lack of communications or a striking case of amnesia." On June 30, 1951, de Lattre blocked the signing of a bilateral agreement between the Vietnamese government and the ECA on the grounds that it had first to be submitted to the French Union for approval, a process that might take months. The Associated Press reported this as a "slap in the face" to the new Vietnamese government, which was seeking to negotiate its first foreign treaty. De Lattre now exploded in anger at the American press, causing Heath to lecture him on the rules protecting freedom of the press in the United States, and the right of the Vietnam government to sign agreements independently of France.[25]

But there was validity to de Lattre's charges. A careful career diplomat, Heath defended the ECA to de Lattre but complained bitterly about it to Washington. Heath suggested that the ECA and STEM coordinate their activities with the French. This brought an angry retort from Robert Blum: STEM had a vital role in building popular anti-Communism; he argued, he would not "trim our sails at every whim of the French," who undermined themselves by their policies and would clearly one day have to leave. Blum said the United States must look to its own future influence with the people of Vietnam independently of France. Acheson rejected French complaints against the USIA; the Americans insisted on their right to circulate books and offer lessons in English to the Vietnamese public. But Heath would not be deterred. The major interest of the United States in Vietnam, he wrote in a revealing essay, was real estate: strategic position, rice, rubber, and tin. These must be denied to Communism. The French were doing the fighting, but only for the goal of preserving the French Union. The United States must accept the French Union or be prepared to see the French leave. The ECA was playing into Communist hands, facilitating the "Commie aim" to split

25 MAE, Asie 1944–55, Indochine, 264, Note of July 3, 1951, Bonnet to Schuman, July 6, 1951. FRUS, 1951, VI, Pt. 1, Indochina, March 8, 1951, pp. 388–91; March 18, 1951, pp. 404–6; May 15, 1951, pp. 418–20; June 19, 30, 1951, pp. 428–9, 439–41.

the United States and France, and adding to the danger that the French would choose appeasement as a way out of their dilemma. Heath won the argument, and ECA officials were warned they must inform the French of their projects and refuse to listen to Vietnamese complaints against the French: "Hear no evil, speak no evil, see no evil," as ECA administrator Barry Bingham sarcastically put it.[26]

De Lattre's visit to Washington was ostensibly at the invitation of the joint chiefs of staff in recognition of his role during the Second World War under American command, but in reality it was a working visit devoted to the Vietnam situation. It was also a publicity exercise for the American public: the "fighting general" made the cover of *Time*, received a flattering editorial in *Life*, and appeared on U.S. television on "Meet the Press," receiving, according to the show's host Robert Spivak, an "overwhelmingly favorable reception all over the country." De Lattre caused a sensation by promising victory within eighteen months to two years. His intent was to convince Washington of the need to speed arms deliveries and increase their amount, and emphasize that Vietnam was not a colonial struggle but part of a broader anti-Communist effort, the two axes of which were Korea and Indochina. Indochina was the more important of these conflicts, for the loss of Korea meant only the fall of the outer edge of the Asian continent, while the Gulf of Tonkin was the key to all non-Communist Asia. If it fell, not only would Burma, Thailand, and Malaysia be lost, but "India will burn like a match," and the barriers to the Suez and Africa would collapse as well. Never was the domino theory to find again such eloquent expression.

In asking aid, de Lattre complained that he should not be made to feel like a beggar: "I am your man just as General Ridgeway is your man. Your own spirit should lead you to send me these things without my asking." Lovett assured de Lattre the feelings were mutual. Bonnet was in rapture: De Lattre's speech was "magisterial. . . . He demonstrated, with a clarity that struck M. Lovett, that the wars under way in Asia were one and the same war." Robert Lacoste termed the trip a brilliant success: De Lattre had left a deep impression and prepared collective action where France had labored alone for five years. The general himself saw the trip as having secured recognition from Washington of the importance of the French effort, a speedup in arms deliveries, a renewed American commitment to the Vietnam army, and a new climate of comprehension in the United States.[27]

Acheson agreed that de Lattre's forceful personality had "advanced

---

[26] FRUS, 1951, VI, Pt. 1, Indochina, May 15, 1951, pp. 418–20; July 12, 13, 20, 1951, pp. 450–9.
[27] Papiers de Maréchal de Lattre de Tassigny, N541, September 18, 21, 24, 26, 27, 1951. Available through the courtesy of Madame la Maréchale, Paris. Further documentation in FRUS, 1951, VI, Pt. 1, Indochina, September 14, 20, 1951, pp. 502–4, 515–20; MAE, Asie 1944–55, Indochine, 260, Bonnet to Schuman, September 18, 1951; 264, Note by the Secretary of National Defense, October 13, 1951.

awareness in the Department and the public of the extreme importance of Indochina and the urgency of the situation there." But Acheson denied suggestions that de Lattre had effected a turnabout in American thinking; the United States needed no lessons on the importance of Indochina. De Lattre was a "convinced egotist who has recently passed through a grave crisis carried away by enthusiasm after unexpected success." The crisis was the death of de Lattre's son in action in Vietnam earlier in the year. Within three months of his Washington triumph the general was himself dead of cancer, his will to live, according to his wife, diminished by his personal tragedy. Hearing of de Lattre's ill health, General Collins feared that all was now lost. General Bradley advised further military talks with the French, but Collins thought not; the French always said "We can't do anything, you can, so if you don't do anything, that's your responsibility." By the year's end Bruce saw French hopes for victory dashed and the public eager for peace. Mendès France was gaining support, Monnet wanted the war ended because of its effect on France's European position, and even Paul Devinat said there was no arguing with Mendès France's logic. De Lattre's promise of victory in eighteen months or two years had been "whistling in the wind." The snowball was forming, Bruce said. The alternatives were massive aid, internationalization of the war, or withdrawal.[28] There was no question, of course, of how Washington would choose. Massive aid began in 1952, along with increased American influence and involvement, with the French retreating to a holding action, in part prevented from leaving by having invited Washington in. The dénouement of that situation was to be the French collapse of 1954 and the disintegration of Franco–American relations.

II THE AMERICANS, THE NAVARRE PLAN, AND DIEN BIEN PHU

During 1952 the war reached a stalemate. The French would undertake no offensive action, and doubts fueled by the antiwar movement multiplied in Washington about French willingness to continue fighting.[29] The disappointment following the death of General de Lattre was exacerbated by developments in North Africa, where a promising reform effort, taken under American pressure in 1951, came to grief. In March 1952 the French ended their experiment with a nationalist government by the neo-Destour in Tunisia, arrested its ministers, and formed a new cabinet composed of men the American consul characterized as stooges. The Tunisian question

[28] FRUS, 1951, VI, Pt. 1, Indochina, September 26, 1951, pp. 524–5; October 12, 15, 1951, pp. 530–2; December 21, 26, 1951, pp. 570, 576.

[29] For a systematic treatment of the attitude of the French left toward the Indochina war, and the concern about French antiwar sentiment in Washington, see Edward Rice-Maximin, *Accommodation and Resistance: The French Left, Indochina and the Cold War, 1944–54* (Westport, CT: Greenwood Press, 1986).

was raised by the African–Asian bloc in the United Nations, and contrary to past practice, Acheson felt unable to vote with France in keeping it off the agenda of the General Assembly. The American delegation abstained in what Acheson characterized as one of the hardest decisions he had ever had to make. In September, following the failure of French reform efforts, Washington dropped its opposition altogether, and the Tunisian question came up for discussion in the world body. Predictably, Paris exploded. Washington, already unpopular because of its reduction in offshore aid and the accusation by Pinay of interference in French affairs, now became "public enemy number one . . . it is difficult to forecast to what point and how rapidly our relations with France may deteriorate."[30] Washington retreated and pushed through a mild resolution that simply encouraged French negotiations with the nationalists. But the damage was done, without the Truman administration having mitigated the effects of French colonialism in North Africa or Indochina.

In Indochina General Salan, de Lattre's successor, adopted a defensive strategy and would no longer promise victory in any specific time frame. The CIA predicted a gradual deterioration of the French position leading to withdrawal, while Jean Monnet warned that an end to the war was essential if France was to meet its obligations in Europe.[31] But Washington preferred to regard such predictions as "inconceivable": France would not so easily sacrifice its aspirations to be a Great Power, and would continue to fight if the United States financed its budget deficits and built national armies for the Associated States. The army thought that "the out-phasing of French influence is essential to the emergence of efficient leadership which can unite all factions [in Vietnam] into a cohesive national government," but it was essential to "keep the shield of French military power while gaining full independence for Vietnam, including the right to leave the French Union." The military offered no means of reconciling these contradictory goals other than offering more aid. By 1953, in consequence, "la salle guerre" became France's leading dollar export.[32]

The Americans were meanwhile drawn into the quagmire of internal Vietnamese politics; Heath began to advise Bao Dai on the choice of premiers and the best means of resisting French intervention, observing that the emperor felt he "could count on me [Heath] as a sincere friend and advisor." Heath had no illusions about the Vietnamese mandarinate, however. Bao Dai and Ho Chi Minh each controlled about 11 million people, but Bao Dai received billions from Paris and Washington, while Ho Chi Minh's forces

30 FRUS, 1952–4, XI, part 1, Tunisia, September 11, 26, 1952, pp. 808–13; October 7, 8, 1952, pp. 813–5; October 20, 23, 31, 1952, pp. 822–39.
31 FRUS, 1952–4, XIII, 1, Indochina, January 2, 3, 6, 17, 1952, pp. 1–21; March 3, 1952, pp. 53–60; March 12, 1952, pp. 66–7.
32 FRUS, 1952–4, XIII, 1, Indochina, March 15, 1952, pp. 69–71; March 25, 1952, pp. 77–80; April 8, 1952, pp. 99–100; May 10, 1952, pp. 129–31.

were ensconced in "malarial foothills at subsistence levels." Yet the Vietminh were winning the war. The government of Nguyen Van Tam, according to Consul Sturm, even "nauseated the French;" it was composed of
"puppets, cops, sadists, reactionaries, criminals, assassins, men of faded mental
powers," and would achieve only victory for the Vietminh, "a poor return
for French blood and American money."[33]

Nevertheless, on May 28, 1952, during the signing of the EDC treaty,
Acheson declared that the "French effort is not made in the French interest
but in the general international interest," and he promised increased aid.
But the French had lost their taste for the war; they were conducting a
holding operation that was designed to maintain their position militarily
while endeavoring to negotiate an honorable withdrawal.[34] Jean Letourneau came to Washington in June 1952 to negotiate a new aid agreement,
but he could offer only a picture of pessimism and lethargy. The Chinese
would never permit the defeat of the Vietminh, even if the French were able
to accomplish it. No military decision was possible; Paris hoped an armistice in Vietnam would follow that being negotiated in Korea. The Americans were shocked, and pressured Letourneau to retract his statement.
Acheson told the NSC that Letourneau meant the French wanted negotiations only when their military position was stronger. The NSC resolved that
the United States must "influence the policies of France and the Associated
States toward actions consistent with U.S. objectives," and assured Paris
that it would use air and naval power to deter Chinese intervention. Acheson said the United States must "impress on the French the folly of giving
up the offensive strategy so brilliantly launched and carried out by de Lattre
in favor of a mere holding operation."[35]

But the pressure had no effect. The atmosphere remained clouded by differences over North Africa and acrimony over the $125 million reduction
in aid. In Washington electoral concerns were paramount, and the State
Department was conducting its own "holding operation" pending the arrival of a new administration. Paris feared the Republicans: Auriol told
Monnet France should not ratify EDC until the victory of Stevenson was
assured, because Eisenhower was in the hands of "gangsters." Monnet agreed
the Republicans were a danger. The CIA again pronounced the military
situation to be a stalemate, and the American military found the French
unable to make good use of the aid that was arriving.[36] Heath remained

33   FRUS, 1952–4, XIII, 1, Indochina, January 30, 1952, pp. 23–4; May 10, 1952, pp.
     129–31; June 10, 1952, pp. 177–9.
34   Philippe Devilliers and Jean Lacouture, *End of a War: Indochina, 1954* (New York:
     Praeger, 1969), pp. 29–30.
35   FRUS, 1952–4, XIII, 1, Indochina, June 14, 1952, pp. 183–7; June 16, 1952, pp.
     189–95; June 17, 1952, pp. 197–202; June 20, 1952, pp. 204–8; July 27, 1952, pp.
     225–7; August 1, 1952, pp. 231–3.
36   FRUS, XIII, 1, Indochina, August 29, 1952, pp. 237–9; September 8, 1952, p. 250;

optimistic. Two more divisions, he thought, could turn the tide, and he was delighted that Vietnam had finally achieved real independence. But in the State Department Charlton Ogburn challenged both these claims, particularly that of Vietnamese independence: "it is not true and Ambassador Heath must know it is not true. It may be sound policy for us to act publicly as if it were true, but that is quite different from asserting it under a confidential classification." Reevaluation of American policy was clearly necessary but must be left to the new administration.[37]

John Foster Dulles brought differences of style, not substance, to American foreign policy. There was no more fervent backer in Washington of the EDC or more firm believer in the domino theory with regard to Vietnam. Dulles considered himself a Francophile, and made France the focal point of his European and Asian policies, which revolved around EDC and Indochina. Bonnet warned Paris that intensified pressure was to be expected as soon as the new administration took up its post. Failing EDC, the Republicans would push ahead on their own with German rearmament. In Indochina they would demand victory, in exchange for which they were prepared to step up assistance.[38] Bonnet was correct. At a State Department–joint chiefs conference in January 1952, Admiral Radford, the new chairman of the joint chiefs of staff, demanded a military plan to end the war. The French needed a more aggressive spirit; the United States must be "hardboiled" and force them to adopt an aggressive policy. Heath agreed Paris should be told to come up with a plan to win the war "in so many months . . . or years." In Washington the new MSA administrator Harold Stassen warned the French that future aid packages would depend upon progress toward ratification of EDC.[39]

In Paris the new government of René Mayer was developing its own agenda. Dulles must be told on his forthcoming visit that France had a "double vocation," in Europe and the world. There would be no ratification of EDC unless the United Kingdom and United States undertook firm commitments, sufficient aid was forthcoming, and the Americans paid an appropriate share of the cost of the war.[40] On EDC, the blackmail worked both ways: The Americans said no aid unless the treaty was ratified, the French said no ratification without aid. On Indochina the French recognized, "If we want additional aid from the United States, we must offer to their imagination

November 13, 1952, pp. 279–83. Vincent Auriol, *Journal du Septennat*, vol. 6 (1952), August 7, 1952, p. 489.

37   FRUS, 1952–4, XIII, 1, Indochina, December 22, 29, 1952, pp. 328–9, 332–6.
38   A.N., Papiers René Mayer, 363 AP 22, January 16, 1953.
39   FRUS, 1952–4, XIII, 1, Indochina, February 4, 1952, pp. 382–4; March 12, p. 405; March 19, 1953, pp. 416–7. MAE, Asie, 1944–55, 261, Minutes of Washington Conversations, March 17, 1953.
40   MAE, Asie 1944–55, Indochine, 261, January 30, 1953, "Introduction" to forthcoming talks with Secretary Dulles.

larger perspectives than simply the maintenance of a sterile and costly status quo." Perspectives of victory in an anti-Communist struggle were the best means of extracting foreign aid from the budget-conscious Republicans. But René Mayer feared "an American grasp of Indochina;" Jean Letourneau observed that "the day that the American financial effort becomes superior to ours, we risk seeing the direction of operations escape us." René Pleven thought it necessary to "get out of the heads of the Americans the idea that increased aid must be matched by an increase in our effort." But the Quai warned that was just what the Americans had in mind: "a plan of action of great scope in which each request for aid would be formulated in terms of successive goals that we promise to accomplish." To the American pragmatists the war was a simple question of cost accounting. How much more would it cost, they naively had asked of the French, to win the war in two years as opposed to four?[41]

Mayer came to Washington in March 1953. He was regarded there as a "real friend . . . in our corner . . . dedicated to U.S. objectives in Europe." All the more reason to pressure him. Dulles instructed the Paris embassy to tell Mayer to come to Washington with a plan to end the war within twenty-four months. If he did, Dulles and Eisenhower agreed, aid to the French would be stepped up considerably.[42] Thus were born the Navarre Plan and the tragedy of Dien Bien Phu. On the presidential yacht *Williamsburg*, on March 26, 1953, Eisenhower impressed upon Mayer his desire to hear of any French program for victory in Vietnam. Mayer was evasive, as was Letourneau in meetings at the Pentagon, and it is not clear that the French had a plan before they arrived in Washington.[43] But the Americans needed to be told something if the promised increase in aid was to be granted. Letourneau improvised a two-step program: first, pacify the south and build up the Vietnamese army to hold it; second, carry out a decisive blow in the north in 1955. Letourneau put the increased cost at $300 million, and agreed that two American officers come to Indochina to discuss the military aspects of his idea with General Salan.[44]

The joint chiefs of staff did not regard Letourneau's vague notions as an operational plan, but General John O'Daniel was sent to Saigon to meet with General Salan and give him American ideas of how the war might be

---

[41] A.N., Papiers Georges Bidault, 457 AP 44, Dossier 2, "Relations Franco–américaines," MAE Note of January 21, 1953; 2 (B), Conversations Foster Dulles, Réunion interministerielle de 31 janvier, 1953; "L'Aide américaine," Note sur une nouvelle orientation possible de l'aide américaine, 10 mars, 1953. 457 AP 45, Dossier 1, "Voyage en Amérique, Mars 1953," MAE Note de 17 mars, 1953. 457 AP 52, Dossier 1, "1953," Note, Vues de M. Letourneau, le 31 janvier, 1953.

[42] FRUS, 1952–54, XIII, 1, March 19, 24, 1953, pp. 416–20.

[43] George Herring, in Artaud and Kaplan, eds., *Dien Bien Phu*, p. 74.

[44] FRUS, 1952–4, XIII, 1, Indochina, March 26, 1953, pp. 429–32; March 30, 1952, pp. 435–49; April 3, 7, 1953, pp. 455–64; A. N., 363 AP 22, Papiers René Mayer, April 2, 3, 1953.

won. The French knew O'Daniel would be guided by the American experience in Korea, and Salan was instructed to reject any parallel with that war. The result was an interesting dialogue of the deaf. Salan told O'Daniel that it was impossible to pacify the south with Vietnamese police, that battalions, not divisions, were the appropriate unit size, and that the Vietnamese lacked the training to be officers. O'Daniel vented his frustration and insisted that France could learn lessons from the Korean war, but Salan held firm.[45] Not surprisingly, the Pentagon was incensed; the French had been trying to clean up the south for seven years and there was no reason to suppose they would succeed now. An audacious effort was needed to cut Vietminh supply lines to China, but first France must create Vietnamese-officered divisions. Dulles agreed: Should U.S. aid cease, he wondered, if the French fail "to do what the U.S. told them?" General Collins advised against it. But the Americans should certainly "use maximum effort and persuasion to get them to adopt a sensible program." On April 22, 1953 Dulles was again at the Quai. The continuation of aid, he said, must depend on a program promising a satisfactory outcome of the war within "a couple of years." Letourneau insisted the French plan would achieve that, and Dulles in turn promised continuation of the $525 million aid figure of the previous year. Any increase in that figure would depend upon French military performance. The whole of American budgetary assistance to France was now earmarked to cover the cost of the war; and the French were now totally dependent on the bloody conflict for continued relief from their balance of payments difficulties.[46]

At the Pentagon exasperation with the French deepened. General Collins wanted to "put the squeeze on the French to get them off their fannies." General Vandenberg complained that the French did not cooperate as an ally should; they resisted suggestions in Vietnam and put restrictions on American troops in North Africa. "All these things amount, I think, to a general indictment of the way in which the French are working with us." General Vandenberg demanded high-level talks with Paris, where the Americans would "talk turkey to them about what they should do in Indochina." General Nash accompanied Dulles to Paris to communicate the Pentagon's concerns; the tempo of the plan was too slow, he told René Pleven, the French must apply "more steam." General Salan had clearly revealed his inadequacy in his interview with General O'Daniel; new leadership was necessary.[47]

[45] FRUS, 1952–4, XIII, 1, Indochina, April 13, 1953, pp. 465–68. A.N., Papiers Georges Bidault 457 AP 52, Dossier 1, January 31, 1953, Vues de M. Letourneau: "We must not allow ourselves to be influenced by new American suggestions to conduct the Indochina war according to the same principles as the Korean war."

[46] FRUS, 1952–4, XIII, 1, Indochina, April 18, 20, 21, 22, 1953, pp. 472–83. FRUS, 1952–4, VI, 2, France, April 23, 1953, pp. 1347–9.

[47] FRUS, 1952–4, XIII, 1, Indochina, April 24, 26, 1953, pp. 500–10.

Pleven promised to change generals, and the Americans next concerned themselves with who should be appointed. President Eisenhower liked General Guillaume, the resident-general in Morocco; the NSC discussed whether it was "in a position to force the French to send him to Indochina." Dulles said he would raise the issue with Bonnet. Eisenhower condemned French colonialism, agreeing that without independence for Indochina, the United States was "pouring money down a rathole." Dulles instructed the Embassy to tell the French that a forceful and inspirational leader was needed in Vietnam—if not General Guillaume, General Valluy might do. Mayer rejected both American choices, suggesting instead General Navarre, whom he characterized as forceful, strong, and a leading expert on military intelligence. Washington agreed, Navarre arrived in Indochina on May 19, and an American military mission was dispatched to meet him there on June 10. In the meantime the French further buckled under American pressure and devalued the piaster, thus allowing much greater purchasing power for the U.S. dollar but angering the Vietnamese elite.[48]

Despite these minor victories frustration only grew in Washington. The Vietminh invaded Laos, further demonstrating French military weakness. Washington wanted to take the aggression to the United Nations, but the French resisted fiercely, fearing the effect on North Africa. In France neutralist sentiment grew apace; Dillon expressed concern about the campaign of the group around *L'Express,* most of whom supported Mendès France. Their influence would certainly increase unless genuine hope appeared for a solution in Indochina some time soon. In Vietnam the French would allow the Americans no role in operations and hamstrung their own commanders. Navarre would provide the test: "If the new French leadership continues the lethargy of the old we shall be forced to take a very close look at motivation in Paris." Dulles cautioned, however, that no bill of particulars must be given the French. "Our influence and pressure must be exerted so that the French themselves will come up with and implement needed decisions in the military, political, and economic fields." Withdrawal from Indochina was "inconceivable," and would "start an inevitable chain reaction which would destroy France's position as a world power."[49]

In late June O'Daniel had several meetings with Navarre, finding him offense-minded and open to suggestions. Navarre agreed to an offensive in the South during the forthcoming rainy season, and leaving "mopping up" operations there to the Vietnamese. In the fall he promised a new offensive in the North aimed at Vietminh supply lines. O'Daniel was happy that Navarre had absorbed American ideas and recommended that Washington

48   FRUS, 1952–4, XIII, 1, Indochina, April 28, 1953, pp. 516–9; May 6, 7, 1953, pp. 543–51; May 9, 1952, pp. 561–2; May 15, 1953, pp. 567–8; May 18, 1953, pp. 570–1; May 20, 1953, pp. 571–5; May 26, 1953, pp. 583–4.
49   FRUS, 1952–4, XIII, 1, Indochina, May 23, 24, 1953, pp. 579–83; June 5, 1953, pp. 503–4; June 10, 1953, pp. 604–8.

support the plan fully. Heath noted that the new French plan clearly reflected the American general's impact.[50] In June 1953 a moment of panic occurred in Paris, as Mendès France narrowly missed forming a government; his 301 votes, if the Communist deputies were added, the Ambassador noted, came to 406 votes in the National Assembly in favor of withdrawal from Indochina. But the French had thought better of themselves and supported Joseph Laniel, who was committed to victory. Washington was favorably impressed by Laniel's traditional, solid, Norman conservatism. The State Department thought his the first government in seven years that was ready to grant independence to the Vietnamese and pursue an aggressive plan for military victory. Laniel promised Dillon he would send nine more battalions to Vietnam to implement the Navarre Plan. There was a price tag, however, of an additional 150 billion francs, which Washington must pay. Without the new aid, Laniel said, he would be forced to resign, a neutralist government would be in power by October, and Indochina would go "down the drain." Laniel appeared to represent Washington's last chance. Behind him stood the bogey of Pierre Mendès France, which the French now brandished at every opportunity, lest Washington's willingness to pay show signs of flagging.[51]

On September 2, 1953 the Pentagon recommended that the Navarre Plan be funded, "conditional upon implementation, performance, and continued French willingness to receive and act upon United States military advice." At a State Department–joint chiefs meeting, MacArthur argued that $385 million additional aid must be provided the French or a political reversal would occur. Admiral Radford agreed: The French should be given the money if only to eliminate their "excuses." Dulles was more optimistic; much was to be expected from the Laniel–Navarre tandem, the Vietnamese would get their independence and the Navarre Plan was both practical and feasible. Vice President Nixon wanted to give the French more money. Dulles said an additional $100 million might be forthcoming later if needed, but the

---

[50] Devilliers and Lacouture insist the Navarre Plan was never meant to achieve more than an honorable negotiated peace: *End of a War*, pp. 35–7. But it must also have served the purpose of convincing Washington that France meant to fight for victory, which was the condition of American aid. General Navarre makes no reference in his memoirs to the American role in the formulation of the plan but notes that O'Daniel enthusiastically approved it afterward. Henri Navarre, *Le Temps des Verités* (Paris: Plon, 1979), pp. 335–6.

[51] FRUS, 1952–4, XIII, 1, Indochina, June 24, 1953, p. 617; June 30, 1953, pp. 624–6; July 2, 1953, pp. 631–2; July 10, 1953, p. 654; July 12, 1953, pp. 656–7; July 17, 1953, pp. 683–9; July 22, 1953, pp. 693–5; July 27, 1953, pp. 699–701; July 29, 1953, pp. 701–3; August 5, 1953, pp. 714–7. A.N., Papiers Georges Bidault, 457 AP 52, (1), July 10, 1953: a penciled, undated note by Bidault is revealing of French negotiating tactics. "Purely French affair . . . tell them that we will leave – Withdrawal of forces, will they believe it? 1) frighten them (Mendès) 2) increased help 3) political conference, increased solidarity 4) Navarre asks an additional financial and human effort – what will you give us if . . . ?"

present amount "finances as large an effort as the French were physically able to make." Washington was now clearly willing to pay whatever the war might cost.[52]

Dulles demanded assurances from Paris that American views on the conduct of the war would be taken into account in French planning and operations: "Complete execution of the recommendations of General Navarre was subject to the grant of this additional aid," and if the French failed to execute the plan, the United States would not be bound by the stated aid figure. Bidault and Dulles exchanged letters on September 29, 1953. Paris promised to "perfect" the independence of the Associated States, take the offensive to destroy enemy forces, implement the Navarre Plan, provide additional military strength, and take into account U.S. views on French strategic plans in Indochina. The United States would provide, during fiscal year 1953–4, $460 million in direct budgetary assistance, $385 million in supplementary aid to finance the Navarre Plan, $85 million in end-item military hardware, and $217 million in offshore procurement. American military aid to France had passed the billion-dollar mark, the bulk of it Vietnam-related.[53]

On November 19, 1953 Navarre announced with pride the successful parachute drop at Dien Bien Phu, which established a strongpoint in the heart of Vietminh country and interdicted the enemy's supply lines to Laos. O'Daniel jubilantly reported that the French had gained the initiative in the war; he visited the outpost and told Navarre that similar successes offered an ultimate "solution" to the problem of the war. It may be doubted that this operation was entirely in the spirit of the Navarre–O'Daniel plan, but Washington was gratified just the same.[54] In Bermuda in December 1953, Bidault told Eisenhower and Churchill that the French military position in Indochina was "better than ever before." O'Daniel agreed that Navarre had made great strides, although problems remained: The Vietnamese government still lacked popular support, and the political will to win in Paris appeared lacking. More than ever, Washington resolved to support the French effort. With the military success on the ground, Vice President Nixon concluded, all that remained was to "stiffen the French at home."[55]

[52] FRUS, 1952–4, XIII, 1, Indochina, September 2, 1953, pp. 743–6; September 4, 1953, p. 755; September 8, 1953, pp. 762–7; September 9, 1953, pp. 791–3. Dwight D. Eisenhower Library (Abilene, Kansas), Anne Whitman File, National Security Council Series, Box 4, NSC 161, September 9, 1953.

[53] FRUS, 1952–14, XIII, 1, September 29, 1953, pp. 812–19. A.N., Papiers Georges Bidault, 457 AP 52 (1) September 19, 29, 1953 (French text of U.S. notes).

[54] Navarre, *Le Temps des Verités*, p. 336. G. Herring and R. Immerman, in Artaud and Kaplan, eds., *Dien Bien Phu*, argue that the air drop was undertaken to please Washington but was aimed at the defense of Laos rather than the promised offensive: p. 105. Reprinted from the *Journal of American History*, 71, no. 2 (September 1984): 343–63.

[55] FRUS, 1952–4, XIII, 1, Indochina, November 19, 1953, p. 881; November 27, 1953,

Both American moments of optimism in Vietnam, the first provided by the dashing de Lattre, the second by Navarre, proved ephemeral. On January 3, 1954 Navarre confided to Heath that he could see a way for the Vietminh to take Dien Bien Phu, although its loss would not affect the war. On January 8 Dulles told the NSC that Dien Bien Phu was surrounded and the Vietminh could take it with three divisions if they were willing to accept the losses. With the situation collapsing, the Americans now for the first time faced the possibility that their own intervention might be the only way to salvage the situation. Eisenhower immediately declared that he was bitterly opposed to any American involvement in the war on the ground, a line he was to continue, with some modification, through the Geneva conference. If U.S. forces entered the war, he said, "the Vietnamese would simply transfer their hatred of the French to us." The president on the other hand ordered complete satisfaction to all French requests for materiel where possible.[56]

Navarre, changing his earlier estimate, now thought if Dien Bien Phu were lost, it would affect the entire course of the war. Washington tried to give the stronghold less significance. It was only one battle in a larger war that could still be won. Whatever happened at Dien Bien Phu, the American military thought, "a defeat or abandonment of the struggle by France would diminish France's value as a factor in free world defense." Such an outcome could not be tolerated. In a rare moment of lucidity, Dulles disputed the military's analysis. Getting out of Indochina, he said, would actually increase French military strength in Europe, to the net benefit of NATO. But the secretary would not act on the basis of that insight, because "the U.S. must worry about its own interests, not those of France." It must employ "every feasible means to influence the French government and people against any conclusion of the struggle on terms inconsistent with basic U.S. objectives."[57]

U.S. policy in France now began to unravel quickly, in part because basic American objectives were inconsistent. Parallel with Washington's effort to bolster the French will to win in Indochina went a heavy-handed campaign to force the French into the EDC. But each of these policies depended upon a different majority in the French National Assembly. The Deputies who were favorable to EDC opposed the war; the most diehard colonialists opposed EDC. The contradiction became apparent during the Four-Power conference at Berlin in February 1954. By then the Navarre Plan was dead and the French had reverted again to a holding operation in hope of salva-

pp. 884–5; December 7, 8, 1953, pp. 901–12. DDE Library, AW File, NSC Series, Box 5, NSC 177, December 23, 1953.

[56] FRUS, 1952–4, XIII, 1, January 3, 1954, pp. 937–8; January 8, 1954, pp. 947–54. DDE Library, AW File, NSC Series, NSC 179, January 8, 1954.

[57] FRUS, 1952–4, XIII, 1, Indochina, January 12, 14, 15, 1954, pp. 954–69. DDE Library NSC 180, January 14, 1954.

tion through negotiations. The French hinted they might strike a deal with the Russians and reject EDC, which Moscow bitterly opposed, in exchange for a negotiated solution in Indochina.[58] No such bargain was struck, but Dulles could not prevent Bidault from placing the Indochina question on the Agenda of the Geneva Conference, scheduled to open in April. American intransigence on the Indochina question would put the partisans of EDC in Paris in a difficult position. If he resisted too strongly, Dulles feared, he would lose Indochina and EDC together.[59]

On March 14, 1954 the Vietminh attacked Dien Bien Phu, and by March 16 Heath was reporting that enemy fire had quickly rendered the air strips there unusable, creating the fear that the fortress would fall. Eisenhower was exasperated. He could not understand why the French had wanted or invited such an attack. Dulles replied that he had warned them Geneva would bring it on. Allen Dulles gave the French a 50–50 chance of surviving. The secretary immediately perceived that the crisis of American diplomacy and influence in France was at hand. "We are witnessing," he said, "the collapse or evaporation of France as a great power in most areas of the world." The question was, who would fill the void, the Communists, or the Americans? The United States, Dulles said, will have to "beat the French into line, or accept a split with France." Neither alternative now appeared very attractive. In desperation the Americans were to try the former, fail, and find themselves obliged to accept the latter.[60]

On March 21, 1954 General Ely arrived in Washington to sound out the Americans about assistance in case China came to the help of the Vietminh. In an initial conference with Admiral Radford on March 22, the latter apparently urged overt American assistance on General Ely in the form of air strikes, carrier based, but also by means of B-29s operating out of the Philippines. Despite what he was told later, Ely apparently went home believing that a French request for such air strikes would be honored in Washington.[61] More important, the French government believed it as well. Eisen-

[58] Jean Chauvel advocated offering Communist China admission to the United Nations and economic aid in exchange for a free hand for the West in Indochina; see MAE, Asie 1944–55, Dossiers Généraux, 262, Papiers Jean Chauvel, Note of April 8, 1954. Ironically, Washington suspected Mendès France of harboring such schemes, when it was Bidault who actually gave them serious consideration. See Denise Artaud, in Artaud and Kaplan, eds., *Dien Bien Phu*, pp. 379–403.
[59] FRUS, 1952–54, XIII, 1, Indochina, February 4, 5, 9, 1954. FRUS, 1952–4, V, 1, West European Security, EDC. February 23, 1954, 880.
[60] FRUS, 1952–4, XIII, 1, Indochina, March 14, 16, 18, 1954, pp. 1119–33. DDE Library, NSC 190, March 26, 1954.
[61] Admiral Radford denied that he made any such promise: see *From Pearl Harbor to Vietnam: The Memoirs of Admiral Arthur W. Radford*, ed. Stephen Jurika, Jr. (Stanford, CA: Hoover Institution Press, 1980), pp. 394–6. But General Ely wrote that President Eisenhower told Radford in Ely's presence to give satisfaction to any re-

hower had offered all possible help to the beleaguered garrison, Dulles made a very strong speech of support, and Radford assured General Valluy that the air support would be forthcoming.[62] Thus was born Operation *Vautour* (Vulture), which became the focal point of American discussions about possible intervention to save Dien Bien Phu.[63] Radford in fact argued in favor of air strikes with the support of Vice President Richard Nixon. But Dulles did make it clear to Ely that the French request was tantamount to direct American intervention in the war, which required the consent of Congress. Moreover, if the United States was to fight, as a Great Power it must be assured of success, which meant full partnership with the French in the conduct of the war. Ely was clearly unhappy at this prospect; did the Americans lack confidence in the French command? Dulles replied that the Americans had experience in these matters and could offer pertinent advice that the French should consider. To Radford two days later, Dulles was more blunt. Ely had requested more materiel, and Radford was sending them more B-26 bombers. But the French gave no assurances of improved performance or willingness to accept American training of the Vietnamese. Dulles noted that "France is creating a vacuum in the world wherever she is . . . we may have to think of cutting loose on our treaties with France . . . we must have a policy of our own even if France falls down. We could lose Europe, Asia, and Africa all at once if we don't watch out."[64]

In the following days Dulles consulted with Congress and the British in an effort to elaborate a policy governing possible American intervention in the Vietnam War. The consultations brought mostly negative results from the point of view of the French. Congress wanted the war internationalized, the United Nations brought in, and full independence granted to Vietnam. On April 2 the joint chiefs concluded that an American air strike in support of the French at Dien Bien Phu offered no likelihood of success. On April 3 Dulles suggested to Bonnet the creation of a broad coalition of anti-Communist powers in Asia. The answer was already clear, therefore, when

---

quest the French made. Ely interpreted this to include air strikes. Paul Ely (Général d'Armée), *Memoires: L'Indochine dans la tourmente* (Paris: Plon, 1964), p. 64.

[62] Mendès France commissioned an analysis of this question after taking power in June and came to the same conclusion. See Documents Pierre Mendès France (Institut Pierre Mendès France), Indochine, IV Dossier O,a,ii, "Négociations secrètes avec les américains . . ." April–May 1954, Note Complementaire sur l'Affaire de Dien Bien Phu.

[63] Melvin Gurtov, *The First Vietnam Crisis: Chinese Communist Strategy and United States Involvement, 1953–54* (New York: Columbia University Press, 1967), p. 80. Laniel wrote that Ely told him of the latter's clear impression that a French government request for air intervention at Dien Bien Phu would be honored in Washington. Joseph Laniel, *Le Drame Indochinois: De Dien-Bien-Phu au Pari de Genève* (Paris: Plon, 1957), pp. 83–4.

[64] FRUS, 1952–4, XIII, 1, Indochina, March 21, 22, 24, 1945, pp. 1137–51.

Dillon was called to the Hotel Matignon on April 4, with a French cabinet meeting in progress, and was asked by Bidault and Laniel for American carrier-based air strikes to save Dien Bien Phu.[65] Dillon forwarded the request to Washington, where it was refused.

The French were angered by Washington's response. They were in need of a short-term intervention to save Dien Bien Phu; instead Washington offered a diplomatic effort over the long term of uncertain outcome. Formation of such an alliance was likely to wreck the Geneva conference, moreover, which offered the only chance for a negotiated peace. Massive American air attacks at Dien Bien Phu would hardly have helped at Geneva either, but that was a risk Paris was prepared to take to save the garrison. For long-range solutions, the Quai said, the American timing was all wrong. The Dulles plan would require weeks or months to implement, while the fate of Dien Bien Phu was a question of days or hours. Dillon, at least, appeared to understand this: "He realizes the seriousness that would result from a crisis born of misunderstanding in this matter."[66]

But Eisenhower flatly ruled out any unilateral American military intervention: "We cannot intervene and become the colonial power which succeeded France." The NSC established the conditions under which the United States could join in the war; these were that Congress approve, a coalition of Asian and British Commonwealth nations participate, a political understanding be reached with the French that included full independence for Vietnam, and the French promise not to reduce their own commitment of forces. The NSC decided to begin negotiations with the British and other nations, and it approved the sending of additional planes and technicians to Vietnam to assist the French. But it was apparent that the Americans would not intervene to try to save Dien Bien Phu. Indeed, Eisenhower offered the opinion that even if Dien Bien Phu fell it did not necessarily mean defeat of the French, nor would the rest of Southeast Asia go Communist either. The domino theory also collapsed at Dien Bien Phu, although it was to be revived later.[67]

Bidault warned Dillon that Dien Bien Phu was a symbol; if it fell, the French would withdraw from Vietnam. Dulles thought the French were trying to blame their defeat on Washington in a manner "reminiscent of Reynaud's hysterical appeals in 1940." There were other reasons for American recrimination: after working hard to arrange an emergency airlift of two battalions from France to Indochina, the Pentagon learned the troops were not ready to leave because they were due to take furloughs first. The aircraft

[65] FRUS, 1952–4, XIII, 1, Indochina, April 1, 1954, p. 1206; April 2, 1954, p. 1224–5; April 3, 1954, p. 1226; April 4, 5, 1954, p. 1237. Gurtov, *First Vietnam Crisis*, pp. 94–9.

[66] A.N., Papiers Georges Bidault, 457 AP 52, "Conversations Franco–américaines," April 5, 7, 1954.

[67] DDE Library, NSC 192, April 6, 1954. Gurtov, *First Vietnam Crisis*, pp. 94–9.

carrier *Belleau Wood*, given to the French a year earlier, was carrying French
planes sold to India rather than operating in Indochina. The French asked
for B-29 aircraft, but they lacked both the pilots to fly them and the technicians to maintain them, and the heavy bombers were inappropriate for
use in Indochina. Whatever Washington provided, the French would ask for
more, so as to have the Americans to blame when the battle was lost. Eisenhower wondered why the French did not mount a relief column from Laos
to lift the siege of Dien Bien Phu – did Paris lack the will to win? Dulles met
Bidault on April 14, to hear the Frenchman reject the American terms. This
was not the moment for a Southeast Asia coalition, he declared, and Paris
could not accept that Vietnam be granted the right to withdraw from the
French Union. The Americans wanted to turn loose from their historic ties
with France "countries which have never played a civilizing role in the history of the world." Under such conditions the French public would cease to
support the war.[68]

On April 22, 1954 Navarre announced that Dien Bien Phu could only be
saved by air strikes within the next seventy-two hours. Bidault, shaken, renewed his requests for American intervention. If necessary, American planes
could fly with French markings to hide Washington's role. Dulles observed:
"France is collapsing under our eyes. . . . If Dien Bien Phu falls the government will be taken over by defeatists." But the American terms could not
be met in time to save Dien Bien Phu, nor could air strikes be effective there.
Dulles urged the French to hold on despite the loss of a battle, and show the
world France still "has the spirit of a great nation." Laniel told MacArthur
that, if Dien Bien Phu fell, France would settle at Geneva and the EDC
would be destroyed as well. MacArthur replied this would be "catastrophic"; France would become "a weak and defeated nation," and the
United States would have to rethink their entire political relationship. Undeterred, General Ely brought a new request for air strikes to Admiral Radford the next day. But it was all to no avail, the Americans would not intervene. Bonnet reported on April 25: "The chances of obtaining massive and
immediate intervention by American air power without agreement of
countries interested in the defense of Southeast Asia are non-existent." President Eisenhower so informed the ambassador personally, and Vice President Nixon confirmed that the president would not permit American troops
to be involved in another land war in Asia. Dulles appealed to the British to
join with Washington in building an Asian coalition, but the British would
not be involved in any action that might ruin the chances of peace at Geneva.[69]

[68]   FRUS, 1952–4, XIII, 1, April 8, 9, 1954, pp. 1292–8; April 13, 1954, pp. 1323–6;
       April 21, 1954, pp. 1328–34. A.N., 457 AP 52, Papiers Georges Bidault, "Conver-
       sations Franco–américaines," April 14, 1954.
[69]   FRUS, 1952–4, XIII, 1, Indochina, April 22, 23, 1954, pp. 1360–75. A.N., 457 AP
       52, I (2) "Situation Militaire," April 22, 23, 1954; "Conversations Franco-améri-

The NSC discussed the French request on April 29; the Americans were troubled that it came from Laniel, Bidault, and Pleven, not the French cabinet as a whole. They were asking on behalf of the select cabinet committee that was charged with the conduct of the war. Harold Stassen still favored intervention, supporting Radford and Dillon, but Eisenhower remained determined not to put American "boys" in a land war in Asia. General Cutler raised the possibility that "new weapons" be employed to save Dien Bien Phu. On April 7 a Pentagon study group had concluded that three tactical atomic bombs could save the garrison, but MacArthur quashed the idea, insisting that there would be a world outcry against the United States if nuclear weapons were used.[70] No help for Dien Bien Phu was forthcoming, with nuclear or conventional weapons. Dulles complained on May 6 that France was divided, drifting, its leaders "don't even dare to have a cabinet meeting." The American conditions for assistance remained unmet, and unless the French fulfilled them Washington could do nothing. The best Dulles could offer was that Paris use the empty threat of American intervention as a negotiating card at Geneva. But Chauvel noted that Moscow and Beijing already understood that the United States would not intervene; France must negotiate from a position of weakness.[71] Bidault later claimed that Dulles offered him the use of two nuclear bombs to save Dien Bien Phu. There is no mention of this conversation either in the American documents or in the Bidault papers, however, and Dulles later angrily denied that he had made any such offer.[72]

Dien Bien Phu fell on May 7, and it appeared that the French would now accept the best terms they could get at Geneva. There began a month of

caines," April 24, 25, 1954; 457 AP 54, II (1), "Position Anglaise," April 27, 1954; "Position Américaine," April 26, 29, 1954. For detailed analysis of the British position, see Geoffrey Warner, in Artaud and Kaplan, eds., *Dien Bien Phu*.

[70] FRUS, 1952–4, XIII, 2, Indochina, Duration of the Geneva Conference, April 29, 1954, pp. 1431–50; May 5, 1954, pp. 1466–70; May 6, 1954, pp. 1481–93. The earlier discussion of nuclear weapons appears in XIII, 1, Indochina, April 7, 1954, pp. 1270–2. Also see DDE Library, NSC 195, May 6, 1954.

[71] MAE, Asie 1944–55, Dossiers Généraux, 262, Papiers Jean Chauvel, Note of April 30, 1954.

[72] DDE Library, NSC 195, May 6, 1954. Edgar Faure, *Memoires* (Paris: Plon, 1982), I, *Avoir toujours raison . . . c'est un grand tort*, 554–5. Pierre Rouanet, *Mendès France au Pouvoir* (Paris: Robert Laffont, 1965), pp. 77–80. *Resistance: The Political Autobiography of Georges Bidault* (New York: Praeger, 1967), pp. 196–200. Herring and Immerman find implausible the idea that Dulles offered the bombs to Bidault (whom he regarded as unstable), as I do. Laurent Cesari and Jacques de Folin, however, note that the French actually studied the idea, only to conclude it would be of no use (in Artaud and Kaplan, eds., *Dien Bien Phu*, pp. 121, 150). Jean Chauvel also claimed he heard Dulles ask Bidault "Do you want two bombs?", an offer Bidault allegedly refused. Jean Chauvel, *Commentaire: III, De Berne à Paris (1952–62)*, (Paris: Fayard, 1973), p. 46.

Franco–American negotiations on the conditions of an American intervention in the event the Geneva conference failed. Washington expected and
desired the conference to fail; the French had to take the possibility seriously, and the threat of an Americanization of the war remained their only
negotiating point. Dulles laid down seven conditions for American intervention in the war: An official request must come from the French government
and the Associated States; a coalition of Asian nations must be created; the
United Nations must be involved; independence must be granted Vietnam
with an option to withdraw from the French Union; France must promise
not to reduce its own troop commitment in Vietnam; the Americans would
take over the training of Vietnamese forces; and the French National Assembly must ratify the French request.[73] In retrospect it does not appear
that these conditions could be met, or that Paris and Washington would
agree to fight the war in partnership. Bidault appeared to take the negotiations seriously, however, because he needed them at Geneva, and there was
some satisfaction in conducting talks with Washington from which London
now felt excluded – a pitiful recompense for years of rejection from the
Anglo-Saxon club. The French made an effort to fulfill the conditions, recognizing that the last, approval by the National Assembly, was unobtaina-
ble, the weak point in the plan that would inevitably bring the rest of the
edifice down. Bonnet suspected the United States was deliberately creating
conditions that could not be fulfilled in order to hide its own unwillingness
to commit ground forces to Indochina; hence the equally unacceptable demand that France not withdraw any troops of its own. If the war continued,
Paris suspected this provision meant it could expect air and naval support
only. Dillon got Washington to drop its insistence that Paris grant the Associated States the right to withdraw from the French Union. Under Secretary of State Walter Bedell Smith assured Bidault that restrictions against
the use of American ground forces would not apply to the marines, which
could be deployed in strength as part of any naval operations plan. But
Bonnet could get no confirmation of Bedell Smith's views in Washington,
where everyone seemed to think the marines would not be used; Asians
should defend Asia. When Bidault sought clarification, Dillon could only
assure him that "an appeal clearly made by France would be heard." This
was scant comfort in the aftermath of Dien Bien Phu. By then the Laniel
government had fallen. Bonnet reported that Washington was "contradictory and confused," and Bidault saw no purpose in continuing the negotiations; the Americans elicited promises and committed themselves to nothing. On June 18 Dulles confirmed officially for Bonnet what had been apparent
throughout the month: The Americans could not promise ground troops;

73 FRUS, 1952–4, XIII, 2, Prelude to Geneva, May 7, 1954, pp. 1498–1503; May 11,
    12, 1954, 1526–43.

"The Secretary of State and I both recognized that in consequence a large gap remained between the positions of Washington and of Paris."[74]

Dulles drew the conclusion that France's moral fiber was gone; the French wanted not American cooperation, but an end to the war. The prospect was for a new government of the left that would capitulate in Indochina and be hostile to the European Defense Community, the two poles of Washington's French policy. "A French collapse seemed to be in prospect," Dulles told the Security Council on May 13, 1954, "as grave as the collapse of 1940 with the distinct possibility of a French Government which would collaborate with the Soviets just as the French Government of the summer of 1940 collaborated with the Germans."[75] Remarkable as it may seem, Dulles never fully abandoned that view of the government of Pierre Mendès France, despite intermittent efforts to cooperate with and influence it. With the coming of Mendès France the tortured history of the extraordinary postwar American influence in France came to an end.

[74]   A.N., 457 AP 54, Papiers Georges Bidault, I, 3 (3), June 15, 16, 17, 18, 1954; II, 1, "Position Américaine," May 10, 12, 17, 27, June 7, 10, 1954. See also the "Report Brilhac," in DPMF, Indochine, IV, O,a,ii. Gary R. Hess, in Artaud and Kaplan, eds., *Dien Bien Phu,* pp. 193–233.
[75]   DDE Library, NSC 197, May 13, 1954.

9

France declares its independence

I THE EUROPEAN DEFENSE COMMUNITY

As It Stepped up Pressure on the French in Indochina, the United States increased its efforts to force the French to ratify the treaty establishing the European Defense Community. France was now the linchpin of American policy in Europe and Asia, and in both areas Washington's frustration grew in proportion to French inability or unwillingness to act. The governments of René Mayer and Joseph Laniel, which held power from January 1953 to June 1954, enjoyed American support and confidence, yet each refused to submit the EDC treaty for parliamentary ratification. Both had good reason. The conservative majority that governed France since the 1951 elections was divided over the treaty. If a majority in favor of ratification existed in the National Assembly, it would have to include the Socialists. Rather than seek the support of the left, Mayer and Laniel tried to obtain additional protocols to the treaty from France's five partners, and assurances from the United States and Britain, in an effort to make the EDC acceptable to conservative and Gaullist members of the coalition.

These efforts dragged on interminably through 1953 and 1954, as the Indochina war wound down to its inglorious end. In desperation the Americans multiplied their pressures to secure ratification before the Geneva conference, for lurking in the background was the increasingly powerful and threatening figure of Pierre Mendès France. The lengthy cabinet crisis following Mayer's fall in May–June 1953 was punctuated by a brilliant speech of Mendès France that established his candidacy for premier. It had long been clear that Mendès intended to negotiate a peace in Indochina. The Americans regarded him with a mixture of admiration and suspicion. His advocacy of financial policies of rigor had pleased the Americans in 1945, and his participation in the IMF won him respect as an economist. Through 1953 embassy analysts wrote about him with sympathy, and even his June

1953 speech, which won him 301 votes, only 13 short of the majority necessary to form a government, won him plaudits and praise. But it was also
clear that Laniel, who succeeded in forming a government after Mendès
failed, represented the last hope for Washington if its policies were to be
achieved. Without victory or a favorable settlement in Indochina, Mendès
France was certain to succeed the next time, and it appeared that he would
not only liquidate French participation in the war, but perhaps destroy the
EDC as well.

The defeat at Dien Bien Phu in May 1954, formation of the Mendès France
government in June, and the settlement that followed at Geneva, confirmed
Washington's worst fears. It was not only the conclusion of the war, but the
nature of Mendès France's modus operandi that displeased Washington.
From the outset he showed a disposition to act rapidly and decisively, a trait
that should have pleased the Americans had it not been for his failure to
consult them about his decisions. None of the intimacy that had characterized American–French relations since late in 1947 was in evidence under
Mendès France. His "brain trust" was styled after the American New Deal
but consisted of people whom Washington knew little and trusted less. The
Americans dissociated themselves from the Geneva settlement, recognizing
that events in Indochina and Paris had escaped their control. They then
watched with irritation as Mendès France sought still new protocols to the
EDC treaty in an effort to build a majority necessary to ratify it. The Americans believed that a majority in favor of EDC already existed, and they
objected to the new protocols, which went further than anything suggested
by Mayer or Laniel, in removing from the treaty its supranational aspects.
Consequently Washington supported a united front of France's partners in
opposition to Mendès's proposed changes, only to react in shock when he
brought the treaty to the National Assembly without engaging his government's confidence, thus consigning the treaty, in Molotov's phrase, to the
archives of history.

There followed the nadir of postwar Franco–American relations and the
virtual collapse of the postwar influence and power the Americans had enjoyed in French affairs. Convinced that Mendès was little better than, if not
actually, a tool of the Soviets and a neutralist, John Foster Dulles cut off
American aid to France and entertained the schemes of Mendès's internal
political opponents to topple his government. A confrontational style once
again governed Franco–American relations, reminiscent of the war years
and previewing the circumstances that prevailed following de Gaulle's return to power in 1958. But Washington saw it had more to lose than to
gain by trying to overthrow Mendès, and the British appeared to admire
him and supported his policies. As it became apparent that Mendès would
in fact negotiate terms for German rearmament, Washington put aside continuing frictions with him over Indochina, and entered talks at London and
Paris that fashioned a substitute for EDC. The Brussels pact was revived,

Germany and Italy admitted to it, and Germany rearmed under its auspices and admitted to NATO, while foreswearing both nuclear and chemical weapons. The new arrangements fulfilled two basic French objectives, the absence of which had caused France's opposition to EDC. Britain was now associated with European defense and the supranational clauses in the treaty were eliminated. France was not yet convinced of its vocation as a European, rather than an Asian and African, power. The Americans destroyed the last of French illusions in Asia, pushing the French aside in Indochina, by the end of 1954. For Paris to abandon its North African ambitions required seven more years of war.

The French had lost their initial enthusiasm at the time of the signing of the EDC treaty; a note by the Quai in May 1952 observed that the supranational provisions would work to the detriment of France. The Germans were better negotiators and enjoyed Washington's support; the final draft allowed the reconstitution of the Wehrmacht, the very contingency EDC had been devised to prevent. France was dominant in the coal and steel pool but would be subordinate to Germany in EDC. The perception of the treaty had changed, and even Ambassador Dunn understood that its origins in a French policy initiative were now "lost from sight." The psychological picture was of the United States forcing France to accept EDC, and thus German rearmament. Washington must emphasize, Dunn said, that it was a French project that "we are not paying them to complete." The alternatives to EDC were full restoration of German sovereignty, reconstitution of the Wehrmacht, and the reversion of the Americans to a peripheral strategy of defense behind the Pyrenees. Acheson told Dunn to "bring the French press to emphasize" that EDC would bring a lasting American presence in Europe, the goal of French policy ever since the end of World War I. Washington offered the French considerable inducements to sign: economic aid, support in Indochina and North Africa, and an increased role for France in NATO planning.[1]

The Republican administration that took office in January 1953 seemed to grow more enthusiastic for EDC in proportion to increasing French reluctance. Eisenhower told Bonnet that the EDC and European unity were "major objectives of primary importance for the success of allied policy." To be sure, the United States sought to persuade, not pressure, recognizing that France was the leader of Europe. But Bonnet warned the Quai of the dangers of disappointing the Americans; the "administration of businessmen who want results" was ready to go ahead on its own to rebuild the Wehrmacht. In the Quai, where enthusiasm for the treaty was never great,

---

[1] Archives Nationales (A.N.), Papiers René Mayer, 363 AP 28, May 27, 1952. FRUS, 1952–4, Vol. V, Part 1, Efforts to Secure Ratification of the European Defense Community, June 22, 1952, pp. 688–90; September 6, 1952, pp. 692–4.

Bonnet's warnings were taken with a grain of salt. Any unilateral action by the United States

> would create a very serious crisis in Franco–American relations, and correspondingly profound disarray in French opinion. Our American friends appear to have an extremely simplistic conception of the unity of Europe, inspired by the American precedent of 1787 and ignoring the seriousness of the problems faced by the European states, particularly France, a power having worldwide responsibilities.

The French Union and the construction of a Federal European state were mutually exclusive; EDC went beyond acceptable limits. France must retain its position in North Africa and Indochina.[2] France and the United States were on a collision course, yet Washington persisted in its pressure, and the French government continuously postponed the issue.

Dulles arrived in Paris on February 2, 1953 and conferred with Mayer and Bidault. Mayer told the secretary that the protocols were necessary in order to provide for French removal of troops from EDC if they were needed either internally or within the French Union. Moreover, Mayer insisted that new American assurances of troop support in Europe were necessary, Britain must define its relationship to EDC (which it refused to enter), and the Saar question must first be settled as well. Bidault said the French Union was "sacred and vital" to France, and provided the Americans with important bases in North Africa. In Libya, in contrast, "a few camel merchants" had been granted their independence, and they excluded the Americans. Dulles insisted that the United States did not favor the disintegration of the French Union and would not object to the new protocols. But France had struck the American imagination with EDC, Dulles warned, and American opinion would be grievously disappointed were the French now to abandon it. Harold Stassen, the new director of the Mutual Security Agency, was more blunt in economic talks with the French, warning: "The fate of the EDC treaty will strongly affect the availability of [American] aid."[3]

The protocols quickly became another excuse for French government procrastination. Dillon worked with Hervé Alphand to draft language acceptable to both governments, but Bidault used his own version anyway. Dillon could not protest without revealing his relationship with Alphand, unlike most at the Quai, a strong supporter of the treaty. Dulles appointed David Bruce, until the then Under Secretary of State, as the American "Observer" to the EDC Interim Committee, as well as Representative to the

---

[2] A.N., Papiers Georges Bidault, 457 AP 44 (1), CED, January 3, 1953. Papiers René Mayer, 363 AP 22, January 16, 1953; 363 AP 23, January 23, 26, 1953.

[3] A.N., Papiers René Mayer, 363 AP 22, Feburary 2, 1953; 363 AP 23, February 2, 1953, Conversations with John Foster Dulles. Also in Ministère des Affaires Etrangères (MAE), Asie 1944–55, Indochine, 261.

ECSC; Bruce's major task was to lobby for ratification. In a message to Anthony Eden, Dulles despaired of meeting the French requirements for ratification; there seemed no sense in even trying, for they would only "ask more and more." The best procedure would be to get the other nations to ratify first: "Forget the French for now, they will ratify under cumulative pressure later." On March 10, 1953 Dulles selected the Dutch to be first to ratify EDC (an honor, he complained, that nobody seemed to want). Eisenhower called in the Dutch ambassador and sent a message to Prime Minister Van Zeeland. Dulles tried his hand with the Italians, but they raised objections; Dulles told de Gasperi that unless Italy ratified, its "position of leadership and respect" in Europe would be lost. De Gasperi, however, was unmoved.[4] Nor were the French fooled: the Dutch would ratify first to look good, Paris thought, but only because they serenely expected France to kill the treaty. According to Jean Chauvel, Bidault never intended to rescuscitate the EDC "cadaver."[5]

Anticipating René Mayer's visit to Washington, Dulles was frustrated by the French situation. Mayer was sincere in desiring ratification, he thought, but Bidault was more complicated: "No one could know quite where he is." Strangely, Bidault was intransigent on the protocols for the sake of the Gaullists, yet they would oppose the treaty anyway. Bruce thought Bidault was really seeking support for the December presidential election; he was "crafty, unreliable, playing a deep game, a loner, who counsels with few." Dillon advised that René Mayer be pinned down in Washington on the French determination to ratify and the proposed timing.[6]

Bruce complained to René Mayer of opposition to EDC among officials in the Quai; Mayer promised he would take "drastic steps" to bring them into line. In the National Security Council Dulles sounded pessimistic: Mayer was "wholly dedicated to our objectives in Europe," but also the last American hope for EDC. If he failed, there would be no choice but to proceed with the unilateral restoration of German sovereignty. Richard Bissell and Tomlinson recommended a show of strength by Washington; the United States should slow the delivery of end-items, delay Offshore Procurement contracts, shift MAAG from a national to a European basis, block new loans, and slow defense support. "Once the French military understands that there may be no French continental forces unless there is an EDC, their attitude and the prospects of EDC ratification in France will improve con-

---

4   Foreign Relations of the United States (FRUS), 1952–4, V, 1, EDC, February 12, 13, 1953, pp. 721–37; February 18, 1953, pp. 734–7; March 10, 1953, pp. 761–3; March 12, 1953, pp. 766–9; March 19, 1953, p. 777.
5   Ministère des Affaires Etrangères MAE, Europe, Généralités, EDC, 27, Garnier (the Hague) to Bidault, January 27, 1953; Jean Chauvel, *Commentaire*, III, p. 29.
6   Foreign Relations of the United States (FRUS), 1952–4, V, 1, EDC, March 5, 6, 1953, pp. 748–55; March 12, 1953, pp. 766–9.

siderably. This is also the judgment of a number of sympathetic French officials."[7]

Dulles accepted this advice and resorted to the aid weapon. Eisenhower warned Mayer that the American people would not support aid to France if the French used "dilatory tactics" to postpone ratification; Dulles told Bidault the United States would make its aid to France conditional on the treaty's progress. But threats of economic pressure had no apparent effect on the French. The MSA European representative, Theodore Draper, warned that France would be the obstacle to EDC in Europe so long as it remained "burdened financially by the Indochina war, politically by an unworkable constitution, and psychologically by the fear of German revival."[8]

Fearing that the stick would not work, Washington resorted to the carrot. Despite all the threats the Americans put together an impressive aid package for the French for 1954. The Republicans were to prove much more generous than the Democrats, their generosity made easier by the devotion of virtually all the funds to the military. In practice it proved impossible to cut off funds in Indochina to make the French ratify EDC; given Washington's anticommunism, Paris held the upper hand.[9] The aid package of April 26, 1953 included a special $60 million grant to deal with the emergency Vietminh invasion of Laos, a $100 million loan from the Export-Import Bank, $100 million for heavy weapons, $460 million in direct budgetary assistance for Indochina, an unstated additional sum to be devoted to the building of national armies in Indochina, and all end-items and Offshore Procurement to be additional to these sums. The amount for the Indochinese national armies was to take the form of the lump sum $385 million the United States agreed to pay to finance the Navarre Plan in September 1953. In all it was over $1 billion in aid. If this largesse was meant to bolster Mayer or to assist him in securing EDC ratification, it fared no better than the earlier threats to withhold assistance. Mayer's government fell on May 21, 1953, without having attempted to ratify the treaty.[10]

The Americans had many reasons to regret Mayer's fall. The crisis dragged on interminably, punctuated by the disturbing effect of Mendès France's narrow defeat on June 3. The implications of that failure were frightening. If one added 99 Communist votes to Mendès France's total of 301 there were 400 deputies in the National Assembly ready to vote for French withdrawal from Indochina. Some of these votes, to be sure, were for sale: Paul

[7] FRUS, 1952,–4, VI, 2, France, March 24, 25, 2953), pp. 1319–25.
[8] FRUS, 1952–4, VI, 2, France, March 26, 1953, p. 1329; April 26, 27, 1953, pp. 1352–6.
[9] See the essay by Denise Artaud, in Artaud and Lawrence Kaplan, eds., *Dien Bien Phu: L'Alliance atlantique et la défense du Sud-Est asiatique* (Lyon: Editions de la Manufacture, 1989), pp. 379–400.
[10] FRUS, 1952–4, V, 1, EDC, March 26, 1953, pp. 781–4; VI, 2, France, March 26, 28, 1953, pp. 1329–40; April 26, 1953, pp. 1352–5.

Antier, head of a small group of nine deputies representing the peasantry, offered to oppose Mendès and switch to support of EDC if the Americans would give him a subsidy to keep his newspaper going. The embassy rejected this "brazen blackmail," recognizing in Antier a "venal and corrupt" politician. But Mendès France, embassy analysts noted, was drawing wide support; nobody seemed to doubt his integrity, and he was admired for his "courage, consistency, honesty, and intelligence." His economic program was tough and potentially unpopular, but he captured the imagination of his audience with his eloquence and logic. He was least responsible in his Indochina policy, where he had nothing to offer except withdrawal. But he had demonstrated that a left-center majority was possible.[11] The cabinet crisis had shaken the Assembly. Underlying it was increased sensitivity in France about its relationship with the United States, a desire to be free of dependence on American aid even at the cost of considerable sacrifice. American leadership was in question.[12]

Moreover, American prestige in France, Dillon complained, was at a new low. The execution of Julius and Ethel Rosenberg as atomic spies led to massive demonstrations in which representatives from all parts of the political spectrum participated. Foreseeing the damage, Dillon pleaded for a commutation of the sentence in the name of the "higher national interest," but his request went unheeded in Washington. The Richards Amendment emerged from Congress despite Dulles's opposition. It earmarked one half of future American military aid to Europe for the EDC, as an inducement in favor of ratification. Dillon reported that French confidence in American leadership was in decline because of the divergence of voices in the administration, McCarthyism, the conservative rhetoric in Washington that appeared to shed doubt on American commitment to peaceful coexistence, the lack of consultation with France on East–West relations, and increased French assertiveness.

French public opinion was confused and ill-informed about EDC, and probably more concerned about economic issues. Polls showed as many as 64 percent favored the unity of Europe, but 57 percent thought the existence of German troops would threaten French security.[13] And neutralist sentiment was growing. In *Le Monde,* Robert Borel and Jean-Jacques Servan-Schreiber challenged American influence. Borel complained that American pressure prevented French peace initiatives to the USSR, or recognition of China. Ratification of EDC was promised to Washington when it lacked

[11] National Archives and Records Administration (NARA), 751.00/6-353, June 3, 1953; 751.00/6-553, June 5, 1953; 751.00/6-1753, June 17, 1953; 751.00/7-953, July 9, 1953.

[12] NARA, 751.00/6-2553, June 25, 1953.

[13] Jean-Pierre Rioux, "L'Opinion publique française et la Communauté européene de Défense: querelle partisan ou bataille de la mémoire?," *Relations Internationales,* 37 (Spring 1984): 37–53.

support in the National Assembly, while Paris pursued Offshore Procurement contracts instead of pressing Washington to lower its tariffs. Servan-Schreiber charged that France blocked Indochina negotiations for the sake of its aid: "We continue this war in Asia in order to justify to the Americans their subsidy to our standard of living."[14]

The formation of the Laniel government gave the Americans scant comfort, in view of the narrow escape from Mendès France. Bidault remained as foreign minister, and Laniel was less accommodating on EDC than Mayer had been. In July a meeting of the foreign ministers of the Big Three took place in Washington. Dulles and Eden increased pressure on Bidault to ratify the EDC treaty, which dominated the conference. Dulles tried every argument, from the prosaic to the apocalyptic. Congress would link all future European aid requests to EDC, he warned; the authority of the Eisenhower administration was at stake, and failure would "sound the tocsin of our civilization." Dulles demanded a date of ratification, but Bidault refused. Why was EDC the main subject of a conference in which two of the three participants were not even parties to the treaty? France alone was to take part in EDC; it must not appear to be doing the bidding of its Anglo-Saxon partners. In May Churchill had proposed a summit meeting with Moscow on the German question. Ratification of EDC would have to wait until a conference of the Big Four powers was concluded, Bidault said. Only when Russian intransigence had clearly been demonstrated to the French people would a conducive climate exist for ratification. Dulles disagreed: EDC should first be ratified so that the West could negotiate from a position of strength. But Dulles agreed to the summit, scheduled for Berlin in January 1954, and thus handed Bidault a victory and an excuse to postpone ratification, barely compensated for by Bidault's agreement to a communiqué in favor of EDC. In Paris, Maurice Schumann congratulated Bidault on behalf of Laniel and the government: "The pressure exercised upon you the 10 and 11 July 1953, recalls the famous meeting of 12 September 1950 in New York of the Atlantic Council, during which the voice of France was alone raised against the immediate restoration of an autonomous German military force."[15] By delaying EDC, France was still fighting the battle against German rearmament.

Laniel's government was the less likely to ratify as its position became unstable. In August it confronted a wave of strikes in the public sector, animated by the reformist Force Ouvrière, whose constituency favored EDC. The embassy did not pressure Laniel to make concessions, but demanded

[14] *Le Monde*, March 29–30, May 20, June 17, 1953. FRUS, 1952–4, VI, 2, France, August 4, 1953, pp. 1372–5.

[15] A.N., Papiers Georges Bidault, 457 AP 46 (1), "Conférence de Washington du 10 juillet, 1953," Schumann to Bidault, July 12, 1953; Bonnet to Paris July 10, 11, 12, 1953; Compte Rendus des entretiens des trois ministres des affaires étrangères, Washington, 10–14, 1953.

assurances that force would not be used against the workers. Dillon was promised that trade union rights would be respected. Reassured, the Americans cast about for ways of bolstering Laniel. Laniel was authorized to say the United States would pay for the Navarre Plan, and additional aid for Indochina was rushed through by September. Dillon sounded out the major party leaders in an effort to gauge the government's chances of survival. Reynaud and Mollet among others convinced him that Laniel was stable and the opposition quiescent. No evidence of a Popular Front was yet apparent. But labor dissatisfaction was real, Dillon warned, and the trend to the left demonstrated by Mendès France would continue unless the situation in Indochina were reversed. Laniel was the "last chance" for France to stay in Indochina.[16]

If Laniel failed, the alternative was clearly Mendès France. What would a Mendès government really do? Ridgeway Knight's analysis of September 3, 1953 showed there was perfect clarity about *Mendèsisme* in the State Department that was to be ignored by Dulles when he faced the reality of a Mendès France government later. Knight said that Mendès would regard Indochina as a free-world problem, not a specifically French one, and negotiate French withdrawal unless France received greater solidarity from its allies. But internally he was a "conservative with a progressive heart," whose economic policies of rigor were more likely to anger than to please everybody, and he was deeply anti-Communist and anti-Soviet. Mendès regarded the Soviet military threat as exaggerated and wanted to cut military spending, and he would try to establish a European "counterweight" to American policy. But he was not viscerally anti-German and might ratify EDC. In a meeting with Knight Mendès said he resented the distortion of his views in Washington. He was not seeking an end to the war at any price, and recognized that the United States was much too important to France for him to allow personality differences to matter in the making of policy.[17]

It soon became apparent that no action could be got out of the French until after the presidential election in December. Frustrated, on October 5, 1953 Dulles ordered "all out" pressure for ratification. Press them, "pin them down," and accept no more nonsense about new protocols, Dulles ordered. Washington now meant business.[18] On October 18 Dulles told Bidault that nothing less than the future of European and Western civilization were at stake, France must ratify EDC. The secretary complained again bitterly about opposition to the treaty among officials in the Quai, about

[16] NARA, 751.00/8-1453, August 14, 1953; 751.00/8-2053, August 20, 1953; 751.00/8-2253, August 22, 1953.

[17] NARA, 751.00/9-353, September 3, 1953, Ridgeway Knight, "Main Characteristics of a Mendès France Government"; 751.00/9-1153, September 11, 1953.

[18] FRUS, 1952-4, V, 1, EDC, September 8, 1953, pp. 800–2; September 17, 1953, pp. 807–8; October 5, 1953, pp. 815–9; NARA, 751.00/9-2853, September 28, 1953; 751.00/10-953, 751.00/10-1053, October 9, 10, 1953.

whom, despite promises, Mayer had done nothing. Bidault admitted the problem but was evasive about what he would do. On October 23 Dillon and Douglas MacArthur III saw Laniel. Failure to ratify, the premier was told, would lead to a "reexamination of our European policy." Such threats were to escalate in the coming months. Laniel promised to try right after the presidential election. On November 8 Dulles instructed Dillon to tell Laniel that Washington's patience was running out. France's future role as a great power depended upon rapid ratification of EDC.[19]

Dulles's famous statement of December 14, 1953, in the midst of the French presidential election, was designed to administer the necessary shock to the French to bring them to their senses. "It was essential to give French public opinion a jolt," Dulles told Eden, and put an end to the absurd comedy at Versailles, where repeated ballots failed to elect a successor to Vincent Auriol. Indeed, Dillon counseled that perhaps it was time to bring down Laniel and permit the emergence of a new majority favorable to EDC. While visiting Paris, Dulles announced that if the ancient enmity between France and Germany were not ended and EDC not ratified, Washington would be forced to undertake an "agonizing reappraisal" of its European policy. The implicit threat in these words was that Washington would revert to a peripheral strategy and abandon hope of defending Western Europe in case of a Soviet attack.[20]

There was in reality little substance to Dulles's blustering, however. The French understood that it was not in the American interest to leave Western Europe to its own devices.[21] The State Department could devise no meaningful alternatives to EDC; if it failed Washington would still be forced to negotiate with France before it rearmed Germany. The French knew this. Dulles's statement caused bitter reaction in Paris, charges of blatant American interference in French affairs, and much speculation about the content of what the French translated as "une révision déchirante" of American policy. But the statement affected nothing. It did not "puncture the wishful thinking that the United States would support a nationalist France," as Dillon thought, nor did it provide the "shock treatment" necessary to deal with French paralysis and procrastination. All continued in Paris as before.[22]

Dulles reappraised, but changed nothing. On February 16, 1954 he wrote Eisenhower from the Four-Power Conference in Berlin that American policy

[19] FRUS, 1952–4, V, 1, EDC, October 18, 1953, pp. 826–8; October 23, 1953, p. 829; November 8, 1953, pp. 838–9.

[20] Edward Fursdon, *The European Defense Community: A History* (New York: St. Martin's Press, 1980), p. 232. FRUS, 1952–4, V, 1, EDC, December 10, 1953, pp. 863–5; December 15, 1953, pp. 868–70.

[21] Bonnet, however, reported that EDC failure would bring either German entry into NATO, bilateral rearmament of Germany, or a peripheral strategy, and Jean Daridan feared "incalculable damage to French–U.S. relations." MAE, Europe, Généralités, CED, 27, March 29, 1954, Daridan to Bidault; 28, April 8, 1954, Bonnet to Bidault.

[22] NARA, 751.00/12-1953, December 19, 1953. *Le Monde*, December 16, 17, 1953.

remained to support French leadership on the continent and a tripartite role for France with the United States and United Kingdom in world affairs. "But if in the next several months France rejects EDC it will be impossible for the U.S. to maintain the fiction that France is capable of the role of leadership in European and world affairs and will have demonstrated its incapacity for such leadership."[23] In Berlin Dulles and Bidault had further talks about EDC. The French prerequisites for ratification were still some form of British association with the Defense Community, an American commitment to keep its troops in Europe, settlement of the Saar, and a mechanism in the European Political Community to provide for democratic control of the European army.[24]

Dulles did not think these conditions too onerous to meet. He agreed to look into making a stronger U.S. commitment to European defense, and he was willing to pressure Adenauer on the Saar. But Paris was on warning: The alternatives were EDC or the end of France as a great power. The French insisted at Berlin that the Indochina war be discussed at the forthcoming Geneva conference. Dulles reluctantly gave American assent, but warned Bidault that Geneva must not be used as a reason not to proceed with EDC or "the results would be grave from the standpoint of Franco–American relations." On March 2, 1954, however, Bruce noted that Laniel and Bidault were still trying to avoid a parliamentary debate. It was again time for "maximum desirable pressure" to be put on the French. MacArthur went to see Laniel in the company of Paul Reynaud, while Dillon made a personal appeal to Bidault. The Americans pressed Laniel to accept the principle of direct election of the European parliament. "He is throwing away 80 Socialist votes for 40 doubtful [Gaullist] ones," Bruce complained. Laniel's was an "irresolute government which prefers to procrastinate hoping like Mr. Micawber an outside power will save it from its own irresponsibility."[25]

On March 5 Dulles approached the National Security Council to request further assurances to the French about keeping American troops in Europe. The meeting turned into another opportunity for the expression of American anger at Paris. Eisenhower wanted to know: "Must we go on forever coddling the French?" Bedell Smith saw nothing new in the desired assurances; the United States had often pledged to keep its troops in Europe. But the others were more irritated at the continued French-created obstacles to conclusion of the treaty, which never seemed at an end. Under Secretary of Defense Roger Kyes complained: "We have reached the point of being mere

23   Eisenhower Library, Dulles–Herter Series, February 16, 1954.
24   MAE, Europe, Généralités, CED, 27, January 15, 1954, Note: "German rearmament must be balanced by the assurance of an Anglo-Saxon counterweight on the continent."
25   FRUS, 1952–4, V, 1, EDC, February 17, 1954, pp. 875–7; February 23, 1954, pp. 879–80; February 27, 1954, pp. 880–2; March 2, 1954, pp. 883–4.

whipping boys for the French." The United States should tell them to ratify or "we will pull out." Secretary of Defense Wilson was "sick and tired of the U.S. pulling French chestnuts out of the fire." Eisenhower showed some restraint, however: "Don't try that on the French," he said, "they say they held the fort [in 1939] while the U.S. decided whether to save its own skin." With that the NSC agreed to provide Paris with the necessary assurances.[26]

In exchange for the assurances Dulles extracted a promise from Bidault that the EDC debate in the National Assembly would take place in April. But word of the deal leaked in the American press, to Bidault's embarrassment. "I pray God," he told Dulles, "that a calendar of American origins, unofficially proposed for our labors, and whose existence is known to several people, will not be brought to the attention of the public." Bidault used the leak as an excuse to postpone the target date for the debate until May. It was now the turn of Dulles to be upset; the new date for the EDC debate coincided with the Geneva conference. Bruce was furious.[27] He recommended the most severe punitive measures against the French: A united front should be formed between the United States and the United Kingdom, including talks between Dulles and Eden "leaving the French out." Unilateral action should be taken to restore German sovereignty, there should be a slowdown in Offshore Procurement, American "stickiness" in Geneva, and further pressure on the French with regard to the Saar. "We have tried reason, persuasion, generosity, understanding, sympathy, patience: all have failed and I see no alternative but to deal with the French as cold-bloodedly as they deal with us." Dillon predicted a majority of 350 votes in the Assembly in favor of EDC, but to get it Laniel would have to fall and the Socialists enter the government. If necessary, EDC might have to be achieved through a cabinet crisis.[28]

On April 2, 1954 Bidault promised the Americans that a date would be fixed for the ratification debate on April 15, but it could take place only after the May Congress of the Socialist party. On April 12 the British announced their intent to establish a relationship with EDC, and on April 16 the Americans gave their assurances on maintaining their troops in Europe. The French meanwhile scheduled the Assembly debate for May 18, 1954. But Laniel told MacArthur that in the interim the government might fall, and if Mendès France came to power he would kill Indochina and EDC both. The premier was trying for Gaullist support to get his majority for the treaty; MacArthur told him not to bother, the Socialists were a better bet.

[26] Eisenhower Library, NSC Series, NSC 187, March 5, 1953.
[27] MAE, Europe 1949–55, Généralités, CED, 27, March 4, 1953, Bonnet to Bidault; March 23, Rivière (Brussels) to Bidault, on the leak of the supposed "calendar" for ratification.
[28] FRUS, 1952–4, V, 1, EDC, March 6, 7, 1954, pp. 892–6; March 20, 22, 1954, pp. 900–10.

MacArthur again warned Laniel of "grave consequences" if there were any further postponement of EDC, and complained that France lacked the capacity to act and take the necessary courageous decisions. The American diplomat resorted to a fable to make his point. The NATO countries were like mountain climbers bound together by a rope, the French having become frozen with fear on a ledge, unable to continue and thus holding the others back. The others would have no choice, if persuasion failed, but to cut the rope and leave the French behind. For his part, MacArthur said he was sad to see Laniel, whom he knew to be a good friend of the United States, ruin French–American relations, and make of France another Belgium.[29]

On February 22 Bidault had informed Dulles that the situation of Dien Bien Phu was hopeless. The fate of EDC immediately became bound up with the Indochina fortress and the French request for American air strikes to save it. Laniel told MacArthur that EDC could not be ratified if Dien Bien Phu fell. The premier's support was eroding in the cabinet, several members of which had rallied to Mendès France. MacArthur said that if EDC were not ratified, the Americans would put the contractual agreements with Germany into effect and adjust their entire European strategy accordingly. There would be no air strikes to save Dien Bien Phu, but MacArthur could not understand how French greatness could be made to depend on a small Indochina outpost. Dillon, for his part, was disgusted. Nothing in French government behavior in the past two years, he said, "should lead even the most trusting of friendly nations to believe its protestations." Even after setting the date for the Assembly debate, the French government had not said whether it would support EDC. "With Anglo-Saxon generosity and credulity we have more ardently espoused the cause of European integration than its originators, the French." There was perhaps a lesson there, but Dulles failed to see it. Dien Bien Phu fell on May 7, and May 18 came and went with no Assembly debate. Dulles ordered American pressure on the French continued. But Dillon observed it was now of no use, Dien Bien Phu had bound EDC up with Geneva, and only American–French united action there might save it. If Laniel fell, a new government would sign an Indochina peace and end EDC. There was to be no united action at Geneva, and on June 12, 1954 Laniel resigned. Indochina, EDC, and American policy in Europe became dependent upon Pierre Mendès France.

II   THE UNITED STATES AND
PIERRE MENDÈS FRANCE

French press reports of initial reaction in Washington to the government of Pierre Mendès France were favorable; the new premier had refused to count

---

[29]   FRUS, 1952–4, V, 1, EDC, April 2, 1954, pp. 924–6; April 13, 14, 1954, pp. 930–8.

Communist votes in his majority and was believed to be ready to accept German rearmament. Moreover, "Washington will be glad to meet a French politician who does not come here in order to beg for dollars." But the Americans had watched Mendès France with foreboding for too long to rally to him now. Jean-Jacques Servan-Schreiber called at the Embassy early in May; he told Dillon then that Mendès would not count Communist votes in his favor, was friendly to the United States, and was not a neutralist. Other associates of Mendès also sought to reassure the embassy: These included François Mitterrand, Robert Schuman, and Jacques Soustelle. But Dillon remained distrustful. Mitterrand, he reported on May 11, had made a "totally illogical and purely destructive" speech in the National Assembly asking for an immediate Indochina debate, and Mendès France attacked Bidault in a manner that was "unusually low," accusing him of wanting to continue the war in Indochina. Mitterrand followed up again just before Laniel's fall, making "as usual a wholly negative" attack in a manner "worthy of the best traditions of the Comédie Française."[30]

Washington understood that the new government intended to end the war even at the cost of major concessions. This was unacceptable; American policy had been to keep France in the war and to internationalize it, but with conditions. The United States would intervene if France recognized full independence for Vietnam including the right of withdrawal from the French Union, and accepted a role for the United Nations. But the American offer became less firm as the Geneva conference dragged on and the local situation in Vietnam deteriorated. On June 1, 1954 Eisenhower flatly ruled out any American participation in the war except in the event of a true internationalization as had been the case in Korea. Pleven charged that the Americans had let the French down. Eisenhower was incensed; the French refused American help except on their own terms. They played a double game, refusing to meet American conditions while they trumpeted an alleged American commitment to intervene – in effect, blackmail. Paris was careening in all directions in a frantic effort to place responsibility for its defeat on the United States. But there was duplicity on the American side as well. The chances for American intervention were nil, even if Paris met the stated conditions; the joint chiefs would commit no ground forces, and Australia and New Zealand were unlikely to join. Dillon thought the French should be told of this so they could accept the best terms possible at Geneva and save their expeditionary corps in the North from disaster. If the French were further defeated in the Delta while the Americans stood by, Dillon warned, the result would be the end of NATO.[31]

[30] *Le Monde*, June 19, 1954. NARA, 751.00/5-1154, May 11, 1954; 751.00/6-954, June 9, 1954; 751.00/6-1354, June 13, 1954.

[31] NARA, 751.00/6-1454, June 14, 1954. FRUS, 1952–4, XIII 2, Indochina, May 30, 1954, pp. 1636–9; June 10, 1954, pp. 1675–9; June 14, 1954, pp. 1687–9.

Bidault warned Dulles that, in the absence of an American commitment to intervene, France could not continue to fight. Dulles replied that Laniel had never given a promise of French intent to stay on if the Americans entered the war. Bonnet protested; there had been agreement on the conditions of American intervention, he said, but the United States had backed off. Dulles was angered. When there was a French government with adequate backing in its own country to fight, he said, the United States would sit down with it and give a reply. The secretary added that he had predicted the current disaster in February, in Berlin, when the French had insisted on putting Indochina on the agenda at Geneva.[32]

Washington grasped at straws in the hope of forestalling Mendès and getting a government with which it could deal. Dulles instructed Dillon to seek a dissolution of the Assembly and new elections; he should make no statement, but try to convince the anti-Communist parties to go along. Dillon approached Laniel, who agreed to try, but the Radicals in the coalition would not agree. Laniel said he had been defeated on EDC, not Indochina, in any case, and he bitterly attacked the Mendès group: Soustelle and Palewski, although Gaullists, were really Soviet fellow-travelers, and Mitterrand was a "concealed supporter of the Soviet line." Servan-Schreiber's *L'Express* had Communist connections and Mendès himself was "brilliant, logical, but entirely untrustworthy." Dillon clearly did not believe all of this. But he did think that Mendès was "maneuvering for votes on both sides of key issues by equivocal statements capable of ambiguous interpretations." Dillon hoped Mendès's "reputation of flexibility and opportunism would prove his undoing."[33] The only cause for optimism lay in the government's weakness. Although a clear majority of the deputies were with Mendès, the party leaders were still opposed to him. Guy Mollet told Dillon the Socialists would not participate in the cabinet and it would fall rather quickly in July, as soon as Mendès's attempt to compromise on EDC failed.

Other Americans had better appreciation of Mendès France. Martin Herz noted the youth and dynamism of the new cabinet, which represented a "revolt of the backbenchers." Mendès had made a hazardous gamble and his majority was unstable, but he had achieved a personal victory "rare in the annals of parliamentary history." He was symptomatic of something deeper in French politics, a lasting change from the tradition of postwar French leaders to a group or generation that was more independent and nationalistic, with which the United States would do well to come to terms. France was now likely to seek its own path, independent of American influence. Success in Indochina would make Mendès "the Pinay of 1954." Herz, too, thought that the opposition of the entrenched party leaders would

---

[32] FRUS, 1952–4, XIII, 2, Indochina, June 16, 1954, pp. 1710–3.
[33] NARA, 751.00/6-1554, June 15, 1954, 751.00/6-1654, June 16, 1954.

eventually destroy Mendès, but his effect on France was likely to be last-ing.[34]

The expectation of Mendès's fall reinforced Washington's willingness to distance itself from the Indochina settlement. It soon became apparent that Mendès was insufficiently anti-Communist as well. The State Department's antisubversion expert, Raymond Murphy, reported that the replacement of Jean Baylot as prefect of police indicated the new government was, as feared, "soft on Communism." Baylot had understood Communist intrigue, purged the police, arrested "Duclot" (sic), and arrested worker-priests and exposed them to the Vatican. "The U.S. has lost a real friend in Baylot who is being given as a sop some kind of appointment in the Saar."[35] Washington's sus-picions were confirmed the day after Mendès's investiture, when the new premier told Bedell Smith that he intended to invite the Chinese foreign minister, Chou En-lai, to Paris. Smith warned Mendès against any de facto recognition by France of Communist China, and insisted Washington be informed of any development at Geneva from which it might have to dis-sociate itself, such as a negotiated peace on unacceptable terms. Washington must be forewarned so it could react "gradually," cushioning any "shock" that might result to Franco–American relations. Mendès asked that the Americans use their influence with the new pro-American premier of Viet-nam, Ngo Dinh Diem, to get him to accept a negotiated solution. Smith said he could not promise to force Diem to accept what the Americans them-selves rejected. What Smith did not tell Mendès was that the displacement of French influence by the Americans in South Vietnam, in the event of a partition, had become the new design of Dulles's policy. Full American sup-port of a South Vietnamese government, Dulles wrote Eisenhower on July 1, would "radically alter the situation" in Indochina. The French would have no choice but to accept, and the Communists would desist from chal-lenging the new arrangements if they were confronted with American will-ingness to fight.[36]

On June 23, 1954 Bedell Smith told Eisenhower that Ho Chi Minh would get the support of 80 percent of the Vietnamese people in any free election. American policy in Geneva and Vietnam became to postpone or avoid free elections. On the same day Dulles observed that France, for the first time, had a government fully responsive to the wishes of its people. The State Department noted that consequently French policy was sliding out of con-trol toward an unacceptable peace. Washington was unable to live with the result of democratic choices either in Vietnam or France. The State Depart-

[34] NARA 751.00/6-1854, June 18, 1954, 751.00/6-2354, June 23, 1954.
[35] NARA 751.00/6-2854, June 28, 1954; 751.00/7-1054, July 10, 1954; 751.00/7-1954, July 19, 1954.
[36] FRUS, 1952–4, XIII, 2, Indochina, June 20, 1954, pp. 1725–7; Dulles to Eisen-hower, n.d., p. 1774. On the American displacement of France, see Pierre Melandri, in Artaud and Kaplan, eds., *Dien Bien Phu*, pp. 303–22.

ment and joint chiefs recommended the interruption of the $785 million in war-related American aid to France if necessary to block a settlement in Indochina. On June 28 a French aide-memoire informed London and Washington of the likelihood of a partition of Vietnam being worked out as part of the Geneva settlement. Washington could be helpful, Paris said, if it would publicly endorse such a settlement, warn the Communists against the consequences of a failure at Geneva, and counsel "wisdom and self-control" on the Vietnamese.[37]

This was not what Washington wanted to hear; its reply was intended instead to "stiffen the French position." Washington demanded that seven points be fulfilled before it would "respect," but not endorse, an Indochina agreement. These included the integrity of South Vietnam, Laos, and Cambodia, their full sovereignty without any conditions that might risk their subsequent loss to the Communists (i.e., elections), allowance for the possible reunification of Vietnam in the future, and the supervised transfer of population. The United States recognized it would have no choice but to support any Indochina settlement against violation by the Communists, but Paris would not be told of this so long as the provisions of the agreement were unknown: "we must not throw away our last negotiating lever with precipitate agreement to the French request." Washington was powerless to prevent a settlement because the president had ruled out military intervention and the British were supporting the French position.[38]

Mendès France met with his advisors on June 24 to consider the American position. Chauvel thought France should go ahead and negotiate partition of Vietnam – the Americans were unreliable, he said, and were guided only by an ill-defined anti-Communist crusade. Mendès agreed France must act quickly, while the American "uncertainty can leave us a greater freedom to maneuver." But as Bidault had done, Mendès wanted to use the threat of American intervention to extract concessions from the Vietminh. It was fear of a wider war that had brought them to the conference table in the first place, he believed, and the American threat "is the more useful to the extent that it remains latent." Mendès instructed Bonnet to tell the Americans he intended to save Indochina from communism. But Dulles must be made to understand that his presence in Geneva was necessary in order to demonstrate Western unity, or the world would perceive the crisis in Franco–American relations the American Secretary said he was trying to avoid. To Chou En-lai, in Geneva, Mendès counseled restraint on the Vietminh. A demarcation line farther to the north, accepted by the Americans, would be worth more in the long run than one farther south, that was unrecognized

---

[37] FRUS, 1952–4, XIII, 2, Indochina, June 24, 25, 1954, pp. 1741–8; June 28, 1954, pp. 1755–7

[38] FRUS, 1952–4, XIII, 2, Indochina, June 28, 1954, p. 1757; June 30, 1954, p. 1767.

by Washington. The Vietminh offered to accept the sixteenth parallel as the provisional boundary on July 13; Mendès told Dulles that it was fear of the latter's arrival in Geneva that had made them do so.[39]

Dulles was angered; he had little information about the negotiations, nor was Washington consulted any longer about French military plans. Paris was warned that the United States would not accept any arrangement short of the seven conditions, and there was a serious danger of rupture in Franco–American relations if the final settlement contained provisions that jeopardized the freedom of the South. An article in the *New York Herald Tribune* by Walter Kerr made known the State Department's feeling that the Mendès France government dealt less openly and frankly with the United States than had its predecessors. Mendès was now upset in turn. He wanted to avoid any such implication, he told Dillon, despite the inevitable disagreements among friends. Dillon said "the Department felt we were not fully notified in advance of French decisions." Naturally it had no right to ask, but would welcome being informed anyway. Mendès noted Washington had been told in advance of his meeting with Chou En-lai.[40]

On July 6 Mendès requested clarification of the American attitude with regard to elections, and what Washington meant when it said it would "respect" the settlement. He also requested the presence of either Secretary Dulles or Under Secretary Bedell Smith in Geneva for the final phase of the negotiations. As a measure of his unwillingness to accept peace at any price, Mendès said, if the negotiations failed he would ask the mobilization of draftees to fight in Vietnam as his last act before resigning. But the Americans must pressure Diem into accepting a settlement. Dulles said he wanted elections delayed as long as possible; "respect" meant the United States would not oppose the agreement by force. Dulles complained of a "lack of intimacy" with the new French government, which he attributed to the fact that the Americans had not worked closely with its "personalities" in the past. Dulles again insisted he wanted to avoid any spectacular dissociation from France that might be harmful to the interests of both countries. A high-level American presence in Geneva in case of an unacceptable agreement risked causing "irreparable harm" to Franco–American relations.[41]

Paris intensified its pressure. Mendès promised he would accept no terms that did not meet the American seven points, and he promised to keep Washington better informed. An American presence at Geneva was "absolutely essential and necessary" to make the Communists believe a united

[39] Pierre Mendès France, *Oeuvres Complètes, 3, Gouverner, c'est choisir, 1954–55* (Paris: Gallimard, 1986), pp. 83, 110, 118, 120. Also Documents Pierre Mendès France (DPMF), Carton V, Dossier O c, Conférence de Genève, Mendès France to Bonnet, July 9, 1954; O c, iii, Genève, Mendès France to Dulles, July 14, 1954.
[40] FRUS, 1952–54, XIII, 2, Indochina, July 3, 4, 1954, pp. 1780–5; VI, 2, France, July 6, 1954, pp. 1428–9.
[41] FRUS, 1952–4, XIII, 2, Indochina, July 6, 7, 8, 1954, pp. 1785–96.

front existed among the Western powers. Dulles again refused; a united front did not exist, and Washington believed the French contemplated "departures" from the seven points, a "whittling away process" that would lead to the loss of South Vietnam. Mendès insisted this was not the case; the Americans could have veto power over the final settlement if they wished, but they must support it if it was to work. The only alternative was total capitulation.[42]

On July 11 Eisenhower ordered Dulles back to Europe, or the French "will then blame us for everything that goes wrong." On July 13 Dulles met with Mendès France and Anthony Eden. Dulles was still adamant; the Russians wanted to destroy EDC and harm American–French relations, Dulles said, and he feared a full break might occur at Geneva between France and the United States if the settlement were unacceptable to Washington. Mendès replied that the danger of a break was the same if the Americans were not there. Dulles said the United States could not accept a "new Yalta." Perhaps the American absence could even be helpful to Paris, he suggested, which could use the possible threat of a severe American reaction in order to secure better terms. But Eden flatly ruled this out: He would not be party to an attempt to portray the United States in the background as a "bogey man," an image that fit so well with Communist propaganda. Mendès France said he would take personal responsibility in the event the United States felt it must disavow the settlement. "He then solemnly said in his official capacity 'I ask you to come and help us.' " Dulles said he understood the "weight" of Mendès's request and would defer a reply. The premier returned to the issue the next day. The seven American conditions would be met, he promised. If not, "I engage myself, on behalf of France, to make known publicly the conditions under which you have acceded to my request." Dulles then gave his assent; Bedell Smith would go to Geneva. The secretary acknowledged "a new chapter in the honorable and precious tradition of Franco–American cooperation."[43]

The terms of the Geneva settlement intensified the underlying suspicion that alienated Washington from the most profound and important political experiment the French were to undertake during the period of the Fourth Republic. The United States refused to endorse partition and was unhappy about the promise of elections that threatened to result in the emergence of a Communist state in the South. Bedell Smith did "take note" of the accords and declared the United States would respect them. Washington further declared it would view any violation of the agreements with grave concern. Dulles even had a good word for Mendès. It was a "good augury" for France,

---

[42] FRUS, 1952–4, XIII, 2, Indochina, July 9, 10, 11, 1954, pp. 1800–14; DPMF, V, O c, iii, Genève, Massigli (London) to Mendès France, July 8, 1954; Parodi to Geneva, London, and Washington, July 9, 1954; Bonnet to Mendès France, July 9, 1954.

[43] FRUS, 1952–54, XIII, 2, Indochina, July 13, 14, 1954, pp. 1813–34; Mendès France, *Oeuvres*, 3, pp. 119–23.

the secretary thought, "that he has demonstrated a capacity to take decisions and carry them out."[44] But the war's end put Franco–American relations on a new footing in another crucial sense. Mendès France noted before the National Assembly that American aid to France had become linked in its entirety to the Indochina war: ". . . we have found in the Indochina war the equivalent of resources that normally our exports should procure for us. . . . The end of the hostilities in Indochina will result in a diminution of our dollar reserves." To be sure, Mendès claimed that he had repaired the breach in France's relations with Washington left by Bidault. But in fact the gap between the two countries was to become wider by far under Mendès than it ever had been under Bidault or Schuman, who between them had managed French foreign policy since 1945.[45]

It soon became apparent that Mendès would go his own way on EDC just as he had done in Indochina. Dillon was at first optimistic. On July 1 he observed that Mendès France and his people were showing a "complete spirit of cooperation" on EDC, and he believed that even the Quai was coming around to support of the treaty. Indeed, the evidence suggests Mendès thought there was no alternative to ratification; failing EDC, France faced the possibility of the rearmament of Germany without restrictions, the growth of reunification sentiment there, and the isolation of France from her allies.[46] But Mendès did not believe the treaty capable of gaining a majority as it was. Noting the ambiguity of his previous declarations on EDC, Paul Henri Spaak invited the new premier to Brussels to explain his position to France's five prospective partners. Mendès was irritated at this because it came during his self-imposed deadline at Geneva. He regarded Spaak's timing as maladroit and inopportune, and wondered whether the Belgian had not in fact been put up to it by the Americans.[47]

On July 6, in any event, Mendès disappointed Dillon, telling him that the treaty would need to be amended further. Alarmed by this news, Dulles brought the question up with Mendès France on July 13. The exchange between the two men was of interest. Mendès noted his past experience in economics and the irony in his having to serve as foreign affairs minister, since he was a "neophyte" in foreign policy. Dulles took this as an opening to lecture Mendès on international relations. If EDC did not pass, the secretary said, France would be susceptible to Soviet pressure, the United States

44 *Le Monde*, July 18–9, 1954. FRUS, 1952–4, XIII, 2, Indochina, July 15, 1954, p. 1836; July 20, 1954, pp. 1855–6; July 21, 1954, p. 1865.
45 Pierre Mendès France, *Oeuvres*, 3, p. 153.
46 MAE, Europe 1949–55, Généralités, CED, 28, "Note," June 26, 1954; also DPMF, CED, II, Conférence de Bruxelles, "Note explicative," n.d.
47 MAE, Europe, 1949–55, Généralités, CED, 29, Rivière (Brussels) to Mendès France, June 23, 1954; Parodi to Brussels, June 24, 1954; Massigli (London) to Mendès France, June 26, 1954.

would withdraw to a peripheral strategy, and the damage to France would be "incalculable." Neophyte or not, Mendès was not impressed. No majority in favor of the treaty existed at present in the National Assembly; the treaty must be amended by new protocols so as to make it capable of rallying the vast majority of the French around it. Dulles disagreed. One vote was enough for a majority: Had not a majority of one vote been sufficient to establish the constitution of the Third Republic? Mendès assured Dulles his understanding of French history was simplistic; in any event Mendès would not press for the treaty unless assured of a large majority.[48]

With the Geneva agreements signed, EDC became the next item on the premier's agenda, and the internal French propaganda campaign reached new heights. Dillon argued that French industrialists were financing the anti-EDC campaign while they profited from American OSP contracts. Dulles was hesitant, but Dillon insisted further contracts be stopped: Indochina had made Mendès strong, but he would not be able to withstand this kind of pressure, and his power would be short-lived. Dulles agreed. Dillon still thought Mendès could be made to ratify the treaty. The premier was strong, but power was in his person, not the coalition. Neutralists supported Mendès, but there was no evidence that he personally was neutralist; on the contrary, he continued to stress French–American cooperation. But nobody really knew what Mendès might do. He "rides on momentum," Dillon said, imposing time deadlines on himself as he moves toward his targets.[49]

Dulles was not disposed to gamble on Mendès's cooperation. No sooner were the Geneva agreements signed, than France and the United States began to clash in Vietnam. Mendès intended to preserve French interests in the South. On July 28 he proposed an ambitious plan of economic assistance to the new state with the intent of strengthening it in time for the 1956 elections, the program to be coordinated by France and including the United States and the United Kingdom. But reforms were equally necessary, and Mendès hoped to convince the Americans that Diem was hopelessly incompetent, unable to undertake the reforms, and lacked a power base to secure his regime.[50] However, Dulles complained to Paris that the French in Vietnam were trying to undermine Diem, and the CIA advised against holding elections, for which the outlook was very poor. The French, moreover,

---

[48] FRUS, 1952–4, VI, 2, France, July 1, 1954, pp. 1424–6; July 6, 1954, pp. 1429–30; July 13, 1954, pp. 1431–6. V, 1, EDC, July 13, 1954, pp. 1819–26. The French version of the July 13 talks is in Pierre Mendès France, *Oeuvres*, 3, 119–23.

[49] FRUS, 19592–4, VI, 2, France, July 21, 23, 26, 1954, pp. 1437–41. NARA, 751.00/7-2654, July 27, 1954.

[50] MAE, Asie 1944–55, Indochine, 193, Mendès France to Washington and London, July 28, 1954. Documents Diplomatiques Français (hereinafter DDF), 1954 (21 Juillet–31 Décembre, Paris, Imprimerie Nationale, 1987), Ely to La Chambre, August 11, 1954, p. 111.

were seeking to protect colonial interests, and were maintaining a presence in the north. France and the United States continued to clash over support for Diem and adherence to the terms of the Geneva agreements.

On August 5 Dillon and Bruce both reported with alarm that the anti-EDC group in the French government were "back in business" and close to Mendès. But the worst example of the new French government's perfidy came on August 12. Mendès France announced that before seeking ratification of EDC by the Council of the Republic, he would seek negotiations with the Soviet Union in quest of a definitive German settlement. All of the secretary's worst fears about Paris were now confirmed. Dulles declared that he was "deeply shocked and disheartened" by Mendès's announcement, the implications of which "undermine the very basis of French–American relations and the future of the NATO alliance." France was apparently ready to drop EDC in exchange for elections in a neutralized, united, Germany. The result of such policies would be the destruction of Adenauer and the ruin of plans for Western security. Mendès sought to correct Dulles's impression. He cabled Bonnet that he had told Molotov there could be no discussion of EDC until the end of the Geneva conference. Mendès had ruled out any hint of a "planetary deal" over EDC.[51] France meant only to find out if the Russians had something genuinely new to offer in Germany. Mendès was opposed to a neutralized Germany. He had no intention of delaying the vote on EDC and was willing to stake the life of his government on its passage, but his personal prestige was insufficient to secure ratification. "It is clear that Washington has mistaken my meaning," Mendès wrote. "I protest against this unjustified misunderstanding. . . . I insist that the American government take account of this fact in which it obstinately refuses to believe. I ask to be helped in the effort I am making toward this end, and I ask to be understood and believed." To gain a majority the treaty had to be amended so as to guarantee a veto power for France on institutions of the Community and mitigate its supranational aspects.[52]

Mendès France's hopes for American backing of his new treaty protocols were destroyed in the wake of the Moscow initiative. Bonnet reported that Bedell Smith was so preoccupied with the French approach to Moscow that he would not consider support for the protocols.[53] Dulles cabled Brussels on August 14 that he was "deeply disturbed"; the West could not accept any arrangement that made its action dependent upon Soviet desires. The

---

[51]   In fact, Mendès told Molotov in Geneva that he saw no alternative to French ratification of EDC: DPMF, CED, Carton 2, B, Débats, Sous-Dossier 1, "Entretien de M. Mendès France avec M. Molotove à Genève," July 21, 1954.

[52]   FRUS, 1953–4, V, 1, EDC, August 5, 1954, p. 1024; August 12, 13, 1954, pp. 1026–33. Pierre Melandri, in François Bédarida and Jean-Pierre Rioux, *Pierre Mendès France et le Mendèsisme* (Paris: Fayard, 1985), p. 273. Pierre Mendès France, *Oeuvres*, 3, 226. DDF, 1954, Mendès France to Bonnet, August 13, 1954, pp. 141–2.

[53]   DDF, 1954, Bonnet to Mendès France, August 16, 1954, pp. 156–7.

United States must convince France's EDC partners to reject the French proposals, which discriminated against Germany, vitiated the supranational aspects of the treaty, and required resubmission to the parliaments of the signatory states. Bruce thought Mendès France would drop his proposals if the other parties to EDC stood firm; Mendès's "irretrievable error" could be corrected only if the others refused to compromise. American aid and military guarantees to Europe were also suspended pending the outcome of the Brussels negotiations. Virtually irresistible American pressure encouraged the other powers to stand firm against "unrealistic concessions or destructive compromises" with the French on EDC.[54]

Under these conditions it is little wonder that Mendès France got no concessions to the French point of view in Brussels. The British, to be sure, favored making some effort to meet the French position. Eden did not share Dulles's distaste for Mendès, and the supranational aspects of the treaty were the major reason Britain was not a part of it.[55] Dulles insisted the treaty was worthless without its supranational provisions, however. On August 18 André Mayer brought Dulles a personal letter from Mendès explaining that changes in the treaty were needed to secure its ratification in the National Assembly. Mayer got a stern lecture in exchange. Mendès was "ill-advised," and did not appreciate the gravity of the situation. The United States had been through these French tactics before: New protocols, guarantees, meetings with the Russians, all had been tried and the treaty remained unratified. American patience was at an end. Dulles made a personal appeal to Mendès once more. If EDC failed, he warned, the United States, Britain, and the Brussels powers would go ahead without France to reestablish German sovereignty and rearmament.[56] France was isolated.

On August 12 Dillon found Mendès "very shaken" but resolved to stand firm. Parodi wrote Mendès: "You are subjected to the strongest pressure, the most brazenly concerted and indiscreet that I have until now seen being exercised on a French government." Mendès was fatigued, cynical, and pessimistic, but fully confident in his judgment of the parliamentary situation; his protocols reflected political necessity. He told Tomlinson EDC was certain now to be defeated; he hoped the Big Three were prepared to map new plans and limit the damage from its collapse. Tomlinson warned that France would be isolated if the treaty failed. But Mendès did not believe that. He

---

54 FRUS, 1952–4, V, 1, EDC, August 13, 14, 15, 16, 1954, pp. 1036–43.

55 MAE, Europe 1949–55, Généralités, 30, "Aide-Memoire to the French Government," August 17, 1954. While the British saw "very substantial amendments which would weaken the force of the treaty" in Mendès's proposals, they advised that "all concerned should go as far as possible to meet the proposals of the French government and above all that they should not be rejected out of hand."

56 FRUS, 1952–4, V, 1, EDC, August 19, 20, 21, 1954, pp. 1049–60. Papiers Jean Monnet, AMI, CED, 23/8/1, August 18, 1954, Pierre Mendès France to John Foster Dulles. Pierre Mendès France, *Oeuvres*, 3, 234.

agreed with Parodi that "we hold too strong and essential positions in Europe and also in Indochina for anyone to bypass us." To Eden Mendès noted that France could never be isolated in Europe "whose culture she symbolizes." Even after the treaty's failure, France intended to remain party to any negotiations involving the rearmament of Germany.[57]

On August 24 Mendès told Dillon that the United States was misinformed about the French parliamentary situation.[58] The Americans had gambled that they had more support in the French National Assembly than Mendès. In the process, they had needlessly humiliated France. Could they really have expected Mendès France to stake the confidence of his government on a treaty in the integrity of which he no longer believed? On August 25, 1954 the embassy reported that Mendès was entering the debate without a desire to win, and predicted a 295–278 vote against the treaty with 53 abstentions. It was now clear Mendès had never meant to seek ratification over the objections of the nationalist right, as he had told Dulles on July 13, 1954. Bedell Smith warned Bonnet that defeat of EDC would mean a full reconsideration of American strategic thinking, but nobody in France believed American threats to abandon the European continent. Finally, Adenauer had needlessly insulted Mendès in Brussels, refusing to see him for four days. Mendès had concluded that France would be isolated within the EDC as well as outside it. Bruce proposed a desperate last minute appeal from the United States and the United Kingdom to the six to reconvene the Brussels negotiations, thus dramatizing French isolation. But Eden rejected this idea as useless, as it was. The treaty went down to defeat on August 31, 1954, with 319 negative votes.[59]

With the Geneva agreements signed and EDC defeated, the whole of Washington's postwar policy in France seemed to be in ruins. Dillon pleaded for sympathetic understanding of the French, but with the same patronizing attitude that prevented Washington from ever treating the French as equals. Dillon counseled against attempts to omit France from Western discussions or isolate her. The United States must refrain from punitive acts, be firm, but keep an open door. If the French made trouble in Germany then the Americans should cut off aid. OSP should be cut in the meantime so as not to reward those arms manufacturers who had opposed the treaty. But Washington should keep in mind that the French remained attached to the

---

[57] 1952–4, V, 1, EDC, August 21, 1954, pp. 1061–3. Pierre Mendès France, *Oeuvres*, III, 817.

[58] FRUS, 1952–4, V, 1, EDC, August 22, 1954, pp. 1064–7; August 24, 1954, pp. 1071–7.

[59] DPMF, CED, I, S.D. 3, Mendès France before the Commission of the National Assembly: "an unprecedented negotiation, painful and humiliating for he who spoke in the name of France." MAE, Europe 1949–55, Généralités, 30, Bonnet to Mendès, August 27, 1954. FRUS, 1952–4, V, 1, EDC, August 26, 27, 30, 1954, pp. 1079–92. NARA, 751.00/8-2554, August 25, 1954.

West. Their intelligence and vitality persisted underneath their momentary display of selfishness, defeatism, neutralism, negativism, and cynicism. Their individualism was the best antidote to Communism but unfortunately had the effect of making decisive government impossible. It may be, Dillon went on, that "we shall have to relegate France to a museum in our future strategic planning." France was ill; shock treatment and therapy were needed. "But the voltage must be controlled so as not to kill the patient."[60]

Dulles was in no mood for counsels of moderation, however, and briefly indulged an unlikely scheme to overthrow Mendès France. Georges Bidault called on Dillon in September 7, to express his bitterness at Mendès and hopes that the United States and Britain "would not help him too much." The only real solution, Bidault said, was to "drive him out," and he invited Washington to help. Initially, Washington was skeptical; Bedell Smith thought Bidault's animus to Mendès "understandable," but disturbing, for the French premier had declared his intention of working toward a solution to the German problem. Mendès could be sincere despite the "distorted perspective and distrust he has generated," while Bidault was clearly an opportunist. Better to work with Mendès than run the risk of getting no German settlement at all that France could live with. Smith wanted this point made to Bidault, Mollet, Pinay, Reynaud, and others who might try to overthrow Mendès. Likewise Chancellor Adenauer should be informed of the American intent to do business with Mendès France.[61]

But Bidault was not alone; Maurice Schumann proposed to Dillon that the United States and Britain dramatize Mendès's isolation by refusing to negotiate with him. Mendès would fall, Schumann would become foreign minister, and EDC would be revived and ratified. Dillon was unsure: "Mendès France can negotiate German rearmament and will do so," while it was now clear there was no majority in favor of EDC in the National Assembly. On the other hand if no solution agreeable to Adenauer could be achieved, "then we might be forced to try the course which Schumann recommends." Schumann had a plan: following Mendès's fall, the next government formed would immediately engineer its own defeat. There would then have been three governments overthrown in the eighteen-month period since René Mayer's fall on May 21, 1953, which constitutionally required a dissolution of the Assembly and new elections. The new elections would produce a majority in favor of the treaty. Christian Pineau, who represented those Socialists favorable to EDC, supported Schumann's plan. Bedell Smith was now intrigued. The eighteen months ran out on November 21. Could Schumann's scenario be achieved by then, he queried Dillon.[62]

Why would Washington have seriously considered such a plan? Dulles's

60 FRUS, 1952–4, VI, 2, France, August 31, 1954, pp. 1443–5.
61 NARA, 751.00/9-754, September 7, 1954.
62 NARA, 751.00/9-1654, September 16, 1954.

frustration following the defeat of EDC was extreme, and the "agonizing reappraisal" of American policy began at once with a suspension of MDAP shipments to France, and the stoppage of OSP contracts. Dulles planned a trip to Europe to see Adenauer and Eden, informing Mendès that time was too short for a Paris stopover. The French "must learn there are some consequences of their EDC decision." Mendès France got the message. He was "deeply hurt" by Dulles's action, but warned Dillon that the notion of "punishment" to him personally was much less important than the harm that might be done to a constructive solution to the German problem. Dulles did not believe, however, that Mendès intended to achieve a German settlement. To Eisenhower, Dulles noted a "rising tide of concern about Mendès's Russian contacts . . . he has killed EDC and now may kill German membership in NATO." To the National Security Council Dulles said the Soviets had "used Mendès France to kill EDC." The question now was whether they would similarly "use" him to kill NATO.[63]

In South Vietnam American commitment to Diem intensified in proportion to French efforts to unseat him. Dulles wrote Mendès on August 18 that he saw no alternative to Diem, and asked French cooperation in supporting him. On September 27 General Ely and Associated States Minister Guy La Chambre met with Bedell Smith in Washington, and agreed to support Diem; Washington, in turn, promised to coordinate economic aid with France.[64] But the CIA reported French scheming with their former creatures, especially General Hinh, against Diem, and Bonnet had earlier told Bedell Smith that the French thought Diem was "on the way out." Strong representations were made to Paris to cease its support of Hinh. Meanwhile, Dillon noted that several French officials favored dealing with Ho Chi Minh, and a French delegation under Jean Sainteny had gone to North Vietnam to negotiate the preservation of French interests there. The French regarded South Vietnam as destined to go the way of the North, and hoped to salvage what they could by an entente with the Communists. Admiral Radford demanded that France "call Hinh off," but Dulles feared their policy was secretly to back him. "We don't know Mendès France's game." Mendès was either collaborating with Ho Chi Minh or leaving policy in Vietnam to French colonial interests or both. It might be time to stop all support to France in Indochina. Dulles agreed with Adenauer: "Mendès France was not a Communist tool, but could be led to play the Communist game."[65]

63 FRUS, 1952–4, V, 2, The German Problem, August 30, 1954, pp. 1114–6; September 15, 1954, p. 1196; September 18, 1954, p. 1227; September 27, 1954, pp. 1283–8. Eisenhower Library, Dulles–Herter Series, September 17, 20, 1954.
64 MAE, Asie 1944–55, Indochine, 193, Dulles to Mendès France, August 19, 1954; Washington Conversations, September 28, 1954.
65 FRUS, 1952–4, XIII, 2, Indochina, Geneva Aftermath, August 23, 1954, pp. 1977–80; August 27, 1954, p. 1992; September 17, 1954, p. 2034; September 24, 25, 1954, pp. 2056–9.

In the event there was no overt attempt to bring Mendès France down. Dillon saw "no mileage in working for Mendès's downfall as Adenauer and Bidault wish," because the United States needed French participation in a solution to the German problem. Mendès heard of the attempts to draw the Embassy into plans to unseat him, and the campaign was also leaked to the French press, threatening another nationalist and anti-American reaction as had occurred under Pinay. Dillon told inquiring journalists to inform their "contacts" in the French government (i.e., Mendès), that while the United States had no admiration for the way in which Mendès had handled EDC, it did not follow the tactics of trying to bring down friendly governments. On the contrary, the Americans hoped to negotiate a successful agreement with Mendès France on German rearmament, and if this happened, he would be "a popular hero in the U.S." But most important, the British were dead set against any such scheme. On September 27, 1954 the matter was brought up in London by Ambassador Douglas; he was told that the British believed that the best policy was to work with Mendès for a successful negotiation of the London accords on Germany. In reply Douglas declared: "We shared Ambassador Jebb's concern regarding the machinations of our French friends and we could not envisage the overthrow of Mendès as leading to the early accomplishment of our European defense objectives." The State Department formulated its own doubts; they had failed to isolate Mendès at Brussels; one could not "chasten and educate" him by "mild shock treatment." Slaps to him encouraged the anti-EDC people to seek his downfall, and the United States needed their votes behind him in support of the London accords.[66]

Dulles did decide to do what he could to weaken Mendès France. Harold Stassen noted that France received huge amounts of American aid while its currency reserves increased; Bedell Smith suggested the aid be cut off. Dulles said "We would like to see the reserves of the Bank of France come down . . . [and] capital start moving out of France." Stassen suggested "study and stall" tactics on French aid requests. Smith said the phase-out of the French Expeditionary Corps in Vietnam must be gradual, since it was the only force maintaining order in the country, but if the French threatened to withdraw it suddenly, we should "call their bluff." On September 29, 1954 Finance Minister Edgar Faure conferred with Stassen regarding French aid requests for 1955. Stassen was noncommittal, promised nothing for 1955, and said remaining 1954 aid would have to be renegotiated in view of unrealized objectives in Vietnam. Faure cited the continuing needs of the French Expeditionary Corps and asked about the slowdown in the placement of OSP contracts. Stassen noted that the Richards Amendment reserved half of

---

[66] FRUS, 1952–4, V, 2, The German Problem, September 11, 1954, pp. 1177–8; September 24, 1954, Jones to Merchant. NARA, 751.00/9-1654, September 16, 1954, 751.00/9-2254, September 27, 1954.

American military aid to EDC, which did not exist, and advised Faure that the French should not anticipate any new orders from OSP in the near future.[67]

Mendès decided he could do nothing but accept Washington's lead on the Vietnam question. In Paris he promised Dillon he would support Diem, and accepted the transfer of the $385 million of emergency American aid for Indochina directly to the Associated States. A communiqué followed La Chambre's and Ely's meetings with Bedell Smith stating the existence of full American and French agreement on Vietnam. Mendès observed to Guy La Chambre that "We have numerous problems with them elsewhere [the United States] and we do not need additional causes of opposition in Vietnam." Similarly, with regard to the Southeast Asia Treaty Organization being negotiated in Manilla at that time, Mendès ordered La Chambre to give Dulles the diplomatic victory he wanted. Dulles was momentarily pleased. But in Vietnam American accusations of French support to anti-Diem politicians continued. Dulles complained that despite Mendès's promises, French officials in Indochina did not support Diem, and Radford continued to insist Paris be made to restrain its clients there. Eisenhower now thought it was time to "get rough with the French. We have to cajole them in Europe but not in Indochina." The NSC decided on a crash program of support for Diem. A national constabulary or police would be built that was loyal to him only; the army, controlled by Hinh and the French, would be circumvented.[68]

A letter was duly dispatched to Diem telling him of the American decision. He was delighted, but Paris was not. Guy La Chambre told Dillon the government was "surprised and disturbed" by the American action, but France would accept: "We prefer to lose in Vietnam with the U.S. rather than to win without them." France would rather support Diem knowing he was going down to defeat, rather than pick someone who "could retain Vietnam for the free world," if that meant losing American friendship. This kind of sarcasm did not go over well in Washington. In the NSC Herbert Hoover, Jr., attributed Mendès's unhappiness to a "secret deal" between France and the Vietminh. Eisenhower thought the French were irritated by the cuts in their "cash handouts." Hoover thought the British were a part of the deal with Ho Chi Minh, and Eisenhower resolved to confront Eden and Churchill to find out if it were true. Dulles thought that the French were still seeking to retain Cochin China as a colony. The reality was much more prosaic. Daridan warned La Chambre that Diem's situation was deteriorating; La Chambre observed that "the Americans behave like imbeciles and

[67] FRUS, 1952–4, XIII, 2, Geneva Aftermath, September 25, 1954, p. 2069; September 27, 1954, p. 2079; September 29, 1954, p. 2096. MAE, Asie 1944–55, Indochine, 194, September 28, 1954, Faure–Stassen economic talks.
[68] FRUS, 1952–4, XIII, 2, Geneva Aftermath, September 28, 19, 1954, pp. 2097–8; October 21, 22, 1954, pp. 2147–57. Pierre Mendès France, *Oeuvres*, 3, 300, 310.

we too for not being able to tell them." In the end Eisenhower decided to dispatch General Lawton Collins to Vietnam as his representative. Arriving there on November 3, the general reported that he would phase out the French presence more rapidly than had been contemplated. The financial means to do so were readily available. Dulles noted that the French kept their Expeditionary Corps in Indochina in order to earn dollars from the U.S. subsidy. In view of the truce, the United States would cease payments, offer a lump sum to defray expenses to the end of 1954, and cease all aid thereafter. The French could maintain 6,000 cadres in Vietnam, but their pay would come from the Vietnamese government, not from Washington.[69]

Dillon warned that without the assistance program Washington would lose the lever it enjoyed to influence the level of French forces in Europe, and Mendès France might be endangered politically. But that was the result that Dulles intended. French and American policies in Vietnam were irreconcilable, ending finally in 1955 with French withdrawal. The French opposed direct aid to Diem and the Collins mission, and supported the anticipated 1956 elections in Vietnam that were part of the Geneva agreement. Washington did not. France believed Diem needed to carry out land reform and make peace with the army and the sects. Heath believed his problems would be over if he could get rid of General Hinh. But more seriously, Dillon warned that this "fundamental divergence in U.S.–French positions" had serious implications for East–West relations. The French favored a rapprochement between North and South and expected the 1956 elections to bring the Vietminh to power. They did not believe that South Vietnam could survive, or that the Americans would put in troops to defend it. Paris was counting on doing business with a Communist neutralism in Vietnam, Dillon thought. To Dulles it was the same attitude Mendès had revealed on the German question. Rather than strengthen West Germany or South Vietnam, he preferred to deal with Moscow in quest of neutralization and reunification, in the long-term pursuit of a policy of peaceful co-existence with Communism. Moreover, Washington had further reasons for suspicion of Mendès France on account of the "Affaire des Fuites."[70]

The "Affair of the Leaks," or Dides case, involved one of those typical scandals upon which French politics appeared to thrive. French government secrets apparently were getting into the hands of the French Communist party, which was taken to mean that they were being transmitted to Moscow. Commissaire Dides, who worked for the Paris prefect of police, ran an anti-Communist spy network of doubtful reliability. It is still not clear whether his informant, Baranès, was a police implant in the PCF, a PCF implant in

[69] FRUS, 1952–4, XIII, 2, Geneva Aftermath, October 25, 26, pp. 2176–85; October 31, 1954, pp. 2198–9; November 5, 1954, pp. 2213–6. DDF, 1954, Daridan to La Chambre, October 4, 1954, p. 515.

[70] FRUS, 1952–4, XIII, 2, Geneva Aftermath, November 6, 1954, pp. 2218–20; November 15, 1954, pp. 2246–50.

the police, or both. To make matters worse, the French counterespionage services, the SDT, had its own agenda in the case in rivalry with the Prefecture of Police. Where Washington fit in all this remains in large part mysterious, especially since the Dides anti-Communist network may also have been aimed at damaging Mendès France.[71] *L'Humanité* charged on September 29 that Dides was giving information to the FBI as well as to the French police. This was certainly the case. On September 30 Dillon reported that Lallier, the attaché of the FBI in the embassy, complained of being shadowed by the French police. Indeed, the police observed Dides and Lallier having lunch twice during the height of the affair; from a phone tap they ascertained that Dides informed the FBI agent he had something interesting to tell him.[72] Bureau Director Hoover asked the advisability of protesting this surveillance to the French government. Lallier and Dillon agreed this was inadvisable because it "would merely attract publicity with respect to the U.S. connection with the affair, which the non-Communist press is playing down." At a minimum, Dides was keeping the FBI informed about the extent of Communist influence and power in the French administration.[73]

Queried by John Foster Dulles, Allen Dulles called the Dides affair "strange and unimportant," low-level espionage; he had lots of cables but no time to read them. One of the principals, he thought, was "trying to get something on all of us," but he didn't know what it was. Calling again the next day, Allen Dulles assured his brother the case should not cause Washington any embarrassment. There had been an FBI man with an associate of one of those arrested. "Hoover didn't know, but it was OK for the FBI to be in on it." John Foster Dulles thought it was disturbing "the way these fellows were carrying on these activities against anti-Communists," and Allen Dulles agreed it was. The CIA chief promised to follow the case closely. It soon appeared that more than low-level counterespionage was involved. Dillon reported that the Dides case involved the leak of September 10 minutes of a discussion of the National Defense Council regarding a Strategic Air Command unit in Morocco, and the stationing of American nuclear weapons in North Africa. Dillon had secured permission from Laniel in 1953 for the United States to stock nuclear weapons at its North African air bases. He now contacted Jean Mons, secretary of the National Defense Council, who assured Dillon that nothing relating to American security in North Africa had been leaked. But Mons was under suspicion in the affair, and Dillon

---

[71]   The FBI, which was certainly involved in the case, says it has no relevant archives. The CIA will not say whether it has any archives. The State Department has materials relating to the affair but will not release them.

[72]   DPMF "Fuites," I, Dossier 2, "Note Chronologique."

[73]   NARA, 751.00/9-2954, 9-3054, September 29, 30, 1954. Dides told Sûreté head Roger Wybot that he saw it as his duty to keep Lallier informed about the Communist danger in France. DPMF, "Fuites," Carton II, Dossier 7, report by David Weil.

suspected that more might have been leaked than the French cared to admit.[74]

Mendès France assured Dulles personally that although classified materials were passed on in the Dides case, it had not been "the most precise or sensitive subject matter discussed." Achilles determined that the nuclear information had been closely held by very few persons other than (Robert) Schuman and Bidault; indeed, Mendès himself had not yet been briefed, and Mons was really the only one au courant. But Mons's secretary, René Turpin, was finally charged with having passed on the classified materials, and his associate, Roger Labrusse, was the person with whom all emergency evacuation plans for Americans in France had been discussed. Dulles ordered new evacuation plans drawn up without the French being informed. But Dillon nevertheless felt the case had got beyond his capabilities to handle, and he asked that it be turned over to William Tyler, an Embassy specialist who had "unique" contacts. The political implications of the so-called Dides case were so serious, Dillon wrote, that only Tyler could obtain the clarifications necessary in the "highly complex and dangerous political atmosphere that obtains here."[75]

Dillon eventually concluded that there had been only a minimum security breech, but the public aspects of the affair continued to rankle. *France-Observateur* charged that Dides had been passing information to the United States in order to help discredit Mendès France; in effect, a parallel police existed in France under the supervision of the FBI. These allegations escalated. The Dides case was claimed to be a U.S.-inspired plot, running from Allen Dulles through the American Embassy through Dides to the government-sponsored, CIA-financed, peace movement, *Paix et liberté*. Jean Paul David, whose offices were searched by the police, protested his innocence, but his American-financed organization was involved with the Dides network.[76] Mendès France later came to believe that the affair was an attempt by his political opponents to destroy his government; he did not at the time have any proof that the Americans were involved, however.

The atmosphere surrounding the case motivated Mendès's enemies to intensify their efforts to unseat him. Bidault told Dillon that Mitterrand had told all prefects to cease their actions against the Communists; the minister

74   Eisenhower Library, Dulles Papers, Telephone Calls, September 24 and 25, 1954. NARA, 751.00/9-3054, 10-254, September 30, 1954, October 2, 1954. DPMF, "Fuites," II, Dossier 1, Wybot–Mons interview, confirms that the NDC minutes allegedly leaked to the PCF contained discussion of U.S. nuclear weapons.

75   NARA, 751.00/9-3054, 10-254, 10-454, September 30, October 2 and 4, 1954. FRUS, 1952–4, V, 2, German Problem, September 27, 1954, p. 1284. Tyler's role, and that of the CIA station head Robert Thayer, remain hidden from view.

76   DPMF, Fuites, I, 7, J. P. David to Mendès France; II, 3, David to Mendès, November 24, 1954; Mendès to David, November 26, 1954.

of the interior had himself leaked the Navarre Plan to the Communists the previous year.[77] Dillon, perhaps to find out for himself, lunched with Mitterrand, who said he knew no Communists and had relations with none, and had personally shut off any investigation of the charge that Dides had relations with the Americans.[78]

Despite the aid freeze, Vietnam, and the Dides affair, Washington dealt with Mendès France successfully in a resolution of the German problem. It was Mendès's idea to revive the Brussels treaty of 1948, to which Germany and Italy were invited to adhere. Through the mechanism of the Brussels treaty, Mendès France managed to gain the benefits of EDC without, from the French standpoint, suffering the disadvantages. German rearmament would occur by treaty and in an integrated European framework, while the two major French objections to EDC were eliminated: there was no supranationality in the Brussels mechanism, and the British were fully associated.[79] Even Dulles admitted that the essentials of EDC had been saved after the London–Paris accords were signed. But Dulles would offer no tribute to Mendès France, public or private. The United States, he said, played a background role in the negotiations to avoid the appearance of pressure. "But of course our presence has been the indispensable ingredient without which the whole affair would have fallen apart, and it will be necessary for us to continue our support of the European army." In the NSC, Dulles praised Adenauer as a European and a statesman who saw "the big things," while Mendès France was the nationalist, who saw only the little things. But it had all turned out alright in the end.[80]

The freeze on American aid had no effect on Mendès, who refused even to discuss economic questions during his visit to Washington, thus refusing even the appearance that questions of aid had an impact on political differences extant between the two countries. The differences remained, despite the public opinion success that the milk-drinking Frenchman enjoyed on his American visit. Mendès promised to support Diem, but insisted on the retention of French rights and administrative methods in Vietnam. But it was clear the Americans meant to push the French out of Vietnam: Dulles stated his intention to build a strong non-Communist government, notwithstanding the Geneva agreements. Mendès requested American support and a guarantee for an agreement with Germany on the Europeanization of the Saar; he was told this was constitutionally impossible. Mendès reiterated a traditional French request for a three-power standing group in NATO and got the usual American refusal. On Algeria there was total disagreement.

[77] NARA, 751.00/10-554, 751.00/10-654, 751.00/10-1254, October 5, 6, 12, 1954.
[78] NARA, 751.00/11-1554, November 15, 1954.
[79] DDF, 1954, Parodi to Massigli, pp. 312–5. The French argreed that Eden, however, should propose the solution to the others.
[80] Eisenhower Library, Dulles–Herter Series, October 3, 1954; NSC Series, NSC 216, October 7, 1954.

This matter had already been before the NSC, where in a fit of pique Admiral Radford said that if a new Vietnam erupted there, the United States should extend military assistance to the Arabs. Dulles angrily rejected that idea. But he would not offer support to Mendès against the Algerian nationalists, despite the premier's claim that France was subject to armed Communist aggression from outside.[81] Washington was apparently charmed only by Madame Mendès France; Eisenhower remarked that it was too bad her husband was so singularly lacking in the same qualities.

On December 24, in a tentative vote, the French National Assembly rejected the London–Paris agreements. Eisenhower was furious. "Those damn French," he fulminated, "what do they think they are trying to do? This could upset the apple cart in Europe." Called in from the golf green, the president apologized to his partner: "Excuse me Ed, I've got to go to work. The French have not only disturbed the whole free world but they're cutting in on my lessons." John Foster Dulles tried to repair the situation in Paris. Informed that several MRP leaders were thinking of voting against the agreements because they were angry at the rejection of EDC, Dulles panicked; he cast about for ways of stopping them. Dillon could not approach any French legislators during a debate. Did Allen Dulles have a pipeline to Schumann and Bidault? Not to Bidault, Allen Dulles said, but possibly to Schumann, he would check. Embarrassed, Allen Dulles reported the next day that he did not have the hoped-for contact. He could get to Robert Schuman but not to Maurice Schumann. The Americans could not, perhaps, be faulted for mixing up their Schuman(n)s. One can only assume that the French, on occasion, did the same.[82]

Pierre Mendès France limped on toward his inevitable fall, his departure from the French scene unregretted by Washington. In the end, paradoxically, the Americans got what they wanted from him. They managed to push aside the French and take control of the Vietnamese situation for themselves, and they got the essentials of what they hoped for in the case of Germany: rearmament, in NATO, in the context of an integrated, if not supranational, Europe. What they could not get was the continuation of business as usual, the feeling that they were a privileged presence on the French scene and a powerful pressure group that had of necessity to be consulted in the making of every major decision. On the contrary, in the mass movement of popular support for Mendès France, they saw the French political scene careening out of control, moving toward solutions they were powerless to prevent. In desperation, the Americans grasped at the leverage of economic aid, only to find it was no longer effective. Paris was now strong enough to do without it, and would sacrifice aid where more impor-

[81] FRUS, 1952–4, VI, 2, France, November 19 and 20, 1954, pp. 1478–86, 1502–6.
[82] FRUS, 1952–4, V, 2, German Problem, December 24, 1954. Eisenhower Library, Dulles Papers, December 28 and 29, 1954.

tant national interests were concerned. In retrospect it appears that the immense hostility occasioned by Mendès France was a reflection of American disappointment at having to resume the use of ordinary diplomatic channels in dealing with the French government. The old methods, to which Washington had become habituated under previous governments, no longer applied. In a conversation with Bedell Smith, Mendès France said that if the Americans wanted to make his job easier, they would withdraw their support from Jean Paul David's *Paix et liberté,* as well as other groups and publications in France.[83] The mere request marked a new beginning in French–American relations.

[83] NARA, 751.00/11-2654, November 26, 1954.

Conclusion

In a Cabinet Meeting of September 18, 1968, Secretary of State Dean Rusk reported on two major foreign policy crises of the summer that had shaken the foundations of the postwar era: the revolts in Paris and Prague. On the Czech crisis Rusk observed: "One of the main problems is knocking down the stories that there was some kind of tacit agreement between the U.S. and Soviets on Czechoslovakia and the bloc. Some of this is due to Soviet black propaganda and some to de Gaulle and his thesis of two super-powers dividing up the world." With regard to the student revolts in the West, Rusk turned to CIA director Richard Helms, who insisted that he had found "no convincing evidence of Communist control, manipulation, or support of student dissidents." But the American leaders were not satisfied with this, leading to the following exchange:

Secretary Rusk: No [Communist] support?
Director Helms: That's right.
President Johnson: But there is support. There is, isn't there?
Secretary Rusk: Well, it is the difference between rape and seduction.
Director Helms: Let's leave it at that.
President Johnson: I just don't believe this business there is no support. . . . Maybe they [the students] are not Communist-led, but they are Communist-agitated.
Director Helms: I'm trying to make that distinction. The difference is there. This report deals with the world situation. I'm trying to stay away from U.S. problems and treat the world.

There followed a discussion of the inadequacy of the French University infrastructure to meet the needs of the 1960s, and the causes of student discontent in general. But despite their irritation with de Gaulle, the Americans regarded the Communist-aggravated students as the greater danger. Earlier, on June 12, Rusk warned the cabinet:

There has been a deep and long concern about the political structure of France post–de Gaulle. The Gaullists are a brittle coalition held up by de Gaulle himself. If the de Gaulle coalition fails, the old fear is that the Communists would emerge. We have a new situation giving some grounds to those old fears now. . . . I want to make one thing clear. We have no interest in de Gaulle being in trouble. It could, for example, contaminate Italy. I hope all of us will restrain any satisfaction we might feel regarding de Gaulle's circumstances. It could mean trouble for all of us.[1]

Thus was revealed a remarkable continuity in American concerns for French stability: anti-Communism as the motivating force, a clear preference for a center coalition, criticism of an allegedly archaic French social structure, and reluctant support of de Gaulle. The very same concerns motivated American policy toward France between 1945 and 1954. The difference was that American influence in France was greater between the years of 1945 to 1954 than at any time previously or since in the history of relations between the two countries. Assessing that influence remains problematic; the American role in France often appeared as intrusive as it was ineffective. Certainly an intimacy was achieved in American–French relations rare in the annals of diplomacy. But it is impossible to say that diplomatic relations were better on that account. On the contrary, the same checkered history that characterized the previous century and a half of relations between the two countries was evident in the immediate postwar years. The myth of a sacred friendship, France as America's oldest ally, was repeated in the speeches of statesmen and politicians ad nauseum. But deep strains continued to exist. Crises erupted with alarming frequency and accusations of duplicity and even dishonesty abounded. Indochina provides the best example: The French accused the Americans of trading dollars for the blood of soldiers, and of failing to assume a fair share of the common burden. The Americans accused the French of inconstancy and ingratitude. The unusual postwar intimacy came to an end amid crisis in 1954. The two nations have seemed to remain since then hostile allies.

The intimacy was unique in several respects. The United States sought not only to influence French policy, but to direct and channel French social and political development. Its efforts in that direction were least successful, yet most resented. Through the Marhsall Plan, the Americans hoped to shape the direction of the French economy. Through the American Embassy and military aid, they hoped to shape French politics in a moderate, centrist direction. These two goals were, unfortunately, mutually exclusive. The Marshall Plan assisted the development of the dynamic, forward-looking sector of the French economy; it supported the modernizing statist-industrialist trend that was firmly entrenched by the wartime experience of both Vichy and the Resistance. But the Americans threw their political support to the unstable centrist coalitions that represented the interests of the

---

[1] Lyndon B. Johnson Library, Austin, Texas, Cabinet Meetings of June 12, and September 18, 1968. The declassified materials on the May 1968 crisis deal mainly with American attempts to understand the crisis; the formulation of policy, and actual exchanges with the French during the events, remain classified.

static traditional bourgeoisie and its peasant allies that provided the political base of the Third Republic, the "stalemate society," or *Société bloquée* of Stanley Hoffmann and Michel Crozier. Gaullism and a left allied with Communism remained Washington's greatest fears. Both emerged as the dominant political forces of the future. The technocratic, modernized society assisted by the Marshall Plan gave birth to the politics of the Fifth Republic, within which the Americans could be satisfied by neither right nor left. The Americans were never able to create the suitable France for which they searched. Perhaps they were foolish even to try.

This was not the only contradiction that helped render American policy in France ineffective. American policy was to reconstruct Germany economically and build it up militarily to become a loyal ally. Yet France, the politically dominant power and influence on the continent, had to be made to accept the restoration of Germany, to which it remained fundamentally hostile. The Marshall Plan was in part designed to placate France into acceptance of German economic reconstruction; NATO was meant to provide the security framework for the restoration of the German military. Neither was fully satisfactory for the French. Paris responded with the Schuman Plan, designed to integrate French and German steel production, and the plan for a European army, meant to subordinate the German military to French overall command. The Schuman Plan became the basis of the movement for European unity. But the EDC blew up in the faces of Paris and Washington, and in the end, the contradiction between German reconstruction and French security was never adequately resolved. And if it became dormant during the de Gaulle years, German unification in the 1990s may well revive it.

Yet another contradiction underlay American participation in the French phase of the Vietnam war. Washington wanted Paris to stay the course but grant Vietnam its independence. France only wanted to fight so long as it was clear that Vietnam would remain within the French Union. And while the Americans encouraged the French to cast aside their colonial illusions and move wholeheartedly toward European integration, even to the point of surrendering traditional aspects of national sovereignty, they ran into a resurgence of nationalism, a measure of imperialism, but certainly a reinforcing of the national state, which became the basis of postwar reconstruction throughout Europe. It is a paradox of the postwar era, as Alan Milward has pointed out, that amid unprecedented efforts at supranational integration, the traditional national states of Europe have assumed larger roles in the lives of their citizens than ever before.[2] The institutions of the welfare state, and rearmament, made the traditional French state more a part of the daily lives of its citizens than it had ever aspired to be before the war.

Even without all these contradictory aims one can argue that the Ameri-

---

[2] Alan Milward, Remarks presented at the Truman Library Conference on NATO, September 21–23, 1989.

can attempt to reshape France was doomed to failure. There were several structural limitations at work: a failure on the part of the American elite to understand fully the nature of French history and culture, and an inability to appreciate the limitations created by historical traditions over which no outside force could hope to exercise control. This emerges most clearly in the ill-fated attempt to create non-Communist trade unions on the American model. For all the American influence exerted, the split of 1947 was a replay of the splits between Communist and non-Communist unions of 1921 and 1939, and the Americans soon vented their dissatisfaction with Force Ouvrière, which would not abandon either its anticlericalism or its colonialism to suit American wishes. For all the inequality in the intimate postwar relationship, France remained a major nation, which could develop only in accordance with its own historical traditions and culture.

It cannot be said that the postwar intimacy was forced upon the French by Washington, and the Americans showed little eagerness to become deeply involved in French affairs. It was the pull of the French, rather than the push outward from Washington, that characterized the different aspects of American involvement, diplomatic, economic, political, and military, between 1945 and 1954. Invariably, though, having invited the Americans in, the French quickly became dissatisfied with what their guests brought with them.

The Americans became involved in French affairs because of their paranoia over French communism, "the main enemy," fear of which became the source and inspiration of so much of Washington's policy throughout the postwar years. Obsessive anticommunism was another reason for Washington's inability, in the last analysis, to find the France it wished to work with. The obsession began with the Free French, and even explains much of Washington's opposition to de Gaulle. The OSS reported that the whole movement of the Free French was subject to pervasive Communist influence, that it threatened to become an auxiliary of Russian strategy, and that de Gaulle was virtually a subordinate of Moscow's "political game." De Gaulle's head of intelligence, Colonel Passy (de Wavrin) was described as in league with the Communist party and Moscow.[3] Not all American analysts believed this, of course. But such attitudes fueled suspicion of de Gaulle harbored among the policymaking elite, and continued to color relations with his successors.

The shadow of the cold war, with its attendant external Soviet military threat and menace of Communist subversion from within, both created and conditioned the American–French intimacy in the postwar era. Communism continued to give rise to irrational fears in Washington, even if the Paris Embassy was able to keep it in some perspective. For example, a frantic cable from FBI Director J. Edgar Hoover early in 1946 warned the Em-

[3] National Archives and Records Administration, Military Branch, Record Group 226, OSS Reports XL 23483, "De Gaulle and the Communists, a New Friendship."

bassy that one Max Shapiro, a San Francisco seaman and member of the American "Workers' Party," was on his way to Paris. "The party is expecting a revolution in France, and the subject is right in the middle of it," Hoover warned. One does not know whether the embassy acted in response to this message. In another such cable Hoover warned the American Embassy that French internal intelligence was controlled by Communists, and Premier "Goin" (sic) was frustrating the efforts of anti-Communists to deal with the situation. Another source of Washington's paranoia was American military intelligence, which occasionally rivaled the absurdities produced by the FBI. On March 8, 1946 American army sources reported a conversation between Maurice Thorez and Russian Ambassador Bogomolov in which the latter detailed Soviet plans for a Russian parachute drop of fifty divisions in Southern France and Northern Spain to seize the Pyrenees and foil American plans for a defense against invasion of Western Europe.[4] The French Communist party was to assist Soviet forces with an internal insurrection carried out by its own paramilitary units.

To this day it remains difficult to get at the source of this misinformation. Some of it came to American military intelligence in France through the mails, unsigned, clearly fabricated by elements of the extreme right. It was taken seriously by military officers, although usually dismissed by the State Department. As noted in Chapter 2, suspect American military intelligence, disbelieved by the State Department, resulted in an American military alert to deal with an expected Communist coup in June 1946. Such materials informed a regular series of reports of the American military attaché in Paris, which became known as the Ronald Reports. These were in turn communicated to the French government, which also tended to take them seriously.[5] Perhaps echoes of the same reports appear in the speculations concerning Communist insurrectionary activities which fill the journal of President Vincent Auriol. The Americans themselves thought the Ronald Reports behind Jules Moch's claim that the strikes of September and October 1948 were carried out at Zhdanov's orders on behalf of the Cominform for insurrectionary aims.

Driven by anticommunism, the Americans became deeply involved in French affairs during the second half of 1946. Washington policy analysts increasingly argued that France was critical to American security – as France went, so might go the rest of Western Europe. The cold war climate created the fear of internal danger of Communist subversion in virtually all the non-

---

[4] Hoover's memos are in NARA, State Department, 851.00B/2-648, February 6, 1948; 851.00/10-1546, October 15, 1946. Military Intelligence, OSS Report XL 48001, March 8, 1946, has the account of the supposed Thorez–Bogomolov conversation.

[5] For a good example see NARA, 851.00B/3-1648, March 16, 1948, which tells of an expected Communist insurrection in the south of France, in much the same terms one may find in the journal of Vincent Auriol. I have been unable to locate the actual "Ronald Reports" in the Archives.

Communist countries of the world. Washington would have preferred a Socialist government in France capable of pursuing a "non-Communist left policy." Urging moderate social reforms upon the French became another continuous concern of the Americans at least until 1950, when military preparedness against the Russians became the overriding consideration. The Americans feared that French conservatives were likely to use Marshall Plan aid to dispense with necessary egalitarian reforms and reconstruct France with its archaic and exploitive social structure intact, which would in turn fuel the resentments that led to communism. These sentiments were widely held at the American Embassy and in Washington. They conformed to the beliefs of American policymakers who felt secure in the conviction that American capitalism had solved the social question by high wages, even higher productivity, and consumerism, and who fervently hoped that European elites would recognize their own enlightened self-interest in doing the same. But Washington was trapped. It wanted enlightened social policies in order to dispense with the French Communists, while continued Communist participation was the only way to achieve such reforms. Communism had become the ultimate horror for Washington; it meant not social reform but Russian domination. Unfortunately, however, its political isolation, which Washington did so much to accomplish, also drove the Socialists into alliances with centrists and the right, leading to defeat of the reforms the Americans desired and decline of the non-Communist left as a major political force in France. Washington thus defeated its own ends. Or it fell into the same political trap that poisoned French politics at least through the 1960s if not until 1981. That is to say, it was as impossible for the left to govern with the Communists as to govern without them.

The Communists, paradoxically, cooperated with American designs. By politicizing the labor unrest in France, they fueled cold war hysteria and contributed to Congress's willingness to pass a huge European aid package, which took the form of the Marshall Plan. It is true, as recent historians have demonstrated, that behind the Marshall Plan there lurked the image of an American-style, consumer-oriented, government-regulated corporate capitalism, which the Americans hoped to impose upon their European allies. And in this, Washington was, over the long term, perhaps successful. As one observer wrote, "Coca-Cola and Hollywood movies may be regarded as two products of a shallow and crude civilization. But American machinery, American labor relations and American management and engineering are everywhere respected."[6] But much of what often passed for Americanization in France was simply modernization. Europeans certainly needed no guidance from Washington in using the State to guide and support capitalist development. In this they were probably ahead of the Americans. And the Marshall Plan cannot, in the last analysis, be divorced from

---

[6] Harry Price, *The Marshall Plan and Its Meaning*, p. 155.

the immediate circumstances of its birth. Its framers were consciously driven and inspired by anticommunism, which they mobilized and used to sell the plan to Congress and the American public.

America's anticommunism and consequent inability to understand or affect the strength of communism in France contributed to another of the impediments to mutual understanding and cooperation in the postwar era: perceptions by Americans and French of each other founded on prejudicial stereotypes. Caffery fretted about the "dumb, instinctive, and unreasoned faith of the [French] working class in the PCF." George Kennan earlier had warned that Russian influence on French affairs was a major impediment to American policy, and complained of a character defect: "Their [French] observers in Moscow are dogged by an inability to recognize crude and elementary phenomena for what they are and by a consequent tendency to seek elaborate and complicated explanations for them."[7] It is tempting to see here yet another clash between French Cartesianism and penchant for ideology and Anglo-Saxon empiricism, and American observers frequently cast their differences with the French in these cultural terms.

As the cold war deepened, the Americans shifted their concern with internal French affairs to foreign policy. France must rearm and provide the missing manpower for the defense of Western Europe against the perceived external Soviet threat. As Marshall Plan assistance was transformed into military aid, American military assistance to France became the means of balancing the French trade deficit, and the essential lubricant to the system of international trade and payments, especially since the Americans were reluctant to reduce tariffs themselves even as they urged such action upon the Europeans. American military assistance also introduced a new source of irritation into Franco–American relations, poisoning ties between the two countries and threatening to rupture them. But Indochina prevented that. The war saved and prolonged for some years the same pattern of humiliation and resentment that had come to characterize American involvement in France since the inception of the Marshall Plan. Instead of addressing themselves to the broader issue of building French military strength, the Americans simply shifted the focus of their aid. Dissatisfied with the terms of sale of the French army as a means of balancing trade, Paris would sell the Americans something better than an army – a real war.

The last gasp of French–American cold war cooperation was during the Laniel government from 1953 to 1954. Washington had by this time fallen to the Republicans, who had no illusions about a "non-Communist left policy" as an antidote to French communism. Dulles wanted internal repression of the Communist menace, and military action to check its expansion abroad. He got both from Laniel. But Indochina proved a frail reed on which to suspend the future of Franco–American relations. The primary

---

[7] NARA, 711.51/4-146, April 1, 1946.

American motive for the war was anticommunism; the French were driven by a stale colonialism. As the French public wearied of the war, and the consequent dependence upon Washington it entailed, they turned to the counsels of Mendès France. And he quickly fulfilled his promises, terminating the French involvement in Indochina. The Mendès France government represented something of a revolution in Franco–American affairs. It was the first French government since the resignation of de Gaulle in 1946 to place French interests before the question of relations with Washington – or put another way, to perceive French national interests independently of Franco–American relations. Mendès went on to terminate Washington's dream of a European Defense Community, Washington briefly tried to bring him down, and the postwar American–French intimacy was over.

Mendès France represented a fundamental turning point in another sense, as American analysts vaguely perceived at the time. His government was the harbinger of the Fifth Republic. In personal style, as well as neutralist-tinged nationalism, he resembled de Gaulle, who was initially one of his admirers. But within his coalition he harbored sympathizers with a new style of Socialism, unafraid of a tactical alliance with the Communists, and alien to the Atlanticist heritage of Léon Blum. American suspicion and hostility to François Mitterrand became another leitmotif of the period. The American aim in France had been to stabilize a regime of the center, based primarily on the MRP, Radical, and Socialist parties, among which Washington found most ready acceptance and support. These were initially the major parties of the Fourth Republic's Third Force coalition. But all of them were in decline. The American fears were the personal power ambitions of General de Gaulle, who might call into existence an opposition either dominated by, or allied with, the Communists. These fears were of course exactly what eventually came to pass. The American attempt to build a suitable France in the postwar period must be judged a failure.

The Americans once again vented their anger over their failures in France by ruminating over their perceptions of defects in the French character. The prejudice started at the top. President Roosevelt, as we have seen, remarked to Stalin that all the French over age forty were hopelessly corrupt. President Truman said he thought the French should be "taken out and castrated."[8] President Eisenhower thought the French were inherently disposed to "cut off their noses to spite their faces"; they repeatedly harmed the best interests of the West, although Georges Bidault seemed to the president less foolish than his "crackpot" colleagues.[9] Eisenhower, unlike Truman or FDR, had years of experience in France. He had not, however, learned French, nor did

---

[8]   Robert J. Donovan, *Conflict and Crisis: The Presidency of Harry S. Truman, 1945–1948* (New York: Norton, 1977), p. 58.

[9]   Eisenhower Library, Correspondance, Letter to Walter Bedell Smith, February 11, 1952.

he understand much of French politics. He did not know how the French president was elected in 1953, and queried Dulles about why it was not by popular vote. He mixed up René Mayer and André Mayer, as his director of intelligence, Allen Dulles, mixed up Robert Schuman and Maurice Schumann. Perhaps these errors were more excusable than his ignorance of the French constitution. Nevertheless, he allowed himself to wax eloquent on French failures. American aid, he asserted, had always been given despite, not because, of French attitudes; they refused to use conscripts in Vietnam, and wanted only commitments from Washington, while they would give nothing in return. They could never make up their minds, and consequently had "abdicated" their position as a world power. It was saddening for the president to contemplate this failure in view of what he thought were the "basic virtues of the great mass of Frenchmen." A sad spectacle indeed when the victors of Verdun and the Marne could not produce a few hundred technicians to keep their planes flying in Indochina.[10] David Bruce, whom Eisenhower thought such a shrewd judge of French character, termed the leaders of the Fourth Republic "timid men" who were unable to overcome their own uncertainties. Nothing Washington could do was likely to help them.

Eisenhower's perceptions were not far from those of Acheson, or Bruce, Harriman, Dunn, Caffery, Marshall, Dulles, Rusk, or the countless other Americans who became intimately involved with French affairs after the war. The American elite, sure of itself, confident in the superiority of its institutions, scornful of the low condition that two devastating world wars, which had enriched the United States, had reduced the nations of Europe, were ill equipped to exercise the kind of empathy and understanding that could have made of their intimate relations with France a less sorry spectacle. Of course the French had their own complexes and stereotypes about *les Anglo-Saxons,* who had no respect for logic or politesse, who were crude and materialistic, and incapable of transcending the mediocrity engendered by their mania for mass production and efficiency. Without indulging in a psychological reductionism, one has to remember that the 1940s and 1950s were an era of racial and national stereotypes that went a long way toward conditioning behavior and creating mutual misunderstandings. The fact that the great powers of the world fought a world conflict against the consequences of racial philosophy carried to an extreme does not mean that they were immune to its poison in milder form. "The French," "Les Américains," evoked a shared complex of stereotypes and attitudes that too often failed to make exception for the differences among individuals. When one

[10] Eisenhower Library, Correspondance, Letter to Walter Bedell Smith, March 26, 1952, mixes up the two Mayers. Letter to General Alfred Gruenther, June 8, 1954, contains the expressions of exasperation with the French.

Frenchman did stand out from the crowd, the Americans regretted that besides his unusual height, he appeared to believe himself by some mystical process to be the offspring of Clemenceau and Jeanne d'Arc.

The racial stereotypes were but another aspect of a basic characteristic of the postwar era, the desire of existing elites to preserve their power and privilege and maintain social hierarchy against egalitarian threats both at home and abroad. The perceived military threat from Moscow, which was thought real, was nevertheless used as a means to repress egalitarian aspirations at home. The French elite perceived a real threat to its hegemony. It could modernize and prosper only by generating capital through self-sacrifice, which implied sharing power and privilege with those who were expected to make the sacrifices. The Americans offered a possible way out of this dilemma, a source of capital for investment that did not require demands for sacrifice on the part of the masses and corresponding cooperation of the lower classes, the price for which might be steps toward a new political and economic order in France. The Americans became as well the source of funding for restored military strength, the ostensible purpose of which was to protect, against the Soviet threat, but which in reality was squandered in colonial wars. The desire of the French elite to maintain its political and economic hegemony resulted in the invitation to the Americans to finance economic reconstruction, restore military strength, and make possible colonial war. In the process the structure of American hegemony and French dependency took shape. The Americans had their own ideas about what France must do; they sought to fashion a France to their own liking. The French sometimes succumbed to Washington's blandishments, sometimes resisted, and most often resorted to manipulation and dissimulation. From those tactics the road was short to psychological reactions of humiliation and recrimination, and the consequent reinforcement of national stereotypes.

There is another irony in this story. The Americans expended much economic and military aid in an effort to restore France as a major anti-Communist power. While that aid was flowing, they built a unique mechanism of influence, which they used as they could to their advantage. But they did not succeed in penetrating France economically. A treaty of commerce and navigation was not signed, and American investment remained hampered by suspicion and mistrust at home and the lack of a receptive and stable climate abroad. For all the influence the Americans tried to exercise between 1947 and 1954, they were able to build nothing that was lasting. Even their extensive system of military bases, the most obvious physical reminder of their presence, was to be dismantled by de Gaulle.

But even as one kind of American influence was phased out, another was poised to penetrate France. Indirect American influence has proven much more pervasive in French life than the direct and clumsy attempts to determine the direction of politics that make up the bulk of this story. While the

French were rejecting American interference with their policies, they were adapting other aspects of American example more to their liking. Productivity, technology, economic methods, academic examples were eagerly studied and adapted, and American business methods became the model of modernization, American consumerism the dominant aspiration. While de Gaulle rejected American political tutelage and the military presence, he allowed the penetration of American investment and encouraged the infatuation with technology. The story of post-1958 American influence on France is that of cultural diffusion rather than political or economic tutelage. Franglais, rock, Mickey Mouse, and shopping malls are perhaps the real legacy of the cruder efforts of American economic intervention and political manipulation that make up the larger part of this narrative. By example the Americans established in France the model of productivity and consumerism they thought best calculated to inoculate society against radical ideology and political extremism. In that sense, perhaps, the Americans sowed better than they knew.

Bibliography

Archives and Published Sources

Archives Nationales, Paris. [A.N.]
    363 AP, Papiers René Mayer
    457 AP, Papiers Georges Bidault
    F 60 and F 60 ter. General Records of the Interministerial Committee on Economic Affairs
Archives of the Central Intelligence Agency, Washington, DC. Diverse Documents dealing with
    France
Archives of the International Ladies' Garment Workers Union, New York. David Dubinsky
    Papers
Archives of the United States Air Force, Office of Special Investigation, Counter-Intelligence
    Summary File
Central Intelligence Agency Research Reports, Europe, 1949–76. University Publications of
    America, Microfilm, Reel 1
Dwight D. Eisenhower Library, Abilene, Kansas
    Ann Whitman File; Cabinet Series, National Security Council Series, Dulles–Herter Series
    Dwight David Eisenhower Papers: Pre-Presidential File, 1916–62 Diaries
    John Foster Dulles Papers
    White House Office: Office of the Special Assistant for National Security Affairs, Records,
        1952–61
Fondation Jean Monnet, Lausanne, Switzerland
Foreign Relations of the United States, 1944–54. Washington, DC.: U.S. Government Printing
    Office, 1972–87 [FRUS]
Harry S Truman Library, Independence, Missouri
    Harry Price Interviews
    Papers of John F. Melby
    Naval Aid Files
    Oral History Interviews
    Papers of Dean Acheson
    President's Secretary's Files: Intelligence File
Institut Pierre Mendès France, Documents Pierre Mendès France, Series CED, Fuites, Indochine
Klaus Barbie and the United States Government: A Report to the Attorney General of the
    United States. Submitted by Allan A. Ryan, Jr., Special Assistant to the Attorney General,
    Criminal Division, Justice Department, Washington, DC. Washington, DC.: Government
    Printing Office, August 1983

Ministère des Affaires Etrangères, Ministère des Relations Extérieures, Quai d'Orsay, Paris. [MAE]

    B Amérique, Etats Unis, Politique Extérieure, 1947–54

    Europe 1949–55, Généralités

    Fonds Nominitifs Henri Bonnet, 1947–54

    Archives Diplomatiques. Y Internationale, 1944–49

    Direction des Affaires Economiques et Financières, A194, 1945–6

    Documents Diplomatiques Français, 1954, 21 Juillet–31 Decembre. Paris: Imprimerie Nationale, 1987

    Asie 1944–55, Indochine

    Asie 1944–55, Dossiers Généraux

National Archives and Records Administration, General Records of the Department of State, Office of European Affairs. [NARA]

    Matthews–Hickerson File

    Agency for International Development, Record Group 286, 1948–52

    General Records of the Department of State, Record Group 59, Decimal File, 1944–54

    Military Branch, Operations and Plans Division, Record Group 319

State Historical Society of Wisconsin. AFL Papers, Files of the Director of Research, Florence Thorne File

United States Congress, 81st Congress, 1st Session, House of Representatives, "Observations and Findings of the Subcommittee to Make Studies in Alaska and the Far East," November 4, 1949

United States Congress, 94th Congress, First Session, Senate, Final Report of the Select Committee to Study Governmental Operations with Respect to Intelligence Activities. Washington, DC: U.S. Government Printing Office, 1976. 6 vols.

United States Vietnam Relations, 1945–1967: Study Prepared by the Department of Defense. Popularly known as the *Pentagon Papers*. 12 vols. Washington, DC: U.S. Government Printing Office, 1971

Memoirs

Acheson, Dean. *Present at the Creation: My Years in the State Department*. New York: Norton, 1969.

Aiglion, Raoul. *De Gaulle et Roosevelt*. Paris: Plon, 1984.

Alphand, Hervé. *L'étonnement d'être, Journal 1939–1973*. Paris: Fayard, 1977.

Auriol, Vincent. *Journal du septennat, 1947–54*. 6 vols. Paris: Armand Colin, 1970–5.

Ball, George W. *The Past Has Another Pattern: Memoirs*. New York: Norton, 1982.

Bergeron, André. *Ma route et mes combats*. Paris: Editions Ramsay, 1976.

Bidault, Georges. *Resistance: The Political Autobiography of Georges Bidault*. Trans. Marianne Sinclair. New York: Praeger, 1967.

Bloch-Lainé, François, and Bouvier, Jean. *La France Restaurée, 1944–54; Dialogue sur les choix d'une modernisation*. Paris: Fayard, 1986.

Bohlen, Charles E. *Witness to History*. New York: Norton, 1973.

Bullitt, Orville H., ed. *For the President, Personal and Secret: Correspondence between Franklin D. Roosevelt and William C. Bullitt*. Boston: Houghton Mifflin, 1972.

Chauvel, Jean. *Commentaire. I: De Vienne à Alger (1938–1944). II: D'Alger à Berne (1944–52). III: De Berne à Paris (1952–1962)*. Paris: Fayard, 1971–3.

Colby, William, and Peter Forbath. *Honorable Men: My Life in the CIA*. New York: Simon and Schuster, 1978.

Davidson, Jean. *Correspondant à Washington, 1945–1953*. Paris: Editions du Seuil, 1954.

De Gaulle, Charles. *Mémoires de Guerre*. 3 vols. Paris: Plon, 1954–9.

De Lattre, Simonne. *Jean De Lattre, mon mari*. Paris: Presses de la Cité, 1971.

Desanti, Domenique. *Les Staliniens: une expérience politique, 1944–1956*. Paris: Fayard, 1975.

Ely, Paul (General). *Mémoires: L'Indochine dans la tourmente.* Paris: Plon, 1964.

Faure, Edgar. *Mémoires. I: Avoir toujours raison . . . c'est un grand tort.* Paris: Plon, 1982.

Frachon, Benoît. *Au Rythme des jours. I: 1944–54: Retrospective de vingt années de luttes de la CGT (textes choisis).* Paris: Editions Sociales, 1967.

Henry-Haye, Gaston. *La grande éclipse franco–américaine.* Paris: Plon, 1972.

Jones, Joseph M. *The Fifteen Weeks (February 21–June 5, 1947).* New York: Viking Press, 1955.

Kennan, George F. *Memoirs, 1925–1950.* Boston: Little, Brown, 1967.

Laniel, Joseph. *Le Drame Indochinois: De Dien Bien Phu au Pari de Genève.* Paris: Plon, 1957.

Lansdale, Edward G. *In the Midst of Wars: An American Mission to South East Asia.* New York: Harper & Row, 1972.

Leahy, William D. *I Was There.* New York: McGraw-Hill, 1950.

Massigli, René. *Une comédie des erreurs: Souvenirs et réflexions sur une étape de la construction européene.* Paris: Plon, 1978.

Mayer, René. *Etudes, témoinages, documents. Réunis et présentés par Denise Mayer.* Paris: PUF, 1983.

Monnet, Jean. *Mémoires.* Paris: Fayard, 1976.

Mons, Jean. *Sur les routes de l'histoire: cinquante ans au service de l'Etat.* Paris: Albatross, 1981.

Murphy, Robert. *Diplomat among Warriors.* Garden City, NY: Doubleday, 1964.

Pierre Mendès France. *Oeuvres Complètes, 3: Gouverner, c'est choisir.* Paris: Gallimard, 1986.

Reuther, Victor. *The Brothers Reuther and the Story of the UAW.* Boston: Houghton Mifflin, 1976.

Sulzberger, Cyrus L. *A Long Row of Candles: Memoirs and Diaries.* Toronto: MacMillan, 1969.

Secondary Sources

Arkes, Hadley. *Bureaucracy, The Marshall Plan and the National Interest,* Princeton: Princeton University Press, 1972.

Artaud, Denise, and Lawrence Kaplan. *Dien Bien Phu: L'Alliance atlantique et la défense du Sud-Est asiatique.* Lyon: Editions de la Manufacture, 1989.

Barnes, Trevor. "The Secret Cold War: The CIA and American Foreign Policy in Europe, 1946–56." Parts I and II. *Historical Journal,* 24, no. 2 (1981): 399–415; 25, no. 3 (1982): 649–70.

Baum, Warren C. *The French Economy and the State.* Princeton, NJ: Princeton University Press, 1958.

Bedarida, François, and Jean-Pierre Rioux. *Pierre Mendès-France et le Mendèsisme.* Paris: Fayard, 1985.

Beloff, Max. *The United States and the Unity of Europe.* Washington, DC: The Brookings Institution, 1963.

Bergounioux, Alain. *Force Ouvrière.* Paris: Seuil, 1975.

Bertin, Gilles Y. *L'investissement des firmes étrangères en France (1945–62).* Paris: PUF, 1963.

Bigsby, C. W. E., ed. *Superculture: American Popular Culture and Europe.* London: Paul Elek, 1975.

Blumenthal, Henry. *Illusion and Reality in Franco–American Diplomacy, 1914–45.* Baton Rouge: Louisiana State University Press, 1986.

Bossuat, Gérard. "L'Aide américaine à la France après la second guerre mondiale." *Vingtieme Siècle,* no. 9 (January–March 1986).

"Le Poids de l'aide américaine sur la politique économique et financière de la France en 1948." *Relations Internationales,* no. 37, (Spring 1984): 17–36.

Braden, Thomas W. "I'm Glad the CIA Is 'Immoral'." *Saturday Evening Post,* May 20, 1967, pp. 10–3.

Brinton, Crane. *The Americans and the French*. Cambridge, MA: Harvard University Press, 1968.

Claude, Henri. *Le Plan Marshall*. Paris: Editions Sociales, 1948.

Colton, Joel. *Léon Blum: Humanist in Politics*. New York: A Knopf, 1968.

Cook, Don. *Charles de Gaulle*. New York: G. P. Putnam's Sons, 1983.

Corson, William R. *The Armies of Ignorance: The Rise of the American Intelligence Empire*. New York: Dial Press, 1977.

Crozier, Michel. *La Société bloquée*. Paris: Seuil, 1970.

De la Gorce, Paul-Marie. *Naissance de la France Moderne. I: L'après-guerre: 1944–1952*. Paris: Bernard Grasset, 1978.

De Santis, Hugh. *The Diplomacy of Silence: The American Foreign Service, the Soviet Union, and the Cold War, 1933–1947*. Chicago: University of Chicago Press, 1979.

DePorte, Anton. *De Gaulle's Foreign Policy, 1944–46*. Cambridge, MA: Harvard University Press, 1968.

Devillers, Philippe, and Jean Lacouture. *End of a War: Indochina, 1954*. New York: Praeger, 1969.

La fin d'une guerre; Indochine, 1954. Paris: Seuil, 1960.

Di Nolfo, Ennio. "The United States and Italian Communism, 1942–46: World War II to the Cold War." *Journal of Italian History*, 1, no. 1 (Spring 1978): 74–94.

Duroselle, Jean Baptiste. *La France et les Etats Unis des origines à nos jours*. Paris: Seuil, 1976.

Elgey, Georgette. *Histoire de la quatrième République. I: La République des illusions (1945–1951). II: la République des contradictions (1951–1954)*. Paris: Fayard, 1965–8.

Elleinstein, Jean. *Goliath contre Goliath: Histoire des relations américano–sovietiques. I: L'Enfance des grands (1941–1949)*. Paris: Fayard, 1986.

Esposito, Chiarella. The Marshall Plan in France and Italy, 1948–1950: Counterpart Negotiations. Ph.D. dissertation, State University of New York at Stonybrook, 1985.

Faenza, Robert, and Marco Fini. *Gli americani in Italia*. Milan: Feltrinelli, 1976.

Faligot, Roger, and Pascal Krop. *La Piscine: Les Services secrets français, 1944–54*. Paris: Seuil, 1985.

Freymond, Jacques. "America in European Eyes." *Annals of the American Academy of Political and Social Science*, 295 (September 1954): 33–41.

Fridenson, Patrick, and André Straus. *Le Capitalisme Français, 19e et 20e siècle: Blocages et dynamismes d'une croissance*. Paris: Fayard, 1987.

Funk, Arthur. "Negotiating the 'Deal with Darlan.' " *Journal of Contemporary History*, 8, no. 2 (April 1973): 81–118.

Charles de Gaulle: The Crucial Years, 1943–44. Norman: University of Oklahoma Press, 1959.

The Politics of Torch: The Allied landings and the Algiers Putsch, 1942. Lawrence: University Press of Kansas, 1974.

Fursdon, Edward. *The European Defense Community: A History*. New York: St. Martin's Press, 1980.

Georges, Bernard, Denise Tintant, and Marie-Anne Renauld. *Léon Jouhaux dans le mouvement syndical français*. Paris: Presses Universitaires de France, 1979.

Gimbel, John. *The Origins of the Marshall Plan*. Stanford, CA: Stanford University Press, 1976.

Girault, René. "Léon Blum, la dévaluation de 1936 et la conduite de la politique extérieure de la France." *Relations Internationales*, 13 (Spring 1978): 91–109.

Godson, Roy S[imon]. *American Labor and European Politics*. New York: Crane Russak, 1976.

Non-Governmental Organizations in International Politics: The American Federation of Labor, the International Labor Movement and French Politics. Unpublished Ph.D. dissertation, Columbia University, New York, 1972.

Grosser, Alfred, *La IVe République et sa politique extérieure*. Paris: Armond Colin, 1961.

Les Occidentaux: Les Pays d'Europe et les Etats Unis depuis la guerre. Paris: Fayard, 1978.
The Western Alliance: European–American Relations since 1945. New York: Continuum, 1980.
Affaires extérieures: la politique de la France, 1944–84. Paris: Flammarion, 1984.
Gun, Nerin E. *Les Secrets des archives américaines. I: Pétain, Laval, de Gaulle. II: Ni de Gaulle, ni Thorez.* Paris: Albin Michel, 1979.
Haight, John McVicker, Jr. "France, the United States, and the Munich Crisis." *Journal of Modern History,* 34, no. 4 (December 1960): 340–58.
American Aid to France, 1938–1940. New York: Atheneum, 1970.
Harper, John L. *America and the Reconstruction of Italy.* New York: Cambridge University Press, 1986.
Henderson, Nicholas. *The Birth of NATO.* London: Weidenfeld and Nicolson, 1982.
Hoffmann, Stanley. *In Search of France.* Cambridge, MA: Harvard University Press, 1963.
and Charles Maier, ed. *The Marshall Plan: A Retrospective.* Boulder, CO: Westview Press, 1984.
Hogan, Michael. *The Marshall Plan: America, Britain, and the Reconstruction of Western Europe, 1947–52.* New York: Cambridge University Press, 1987.
Holter, Darryl. "Politique Charbonnière et guerre froide, 1945–50." *Le Mouvement Social,* no. 130 (January–March 1985): 33–53.
Hurstfield, Julian G. *America and the French Nation, 1939–1945.* Durham, NC: University of North Carolina Press, 1986.
Institut de Science Economique Appliquée. *Les Plans Monetaires Internationaux. 10: Le Plan Marshall. Mouvements de capitaux et liquidités internationales,* by Jean Mouly. Paris: ISEA, July 1955.
Ireland, Timothy P. *Creating the Entangling Alliance: The Origins of the North Atlantic Treaty Organization.* Westport, CT: Greenwood Press, 1981.
Irving, Robert. *The First Indochina War.* London: Croom Helm, 1975.
Jankowski, Paul. *Communism and Collaboration: Simon Sabiani and Politics in Marseille, 1919–44.* New Haven, CT: Yale University Press, 1989.
Kantorowitz, Jack. "L'Influence américaine sur Force Ouvrière: mythe ou realité?" *Revue française de science politique,* 4 (August 1978): 717–40.
Kaplan, Lawrence. *The United States and NATO: The Formative Years.* Lexington: The University Press of Kentucky, 1984.
Kaspi, André. *La Mission de Jean Monnet à Alger, Mars–Octobre 1943.* Paris: Publications de la Sorbonne, 1971.
Kersaudy, François. *De Gaulle et Churchill.* Paris: Plon, 1982.
Kolko, Joyce and Gabriel. *The Limits of Power: The World and United States Foreign Policy, 1945–54.* New York: Harper & Row, 1972.
Kuisel, Richard. "L'American Way of Life et les missions françaises de productivité." *Vingtieme Siècle* (January–March 1988).
Capitalism and the State in Modern France. New York: Cambridge University Press, 1981.
Lacouture, Jean. *Viet Nam, de la guerre française à la guerre américaine.* Paris: Seuil, 1969.
Léon Blum. Paris: Seuil, 1977.
Charles De Gaulle. 3 vols. Paris: Seuil, 1984–6.
Pierre Mendès France. Paris: Seuil, 1985.
Lacroix-Riz, Annie. *La CGT de la liberation à la scission de 1944–47.* Paris: Editions Sociales, 1983.
"L'entrée de la France dans la guerre froide (1944–1947)." *Cahiers d'Histoire de l'Institut de Recherche Marxiste,* 13 (1983): 4–24.
"Négociation et signature des accords Blum–Byrnes (Octobre '45–Mai '46) d'après les archives du MAE." *Revue d'Histoire moderne et contemporaine,* 31 (July–September 1984): 417–48.

La choix de Marianne: les relations franco–américaines, 1944–48. Paris: Messidor/Editions
Sociales, 1985.
"La perception française de la politique américaine en Europe de 1945 à 1948." *Cahiers
d'Histoire de l'Institut de Recherches Marxistes,* 26 (1986).
Les protectorats d'Afrique du Nord entre la France et Washington. Paris: Editions L'Har-
mattan, 1988.
"Autour d'Irving Brown: le Free Trade Union Committee le Département d'Etat et la scission
syndicale française (1944–47)." *Le Movement Social,* 151 April–June 1990, pp. 79–
118.
Lancaster, Donald. *The Emancipation of French Indochina.* New York: Octagon Books, 1974.
Langer, William L. *Our Vichy Gamble.* New York: Knopf, 1947.
Laurat, Lucien, and Marcel Pommera. *Le Drame économique et monetaire français depuis la
liberation.* Paris: Les Isles d'Or, 1953.
Leffler, Melvyn P. "The American Conception of National Security and the Beginnings of the
Cold War, 1945–48." *American Historical Review,* 89, no. 2 (April 1984): 346–81.
*The Elusive Quest: America's Pursuit of European Stability and French Security, 1919–
1933.* Chapel Hill: University of North Carolina Press, 1979.
Lerner, Daniel, and Raymond Aron. *France Defeats EDC.* New York: Praeger, 1956.
Louis, William Roger. *Imperialism at Bay, 1941–1945: The United States and the Decoloni-
zation of the British Empire.* Oxford: Clarendon Press, 1977.
Lynch, Frances M. B. "Resolving the Paradox of the Monnet Plan: National and International
Planning in French Reconstruction." *Economic History Review,* 37, no. 2 (May 1984):
229–43.
Maier, Charles. *In Search of Stability: Explorations in Historical Political Economy.* New
York: Cambridge University Press, 1987.
Malaurie, Guillaume, with Emmanuel Terrée. *L'Affaire Kravchenko: Le Goulag en correction-
nelle.* Paris: Robert Laffont, 1982.
Marantz, Marcel. *Le Plan Marshall, Succes ou Faillite?* Paris: Marcel Rivere, 1950.
Marchetti, Victor, and John D. Marks. *The CIA and the Cult of Intelligence.* New York:
Knopf, 1974.
Margairaz, Michel. "Autour des accords Blum–Byrnes: Jean Monnet entre le consensus na-
tional et le consensus atlantique." *Histoire, Economie et Société,* 3 (1982): 439–70.
McLellan, David S. *Dean Acheson: The State Department Years.* New York: Dodd Mead,
1976.
Melandri, Pierre. *Les Etats Unis face à l'unification de l'Europe, 1945–54.* Paris: A. Pedone,
1980.
Micaud, Charles. *Communism and the French Left.* New York: Praeger, 1963.
Milward, Alan S. *The Reconstruction of Western Europe, 1945–51.* London: Methuen, 1984.
Mioche, Philippe. *Le Plan Monnet: Genèse et Elaboration.* Paris: Publications de la Sorbonne,
1987.
Mitchell, Allan. *The German Influence in France after 1890: The Formation of the French
Republic.* Durham: University of North Carolina Press, 1979.
Munholland, Kim. "The Trials of the Free French in New Caledonia, 1940–42." *French His-
torical Studies,* 14, no. 4 (Fall 1986): 547–79.
Offner, Arnold A. *The Origins of the Second World War: American Foreign Policy and World
Politics, 1917–41.* New York: Praeger, 1975.
Paterson, Thomas G. *Meeting the Communist Threat: Truman to Reagan.* New York: Oxford
University Press, 1988.
Platt, Alan A., and Robert Leonardi. "American Foreign Policy and the Postwar Italian Left."
Political Science Quarterly, 93, no. 2 (Summer 1978): 197–217.
Poidevin, Raymond. *Robert Schuman, homme d'état, 1886–1963.* Paris: Imprimerie Nation-
ale, 1986.

Price, Harry Bayard. *The Marshall Plan and Its Meaning*. Ithaca, NY: Cornell University Press, 1955.

Radosh, Ronald. *American Labor and United States Foreign Policy*. New York: Random House, 1969.

Ranelagh, John. *The Agency: Rise and Decline of the CIA*. London: Wiedenfeld and Nicolson, 1986.

Reid, Escott. *Time of Fear and Hope: The Making of the North Atlantic Treaty, 1947–1949*. Toronto: McClelland and Stewart, 1977.

Rice-Maximin, Edward. "The United States and the French Left, 1945–1949: The View from the State Department." *Journal of Contemporary History* (October 1984).

"The French Communists, the United States and the Peace Movement of the Cold War, 1948–1952." *Proceedings of the Twelfth Annual Meeting of the Western Society for French History (1984)*. Santa Barbara, CA, 1985.

Accommodation and Resistance: The French Left, Indochina and the Cold War. Westport, CT: Greenwood Press, 1986.

Rioux, Jean-Pierre. *La France de la IVe République*. Paris: Seuil, 1980.

Robrieux, Philippe. *Histoire Intérieure du Parti Communiste*. 4 vols. Paris, Fayard, 1980–84.

Rose, Lisle A. *Roots of Tragedy: The United States and the Struggle for Asia, 1945–1953*. Westport, CT: Greenwood Press, 1976.

Rothwell, Victor. *Britain and the Cold War, 1941–47*. London: Jonathan Cape, 1982.

Rouanet, Pierre. *Mendès France au Pouvoir, 1954–1955*. Paris: Robert Laffont, 1965.

Sapp, Steven P. The United States, France, and the Cold War: Jefferson Caffery and American–French Relations, 1944–49. Ph.D. dissertation, Kent State University, 1978.

Schuker, Stephen. *The End of French Predominance in Europe: The Financial Crisis of 1924 and the Adoption of the Dawes Plan*. Chapel Hill: University of North Carolina Press, 1976.

Schwartz, Thomas A. "The Skeleton Key: American Foreign Policy, European Unity, and German Rearmament, 1949–1954." *Central European History*, 19, no. 4 (December 1986): 369–86.

Sommer, René. " 'Paix et Liberté:' la Quatrième République contre le PC." *L'Histoire*, 40 (December 1981): 26–35.

Thibau, Jacques. *La France Colonisée*. Paris: Flammarion, 1980.

Validire, Jean-Louis. *André Bergeron, une Force Ouvrière*. Paris: Plon, 1984.

Van Der Beugel, Ernst H. *From Marshall Aid to Atlantic Partnership: European Integration as a Concern of American Foreign Policy*. New York: Elsevier, 1966.

Viorst, Milton. *Hostile Allies: FDR and Charles de Gaulle*. New York: Macmillan, 1954.

Wall, Irwin M. *French Communism in the Era of Stalin*. Westport, CT: Greenwood Press, 1983.

L'influence américaine sur la politique française, 1945–1954. Paris: André Balland, 1989.

"Les Accords Blum–Byrnes, la modernisation de la France et la guerre froide." *Vingtième Siècle*, 13 (1987): 45–52.

Weil, Martin. *A Pretty Good Club: The Founding Fathers of the U.S. Foreign Service*. New York: Norton, 1978.

Wexler, Imanuel. *The Marshall Plan Revisited: The European Recovery Program in Economic Perspective*. Westport, CT: Greenwood Press, 1983.

Willis, F. Roy. *The French in Germany, 1945–1949*. Stanford, CA: Stanford University Press, 1962.

Windmuller, John. *American Labor and the International Labor Movement 1940 to 1953*. Ithaca, NY: Cornell International Industrial and Labor Relations Reports, 1954.

Yergin, Daniel. *A Shattered Peace: The Origins of the Cold War and the National Security State*. Boston: Houghton Mifflin, 1979.

Young, John W. *Britain, France, and the Unity of Europe*. Leicester: Leicester University Press, 1984.

France, the Cold War and the Western Alliance: French Foreign Policy and Post-War Europe, 1944–49. New York: St. Martin's Press, 1990.

Zahniser, Marvin R. *Uncertain Friendship: American–French Diplomatic Relations through the Cold War*. New York, John Wiley and Sons, 1975.

Zurcher, Arnold J. *The Struggle to Unite Europe, 1940–1958*. New York, New York University Press, 1958.

Index